K. Warner Schaie, a pioneer in the study of gerontology, has written a monumental work representing his lifetime contribution to the study of aging. The book analyzes the Seattle Longitudinal Study, which Professor Schaie began as a graduate student in the 1950s. The study has been impressive in its methodological sophistication, inclusion of a broad array of variables related to intellectual development, and attention to individual differences in intellectual aging.

Up to the 1950s, studies of intelligence focused on children and college students, and the popular notion was that intelligence peaked at age 16 and declined in older adults in a uniform way. In his early work, Professor Schaie discovered that this dominant concept of intelligence was simplistic and that there are many variations in terms of when intelligence peaks and declines, as well as many different factors that affect a person's intelligence. Important practical questions are raised, such as: At what age do developmental peaks occur, and what are the generational differences and within-generation age changes? How do you establish sufficient competence for independent living?

Intellectual development in adulthood

Intellectual development in adulthood

The Seattle Longitudinal Study

K. Warner Schaie
Pennsylvania State University

Foreword by
Paul B. Baltes
Max Planck Institute

CAMBRIDGE
UNIVERSITY PRESS

Published by the Press Syndicate of the University of Cambridge
The Pitt Building, Trumpington Street, Cambridge CB2 1RP
40 West 20th Street, New York, NY 10011-4211, USA
10 Stamford Road, Oakleigh, Melbourne 3166, Australia

First published 1996

Printed in the United States of America

Library of Congress Cataloging-in-Publication Data
Schaie, K. Warner (Klaus Warner), 1928–
Intellectual development in adulthood: the Seattle longitudinal study / K. Warner Schaie; foreword by Paul B. Baltes.
p. cm.
Includes bibliographical references and index.
ISBN 0–521–43014–3 (hc)
1. Cognition – Age factors – Longitudinal studies.   2. Adulthood – Psychological aspects – Longitudinal studies.   3. Aging – Psychological aspects – Longitudinal studies.   I. Title.
BF724.55.C63S32   1996
155.6 – dc20   95–13779
                                                            CIP

A catalog record for this book is available from the British Library.

ISBN 0–521–43014–3 Hardback

Contents

Tables and figures

Tables

Figures

Foreword

In the sciences, we mark our knowledge by a triangulation of several key elements, together constituting the classical foundations of the field: (1) distinguished persons, (2) select concepts, methods, and laws, and (3) critical experiments or studies. For Warner Schaie's book *Intellectual Development in Adulthood: The Seattle Longitudinal Study*, the historical territory is marked, for instance, by such names (in historical order) as Tetens, Quetelet, Galton, Thurstone, and Cattell; by concepts such as psychometric factor theory of intelligence; and by trend-setting longitudinal work such as the Stanford Terman Study, the Duke Longitudinal Study, and the Baltimore Longitudinal Study on Aging.

Although one should be cautious in making predictions about the future, I predict that the present book will become a classic, and that it will age more than gracefully. The impact of *Intellectual Development in Adulthood* will be felt throughout the next century: This volume is setting a yardstick for scholarship, and it contains insights about adult intellectual development which are difficult to deny or forget. Because of this research program on adult intellectual development, the field of life-span developmental psychology will never be the same. And it was primarily for this reason that Warner Schaie in 1993 received the Distinguished Research Award of the American Psychological Association.

The Seattle Longitudinal Study is among the core of longitudinal studies in adulthood and old age that marked the beginning of a burgeoning of interest in life-span psychology and aging. The Study began close to 40 years ago and continues into the future. What makes it different from other longitudinal studies is its commitment to a new design methodology. Specifically, it is the first large-scale empirical demonstration of the need for and utility of so-called longitudinal and cohort-sequential methodologies.

Throughout its history, the Study has been extremely productive, beginning with the now classic opening piece on sequential methods published in 1965 in *Psychological Bulletin*. This seminal article set the stage for the resulting complex and long-term longitudinal design. In the ensuing time, many individual analyses have been published in a multitude of articles and chapters. In the present volume, Schaie succeeds brilliantly in bringing together the entire gestalt of the Seattle Longitudinal Study: its history, its methodological and theoretical underpinnings, and its most significant findings and their implications for future theorizing and research as well as for social policy.

The analyses of the Seattle Longitudinal Study, as Schaie observes in his own acknowledgments, involved many students, associates, and colleagues. During the last decade, the contributions of Sherry Willis, with her unique emphasis on cognitive intervention work, seem of particular relevance. The search for the degree of individual plasticity of intellectual functioning, a hallmark of Willis's conceptual and empirical orientation, provided the Seattle Longitudinal Study with additional vigor and innovation during its phase of advanced maturity. Indeed, one of the special challenges of long-term longi-tudinal work is to manage and create a continuous rapprochement to, and discourse with, the changing intellectual agenda of the field. Schaie has been a master at this, and it reflects his deep under-standing of the historical roots of developmental psychology and the cornerstones of the quantitative (psychometric) approach to the measurement of intelligence.

It is beyond the scope of this foreword to outline in detail the many and varied conclusions about the nature of intellectual devel-opment which Schaie elaborates in this book and supports by the data of the Seattle Longitudinal Study. They can be grouped into methodological and substantive issues.

Let me begin with methodology, because it was its methodological approach which initially represented the most significant innovation of the Study. In psychology, Schaie is the founder of the metho-dology – that is, so-called sequential methods – which combines cross-sectional and longitudinal design strategies into an overarching framework permitting the joint study of individual development and cultural–historical change. The results and insights provided by the Seattle Longitudinal Study through its application of sequential methodology give testimony to the fundamental shortcomings of the traditional cross-sectional and longitudinal methods used in developmental psychology and human development. Rarely, as illustrated in the many cross-sectional and longitudinal gradients which form the basis of the Seattle Longitudinal Study, do simple cross-sectional or longitudinal gradients offer identical evidence as to onset, level, and directionality of change. Rather, as both individuals and sociocultural conditions change with time, it is necessary to go beyond such traditional designs and to employ study arrangements in which multiple cohorts are followed longitudinally as well as cross-sectionally. This is what Schaie recognized in the early 1960s and implemented in the Seattle Longitudinal Study (which, incidentally, in a strict sense is more than a longitudinal study). The Study represents a coordinated series of longitudinal and cross-sectional studies, each of which covers major portions of the adult life span. As a whole, this study design permits generalizable conclusions about the nature and dynamics of age-developmental change, including the zone of variation created by sociocultural conditions.

A further innovative methodological feature of the Seattle Longitudinal Study was added when Sherry Willis joined the project around 1980 and selected subgroups of study participants for cognitive interventions. The goal of this added research focus was to explore intraindividual modifiability (plasticity) of intelligence. A splendid study arrangement resulted, rarely (if ever) true of other long-term longitudinal work. In the Seattle Longitudinal Study, Schaie and Willis were able to combine descriptive with experimental design conditions, and this for multiple cohorts over a span of more than a decade. The effectiveness of these cognitive interventions for the exploration of cognitive plasticity had been tested in earlier basic research on cognitive aging. Now, however, it was possible to employ these interventions with participants whose earlier level of cognitive performance was known, thereby providing a life-span baseline against which the intervention effects could be assessed.

Turning to substantive issues, the data and interpretations presented in this book form a new family of insights into the nature of adult intellectual development. Any modern theory of adult intelligence will need to be seen in the context of the perspectives outlined by Schaie and his colleagues. Among them are the following:

First, adult development of intelligence is not fixed, but dynamic. Part of the dynamic results from the fact that adult development of intelligence is embedded in a general historical context with its own set of constraints and opportunities involving, in addition to personal conditions, such factors as health, education, and work.

Second, adult intellectual development is multidimensional. Intelligence in the psychometric tradition is not a unitary category. Therefore, adult intellectual development is not uniform but can vary by subcategories of intelligence, the so-called primary mental abilities. And the empirical findings bear out this possibility of multidimensionality and multidirectionality. Some of the primary mental abilities develop for longer and decline later than others, and the magnitude of decline varies markedly as well. For most people and most abilities, reliably detectable decline does not begin until the age period of the late 60s and the 70s. Individual differences in these change trajectories, however, are large and typically do not follow a continuous pattern. Rather individual decline appears to occur most frequently in a stair-step fashion.

Third, as demonstrated by the cognitive intervention work associated with the Seattle Longitudinal Study, intraindividual (within-person) potential for further development and plasticity of intelligence continues into old age, at least as long as a given individual does not suffer from severe brain pathology. Therefore, whatever we as researchers observe as a given person's trajectory of age change is only one of many possible instantiations. If conditions had been different for that person (or that cohort), the age-change trajectory in intellectual functioning observed could have been markedly different. A corollary to this conclusion is that there is more latent reserve in the aging mind than we generally expect. Being exposed to facilitative environmental conditions, including our own efforts at optimization, does make a difference in the level of mental functioning we are able to attain during adulthood and maintain into old age. And Schaie also succeeds in specifying some of the societal and personal conditions which operate in this lifelong process of optimization.

Fourth, historical change in intellectual functioning is also multi-directional. As is true for individual aging (where different mental abilities exhibit differential age trajectories), historical change effects were found to vary by mental abilities. Considering conflicting positions in present-day discussions about the impact of various cultural innovations (such as the 20th-century advent of multimedia and information technology) on our minds, these findings from the Seattle Longitudinal Study carry special significance. It is, to my knowledge, the first convincing demonstration of the reality and differential impact of such historical change effects in the modern Western world.

Fifth, despite evidence for sizable plasticity on the individual level, there is also impressive evidence for much within-family similarity in individual differences across generations; that is, correlations involving intellectual functioning across parent–child and sibling pairs were of substantial magnitude. Thus, there are two faces to the plasticity and variability of intellectual functioning across the adult life span. Sizable plasticity in level of individual functioning is juxtaposed with much stability in interindividual differences across age and familial generations. To understand adult intellectual development, it is necessary to keep both these findings in mind. Emphasizing one at the expense of the other, as we often witness in heated discussions on this topic, is inappropriate and fails to do justice to the evidence.

Let me return to the broader framework of this foreword. In my opening observations, I proffered the belief that Schaie's *Intellectual Development in Adulthood: The Seattle Longitudinal Study* will be a classic in the fields of developmental psychology and human development, and I noted its conceptual link to major earlier publications and heralds of the field. In my view, such connections are typical for works that are top candidates for new classics in the field.

The first example of the historical profundity of Schaie's oeuvre concerns Tetens, who, for German-speaking scholars, was the first giant in the field of human developmental psychology. Unfortunately, Tetens's major works, published in 1777, were never translated into English (see my chapter in Lerner, *Developmental Psychology: Historical and Philosophical Perspectives* [1983] for further detail). In his two volumes, entitled *Philosophische Versuche über die menschliche Natur und ihre Entwicklung*, Tetens identified some of the key questions of adult intelligence, very much in line with the main thrust of the present volume: (1) the question of whether performance decrement observed in older persons necessarily indexes decline, or whether certain aspects of apparent performance decrement can be seen instead as evidence for further development and adaptive mastery; (2) the question of the degree to which performance decrement in older persons is a result of the "nonuse" (disuse) of functions; and (3) the question of the degree to which intellectual functioning in adulthood is subject to optimization (*Vervollkommnung*) by means of better experiential and societal conditions. Throughout his writings, Tetens was committed to a view that is essentially contextual, differential, and concerned with modifiability and plasticity and with the active role that society and individuals play as producers of adult development and aging.

The second example of linkage to a classic in the field of human abilities can be found in Quetelet's *A Treatise on Man and the Development of His Faculties*, published in 1835 (1842 in English). This book is perhaps the first comprehensive empirical effort concerned with life-span human development. It is full of empirical data covering the entire life course, including consideration of such psychological variables as crime, morality, and intellectual abilities. Quetelet, like Tetens, and of course Schaie, was much concerned with development in the context of sociohistorical change. And again, like Schaie, he recognized the fundamental significance of using appropriate methodology. In fact, Quetelet's nascent insights, more than 150 years ago, into methodological issues in the study of development are astonishing. For instance, Quetelet, when evaluating his empirical findings on age differences, carefully enumerated a number of problems in research design. He previewed the confounding effects of period-specific historical events on age functions, suggested the need for multiple period (rather than time-specific) data in the study of age changes, drew attention to age-associated survival effects, and touched on issues of measurement validity and equivalence. Each of these issues is at the center of Schaie's Seattle Longitudinal Study.

Two of the classic heralds of developmental psychology and the field of adult intellectual development, then, argued the case for a dynamic and contextual conception of adult intellectual development.

More than a century later, we witness in Schaie's Seattle Longitudinal Study the first successful effort to translate these arguments and perspectives into a comprehensive program of empirical research. Personally – and this is perhaps too egotistical – I wonder to what degree Schaie's European background and international posture, his multilingual abilities and multicultural knowledge have helped him to create this work, which in its basic framework and aspirations transcends the boundaries of a single culture and thereby combines the best of developmental scholarship on both sides of the North Atlantic.

Dear Reader: Enjoy this classic earlier than others, wrestle with the evidence, complex as it might appear, and thereby attain a new view on the dynamic nature and course of adult intellectual development! Some time ago, the Greek philosopher Thucydides warned us against simplicity and convenience in the search for good evidence when he said: "All too accepting are most in the pursuit of truth. They are happy and content with whatever news come first." The passion, persistence, and intellectual creativity which Schaie invested in this program of cohort-sequential and intervention-oriented longitudinal research protects us from snapshot studies of development and therefore from the shortcomings of "whatever news comes first." The Seattle Longitudinal Study makes us look deeper and permits us to see farther.

Paul B. Baltes
Berlin
January 1995

Acknowledgments

As is the case in any long-term study, colleagues, students, and support staff made many contributions to the collection, analysis, and interpretation of data from the study. Much credit for the many aspects of the work that went well goes to these contributors; the responsibility for what went awry is, of course, mine. A very special acknowledgment, however, is due Sherry L. Willis, my wife and colleague, who has codirected the SLS efforts since 1982, and without whose patient support and many helpful suggestions this volume would not exist. Recognized also should be the enthusiastic support provided by the staff and membership of the Group Health Cooperative of Puget Sound throughout our long period of collaboration.

The following colleagues, students, and support staff (in alphabetical order) participated in one or more of the various data collections and analyses and/or contributed to the resultant scholarly products: Christopher Adams, David Adams, Diane Backschies, Margret Baltes, Paul Baltes, Thomas Barrett, Ute Bayen, Timothy Benner, Gisela Bertulis, Joy Bodnar, Hayden Bosworth, Barbara Buech, Michael Cady, Heather Chipuer, Theresa Cooney, Jean Day, Ranjana Dutta, Walter Eden, Carrie Frech, Michael Gilewski, Judith Gonda, Kathy Gribbin, Ann Gruber-Baldini, Brian Hallett, Elaine Hardin, Sarah Haessler, Charlene Herold, Christopher Hertzog, Judy Higgins, Gina Jay, Christine Johnson, Heather Johnson, Iseli Krauss, Eric Labouvie, Gisela Labouvie-Vief, Tamra Lair, Karen Laughlin, Christine Lehl, Helen Leisowitz, Jackie Levine, Heiner Maier, Scott Maitland, Renee Marquardt, Dean Melang, Sherry Murr, Ann Nardi, John Nesselroade, Shirley Paton Norleen, Ann

O'Hanlon, Phyllis Olson, Holly Overman, Iris Parham, Julie Parmentier, Cherill Perera, Robert Peterson, Robert Plomin, Samuel Popkin, Alan Posthumer, Margaret Quayhagen, Sarah Rosen, Christine Roy, Pat Sand, Coloma Harrison Schaie, Carolyn Seszniak, John Schulenberg, Anna Shuey, Michael Singer, Anita Stolov, Vicki Stone, Charles Strother, Alejandra Suarez, Richard Vigesaa, Nathaniel Wagner, and Elizabeth Zelinski.

I would also like to extend my thanks to Robert J. Sternberg, who read the first draft and whose gentle and sensitive advice helped shape the final version of this volume.

The Seattle Longitudinal Study has been funded by grants from the National Institute of Child Health and Human Development (HD00367, 1963–65; HD04476, 1970–73) and by the National Institute on Aging (AG00480, 1973–79; AG03544, 1982–86; AG04770, 1984–89). Current support from the latter institute (R037 AG08055, 1989–98) is funding the collection of data for the family studies, the follow-up cognitive training studies, the sixth wave of the SLS, and the data analyses still in progress. This volume was first conceptualized and parts of it were written while I was a fellow at the Center for Advanced Study in the Behavioral Sciences, Stanford, California, with support from the John D. and Catherine T. MacArthur Foundation. Final revisions were made while I was on a sabbatical leave at the Gerontologiskt Centrum, Lund, Sweden.

1

Introduction and preview

The purpose of this volume is to present in one place the program of studies conducted by me, my associates, and my students over the past 35 years that has come to be known as the Seattle Longitudinal Study (SLS). This study began as my doctoral dissertation at the University of Washington in 1956.

At an early stage of my career I was confronted with addressing the discrepancies between cross-sectional and longitudinal findings in the study of adult intellectual development. I soon became convinced that this issue needed to be addressed by following over time a structured cross-sectional sample such as the one I had collected for my dissertation. As a consequence I designed a follow-up study, put into the field in 1963, that provided some answers but also raised enough methodological and substantive questions to demand a continuing program of studies (including six major and several collateral data collections) that is still in progress.

The SLS has charted the course of selected cognitive abilities from young adulthood through old age. It has investigated individual differences and differential patterns of change. In so doing it has focused not only on demonstrating the presence or absence of age-related changes and differences but has also attended to the magnitude and relative importance of the observed phenomena. An important aspect of the study has been the investigation of cohort differences and their implications for the study of adult cognition. In the more recent phases of the study a number of contextual, health, and personality variables have been identified that offer explanations for differential change and that provide a basis for possible intervention. Within the context of our monitoring of individual change, it has been possible to design cognitive interventions that have been successful in remediating carefully documented declines and in improving the cognitive functions of older persons who have remained stable. Most recently we have begun to study age changes and differences in cognitive ability structure at the latent construct level. We have also conducted analyses of the relative effect of speed and accuracy in age decline and training gain, and we have investigated the relevance of cognitive training to real-life tasks. Finally, we have studied parent–offspring and sibling similarity in adult cognitive performance.

The volume is not designed to provide an extensive overview of theories of intelligence or of the vast literature on adult development. Thus references to the work of other major authors in the field of intelligence or of adult intellectual development are limited to instances where such references provide context or are directly relevant to the issues raised and data collected in the course of the SLS. Quite explicitly, I should state that the Genevan approach to intelligence has not had significant impact on our empirical work. At the time our studies began, Piagetians were simply not interested in adulthood; even though I would readily wish to acknowledge the influence of Piaget's (1972) late-life concerns and the important contributions of recent authors interested in postformal operations (e.g., Commons, Sinnott, Richards, & Armon, 1989) on some of my theoretical writing (see Schaie, 1977–1978). Likewise, our work does not lean to a great extent on the information processing literature and the exciting work on componentializing psychometric abilities (see Sternberg, 1977).

Intuitively I have always subscribed to a hierarchical model of intelligence that considers information processing components as a basic process level, combinations and permutations of skills which result in the products represented by the traditional work on psychometric intelligence. Combinations and permutations of mental abilities in turn represent the basic components underlying practical intelligence as expressed in specific everyday tasks. This model has only recently been explicated more formally (see Schaie & Willis, 1994; Willis & Schaie, 1993). Because of the more general nature of psychometric abilities and their strong relationship to everyday performance, I elected to concentrate my efforts at this middle level of exploration (see Schaie, 1987). I apologize in advance to my many friends and colleagues whose work I may have inadvertently slighted by these limiting decisions.

Why should one study intelligence in adulthood?

For all practical purposes, applied psychology began with the investigation of intellectual competence. Early objectives of this interest may be found in efforts to design procedures for the orderly removal of mentally retarded children from the public school classroom (Binet & Simon, 1905) or in the study of the distribution of individual differences in the interest of demonstrating their Darwinian characteristics (Galton, 1869). What are the mental functions that early investigators sought to describe that we are still pursuing today? Binet's definition remains a classic guide: "To judge well, to comprehend well, to reason well, these are the essentials of intelligence. A person may be a moron or an imbecile if he lacks judgment; but with judgment he could not be either" (Binet & Simon, 1905, p. 106).

In the beginning, empirical studies of intelligence investigated primarily how complex mental functions were acquired early in life (Brooks & Weintraub, 1976). But a concern with following the complexities of intellectual development beyond childhood soon arose, beginning with the theoretical expositions of classical developmental psychologists, such as G. Stanley Hall (1922), H. L. Hollingsworth (1927), and Sidney Pressey (Pressey, Janney, & Kuhlen, 1939). Questions raised by these authors concerned matters involving the age of attaining peak performance levels, the maintenance or transformation of intellectual structures, and the decremental changes thought to occur from late midlife into old age.

Empirical work relevant to these questions was not long in following. In his original standardization of the Binet tests for American use, Terman (1916) had reason to assume that intellectual development reached a peak at age 16 and then remained level throughout adulthood. Large-scale studies with the Army Alpha Intelligence Test (Yerkes, 1921) suggested that the peak level of intellectual functioning for young adults might already be reached, on average, by the even earlier age of 13. But other empirical studies questioned these inferences. One of the most influential cross-sectional study, that by Jones and Conrad (1933), collected data on most of the inhabitants of a New England community who were between the ages of 10 and 60 years. Interestingly enough, age differences found in this study were quite substantial on some of the subtests of the Army Alpha but not on others. In a similar fashion, Wechsler's standardization studies that led to the development of the Wechsler–Bellevue Adult Intelligence scales, found that growth of intelligence does not cease in adolescence. In fact, peak ages were found to differ for various aspects of intellectual functioning, and decrements at older ages were clearly not uniform across the different measures used to define intelligence (Wechsler, 1939).

The practice of intelligence testing attained a peak following World War II with the spread of clinical psychology and the widespread introduction into clinical practice of the Wechsler Adult Intelligence Scale (WAIS) and its derivatives (Matarazzo, 1972). Also important was the almost universal introduction of intelligence and aptitude testing in the public schools and the development of widely accepted aptitude/ability batteries such as the Differential Aptitude Test (DAT) and the General Aptitude Test Battery (GATB; see Anastasi, 1976; Cronbach, 1970).

L. L. Thurstone's (1938) monumental work in creating a taxonomy of mental abilities for children and adolescents was soon followed by even more extensive taxonomies based on work with college students (Guilford, 1967), and work by Cattell and Horn (e.g., Cattell, 1963; Horn, 1970) using male prison inmates ranging in age from young adulthood to early old age. The work by Cattell and Horn is of particular interest, since it posited differential developmental trajectories for fluid abilities (Gf) that were thought to be biologically based and thus subject to early decline, and crystallized abilities (Gc) that were culturally acquired and thus likely to show growth into old age. A broad compendium of factor-referenced tests also became available, allowing investigators to select multiple markers for specific mental abilities (Ekstrom, French, Harman, & Derman, 1976; French, Ekstrom, & Price, 1963).

Disenchantment with ability measurement began to set in following widespread criticism of the misapplication of intelligence tests in education (e.g., Kamin, 1974). Clinicians began to realize that profile analyses of intelligence tests were less useful than had originally been thought and that the information gained on intellectual status often seemed to contribute little to guide therapeutic interventions.

Despite these criticisms, it remains obvious that omnibus measures of intelligence have been rather useful in predicting persons' competence in dealing with the standard educational systems of our country. They have also been useful in predicting success in vocational pursuits whenever job requirements depend on educationally based knowledge or skills or involve high levels of analytic or basic problem-solving skills. Measures of specific abilities, although somewhat more controversial, have nevertheless had utility in predicting competence in those specific situations where special abilities can be expected to be of importance. Many reasonable arguments have been made for the proposition that motivational and other personality variables might have greater potency in predicting adjustment and competence in midlife than does intelligence, but the empirical evidence for this proposition is less than convincing. Certainly when dealing with the elderly it becomes readily apparent that the assessment of intellectual competence, whether or not it may have been irrelevant during midlife, once again reaches paramount importance. Questions such as who should be retired for cause (read incompetence), in the absence of mandatory retirement at relatively early ages; whether there is sufficient remaining competence for independent living; or whether persons can continue to conserve and dispose of their property all involve the assessment of intellectual functioning (see also Schaie, 1988a, 1988b; Willis, 1995; Willis & Schaie, 1994).

If the reader agrees with me that the preceding issues are important to our society, it then becomes necessary to examine in detail the factual issues involved in the development of adult intelligence. We must begin to differentiate intraindividual decremental changes from interindividual differences that result in behavior of older cohorts that appears to be obsolete when compared with the behavior of their younger peers. We need to examine at what age developmental peaks do occur and assess generational differences as well as within-generation age changes. Most important, we must determine the reasons why some individuals show intellectual decline in early adulthood, whereas others maintain or increase their level of intellectual functioning well into advanced old age.

History of the Seattle Longitudinal Study

The origins of the Seattle Longitudinal Study can be traced back to work I did as an undergraduate at the University of California at Berkeley while doing directed studies under the supervision of Professor Read D. Tuddenham. He had introduced me, in an inspiring tests and measurements course, to the basic concepts of factor analysis and the writings of L. L. Thurstone (1938).[1] I soon inferred that, although the work of Wechsler (1939) on adult intelligence might be of great concern to clinical psychologists, the Wechsler–Bellevue test and its derivatives, because of their factorial complexity, did not have the most desirable attributes for the exploration of developmental issues. I also learned that the more explicitly defined Primary Mental Abilities (PMA; Thurstone, 1938) had not been explored beyond adolescence and concluded that such exploration might possibly be a fruitful topic for systematic research.

In an initial study I explored whether the factorial independence of the five abilities measured in the most advanced form of the PMA test (PMA 11–14; Thurstone & Thurstone, 1949) would be retained in adulthood. I then proceeded to ask whether adults would function at the same level as did adolescents. More important, I raised the question whether there might be ability-related differentials in adult PMA performance, and whether such differences in pattern would remain if the PMA test were administered under nonspeeded conditions (Schaie, Rosenthal, & Perlman, 1953).

My appetite having been whetted by some provocative results of the early pilot study, I continued to explore a variety of corollaries of intelligence in adulthood during my graduate work at the University of Washington (Schaie, Baltes, & Strother, 1964; Schaie & Strother, 1968a, 1968d; Strother, Schaie, & Horst, 1957). As part of this work I also developed a new factored test of behavioral rigidity (TBR; Schaie, 1955, 1960; Schaie & Parham, 1975). These activities

---

1   A more extensive account of my scientific autobiography can be found in Schaie (in press).

culminated in a doctoral dissertation designed to replicate the earlier work on differential ability patterns across a wider portion of the adult life span as well as to look at the effect of rigidity–flexibility on the maintenance or decline of intellectual functioning (Schaie, 1958a, 1958b, 1958c, 1959a, 1959b). This dissertation, of course, became the base for the subsequent longitudinal-sequential studies summarized in this volume.

The search for an appropriate population frame for the base study was guided by the consideration that what was needed was a subject pool with reasonably well-known demographic characteristics, one that had been established for reasons other than research on cognitive behavior. That is, if possible the initial selection of volunteer participants for the study should be designed to minimize selection in terms of the potential participants' interest in, concern with, or performance level on the dependent variables of interest. When plans for the study matured, my mentor, Professor Charles R. Strother, was by fortunate coincidence president of the lay board of the Group Health Cooperative of Puget Sound, one of the first broadly based health maintenance organizations (HMOs) in the United States. An arrangement was worked out with the administration of the health plan that permitted me to recruit potential research participants who had been selected by a random draw from the age/sex stratification of plan members aged 22 or older. The appeal for participation was made by the plan's medical director as part of a membership satisfaction survey, the administration and analysis of which was my quid pro quo for gaining access to this population.

Results of the 1956 cross-sectional base study did not support a causal model involving differential patterns of intellectual performance across age for flexible and rigid individuals. The study did demonstrate significant relationships between flexibility–rigidity and intelligence at all ages. More important, however, it provided a sound demonstration of differential patterns of intellectual functioning across age and, by virtue of its design, serendipitously provided the basis for the following longitudinal-sequential studies.

My interest in aging issues continued during a postdoctoral fellowship in medical psychology at Washington University, St. Louis, under the mentorship of Ivan Mensh. There I was able to apply psychological scaling techniques to the assessment of psychiatric complaints in elderly outpatients (e.g., Schaie, Chatham, & Weiss, 1961; Schaie, Rommel, & Weiss, 1959). However, when I entered the job market in the late 1950s there were no positions for someone interested in the psychology of aging, and I accepted a position at the University of Nebraska teaching psychological assessment to students in clinical psychology. My research interest during that period turned to the unobtrusive assessment of personality characteristics by investigating the use of color preference and its relation to moods (see Schaie, 1963; Schaie & Heiss, 1964). But soon my concern returned to the issue of intellectual development in adulthood.

Perhaps the most immediate stimulation leading to the conversion of a one-time cross-sectional study into a series of longitudinal studies was my reading of reports on longitudinal studies of individuals reaching middle adulthood, such as the articles by Bayley and Oden (1955); Jarvik, Kallman, and Falek (1962); and Owens (1953, 1959). Taken together, findings from these studies suggested to me that there was strong evidence that most intellectual abilities were maintained at least into midlife and that some abilities remained stable beyond that period. These findings clearly contrasted with the results of the earlier cross-sectional literature, including my own dissertation data. What seemed to be called for was the follow-up of a broad cross-sectional panel, such as the one I had been able to examine, by means of a short-term longitudinal inquiry. Intensive discussions of such a project with Charles Strother were followed by a grant application to the National Institutes of Health, which funded the study in time to collect the first set of follow-up data in the summer of 1963.

In addition to tracking down and retesting as many of the individuals studied in 1956 as possible, we decided to draw a new random sample from the original population frame in order to provide the necessary controls for examining retest effects and to begin addressing the possibility that sociocultural change affects intellectual performance. The latter concern was stimulated by the thoughtful admonitions previously voiced by Raymond Kuhlen (1940, 1963). Our new sample extended over the original age range

(22 to 70) plus an additional 7-year interval to match the age range now reached by the original sample.

The second cross-sectional study essentially replicated the findings of the base study. The short-term longitudinal study, however, disclosed substantially different information about peak levels and rate of decline. Publication of findings was therefore delayed until a theoretical model could be built that accounted for the discrepancy between the longitudinal and cross-sectional data (Schaie, 1965, 1967). These analyses suggested that comparisons of age-group means needed to be conducted for the repeatedly measured samples as well as for successive independent samples drawn from the same cohort. Results were reported that called attention to substantial cohort differences and that questioned the universality and significance of intellectual decrement with advancing age in community-dwelling persons (Nesselroade, Baltes, & Schaie, 1972; Schaie, 1970; Schaie & Strother, 1968b, 1968c).

It soon became evident that the conclusions based on data covering a single 7-year interval required further replication, if only because two occasions of measurement permit the examination of cross-sectional sequences, but not of longitudinal sequences (see chapter 2; see also Baltes, Reese, & Nesselroade, 1977), the latter requiring a minimum of three measurement occasions. Only longitudinal sequences allow designs that permit contrasting age and cohort effects. Hence, plans were made for a third data collection, which was conducted in 1970. In that cycle as many persons as possible examined on the first two test occasions were retested, and a third random sample was drawn from the residual members of the base population (Schaie, 1979; Schaie, Labouvie, & Buech, 1973; Schaie & Labouvie-Vief, 1974; Schaie & Parham, 1977).

The results from the third data collection seemed rather definitive in replicating the short-term longitudinal findings, but a number of questions remained. Discrepancies between findings in the repeated-measurement and independent-sampling studies suggested the need for a replication of the 14-year longitudinal sequences, and it further seemed useful to follow the original sample over as long as 21 years. A fourth data collection was therefore conducted in 1977, again retesting the previous samples and adding a new random sample, this time from an expanded population frame (Schaie & Hertzog, 1983, 1986). Continuous funding also made it possible to address a number of bothersome collateral questions. These included analyses of the consequences of shifting from a sampling-without-replacement to a sampling-with-replacement paradigm (Gribbin, Schaie, & Stone, 1976); an analysis of the effects of monetary incentives on participant characteristics (Gribbin & Schaie, 1976); an examination of the aging of tests (Gribbin & Schaie, 1977); and the beginning of causal analyses of health and environmental factors upon change or maintenance of adult intellectual performance (Gribbin, Schaie, & Parham, 1980; Hertzog, Schaie, & Gribbin, 1978).

My early introduction to the issues of cohort differences and secular trends led to serious questions as to what the meaning of these effects might be beyond their role as control variables or as bothersome design confounds. I therefore began to pay increased attention to the impact of social structures and microenvironments on cognitive change (see Schaie, 1974; Schaie & Gribbin, 1975; Schaie & O'Hanlon, 1990). This work was influenced early on by the writing of Matilda Riley (Riley, 1985; Riley, Johnson, & Foner, 1972) and later on by the work of Carmi Schooler (1972, 1987), as well as of the many sociologists, anthropologists, and epidemiologists who have contributed to the Penn State social structure conference series (see Bengtson, Schaie, & Burton, 1995; Kertzer & Schaie, 1989; Rodin, Schooler, & Schaie, 1990, Schaie, Blazer, & House, 1992; Schaie & Schooler, 1989).

Until the fourth (1977) cycle of the SLS we followed the then conventional wisdom of assessing each primary ability with the observable marker variable deemed to be the most reliable and valid measure of the latent construct to be estimated. With the widespread introduction of modern methods of confirmatory (restricted) factor analysis, it became obvious that we needed to extend our concern with changes in level of intellectual functioning in adulthood to the assessment of structural relationships within the ability domain. This concern argued for collecting further data with a much expanded battery in which each ability would be multiply marked (Schaie, Dutta, & Willis, 1991; Schaie, Willis, Hertzog, & Schulenberg, 1987; Schaie, Willis, Jay, & Chipuer, 1989).

The fifth (1984) SLS cycle also marks the assumption of a major role in this project by Sherry L. Willis, who brought to this project her skills in designing and implementing cognitive training paradigms. Thus a major part of the fifth cycle was the implementation of a cognitive training study with our long-term participants aged 64 years or older, designed to assess whether cognitive training in the elderly serves to remediate cognitive decrement or to increase levels of skill beyond those attained at earlier ages (Schaie & Willis, 1986b; Willis & Schaie, 1986b, 1986c, 1988).

The database available through the fifth cycle has also made it possible to update the normative data on age changes and cohort differences (Schaie, 1990a, 1990b, 1990c; Schaie & Willis, 1993) and to apply sequential analysis designs controlled for the effects of experimental mortality and practice (Cooney, Schaie, & Willis, 1988; Schaie, 1988d). Finally, this cycle saw the introduction of measures of practical intelligence (Willis & Schaie, 1986b), analyses of marital assortativity using data on married couples followed over as long as 21 years (Gruber & Schaie, 1987; Gruber-Baldini, Schaie, & Willis, 1995), and the application of event history methods to hazard analysis of cognitive change with age (Schaie, 1989a).

Our current research program, initial results of which are provided in this volume, include a set of four related studies. First, with the collaboration of Robert Plomin, a noted developmental behavior geneticist, we have taken advantage of the longitudinal database to collect data to implement a study of cognitive family resemblance in adulthood. We did this by recruiting the participation of a large number of adult offspring and siblings of our longitudinal panel members (Schaie, Plomin, Willis, Gruber-Baldini, & Dutta, 1992; Schaie, Plomin, Willis, Gruber-Baldini, Dutta, & Bayen, 1993; Schaie & Willis, 1995). Second, we have abstracted the health histories on our panel members and have conducted more detailed investigations of the relationship between health and maintenance of intellectual functioning (Gruber-Baldini, 1991a; Gruber-Baldini & Schaie, 1990; Gruber-Baldini, Willis, & Schaie, 1989). Third, we have conducted a 7-year follow-up on the cognitive training study and have replicated the study with a more recent cohort of older persons (Willis & Schaie, 1992, 1994b). Fourth, we are now able to conduct longitudinal analyses of cognitive ability structures and further update our normative data with the collection of a sixth

(1991) wave, using the standard approach of retesting and drawing a sixth new independent sample (Schaie, 1993, 1994a).

Objectives of the Seattle Longitudinal Study

Throughout the history of the SLS, an effort now extending over more than 35 years, our focus has been on five major questions, which we have attempted to ask with greater clarity and increasingly more sophisticated methodology at each successive stage of the study. These are as follows.

1. *Does intelligence change uniformly through adulthood, or are there different life course ability patterns?* Our studies have shown that there is no uniform pattern of age-related changes across all intellectual abilities, and that studies of an overall index of intellectual ability (IQ) therefore do not suffice to monitor age changes and age differences in intellectual functioning for either individuals or groups. Our data do lend some support to the notion that fluid abilities tend to decline earlier than crystallized abilities. There are, however, important Ability × Age and Ability × Cohort interactions that complicate matters. For example, gender difference trends suggest that women decline earlier on the active abilities and men on the passive abilities. Moreover, whereas fluid abilities begin to decline earlier, crystallized abilities appear to show steeper decrement once the late 70s are reached.

Although cohort-related differences in the rate and magnitude of age changes in intelligence remained fairly linear for cohorts that entered old age during the first three cycles of our study, they have since shown substantial shifts. For example, rates of decremental age change have abated, and at the same time there appear to be negative cohort trends as we begin to study members of the baby-boom generation. It is beginning to appear as if patterns of socialization unique to a given sex role in a specific historical period may be a major determinant of the pattern of change in abilities. More fine-grained analyses suggest, moreover, that there may be substantial gender differences as well as differential changes for those who decline and those who remain stable when age changes are decomposed into accuracy and speed.

With multiple markers of abilities, we have begun to conduct cross-sectional analyses of ability structure over a wide age range. Thus far it has been possible to demonstrate configural but not metric factor invariance across wide age/cohort ranges. Finally, we have examined the relationship of everyday tasks to the framework of practical intelligence and perceptions of competence in everyday situations facing older persons.

2. *At what age is there a reliably detectable decrement in ability, and what is its magnitude?* We have generally shown that reliably replicable average age decrements in psychometric abilities do not occur prior to age 60 but that such reliable decrement can be found for all abilities by age 74. Analyses from the most recent phases of the SLS, however, suggest that small but statistically significant average decrement can be found for some, but not all, cohorts beginning in the decade of the 50s. However, more detailed analyses of individual differences in intellectual change demonstrate that even at age 81 fewer than half of all observed individuals have shown reliable decremental change over the preceding 7 years. In addition, average decrement below age 60 amounts to less than 0.2 of a standard deviation; by age 81 average decrement rises to approximately 1 population standard deviation for most variables.

The data from the SLS attain increasing importance in providing a normative base to determine at what ages declines reach practically significant levels of importance for public policy issues related to mandatory retirement, age discrimination in employment, or the determination of the population proportions that can live independently in the community. These bases will shift over time, as we have demonstrated in the SLS that both level of performance and rate of decline show significant Age × Cohort interactions.

3. *What are the patterns of generational differences, and what is their magnitude?* Results from the SLS have conclusively demonstrated the prevalence of substantial generational (cohort) differences in psychometric abilities. These cohort trends differ in magnitude and direction by ability and can therefore not be determined from composite IQ indices. As a consequence of these findings, it was concluded that cross-sectional studies used to model age change will overestimate age changes prior to the 60s for those variables that show negative cohort gradients and underestimate age changes for those variables with positive cohort gradients.

Our studies of generational shifts in abilities have in the past been conducted with random samples from arbitrarily defined birth cohorts. As a supplement and an even more powerful demonstration, we have recently conducted family studies that compare performance levels for individuals and their adult children. We have also recruited siblings of our participants to obtain data that allow extending the knowledge base in the developmental behavior genetics of cognition to the adult level, by providing data on parent–offspring and sibling correlations in adulthood.

4. *What accounts for individual differences in age-related change in adulthood?* The most powerful and unique contribution of a longitudinal study of adult development arises from the fact that only longitudinal data permit the investigation of individual differences in antecedent variables that lead to early decrement for some persons and maintenance of high levels of functioning for others into very advanced age. A number of factors that account for these individual differences have been implicated, some of which have been shown to be amenable to experimental intervention. The variables that have been implicated in reducing risk of cognitive decline in old age have included (a) absence of cardiovascular and other chronic diseases; (b) a favorable environment mediated by high socioeconomic status; (c) involvement in a complex and intellectually stimulating environment; (d) flexible personality style at midlife; (e) high cognitive status of spouse; and (f) maintenance of high levels of perceptual processing speed.

5. *Can intellectual decline with increasing age be reversed by educational intervention?* Because longitudinal studies permit tracking stability or decline on an individual level, it has also been feasible to carry out interventions designed to remediate known intellectual decline as well as to reduce cohort differences in individuals who have remained stable in their own performance over time but who have become disadvantaged when compared with younger peers. Findings from the cognitive training studies conducted with our longitudinal subjects (under the primary direction of Sherry L. Willis) suggest that observed decline in many community-dwelling older people might well be a function of disuse and is clearly reversible for many. Indeed, cognitive training resulted in approximately two thirds of the experimental subjects showing significant improvement; and about

40% of those who had declined significantly over 14 years were returned to their predecline level. In addition we were able to show that we did not simply "train to the test," but rather trained at the ability (latent construct) level, and that the training did not disturb the ability structure.

The dialectical process between data collection and model building that has been part of the SLS has made possible substantial methodological advances in the design and analysis of studies of human development and aging. In addition the study has provided baselines for clinical assessment and has made contributions relevant to education, basic instruction in psychological aging, and a variety of public policy issues.

Plan for the volume

I begin with a brief discussion of the methodological issues that informed our program of research (chapter 2). This involves a review of the age–period–cohort model to examine the relationship between cross-sectional, longitudinal, and sequential data collections. I then deal with the fact that our study is a quasi-experiment and describe the associated internal validity threats and how we have dealt with them. Finally, in this chapter I consider the problem of structural equivalence of observed measures across comparison groups and time.

Chapter 3 contains a detailed presentation of our database. This includes a description of our study participants and of the measurement battery. The latter, in addition to the cognitive ability measures, includes measures of cognitive style, everyday problem solving, self-reported cognitive change, descriptions of lifestyles, health status, and the subjective environment as well as personality traits and attitudes.

The substantive findings of the SLS on cognitive aging are organized into three sections: cross-sectional studies (chapter 4), longitudinal studies (chapter 5), and studies of cohort differences (chapter 6). These presentations are followed by the results of the cognitive intervention studies, including their long-term follow-up and replication with a new cohort (chapter 7).

A number of methodological studies were required in the course of this project (chapter 8). These included a sampling study designed to assess whether it was feasible to move from a sampling-without-replacement to a sampling-with-replacement strategy and a study on the aging of tests, as well as an assessment of the effects of experimental mortality (subject attrition), of the effects of repeated testing, of offering monetary rewards, and of the structural equivalence of our data across samples differing in age, across experimental interventions, and within cohorts across time.

The next three chapters explore interrelationships between the cognitive variables and their context: the relationship between cognitive styles and intellectual functioning (chapter 9), the effects of health on the maintenance of intellectual functioning and the role of intellectual functioning as a predictor of physical health in old age (chapter 10), and a discussion of lifestyle variables that affect intellectual functioning (chapter 11).

Throughout the study some limited data have been collected on a number of personality traits and attitudes. Comprehensive analyses of these variables are presented in chapter 12. This is followed by an account of our family studies of intellectual abilities in adulthood designed to consider similarities in adult parent–offspring and sibling pairs as well as similarity in married couples (chapter 13). Our study participants' perceptions of change in their cognitive functioning over time and their perceptions of the effects of the cognitive training are treated in chapter 14. Finally, there is a brief summary and a listing of those conclusions I believe to be firmly supported by the data presented in this volume (chapter 15).

Much of the material presented in this volume was originally reported in book chapters and scientific journals. An extensive summary of the cognitive abilities part of the study through the fourth (1977) data collection can be found in Schaie (1983a), with updates through the fifth (1984) data collection in Schaie (1988e, 1990a) and Schaie and Hertzog (1986), and brief overviews and previews of the sixth data collection in Schaie (1993, 1994a). Other original sources are cited where the relevant material is presented. However, a substantial portion of the content of this volume was previously available only in the form of convention papers or other manuscripts of limited circulation. Other materials represent sum-

mary previews of as yet unpublished analyses from the most recent
sixth (1991) cycle of the study.

Chapter summary

This chapter describes the scientific odyssey that began with the
author's emerging interest in the complex phenomena of adult cognitive development. It lays out the reasons why one should study
intelligence in adulthood by giving a brief history of the field of adult
intelligence and by pointing out that intellectual competence attains
increasing importance from middle adulthood on, when level of
intellectual competence may determine job retention, whether or not
independent living within the community remains possible, and
maintenance of control over one's financial decision making. An
account is then given of the history of the Seattle Longitudinal
Study, which began as the author's doctoral dissertation. The objectives of the Seattle Longitudinal Study are then described. These
involve the questions (1) whether intelligence changes uniformly
through adulthood or whether there are different life course ability
patterns; (2) at what age decrement in ability can reliably be detected
and what the magnitude of that decrement is; (3) what the patterns
of generational differences are and what their magnitude is; (4) what
accounts for individual differences in age-related change in adulthood; and (5) whether intellectual decline with increasing age can be
reversed by educational intervention. Finally, there is a preview of
the organization and content of this volume.

2

Methodological issues

In this chapter I summarize for the reader a number of methodological issues, including certain research design and analysis paradigms, familiarity with which is essential in order to understand the design of the studies and their findings. I begin with a brief exposition of the relationship between cross-sectional and longitudinal data in the context of the general developmental model. I then present the rationale for both simple and sequential schemes of data acquisition and analysis. Next I deal with the problems of internal validity of developmental studies and sketch out designs for the measurement and control of the most obvious internal validity problems plaguing developmental studies. Finally, I deal with the relationship between observed measures and latent variables and describe how confirmatory (restricted) factor analysis can be applied to assess construct equivalence across cohorts, age, and time in the study of developmental problems.

Cross-sectional and longitudinal data

One of the major contributions of the SLS has been the didactic interplay between data acquisition and the formulation and testing of analytic models of interest to developmental scientists. Once the original cross-sectional study had been converted (in the first follow-up) to a mixed cross-sectional–longitudinal design, it became necessary for me to try to understand the relationship of the two forms of data acquisition in order to interpret the alternative cross-sectional and longitudinal findings occurring in a particular data set. This need led me to explore what I termed a "general developmental model" (Schaie, 1965, 1967), that would help organize and clarify the relationships among these data.

The general developmental model characterizes the developmental status of a given behavior B to be function of three components, such that $B = f(A, C, T)$. In this context, age (A) refers to the number of years from birth to the chronological point at which the organism is observed or measured. Cohort (C) denotes a group of individuals who enter the environment at the same point in time (usually but not necessarily at birth), and time of measurement (T) indicates the temporal occasion on which a given individual or group of individuals is observed or measured.[1] The three components are confounded in the sense that once two of them are specified, then the third is known – similar to the confounding of temperature, pressure, and volume in the physical sciences. Nevertheless, each of the three components may be of primary interest for some questions of interest in the developmental sciences, and it is therefore useful to estimate the specific contribution attributable to each component.

The general developmental model allows us to specify how these components are confounded in research designs traditionally used by developmentalists. In addition, novel designs can be derived from the model that allow us to estimate the components confounded in different ways, even though their unconfounded estimation still eludes us except under specific circumstances and with certain collateral assumptions (Schaie, 1986, 1994b). In turn, these designs lead to new departures in theory building (Schaie, 1988c, 1992).

Simple data collection designs

Most empirical studies in the developmental sciences involve age comparisons either at one point in time or at successive time intervals (see also Nesselroade & Labouvie, 1985). The cross-sectional, longitudinal, and time-lag designs represent the traditional strategies used for this purpose.

Cross-sectional strategy. The hypothesis to be investigated simply asks whether there are differences in a given characteristic for samples

---

1 Each of these components can be defined also independent of calendar time (see Schaie, 1984a, 1986, 1994b).

drawn from different cohorts but measured at the same point in time. This is an important question for the study of interindividual differences. Age differences in behavior at a particular point in historical time may require different societal responses regardless of the antecedent conditions that may be responsible for the age differences. It must be recognized, however, that age differences detected in a cross-sectional data set are inextricably confounded with cohort differences. Since cross-sectional subsamples are measured only once, no information is available on intraindividual change. Unless there is independent evidence to suggest that older cohorts performed at the same level as younger cohorts at equivalent ages, it would be most parsimonious to assume, at least in comparisons of adult samples, that cross-sectional age differences are estimates of cohort differences that may be either inflated or reduced by maturational changes occurring over a specified age range.

Longitudinal strategy. Here the hypothesis to be investigated is whether there are age-related changes within the same population cohort measured on two or more occasions. This is the question that must be asked whenever one is interested in predicting age differentiation in behavior occurring over time. However, longitudinal data do not provide unambiguous estimates of intraindividual change. Unless the behavior to be studied is impervious to environmental influences, it must be concluded that a single-cohort longitudinal study will confound age-related (maturational) change with time-of-measurement effects that are specific to the particular historical period over which the behavior is monitored (Schaie, 1972). The time-of-measurement effects could either mask or grossly inflate maturational changes. In addition, longitudinal studies are subject to additional threats to their internal validity that would be controlled for in cross-sectional designs (see discussion of internal validity below).

Time-lag strategy. In this design, two samples of individuals drawn from successive cohorts are compared at successive points in time. The hypothesis to be tested is whether there are differences in a given behavior for samples of equal age but drawn at different points in time. This strategy is of particular interest to social and educational psychologists. It is particularly appropriate when one wishes to study performance of individuals of similar age in successive cohorts (e.g., comparing baby boomers with the preceding generation). The simple time-lag design, however, also confounds the cohort effect with time-of-measurement effects and therefore may provide cohort estimates that are inflated or reduced, depending on whether the temporal interval between the cohorts represents a period of favorable or adverse environmental influences.

Sequential data collection designs

In order to reduce the limitations inherent in the simple data collection schemes, several alternative sequential strategies have been suggested (see Baltes, 1968; Schaie, 1965, 1973b, 1977, 1986). The term *sequential* implies that the required sampling strategy includes acquisition of a sequence of samples taken across several measurement occasions. To understand the application of sequential strategies, we must first distinguish between their role as sampling designs and as data analysis strategies (see Schaie, 1983b; Schaie & Baltes, 1975). Sampling design refers to the particular cells of a Cohort × Age (time) matrix that are to be sampled in a developmental study. Analysis strategies refer to the manner in which the cells that have been sampled can be organized to disaggregate the effects of age (A), cohort (C), and time of measurement (T). Figure 2.1 presents a typical Cohort × Age matrix identifying the several possible sequential designs. This figure also illustrates the confounding of the three developmental parameters of interest. A and C appear as the rows and columns of the matrix; T is the parameter listed inside the matrix cells. There has been an extended debate on how these effects might be unconfounded. The reader interested in this debate is referred to papers by Adam (1978); Buss (1979–1980); George, Siegler, and Okun (1981); Glenn (1976, 1981); Horn and McArdle (1980); Mason, Mason, Winsborough, and Poole (1973); Schaie (1965, 1967, 1973b, 1977, 1984a, 1986a, 1994b); and Schaie and Hertzog (1982).

Sampling designs. It is possible to distinguish two types of sequential sampling designs: those using the same panel of individuals re-

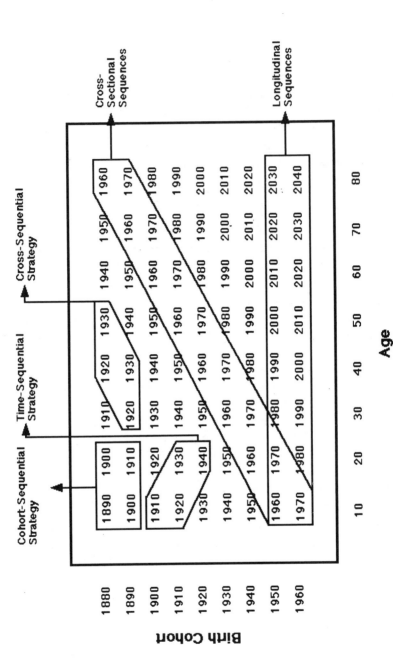

Figure 2.1. Schematic showing cross-sectional and longitudinal sequences and analysis strategies deduced from the general developmental model. Table entries represent times of measurement (period). From Schaie, 1983a, p. 9.

peatedly to fill the cells of the matrix, and those using independent random samples of individuals (each observed only once) from the same cohorts. The matrix shown in Figure 2.1 could be filled by either approach. Using Baltes's (1968) terminology, the two approaches can be called longitudinal and cross-sectional sequences, respectively. A cross-sectional sequence will usually involve the replication of a cross-sectional study so that the same age range of interest is assessed for at least two time periods, obtaining the estimate for each age level across multiple cohorts, where each sample is measured only once. By contrast, the longitudinal sequence represents the measurement of at least two cohorts over the same age range. Here also, estimates from each cohort are obtained at two or more points in time. The critical difference between the two approaches is that the longitudinal sequence permits the evaluation of intraindividual age change and interindividual differences in rate of change, information about which cannot be obtained from cross-sectional sequences. Figure 2.1 has equal intervals for the age ranges and cohort ranges investigated. Intervals do not have to be equal, but unequal intervals introduce special problems in analysis and are best avoided (see Botwinick & Arenberg, 1976).

Analysis strategies. Data matrices of the type shown in Figure 2.1 permit a variety of alternative analytic strategies (see Schaie, 1965, 1977, 1992). Specifically, each row of the matrix can be treated as a single-cohort longitudinal study, each diagonal as a cross-sectional study, and each column as a time-lag study. The sequential designs (except under the special circumstance of reconceptualizing one of the components [see Schaie, 1986]) do not permit complete disentanglement of all components of the $B = f(A, C, T)$ function, owing to the obvious linear dependency of the three factors. Despite this problem, I have suggested that, given the model, there exist three distinct analytic designs, created by considering the distinct effects of two of the components while assuming the constancy or irrelevance of the third component on theoretical or empirical grounds.

The minimum designs indicated in Figure 2.1 provide examples of three analytic approaches. The first, which I have called the *cohort-sequential* strategy, permits separation of age changes from cohort differences under the assumption of trivial time-of-measurement (period) effects. The second, or *time-sequential*, strategy further permits the separation of age differences from period differences, assuming only trivial cohort effects. Finally, the *cross-sequential* strategy permits the separation of cohort differences from period differences.

Longitudinal sequences

When one collects data in the form of longitudinal sequences, as in the SLS, in order to examine intraindividual age changes, it is possible to apply both the cohort-sequential and the cross-sequential strategies for data analysis. Developmental psychologists often find the cohort-sequential design of greatest interest because it explicitly differentiates intraindividual age changes within cohorts from interindividual differences between cohorts (see Baltes & Nesselroade, 1979; Schaie & Baltes, 1975; but see Schaie, 1986). This design also permits a check of the consistency of age functions over successive cohorts, thereby offering greater external validity than would be provided by a single-cohort longitudinal design.

As noted earlier, a critical assumption for the application of the cohort-sequential analysis strategy is the absence of time-of-measurement effects in the data under consideration. This assumption may be parsimonious for many psychological variables, but others may still be affected by "true" period effects or other internal validity threats, such as differences in instrumentation or experimenter behavior across test occasions (see section below on internal and external validity). The question arises, then, how violations of the assumption of no time-of-measurement (T) effects would be reflected in the results of the cohort-sequential analysis. Logical analysis suggests that all estimated effects will be perturbed, although the most direct evidence of the violation would be shown in a significant C (cohort) $\times$ A (age) interaction (see Schaie, 1973b). However, lack of such interaction does not necessarily guarantee the absence of T effects; in extensive studies such as ours, they might well be localized in a small subset of test occasions, thus biasing all estimates.

The essential consequence of the interpretational determinacy in sequential analysis is that, if design assumptions are violated, then all effect estimates will be biased to some degree. The problem of interpretation may be lessened, however, by estimating the relative likelihood of confounded T effects, given a strong theory about the nature and direction of estimated and confounded effects. We have found that the practical application of a strong theory to sequential designs may involve the specification of confounds in an "invalid" design in order to obtain direct estimates of the confounded effects (see Schaie, 1994b).

An example of the planned violation of design assumptions is use of the cross-sequential strategy under the assumption of no A effects, an assumption that most developmental psychologists might find hard to swallow! Such an approach may be quite useful, however, when longitudinal data are available for only a limited number of measurement occasions but extend over a wide range of cohort groupings. The cross-sequential design can then be implemented after only two measurement occasions, whereas a cohort-sequential design would require at least three such occasions. Moreover, the number of measurement occasions required to estimate cohort-sequential designs that span a wide age and/or cohort range would be prohibitive if we insist that no data analyses be performed until the data for the entire cohort-sequential design appropriate for the research question of interest had been acquired. Given a strong developmental theory about the nature of the confound A effects, a misspecified cross-sequential design can provide useful information about the significance of the A effects represented in both the C and T components. As will be seen, the early work in the SLS (analysis of the data from the first two cycles) began with such misspecification in a cross-sequential design in order to permit preliminary inferences regarding the relative importance of C and A effects prior to the availability of data that permitted direct simultaneous assessment of these effects (see Schaie & Labouvie-Vief, 1974; Schaie & Strother, 1968b).

Although it is always preferable to estimate parameter effects from the most appropriate design – one that makes the correct limiting assumptions – one must often settle for something less than the optimal, whether this be a temporary expedient or one dictated by the phenomenon being studied.

Threats to internal and external validity

Although the longitudinal approach has advantages over studies based on one-time observations, it is also beset with many methodological problems, some of which have necessitated a variety of design refinements, which may be noted as the reader follows the account of the SLS from its earlier to its later phases. In this section I wish to alert the reader to some of these issues by discussing threats to the internal and external validity of our study, and I suggest approaches to possible solutions of the remaining problems, which will again be encountered as they are applied to various analyses described in this volume.

Longitudinal studies as quasi-experiments

Longitudinal studies do not conform to the rules for true experiments, since age is a fixed personal attribute that cannot be experimentally assigned. Consequently, longitudinal studies are subject to all the problems inherent in the type of study that Campbell and Stanley (1963) have denoted as "quasi-experiments." These problems may be threats to the internal validity of the study. That is, factors analyzed in a given design that are thought to assess the hypothesized construct may in fact be confounded by other factors not explicitly included in the design. Alternatively, design problems may threaten the external validity of a study; that is, the extent to which valid generalizations from the sample can be applied to other populations.

Internal validity

Eight different threats to the internal validity of quasi-experiments such as longitudinal studies have been described (Campbell & Stanley, 1963): maturation, effects of history, testing, instrumentation, statistical regression, mortality, selection, and the selection–maturation interaction. The first two, history and maturation, have special meaning for the developmental psychologist beyond their threat to the internal validity of any pretest–posttest type of study design. *Maturation*, quite obviously, is not a threat to the validity of developmental studies but rather is the specific effect of primary interest to the investigator. Nevertheless, the measurement of maturation is not always unambiguous, since, given a specific developmental model, it may be necessary to go beyond a test of the null hypothesis negating maturational effects in order to test instead some quite explicit alternative hypotheses that specify direction and magnitude of the expected maturational effect.

By contrast, *historical* effects are indeed the primary internal validity problem for the developmental scientist. History is directly involved in both cohort and time-of-measurement (period) effects. However, cohort effects represent the impact of historical effects on a group of individuals who share similar environmental circumstances at equivalent points in their maturation sequence. On the other hand, time-of-measurement effects represent those events that impact all members of the population experiencing a common historical exposure, regardless of cohort membership. The specific threat to longitudinal studies is that historical effects may threaten the internal validity of designs that attempt to measure the effect of maturation (aging effects).

The traditional single-cohort longitudinal design is a special case of the pretest–posttest design in that it repeatedly measures the same individuals over time. Hence, such studies are affected also by the other six threats to internal validity described by Campbell and Stanley. There are actually two different aspects of *testing*: reactivity and practice. Reactivity involves the possible effect on subsequently observed behavior of being exposed to certain procedures that are part of the experimental protocol. Longitudinal study participants might respond to a second test in a very different manner than would be the case if they had not been tested previously, a behavior change that could be confused with the effects of maturation. Practice effects, on the other hand, may simply mean that, upon subsequent tests, study participants will spend less time in figuring out items previously solved and thus can improve their overall performance.

The internal validity threat of *instrumentation* refers to differences in measurement techniques that covary with measurement occasions. In long-term longitudinal studies, such differences may occur when study personnel change, or when records regarding the study protocol on previous occasions have been lost and slight variations in protocol are introduced inadvertently. Such effects, again, may lead to the erroneous inference of having demonstrated maturational trends, or they may obscure reliable, but small, developmental changes actually occurring.

Statistical regression involves the tendency of variables containing measurement error to regress toward the population mean from one occasion to the next. This problem is of particular importance in two-occasion longitudinal studies. (See Baltes, Nesselroade, Schaie, and Labouvie [1972] and Schaie and Willis [1986b] for examples of applications of the time-reversal method that test for the effect of regression in such studies.) It has been shown, however, that regression effects do not necessarily cumulate over extended longitudinal series (Nesselroade, Stigler, & Baltes, 1980).

Members of longitudinal panels obviously cannot be forced to continue their participation. Consequently, another serious threat to the internal validity of longitudinal studies is that of *experimental mortality*. This term describes the attrition of participants from a sample between measurement occasions, whether such attrition is due to biological mortality, morbidity, or simply experimenter ineptness in maintaining good relations with panel members. Most empirical studies of experimental mortality suggest that attrition is nonrandom at least between the first and second measurement occasions (Cooney, Schaie, & Willis, 1988; Gribbin & Schaie, 1979; Riegel & Riegel, 1972; Schaie, 1988d; Schaie, Labouvie, & Barrett, 1973; also see chapter 8).

Selection refers to the process of obtaining a sample from the population such that the observed effect is a function of the specific sample characteristics rather than of the maturational effect we wish to estimate. The *selection–maturation interaction* refers, of course, to the case where maturational effects may be found in some samples but not in others.

None of the internal validity threats can be controlled for or measured in single-cohort longitudinal studies. When multiple data sets such as ours are available, however, the magnitude of some of the effects can be estimated and appropriate corrections applied to the substantive studies. Specific designs for such analyses have been presented by Schaie (1977, 1988d) and will be applied to some of the data sets presented in chapter 8.

External validity

As quasi-experiments, longitudinal-sequential studies also share certain limitations with respect to the generalizability of their findings (see Cook & Campbell, 1979; Schaie, 1978). Four major issues can be identified. The first concerns experimental units; that is, the extent to which longitudinal data collected on one sample can permit inference to other populations (see Gribbin, Schaie, & Stone, 1976; chapter 8). The second involves experimental settings, or the extent to which findings have cross-situational validity (see Scheidt & Schaie, 1978; Willis & Schaie, 1986a). The third is concerned with treatment variables; that is, the limitations imposed by specific settings or measurement-implicit reinforcement schedules (see Birkhill & Schaie, 1975; Schaie & Goulet, 1977). Finally, external validity may be threatened by certain aspects intrinsic to the measurement variables, to the extent to which task characteristics remain appropriate at different developmental stages as a longitudinal study progresses (see below, and see Schaie, 1977–1978; Schaie, Willis, Jay, & Chipuer, 1989; Sinnott, 1989).

Schaie's "most efficient design"

Given the considerations above, I have collected data in the SLS using an approach that allows some useful analyses early on in the course of a longitudinal study but that over time generates data that can be used to address most of the methodological questions I have raised here. I include a description of this design here (see also Schaie & Willis, 1991a, pp. 248–254) to provide some guidance to those who would start a longitudinal study de novo, as well as to describe the design rationale of the SLS.

As should be obvious from the preceding discussion, the "most efficient design" is a combination of cross-sectional and longitudinal sequences created in a systematic way. In brief, the researchers begin with a cross-sectional study including multiple age groups.

Then, after a period of years, all of those subjects that can be retrieved are retested, providing longitudinal data on several cohorts (a longitudinal sequence). At the same time a new group of subjects over the same age range as the original sample is tested. The new sample together with the first cross-sectional study forms a cross-sectional sequence. This whole process can be repeated over and over (ideally with age groups and time intervals identical), retesting the previously tested subjects (adding to the longitudinal data) and initially testing new subjects (adding to the cross-sectional data).

In the SLS we first tested seven groups of people ranging in age from 22 to 70 in 1970 (see chapter 3). This was a straightforward cross-sectional study. In 1963 those subjects who could be found were retested. Hence, we were able to examine, for each of seven cohorts, what happened to average ability scores as the subjects grew 7 years older. At the same time we recruited new subjects in the same age groups as the original subjects (plus an additional group at the age now attained by the oldest original group) and tested them for the first time. The second cross-sectional study would represent a replication of the first study. A discrepancy suggests the presence of either cohort or time-of-measurement effects. In 1970 we retested the original sample for the third time, adding more data to the longitudinal sequence. Subjects who were added at T_2 in 1963 were also retested, adding a new longitudinal sequence. Again new subjects were recruited to form a third replication of the cross-sectional study. A similar approach was taken on subsequent test occasions, which in our case occurred in 1977, 1984, and 1991.

Data from the "most efficient design" or comparable designs can be analyzed in several ways. The way of greatest interest to developmental psychologists is to contrast age changes and cohort effects (Schaie & Baltes, 1975): a *cohort-sequential* analysis. Such a comparison permits a strong test of an irreversible age decrement model (Schaie, 1973b). At least two cohorts are required, and each cohort must be observed at least at two different ages. In a traditional longitudinal study data would be available only for a single cohort, and one would not know, therefore, whether the observed change holds true beyond the specific cohort studied. For example, one cohort may show an increase and the other a decrease, or one cohort may increase at a slower rate than the other. One cohort may have a higher average IQ than the other at both 60 and 70, though the increase or decrease may be similar for the two cohorts.

In *cross-sequential* analyses, cohort effects are contrasted with time of measurement. At least two cohorts are compared at two or more times of measurement. This strategy may be particularly appropriate for data sets that cover age ranges where, on average, stability is likely to obtain (such as in midlife). No age changes are expected, and the primary interest turns to identifying the presence and magnitude of cohort and time-of-measurement effects. The cross-sequential analysis is helpful when the researcher is interested in, say, the effects of some event or sociocultural change that occurs between the two times of measurement and, in addition, suspects that different cohorts might react differently. In addition, if there is reason to suppose that time-of-measurement effects are slight or nonexistent, then cross-sequential analysis can be used to estimate age changes, since subjects are obviously older at the second time of measurement.

If the cohort-sequential analysis contrasts cohort and age, and the cross-sequential analysis contrasts cohort and time of measurement, there is one logical possibility left: the *time-sequential* strategy, which contrasts age and time of measurement. We might find that the difference between age groups narrows over a given period; or perhaps both age groups change in the same manner, but the gap between them remains sizable. The time-sequential approach would be appropriate also for a test of a decrement-with-compensation model. When a new compensatory method is introduced (say, a computerized memory prosthesis or a drug affecting declining memory), the time-sequential method could show that age differences over the same age range would be smaller at Time 2 than at Time 1.

Repeated measures versus independent samples

In a typical longitudinal study, *repeated measures* are taken of the same subjects at different times. Another possibility is to use the same research design but with *independent samples* at each point on the longitudinal time scale. A longitudinal study usually begins by testing subjects at an initial time point, with plans to retest the same individuals at intervals. The alternative would be to draw a new (independent) sample from the same cohort at each test occasion. The independent sampling approach works well when a large sample is drawn from a large population. If small samples are used, it is of course necessary to make sure that successive samples are matched on factors such as gender, income, and education to avoid possible differences due to selection biases.

The independent-samples procedure, used conjointly with the repeated-measurement procedure, permits us to estimate the effects of experimental mortality and of instrumentation (practice) effects. The independent samples are initially drawn at each occasion; hence, they reflect the likely composition of the single sample the repeated-measurement study would have had if no subjects had been lost between testing – and of course if the subjects had not had any practice on the test instruments.

What analyses can be conducted on successive measurement occasions?

Time 1. The first occasion of any multiple-cohort longitudinal study will simply represent an *n*-group cross-sectional comparison.

Time 2. The second occasion provides a replication of the original cross-sectional study. There are as many 2-point longitudinal studies as there are different age groups in the T_1 design. Both time-sequential and cross-sequential analysis schemes can be applied. A simple cross-sectional experimental mortality by age/cohort analysis can be done by contrasting T_1 scores for those subjects who return and those who do not. Simple cross-sectional practice analyses can be made by contrasting T_1 means for Sample 1 subjects with the T_2 scores of Sample 2 subjects at equivalent ages.

Time 3. A third cross-sectional replication is now available, as well as a second replication of the 2-point longitudinal study. Three-point longitudinal studies are now available from the initial sample. It is now possible to conduct 2×2 cohort sequential analyses. Time-sequential and cross-sequential analyses can be extended to *n* $\times$ 3 designs, allowing estimation of quadratic trends. Alternatively, it is now possible to estimate either experimental mortality or practice effects in the time- or cross-sequential analyses.

Time 4. This adds a fourth cross-sectional replication, a third 2-point longitudinal replication, a second replication of the 3-point longitudinal study, and an initial 4-point longitudinal study. It is now possible to conduct $n \times 3$ cohort-sequential analyses, allowing quadratic estimates, as well as $n \times 4$ time-sequential and cross-sequential analyses that allow estimation of cubic trends. It is now possible to estimate the joint effects of experimental mortality and practice effects in the time- or cross-sequential analyses, and to estimate either of these effects in the cohort-sequential analysis.

Time 5. In addition to adding one further layer to all of the above analyses, this will allow estimation of joint effects of experimental mortality and practice in the cohort-sequential schema.

Structural equivalence

Except for a limited number of demographic attributes and gross anthropometric indices, there are very few observable characteristics that directly contribute to our understanding of human behavior. Behavioral scientists who investigate phenomena in areas such as intellectual abilities, motivation, and personality are rarely interested in their subjects' response to specific items or even the summary scores obtained on a particular measurement scale. Instead such responses are treated as one of many possible indicators of the respondents' location to an unobservable, theoretically defined, or empirically abstracted scientific construct. By the same token, those studying psychopathology are rarely interested in the occurrence of specific clinically observed symptoms, other than that such symptoms serve as indicators of diagnostic syndromes associated with broader import and consequences.

Observed variables and latent constructs

Although we must measure the observable phenotype or surface trait, it is usually the unobserved (latent) genotype or source trait that is the object of inquiry for the definition of developmental change. In fact, directly observable variables in the developmental sciences are primarily used as independent variables. Most dependent variables, by contrast, usually represent latent constructs that must be measured indirectly by means of multiple observations or indicators. This is perhaps fortunate, since the equivalence of single measures of a particular construct over wide age ranges and time periods is often questionable. A variety of techniques are, of course, available under the rubrics of linear structural equation and factor analysis methods that are suitable to examine the relationship between the observed behaviors and their underlying latent constructs (see also Bentler, 1980; Horn & McArdle, 1992; Jöreskog, 1979).

Factor analytic investigations are particularly useful to determine whether the relationships between observed variables and the latent constructs to be represented remain invariant across multiple groups or across time in longitudinal data. Only when factorial invariance has been demonstrated can one assume that quantitative comparisons of differences in developmental trajectories truly reflect changes in the underlying construct (see Baltes & Nesselroade, 1970, 1973). Two types of factorial invariance need to be considered: (1) invariance across multiple groups of subpopulations, such as are usually found in cross-sectional studies, and (2) invariance across time for the same individuals measured longitudinally. LISREL models can be specified that are suitable for statistical tests of the invariance assumption (see Alwin, 1988; Schaie & Hertzog, 1982, 1985).

Structural equivalence across comparison groups

Equivalence of groups must be considered whenever (1) cross-sectional data have been collected and age differences in score level are to be interpreted under the assumption that factor structure is equivalent across the different age groups; (2) when we wish to demonstrate equivalence of factor structure across multiple cohort groups; (3) when the same population is followed by means of drawing successive random samples across time; and (4) when subpopulations are to be compared on multiple dependent variables of interest.

Contradictory findings in the literature on age-group differences in factor structure can often be attributed to problems associated with the analysis of separate exploratory factor analyses of correlations specific to a particular group (see Cunningham, 1978, 1991; Jöreskog, 1971; Reinert, 1970). However, as has been shown by Meredith (1964, 1993), when level of performance differs across groups, it is only the unstandardized factor loadings that can remain invariant across groups. These difficulties can readily be overcome by the joint analysis of multiple covariance matrices in LISREL in which equality constraints are imposed across groups. Likelihood ratio tests then exist that can test the hypothesis that the unstandardized regression coefficients mapping variables on their latent constructs are indeed equivalent across groups (see also Alwin & Jackson, 1981). Alternatively, if large enough population samples exist, one can determine a population factor structure and then test how well a subpopulation structure can be fit by the factor structure obtained for the population (e.g., Schaie, Willis, Jay, & Chipuer, 1989; chapter 8).

Structural equivalence across time

The demonstration of factorial invariance is also important in showing that the relations between observations and latent constructs remain stable across time or that the introduction of an intervention might affect such relationships. When multiple measures of a set of latent constructs are available for two or more occasions across time, the highest covariances among observed variables will often be the covariances of the variables with themselves across measurement occasions. Exploratory factor analyses of such matrices would result in test-specific factors but would be less than optimal in representing change processes over time.

The longitudinal factor analysis procedures developed by Jöreskog and Sörbom (1977) represent a particularly appropriate method for study of factorial equivalence across time. First, they allow testing of the hypothesis that the regressions of variables on latent constructs can be constrained to be equal across the successive longitudinal testing occasions. Second, they permit us to assess interindividual differences in intraindividual change by testing longitudinal changes in factor variance (change in factor variance over time could occur only if there were individual differences in magnitude of change over time). Third, they allow us to estimate the stability of intra-individual differences (high factor covariances across time represent stability of individuals about their own factor means). Extensions of these models suitable for the cohort-sequential designs used in the SLS have been discussed by Jöreskog and Sörbom (1980) and Hertzog (1985), and in the SLS have been applied to longitudinal data (Hertzog & Schaie, 1986, 1988; Schaie, Maitland, & Willis, 1994) and to the evaluation of intervention effects on factorial invariance (Schaie, Willis, Hertzog, & Schulenberg, 1987); see also chapter 8.

For completeness, it should be noted that all the design recommendations provided for the comparison of repeated or independent estimates of performance level can also be applied to the analyses of structural invariance described in this section.

Chapter summary

This chapter discusses the methodological issues that have arisen from the SLS data collections and in a dialectic process have led to subsequent empirical study components. I summarize the general developmental model and specify the relationship between cross-sectional and longitudinal data in the context of that model. A rationale is presented for the simple and sequential schemes of data acquisition and analysis employed in the study. Consideration is then given to the problems of internal and external validity of developmental studies, and designs are presented that are used in the SLS to control for internal validity problems. I include a description of what has been called "Schaie's most efficient design" for multiple-cohort longitudinal studies and describe the analysis modes available at each of the first five test occasions in a longitudinal study thus designed.

The data to be presented in the following chapters concern both observed variables and latent constructs inferred from them. I therefore also discuss the relationship between observed measures and latent variables and describe the applicability of confirmatory (restricted) factor analysis to the assessment of construct equivalence across cohorts, age, and time in the study of developmental problems.

3

The database

The database for the Seattle Longitudinal Study consists of the assessments conducted during six major testing cycles (1956, 1963, 1970, 1977, 1984, and 1991). As part of the 1984 and 1991 cycles, cognitive intervention studies were conducted with a number of participants who were in their 60s or older. In addition, we conducted three pilot studies concerned with the characteristics of the Primary Mental Abilities Test (PMA) and the Test of Behavioral Rigidity (TBR) when used with adults (1952, 1953, 1954). Two collateral studies were undertaken to determine the consequences of shifting to an expanded sampling frame and providing monetary incentives (1974) and to investigate the aging of our test battery (1975). Finally, the basic test battery was administered to the adult offspring and siblings of our longitudinal panel members (1989–1990).

The subject population

All of our study participants (with the exception of those involved in the pilot and family studies) were members of the Group Health Cooperative of Puget Sound at the time they entered the study. Our original 1956 population frame consisted of approximately 18,000 potential participants 22 years of age or older. These individuals were stratified by age and sex, and 25 men and 25 women were randomly selected for each year of birth from 1882 to 1934. After removing individuals who were not in the area, 2,818 persons were actually contacted; of these, 910 agreed to participate. Testing then proceeded in groups of 10 to 30 persons until 25 men and 25 women had been tested in each 5-year birth interval over the age range from 22 to 70 (see Schaie, 1958c, 1959a).

For the second (1963) cycle, in addition to the longitudinal follow-up, approximately 3,000 names were again drawn randomly from the 1956 population after deleting names of all individuals tested in 1956. Of these, 997 persons ranging in age from 22 to 77 were successfully tested. A similar procedure was followed in 1970: retesting survivors of the 1956 and 1963 panels and establishing a new randomly selected panel (aged 22 to 84), consisting of 705 individuals. Our population frame having been virtually exhausted, we determined, by means of a collateral study (Gribbin, Schaie, & Stone, 1976; chapter 8), that it would be feasible to shift to a sampling-with-replacement basis. For the 1977 cycle, we therefore again sampled approximately 3,000 persons from what had now become a 210,000-member health plan. Of these, 609 new subjects were tested. A similar scheme was used in 1984, when 629 new subjects were assessed, and in 1991, when we added 693 new subjects from what by now had become a 420,000-member HMO.

Because of the 7-year intervals, all data were organized into 7-year age and cohort groupings. Tables 3.1 to 3.6 show that, for purposes of analysis, the main study now consists of 21 data sets. These consist of cross-sectional and longitudinal sequences (see Baltes, 1968) as follows.

The cross-sectional sequence

This sequence consists of six independent data sets (see Table 3.1 for detailed breakdown):

> Aa ($n = 500$) – seven cohorts tested in 1956 (mean ages = 25 to 67; mean birth years = 1889 to 1931)
>
> Bb ($n = 997$) – eight cohorts tested in 1963 (mean ages = 25 to 74; mean birth years = 1889 to 1938)
>
> Cc ($n = 705$) – nine cohorts tested in 1970 (mean ages = 25 to 81; mean birth years = 1889 to 1945)
>
> Dd ($n = 609$) – nine cohorts tested in 1977 (mean ages = 25 to 81; mean birth years = 1896 to 1952)
>
> Ee ($n = 629$) – nine cohorts tested in 1984 (mean ages = 25 to 81; mean birth years = 1903 to 1959)

Ff ($n = 693$) – nine cohorts tested in 1991 (mean ages = 25 to 81; mean birth years = 1910 to 1966)

The longitudinal sequences

These sequences involve 15 data sets comprising five 7-year, four 14-year, three 21-year, two 28-year, and one 35-year follow-ups (see Tables 3.2 to 3.6 for details).

Seven-year longitudinal data

Ab ($n = 303$) – seven cohorts followed from 1956 to 1963
Bc ($n = 420$) – eight cohorts followed from 1963 to 1970
Cd ($n = 340$) – nine cohorts followed from 1970 to 1977
De ($n = 294$) – nine cohorts followed from 1977 to 1984
Ef ($n = 428$) – nine cohorts followed from 1984 to 1991

Fourteen-year longitudinal data

Ac ($n = 162$) – seven cohorts followed from 1956 to 1970
Bd ($n = 337$) – eight cohorts followed from 1963 to 1977
Ce ($n = 224$) – nine cohorts followed from 1970 to 1984
Df ($n = 201$) – nine cohorts followed from 1977 to 1991

Twenty-one-year longitudinal data

Ad ($n = 130$) – seven cohorts followed from 1956 to 1977
Be ($n = 225$) – eight cohorts followed from 1963 to 1984
Cf ($n = 175$) – nine cohorts followed from 1970 to 1991

Twenty-eight-year longitudinal data

Ae ($n = 97$) – seven cohorts followed from 1956 to 1984
Bf ($n = 161$) – eight cohorts followed from 1963 to 1991

Thirty-five-year longitudinal data

Af ($n = 71$) – seven cohorts followed from 1956 to 1991

Successively longer studies, of course, involve subsets of those examined earlier. The main SLS database consequently consists of test records on 4,133 participants, of whom 71 were tested six times,

Table 3.1. *Frequency distribution of subject at first test, by cohort, sex, and year of entry into the study*

	Mean year of birth (cohort)												Total
	1889	1896	1903	1910	1917	1924	1931	1938	1945	1952	1959	1966	
1956 sample													
Mean age	(67)	(60)	(53)	(46)	(39)	(32)	(25)						
M	38	35	35	35	36	33	38						250
F	38	37	35	30	35	37	38						250
T	76	72	70	65	71	70	76						500
1963 sample													
Mean age	(74)	(67)	(60)	(53)	(46)	(39)	(32)	(25)					
M	38	64	68	62	70	71	52	42					467
F	39	63	64	81	76	79	70	58					530
T	77	127	132	143	146	150	122	100					997
1970 sample													
Mean age	(81)	(74)	(67)	(60)	(53)	(46)	(39)	(32)	(35)				
M	26	46	42	38	40	44	34	28	31				319
F	24	42	49	42	49	43	50	37	40				376
T	50	88	91	80	89	87	84	65	71				705
1974–1975 sample													
Mean age	(85)	(78)	(71)	(64)	(57)	(50)	(43)	(36)	(29)	(25)			
M	23	47	55	63	58	61	37	15	11	12			392
F	31	69	59	69	58	55	52	13	16	10			432
T	54	116	114	132	116	116	89	28	27	22			824

													Total
1977 sample													
Mean age		(81)	(74)	(67)	(60)	(53)	(46)	(39)	(32)	(25)			
M		27	37	35	35	40	32	37	29	28			300
F		31	33	38	37	37	37	36	33	27			309
T		58	70	73	72	77	69	73	62	55			609
1984 sample													
Mean age			(81)	(74)	(67)	(60)	(53)	(46)	(39)	(32)	(25)		
M			24	39	40	36	33	26	30	27	27		282
F			28	38	42	43	33	39	40	28	56		347
T			52	77	82	79	66	65	70	55	83		629
1991 sample													
Mean age				(81)	(74)	(67)	(60)	(53)	(46)	(39)	(32)	(25)	
M				33	41	41	32	38	34	39	31	27	316
F				34	43	56	41	40	49	40	40	34	377
T				67	84	97	73	78	83	79	71	61	693
Grand total (by cohort)													
M	125	219	261	305	320	326	258	186	135	106	58	27	2,326
F	132	242	268	332	340	350	321	223	178	105	96	34	2,621
T	257	461	529	637	660	676	579	409	313	211	154	61	4,947

Table 3.2. *Frequency distribution of longitudinal subjects tested in 1963, by cohort and sex*

	Mean year of birth (cohort)							
	1889	1896	1903	1910	1917	1924	1931	Total
Mean age in 1963	(74)	(67)	(60)	(53)	(46)	(39)	(32)	
M	25	13	21	22	23	19	19	142
F	23	27	23	18	24	25	21	161
T	*48*	*40*	*44*	*40*	*47*	*44*	*40*	*303*

183 were tested five times, 264 were tested four times, 394 were tested three times, 849 were tested twice, and 2,372 were tested only once. Cumulatively this results in a total of 1,761 subjects followed over 7 years, 912 over 14 years, 518 over 21 years, 254 over 28 years, and 71 over 35 years.

Characteristics of the base population

Our source of study participants provides a population frame that is reasonably close to the demographic pattern of the community from which it was drawn, although somewhat sparse at the lowest socioeconomic levels. In this section I provide data on educational and occupational levels for the six successive cycles and discuss shifts caused by nonrandom subject attrition (for further details on the substantive consequences of attrition, see chapter 8). Data on income were also collected, but because of inflationary factors they are not directly comparable across occasions.

Table 3.7 provides proportions for our 21 data sets by educational level (grade school, high school, college, and graduate training), and Table 3.8 lists similar data for occupational level (Unskilled = cleaning services, maintenance services, laborers, factory workers, fishermen; Semiskilled = protective services, bartenders, personal services, custodians; Skilled = mechanical–technical and clerical occupations; Semiprofessional = managers, proprietors, professions requiring less than an MA degree; Professional = requiring a

Table 3.3. *Frequency distribution of longitudinal subjects tested in 1970, by cohort, sex, and year of entry into the study*

	Mean year of birth (cohort)								
	1889	1896	1903	1910	1917	1924	1931	1938	Total
Mean age in 1970	(81)	(74)	(67)	(60)	(53)	(46)	(39)	(32)	
1956 sample									
M	8	3	13	17	11	11	10		73
F	6	12	15	15	15	15	11		89
T	*14*	*15*	*28*	*32*	*26*	*26*	*21*		*162*
1963 sample									
M	8	19	19	29	36	36	23	9	179
F	6	24	22	45	37	43	38	26	241
T	*14*	*43*	*41*	*74*	*73*	*79*	*61*	*35*	*420*

Table 3.4. *Frequency distribution of longitudinal subjects tested in 1977, by cohort, sex, and year of entry into the study*

	Mean year of birth (cohort)									
	1889	1896	1903	1910	1917	1924	1931	1938	1945	Total
Mean age in 1977	(88)	(81)	(74)	(67)	(60)	(53)	(46)	(39)	(32)	
1956 sample										
M	3	2	10	16	9	8	10			58
F	2	7	14	15	12	11	9			70
T	*5*	*9*	*24*	*31*	*21*	*19*	*19*			*128*
1963 sample										
M	1	11	11	27	31	32	19	10		142
F	3	16	12	40	38	35	36	15		195
T	*4*	*27*	*23*	*67*	*69*	*67*	*55*	*25*		*337*
1970 smple										
M	4	13	18	21	24	28	17	14	10	149
F	4	17	16	25	29	26	28	22	24	191
T	*8*	*30*	*34*	*46*	*53*	*54*	*45*	*36*	*34*	*340*

Table 3.5. *Frequency distribution of longitudinal subjects tested in 1984, by cohort, sex, and year of entry into the study*

	Mean year of birth (cohort)										Total
	1889	1896	1903	1910	1917	1924	1931	1938	1945	1952	
Mean age in 1984	(95)	(88)	(81)	(74)	(67)	(60)	(53)	(46)	(39)	(32)	
1956 sample											
M	1	1	7	10	8	9	8				44
F	0	2	9	14	9	12	7				53
T	*1*	*3*	*15*	*24*	*17*	*21*	*15*				*96*
1963 sample											
M	0	1	5	17	24	21	17	6			91
F	1	4	8	26	29	26	28	12			134
T	*1*	*5*	*13*	*43*	*53*	*47*	*45*	*18*			*225*
1970 sample											
M	1	1	9	14	19	23	14	12	8		101
F	1	2	5	19	23	20	17	17	18		122
T	*2*	*3*	*14*	*33*	*42*	*43*	*31*	*29*	*26*		*223*
1974–1975 sample											
M		7	11	18	23	9					68
F		8	15	29	30	10					92
T		*15*	*26*	*47*	*53*	*19*					*160*
1977 sample											
M		6	6	22	22	29	20	20	15	16	156
F		4	11	16	22	24	17	22	13	10	139
T		*10*	*17*	*38*	*44*	*53*	*37*	*42*	*28*	*26*	*295*

Table 3.6. *Frequency distribution of longitudinal subjects tested in 1991, by cohort, sex, and year of entry into the study*

	Mean year of birth (cohort)										Total
	1896	1903	1910	1917	1924	1931	1938	1945	1952	1959	
Mean age in 1991	(95)	(88)	(81)	(74)	(67)	(60)	(53)	(46)	(39)	(32)	
1956 sample (no. of tests = 6)											
M	1	2	9	8	7	8					35
F	0	2	10	10	7	7					36
T	*1*	*4*	*19*	*18*	*14*	*15*					*71*
1963 sample (5)											
M	0	1	8	12	21	13	5				60
F	1	6	14	24	20	25	11				101
T	*1*	*7*	*22*	*36*	*41*	*38*	*16*				*161*
1970 sample (4)											
M	1	0	9	14	20	12	12	8			76
F	0	1	12	19	16	17	16	18			99
T	*1*	*1*	*21*	*33*	*36*	*29*	*28*	*26*			*175*

Table 3.6. (cont.)

	Mean year of birth (cohort)										Total
	1896	1903	1910	1917	1924	1931	1938	1945	1952	1959	
1974–1975 sample (3)											
M	0	3	10	13	7						33
F	1	5	14	22	6						48
T	*1*	*8*	*24*	*35*	*13*						*81*
1977 sample (3)											
M	1	1	14	13	21	9	19	13	13		104
F	0	3	9	11	18	15	20	11	10		97
T	*1*	*4*	*23*	*24*	*39*	*24*	*39*	*24*	*23*		*201*
1984 sample (2)											
M	—	8	18	29	28	24	23	26	20	17	193
F	—	8	19	31	31	29	34	30	19	34	235
T	—	*16*	*37*	*60*	*59*	*53*	*57*	*56*	*39*	*51*	*428*
Grand total											
M	3	15	68	89	104	66	59	47	33	17	501
F	2	25	78	117	98	93	81	59	29	34	616
T	*5*	*40*	*146*	*206*	*202*	*159*	*140*	*106*	*62*	*51*	*1,117*

Table 3.7. *Educational levels for data sets in the main study as proportions of each sample*

	First test	Second test	Third test	Fourth test	Fifth test	Sixth test
1956 sample						
0–8 years (grade school)	11.0	9.2	4.3	4.2	3.3	2.5
9–12 years (high school)	42.4	38.2	41.0	38.7	27.9	21.3
13–16 years (college)	32.6	35.6	36.6	38.7	38.9	45.0
17 years plus (graduate)	14.0	16.8	18.0	18.5	30.0	31.2
1963 sample						
0–8 years (grade school)	12.9	7.4	4.2	1.6	0.6	
9–12 years (high school)	46.1	43.8	42.3	41.6	38.1	
13–16 years (college)	30.9	37.4	40.6	39.8	43.4	
17 years plus (graduate)	10.0	11.4	12.9	17.1	17.9	
1970 sample						
0–8 years (grade school)	10.1	4.4	3.8	1.1		
9–12 years (high school)	40.4	37.4	29.7	31.9		
13–16 years (college)	35.5	40.6	42.9	44.8		
17 years plus (graduate)	14.0	17.6	23.6	22.2		
1977 sample						
0–8 years (grade school)	9.7	5.9	2.0			
9–12 years (high school)	32.8	27.3	19.9			
13–16 years (college)	38.0	40.2	47.8			
17 years plus (graduate)	19.5	26.6	30.3			

Table 3.7. (*Cont.*)

	First test	Second test	Third test	Fourth test	Fifth test	Sixth test
1984 sample						
0–8 years						
(grade school)	3.6	3.3				
9–12 years						
(high school)	27.9	23.8				
13–16 years						
(college)	41.2	43.9				
17 years plus						
(graduate)	27.3	29.0				
1991 sample						
0–8 years						
(grade school)	0.6					
9–12 years						
(high school)	20.2					
13–16 years						
(college)	49.5					
17 years plus						
(graduate)	29.7					

master's degree or more advanced education). Inspection of these tables indicates that, as suggested earlier, we do experience an upwardly skewed socioeconomic distribution upon completion of the acquisition of our volunteer participants. Further complications arise through nonrandom retest attrition and nonrandom outflow from the population frame, which occurs at a lower rate for the economically advantaged. Nevertheless, our sample structure does represent as reasonable an approximation of the urban population as can be achieved with volunteer study participants, and shifts across samples, although worthy of further investigation, would not seem to interfere seriously with the comparisons to be reported in this volume.

The measurement battery

The test battery includes the psychometric ability and rigidity-flexibility measures that have been collected since the inception of the SLS as well as additional markers for the ability factors included

Table 3.8. *Occupational levels for data sets in the main study as proportions of each sample*

	First test	Second test	Third test	Fourth test	Fifth test	Sixth test
1956 sample						
Unskilled	4.5	4.0	2.5	3.3	7.6	1.3
Semiskilled	10.9	8.6	3.7	4.2	3.7	2.6
Skilled	47.2	45.5	48.1	47.5	26.6	16.1
Semiprofessional	32.2	36.0	40.1	38.3	32.4	6.7
Professional	5.3	5.9	5.6	6.7	5.4	5.3
Retired	NA	NA	NA	NA	24.3	68.0
1963 sample						
Unskilled	5.1	2.9	2.0	5.1	1.9	
Semiskilled	11.3	7.2	7.1	6.1	0.6	
Skilled	56.5	57.7	56.0	34.8	24.4	
Semiprofessional	23.4	29.0	31.7	32.3	8.4	
Professional	3.8	3.1	3.2	6.2	5.1	
Retired	NA	NA	NA	15.5	59.6	
1970 sample						
Unskilled	0.6	0.9	4.7	4.0		
Semiskilled	5.0	5.0	5.1	2.9		
Skilled	48.7	44.1	29.8	28.6		
Semiprofessional	38.0	39.7	31.3	12.0		
Professional	7.7	7.3	12.6	9.1		
Retired	NA	NA	16.5	43.4		
1977 sample						
Unskilled	6.6	5.2	2.5			
Semiskilled	8.0	3.7	1.0			
Skilled	30.6	31.3	16.7			
Semiprofessional	32.8	40.1	23.7			
Professional	22.0	11.7	15.2			
Retired	NA	8.0	40.9			
1984 sample						
Unskilled	4.2	5.4				
Semiskilled	5.2	3.9				
Skilled	29.1	20.4				
Semiprofessional	34.1	22.1				
Professional	15.2	12.3				
Retired	12.2	35.9				
1991 sample						
Unskilled	3.5					
Semiskilled	4.2					
Skilled	20.6					
Semiprofessional	25.4					
Professional	16.6					
Retired	29.7					

in the basic battery. The additional measures included mark the abilities of Perceptual Speed and Verbal Memory, as well as multiple choice items sampling real-life tasks, used as an ecological validity measure. In addition, for some test occasions, measures of certain personality traits, family environment, lifestyles, and health history variables were added.

The cognitive ability battery

The psychometric ability battery was expanded to permit structural analyses that require multiple measures to mark each ability factor. In addition it introduces alternate forms that may have differential validity by age (see Schaie, 1978; Gonda, Quayhagen, & Schaie, 1981). The longitudinal markers included in this battery of necessity (i.e., for consistency across administration) employ the test booklet and answer sheet format used since the beginning of the SLS. All other forms use disposable booklets on which answers are marked directly (see Schaie, 1985). Brief descriptions of the ability factors, the longitudinal marker of each ability (contained in the basic test battery), and the additional measures are given below.

Inductive reasoning. This is the ability to recognize and understand novel concepts or relationships; it involves the solution of logical problems – to foresee and plan. The Thurstones (1949) proposed that persons with good reasoning ability could solve problems, foresee consequences, analyze situations on the basis of past experience, and make and carry out plans according to recognized facts.

> *PMA Reasoning* (R). (Longitudinal marker) The study participant is shown a series of letters (e.g., a b x c d x e f x g h x). The letters in the row form a series based on one or more rules. The study participant is asked to discover the rule(s) and mark the letter that should come next in the series. In this case, the rule is that the normal alphabetical progression is interrupted with an *x* after every second letter. The solution would therefore be the letter *i*. There are 30 test items, with a time limit of 6 min.

> *ADEPT Letter Series* (LS; Blieszner, Willis, & Baltes, 1981). This is a parallel form to the PMA Reasoning test. It has 20 test items, with a time limit of 4.5 min.

Word Series (WS; Gonda, Quayhagen, & Schaie, 1981; Schaie, 1985). The study participant is shown a series of words (e.g., January, March, May) and is asked to identify the next word in the series. Positional patterns used in this test are identical to the PMA Reasoning test. There are 30 test items, with a time limit of 6 min.

Number Series (NS; T. G. Thurstone, 1962). The study participant is shown a series of numbers (e.g., 6, 11, 15, 18, 20) and is asked to identify the number that would continue the series. There are 20 items, with a time limit of 4.5 min.

Spatial Orientation. This is the ability to visualize and mentally manipulate spatial configurations in two or three dimensions, to maintain orientation with respect to spatial objects, and to perceive relationships among objects in space. This ability is important in tasks that require deducing one's physical orientation from a map or visualizing what objects would look like when assembled from pieces.

PMA Space (S). (Longitudinal marker) The study participant is shown an abstract figure and is asked to identify which of six other drawings represents the model in two-dimensional space. There are 20 test items, with a time limit of 5 min.

Object Rotation (OR; Quayhagen, 1979; Schaie, 1985). The study participant is shown a line drawing of a meaningful object (e.g., an umbrella) and is asked to identify which of six other drawings represents the model rotated in two-dimensional space. There are 20 test items, with a time limit of 5 min.

Alphanumeric Rotation (AR; Willis & Schaie, 1983). The study participant is shown a letter or number and is asked to identify which of six other drawings represents the model rotated in two-dimensional space. There are 20 test items, with a time limit of 5 min.

Test stimuli in the Object and Alphanumeric rotation tests have the same angle of rotation as the abstract figures in the PMA Space test.

Cube Comparison (CC; Ekstrom et al., 1976). In each item, two drawings of a cube are presented; the study participant is asked to indicate whether the two drawings are of the same cube rotated in three-dimensional space. The Cube Comparison test has two parts, each with 15 items and a time limit of 3 min.

Number Skills. This is the ability to understand numerical relationships, to work with figures, and to solve simple quantitative problems rapidly and accurately.

> *PMA Number* (N). (Longitudinal marker) The study participant checks whether additions of simple sums shown are correct or incorrect. The test contains 60 items, with a time limit of 6 min.

> *Addition* (AD; Ekstrom et al., 1976). This is a test of speed and accuracy in adding three single or two-digit numbers. The test has two parts, each with 20 items and a time limit of 3 min.

> *Subtraction and multiplication* (SM; Ekstrom et al., 1976). This is a test of speed and accuracy with alternate rows of simple subtraction and multiplication problems. The test has two parts, each with 20 items and a time limit of 3 min.

Verbal Ability. This is the ability to understand ideas expressed in words. It indicates the range of a person's passive vocabulary used in activities where information is obtained by reading or listening.

> *PMA Verbal Meaning* (V). (Longitudinal marker) A four-choice synonym test. This is a highly speeded test with significant loading on Perceptual Speed (Hertzog, 1989; Schaie, Willis, Jay, & Chipuer, 1989). The test has 50 items, with a time limit of 4 min.

> *ETS Vocabulary V-2* (VC; Ekstrom et al., 1976). A five-choice synonym test. The test has two parts, each with 18 items and a time limit of 4 min.

> *ETS Vocabulary V-4* (AVC; Ekstrom et al., 1976). A more advanced five-choice synonym test consisting mainly of difficult items. This test also has two parts, each with 18 items and a time limit of 4 min. Both ETS vocabulary tests are virtually unspeeded.

Word fluency. This ability is concerned with the verbal recall involved in writing and talking easily. It differs from verbal ability in that it focuses on the speed and ease with which words are used rather than on the degree of understanding of verbal concepts.

> *PMA Word Fluency* (W). (Longitudinal marker) The study participant recalls as many words as possible according to a lexical rule in a 5-min period. No additional markers were included for

this ability, because it appears to be factorially more complex than suggested by Thurstone's original work. The test is retained, however, because of the availability of extensive longitudinal data for this variable. In factor analytic work it has been shown to load on Verbal Memory and Verbal Ability (Schaie, Dutta, & Willis, 1991).

Perceptual Speed. This is the ability to find figures, make comparisons, and carry out other simple tasks involving visual perception with speed and accuracy.

> *Identical Pictures* (IP; Ekstrom et al., 1976). (Longitudinal marker beginning in 1975) The study participant identifies which of five numbered shapes or pictures in a row is identical to the model at the left of the row. There are 50 items, with a time limit of 1.5 min.
>
> *Finding A's* (FA; Ekstrom et al., 1976). (Longitudinal marker beginning in 1975) In each column of 40 words, the study participant must identify the 5 words containing the letter *a*. There are 50 columns of words, and a time limit of 1.5 min.
>
> *Number Comparison* (NC; Ekstrom et al., 1976). The study participant inspects pairs of multidigit numbers and indicates whether the two numbers in each pair are the same or different. There are 40 items, with a time limit of 1.5 min.

Verbal Memory. This ability involves the memorization and recall of meaningful language units (Zelinski, Gilewski, & Schaie, 1993).

> *Immediate Recall* (IR). Subjects study a list of 20 words for 3.5 min. They are then given an equal period of time to recall the words in any order.
>
> *Delayed Recall* (DR). Subjects are asked to recall the same list of words as in Immediate Recall after an hour of other activities (other psychometric tests).

Composite indexes. From the original five longitudinal markers, we have consistently derived and reported data on two linear composites. Both indexes were originally suggested by the Thurstones (1949). The first is an Index of Intellectual Ability (IQ), a composite measure likely to approximate a conventional deviation IQ, obtained by summing subtest scores weighted approximately inversely to their standard deviation of each test:

$$IQ = V + S + 2R + 2N + W$$

The second composite score is an Index of Educational Aptitude (EQ) suggested by T. G. Thurstone (1958) as the best predictor from the PMA test battery of performance in educational settings:

$$EQ = 2V + R$$

Measures of self-reported cognitive change

The *PMA Retrospective Questionnaire* (PMARQ; first used in 1984) is given immediately after the five basic longitudinal marker tests have been administered. Subjects are asked to rate whether they think their performance at the current testing session was the same, better, or worse then when they took the tests 7 years earlier. Data collected with this questionnaire show only a modest correlation between subject's estimate of change and magnitude of actual change in 1984 (Schaie, Willis, & O'Hanlon, 1994). The major function of this questionnaire, therefore, is to provide semiprojective data on the subjects' perception of changes in their abilities over time. The PMARQ is also used in the posttest phase of our training studies to obtain the participants' subjective rating of experienced training gain.

Measures of everyday problem solving

A 65-item *Basic Skills Assessment* test developed at the Educational Testing Service (1977) simulates real-life tasks. Examples of such tasks included in the test involve reading a bus schedule, identifying locations on a road map, interpreting a medicine bottle label, finding information in the yellow pages of the telephone book, and so on. In addition to a total score, this test can also be scored for seven subscales that were identified in an item factor analysis conducted on the data obtained in the 1984 cycle.

The first factor score represents the task complexity and is held orthogonal to the remaining six scales, which represent task categories that have similar task attributes. These categories involve:

a. Interpreting labels
b. Interpreting charts
c. Inference from short technical text
d. Inference from short nontechnical correspondence
e. Inference from long text passages
f. Literal comprehension of text passages

Measures of cognitive style

The *Test of Behavioral Rigidity* (TBR; Schaie, 1955, 1960; Schaie & Parham, 1975) contains the following three subtests.

Capitals test. This test was adapted from Bernstein's (1924) study of quickness and intelligence and represents the Spearmanian, or "functional," approach to the study of perseveration and rigidity. Participants copy a printed paragraph that contains some words starting with capital letters, others spelled entirely in capitals, and some starting with lower case letters, with the remaining letters in capitals. In the second half of the test, participants recopy the paragraph, substituting capitals for lower case letters and lower case letters for capitals. Two and a half minutes are allowed for each half of the test. This test yields two scores: *copying speed* (Cap), the number of words correctly copied in the first half of the test; and *instructional set flexibility* (Cap-R), the latter score representing the ratio (rounded to integers) of the number of correctly copied words in the second series to those in the first series.

Opposites test. In this new test, following the work of Scheier and Ferguson (1952), three lists of simple words must be responded to by first giving antonyms, then synonyms, and finally antonyms or synonyms, depending on whether the stimulus word is printed in upper or lower case letters. Each list has 40 stimulus words and a time limit of 2 min. The test yields three scores: an *associational speed* (Opp) score, which is the sum of correct responses in the first two lists; and two *associational flexibility* scores. For this purpose, List 3 is examined for responses that are incorrect, responses started incorrectly, and erasures. The first score (Opp-R1) is obtained by the formula:

$$100 - \frac{\text{Series 3 errors}}{\text{Series 3 total}} \times 100$$

The second score (Opp-R2) involves the formula:

$$\frac{\text{Series 3 correct}}{(1/2 \ (\text{Series 1 correct} + \text{Series 2 correct}))} \times 100$$

TBR questionnaire. Seventy-five true-or-false items include 22 modified flexibility–rigidity items (R scale) and 44 masking Social Responsibility items from the California Psychological Inventory (Gough 1957; Gough, McCloskey, & Meehl, 1952; Schaie, 1959b). Also included are 9 items (P scale) obtained by Guttman scaling of a perseverative behavior scale first used by Lankes (1915).

The TBR yields factor scores for the latent dimensions of Psychomotor Speed, Motor–Cognitive Flexibility, and Attitudinal Flexibility. It also yields several personality trait scores (see below). The three factor scores are obtained by multiplying the standardized factor scores for the eight observed scores from the TBR subtests as follows:

MCF = .25 Cap-R + .35 Opp-R1 + .40 Opp-R2
AF = .50 R scale + .50 P scale
PS = .60 Cap + .40 Opp

For comparison across measures, all psychometric tests were standardized to T-scores with a mean of 50 and a standard deviation of 10, based on all data collected at first test.

Descriptions of lifestyles and demographic characteristics

The *Life Complexity Inventory* (LCI; Gribbin, Schaie, & Parham, 1980) provides information on subjects' demographic characteristics, activity patterns, work characteristics, continuing educational pursuits, and living arrangements. The LCI was initially administered by interviewers and then converted into a mail survey in 1974, and has been administered routinely (as a take-home task) since the fourth SLS cycle. Eight item clusters have been identified for use in relating the LCI to the cognitive variables; these are:

1. Subjective dissatisfaction with life status
2. Social status
3. Noisy environment
4. Family dissolution
5. Disengagement from interaction with the environment
6. Semipassive engagement with the environment
7. Maintenance of acculturation
8. Female homemaker characteristics

Descriptions of health status

Health history abstracts. Health history data for the longitudinal study participants were obtained from time of entry into the study through 1991 for all participants remaining in the study and for those who dropped out for the 7 years following their last assessment, or until their death if the latter occurred earlier.

Health history data consist of the number of annual physician visits or hospital days by diagnosis (coded according to the International Classification of Diseases, ICDA, 8th edition). In addition, the number of continuous illness episodes per year is also coded.

Medication reports. Beginning with the sixth (1991) cycle, medication data have been collected by means of a brown bag procedure, in which subjects bring their current medications to the testing site, where the medication identifiers are recorded. Diseases for the treatment of which these medications are prescribed are identified using the procedure advocated by the American Society of Hospital Pharmacists (1985).

Identification of relatives with dementia. In the sixth cycle we asked all participants to list blood relatives who they thought had been diagnosed as suffering from Disease of the Alzheimer's Type (DAT). Information was also sought on whether such relatives were still living and, if dead, their age at death.

Descriptions of the subjective environment

Family environment. The eight scales of the *Family Environment Scale* (Moos & Moos, 1986) were abbreviated to five items for each scale, and the individual items were converted into 5-point Likert scales. Items were edited to be suitable for inclusion in two versions of the instrument: (1) a form suitable for describing the perceived environment in the *family of origin*; (2) a form suitable for describing the perceived environment in the *current family*. For the latter, two versions were prepared: one suitable for individuals living in multimember family settings and one for individuals currently living by themselves. For purposes of the latter form, "family" was defined as those individuals who the respondent felt were close to him or her and with whom a personal interaction occurred at least once every week.

The eight family environment scales are thought to assess the following dimensions:

> *Cohesion.* (Relationship) Example: "Family members really help one another."
>
> *Expressivity.* (Relationship) Example: "We tell each other about our personal problems."
>
> *Conflict.* (Relationship) Example: "Family members hardly ever lose their temper."
>
> *Achievement Orientation.* (Personal growth) Example: "We feel it is important to be the best at whatever we do."
>
> *Intellectual–Cultural Orientation.* (Personal growth) Example: "We often talk about political and social problems."
>
> *Active–Recreational Orientation.* (Personal growth) Example: "Friends often come over for dinner or to visit."
>
> *Organization.* (System maintenance) Example: "We are generally very neat and orderly."
>
> *Control.* (System maintenance) Example: "There are set ways of doing things at home."

Work environment. In a manner similar to the family environment scales, three scales of the Work Environment Inventory (Moos,

1981) were also abbreviated to five items and converted to 5-point Likert scales. The content attributed to these dimensions is as follows.

> *Autonomy.* The extent to which employees are encouraged to be self-sufficient and make their own decisions. Example: "You have a great deal of freedom to do as you like in your workplace."

> *Control.* The extent to which management uses rules and pressure to keep employees under control. Example: "You are expected to follow set rules in doing your work."

> *Innovation.* The degree of emphasis on variety, change, and new approaches. Example: "You are encouraged to do your work in different ways."

Family contact. A 7-item (6-point Likert scale) form assesses the degree of actual contact between family members. Items inquire about the number of years family members have lived in the same household and the frequency of current personal contact, telephone contact, written contact, and contact through other informants.

Personality traits and attitudes

Social Responsibility (SR). The TBR Questionnaire was designed to include 44 masking items derived from the Social Responsibility scale of the California Psychological Inventory (CPI; Gough, 1957; Gough, McCloskey, & Meehl, 1952; Schaie, 1959b). The scale is of interest because it has allowed us to chronicle shifts in societal attitudes over time (Schaie & Parham, 1974) as well as attitudinal differences within families (Schaie, Plomin, Willis, Gruber-Baldini, & Dutta, 1992).

Derived traits. A factor analysis of the 75 items contained in the TBR questionnaires collected during the first three study cycles resulted in the identification of 19 personality factors, several of which could be matched in content to at least one of the poles of the Cattell et al. 16-PF scale (Schaie & Parham, 1976). More recently we have replicated 13 of these factors for the entire database through the fifth SLS cycle (Maitland, Dutta, Schaie, & Willis, 1992; Willis, Schaie, & Maitland, 1992; see also chapter 12).

Chapter summary

This chapter describes the database for the Seattle Longitudinal Study. The subject population for this study consists of random samples drawn at six 7-year intervals over a 35-year period from a large health maintenance organization, as well as adult children and siblings of many of the panel participants. The sociodemographic characteristics of these samples are quite representative of the upper 75% of the Seattle metropolitan area, although underrepresenting minorities during the early phases of the study. The central measures included in the study are theoretically based on Thurstone's Primary Mental Abilities, sampling the ability domains of Inductive Reasoning, Spatial Orientation, Perceptual Speed, Verbal Ability, Numeric Ability, and Verbal Memory. The cognitive assessment battery is supplemented by measures of cognitive style, lifestyle characteristics, a measure of everyday cognition (practical intelligence), abstracts of the participants' health history, and rating scales measuring perceptions of cognitive change and family and work environments.

4

Cross-sectional studies

This chapter begins with a description of the pilot studies that led to the selection and validation of the measures used in our research program. I then present the 1956 baseline study and compare its findings with the five cross-sectional replications. For purposes of an orderly presentation, I start out with a comparison of the basic cognitive battery that is common to all study cycles. I then present data for the fifth and sixth cycles for the extended cognitive battery and the practical intelligence measure. Finally, I consider the cross-sectional findings for the measures of cognitive style (TBR).

The pilot studies

Our inquiry began by questioning whether factorially defined measures of intellectual abilities would show differential age patterns. Before this question could be examined parametrically, it was necessary to examine the applicability of the PMA test to an older population, with respect to both its level of difficulty and whether the low correlations among abilities observed in childhood would continue to prevail for adults. Two pilot studies concerned with these questions are described in this section. In addition, our interest in cognitive style as a concomitant of intellectual aging required the development of a set of psychometrically sound measurement instruments for the multiple dimensions of rigidity–flexibility. A third pilot study was concerned with demonstrating the construct validity of the resultant measure (the TBR).

Study 1: Suitability of the PMA tests for adults

Sixty-one study participants, gathered from the geriatric practice of a family physician and from the membership of the small first cohort of the San Francisco Senior Citizen Center, were given the PMA tests under standard conditions. For purposes of analysis, participants were arbitrarily divided into four approximately equal groups: ages 53 to 58, 59 to 64, 65 to 70, and 71 to 78. In the absence of adult norms, and to permit comparison across the five abilities measured by the test, raw scores were converted into percentiles, employing norms for 17-year-old adolescents (Thurstone & Thurstone, 1949). Thus, for example, if our participants, on average, were found to be at the 50th percentile, this would imply that their level of functioning would be similar to that of 17-year-olds. The results of this study are shown in Figure 4.1. For the group in their 50s, stability is suggested for Verbal Meaning and Number (performance being slightly above the adolescents' 50th percentile). But performance appears to be substantially lower for the other three tests. Indeed, it was lowest for Spatial Orientation and Inductive Reasoning, measures of the kind of ability later to be termed "fluid" by Cattell (1963). The differential pattern was observed for all age groups, with some further lowering of scores into the 60s and apparent maintenance of the lower level for the group in their 70s (Schaie, Rosenthal, & Perlman, 1953).

On the off chance that the differential pattern might be caused by unequal effects of the slightly speeded instructions for the performance of older individuals, four of the tests were administered to 31 participants without a time limit. Results shown in Figure 4.2 indicate that, if anything, differential performance levels were greater and in the same order as under the standard conditions of instruction.

The first pilot study also investigated the construct validity of the PMA 11–17 when used with older individuals. Intercorrelations between the tests were computed and found to be quite low, ranging from .07 for the correlation between Spatial Orientation and Number to .31 for the correlation between Spatial Orientation and Inductive Reasoning. These correlations did not differ significantly from those obtained for an adolescent comparison group (Schaie, 1958d). Split-half reliabilities computed under the power-test condition were

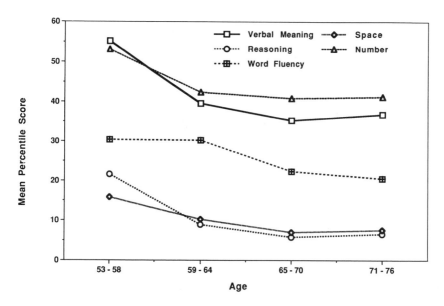

Figure 4.1. Performance of adults on the Primary Mental Abilities test, in percentile scores for an adolescent comparison group. From Schaie, Rosenthal, & Perlman, 1953, p. 191.

also quite satisfactory, all being above .92 after Spearman–Brown correction.

Study 2: Suitability of the PMA tests for older adults

A second pilot study was conducted in 1954 as part of an investigation of community-dwelling older persons (more completely described in Schaie & Strother, 1968a, 1968d). A campus and community appeal resulted in the selection of 25 men and 25 women, all college graduates with professional careers, ranging in age from 70 to 88 (mean age = 76.5). These study participants were all in fair to superior health and free of diagnosable psychiatric symptoms. The differential ability pattern shown in the first pilot study was replicated, with performance on Number, Word Fluency, and Verbal Meaning substantially above that observed for Spatial Orientation and Inductive Reasoning. Also noteworthy was the

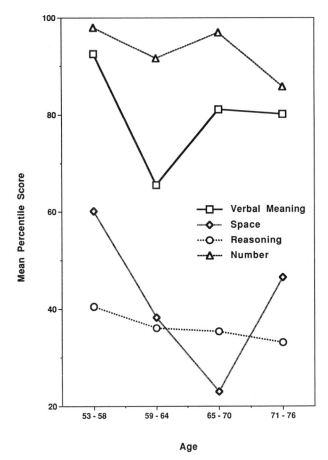

Figure 4.2. The Primary Mental Abilities test administered as a power test to older adults. From Schaie, Rosenthal, & Perlman, 1953, p. 194.

finding that some of the octogenarians in this study still equaled or exceeded the adolescent mean on some of the verbal tests, even though it was most likely that this performance represented a decrement from previously higher levels, suggested by the unusually advantaged demographic characteristics of this sample. In this study, findings also indicated sex differences in favor of the males for the Spatial Orientation and Number abilities and in favor of the females for Verbal Meaning, Inductive Reasoning, and Word Fluency (Strother, Schaie, & Horst, 1957).

Study 3: TBR construct validity

The third pilot study was concerned with demonstrating the construct validity of a set of measures defining the multiple dimensions of rigidity–flexibility. This study began as my masters thesis (Schaie, 1953), in which I factor-analyzed a number of tests representing the functional, structural, and attitudinal approaches to the study of rigidity–flexibility (see Chown, 1959). Although use of an unorthodox method of rotation (Horst, 1956a) made the result of the initial analysis somewhat tenuous, it provided the basis for selecting the variables to be included in the more definitive construct validation study (Schaie, 1955). Because I intended to use the final battery for studies of aging, only those tests were included that could be adapted for use with both adult and elderly populations. For practical reasons, only tests suitable for group administration were retained, and those tests were selected for which social status and education were of minimal importance in influencing results in the initial study.

The measures included in the construct validity study are described in the "measures of cognitive style" section of chapter 3, except for the *Jar test* (Luchins, 1942) and the *Alphabet test* (Bernstein, 1924), which were subsequently dropped from the final battery. The Jar test involves subjects correctly identifying the use of jars of different sizes in measuring a given quantity of water, different methods of solution being appropriate at different times. The so-called *Einstellung* effect is tested by first conditioning the subject to employ a complex method of solution. Critical problems are then presented where a more direct solution is available. The rigidity measure then becomes the number of problems unnecessarily solved in the more complex manner. The Alphabet test involves the letter combinations *abcde* and *lmnopq* written first forward and then backward.

The validation sample consisted of 216 subjects drawn from day and evening classes at the University of Washington, from a social club for older people, from the membership of a liberal church, and from a group of YMCA members. The sample ranged in age from 17 to 79, with a mean age of 38. Educational level ranged from 4 to 20 years, with a mean of 14.2. The subjects' occupational level

Table 4.1. *Factor loadings and factor intercorrelations after oblique rotation (Sample 1)*

Test	Factor pattern		
	I	II	III
Capitals-NR	0.66	−0.02	−0.12
Alphabet-NR	0.66	−0.03	−0.03
Opposites-NR	0.46	0.09	0.14
Water-jar test	0.00	0.31	−0.05
P scale	0.00	0.50	0.07
R scale	0.05	0.56	−0.01
Opposites-R1	0.05	0.00	0.55
Opposites-R2	0.05	−0.10	0.64
Capitals-R	−0.04	0.07	0.39
Alphabet-R	−0.07	0.03	0.25

	Factor intercorrelations	
	II	III
I. Motor–Cognitive Speed	0.427	0.508
II. Personality–Perceptual Rigidity	—	0.422
III. Motor–Cognitive Rigidity		

averaged 6.3 on a 10-point scale from *unskilled* to *professional*. For purposes of cross-validation, a second sample of 200 subjects was drawn from a restricted population of college students between the ages of 19 and 26, with a mean age of 21.4.

The correlation matrix for the first sample was factored using a simplification of Thurstone's multiple group method (Horst, 1956b; L. L. Thurstone, 1947, pp. 170ff.). The reader might note that this approach is an early forerunner of modern confirmatory factor analysis. The first hypothesis specified the existence of a single rigidity factor and a motor-speed factor. This hypothesis had to be rejected, and instead a three-factor combination emerged that upon appropriate oblique rotation (Horst & Schaie, 1956) yielded an acceptable simple structure solution (see Table 4.1).

Factor I was originally named Motor–Cognitive Speed (the current term is Psychomotor Speed), Factor II was identified as

Table 4.2. *Factor loadings and factor intercorrelations after oblique rotation (Sample 2)*

Test	Factor pattern		
	I	II	III
Capitals-NR	0.74	0.03	−0.06
Alphabet-NR	0.68	−0.02	−0.06
Opposites-NR	0.49	−0.01	0.09
Water-jar test	0.00	0.28	0.05
P scale	−0.09	0.57	0.01
R scale	0.09	0.58	0.04
Opposites-R1	0.04	−0.02	0.69
Opposites-R2	0.03	−0.02	0.64
Capitals-R	−0.09	0.02	0.25
Alphabet-R	−0.01	0.10	0.30

	Factor intercorrelations	
	II	III
I. Motor–Cognitive Speed	−0.049	0.075
II. Personality–Perceptual Rigidity	—	0.148
III. Motor–Cognitive Rigidity		

Personality–Perceptual Rigidity (now called Attitudinal Flexibility), and Factor III was thought to be a representation of Motor–Cognitive Rigidity (now called Motor–Cognitive Flexibility). These factors were next cross-validated by factoring the correlation matrix for the second sample and rotating it to the same factor pattern. As indicated by Table 4.2, the resulting pattern replicates that obtained for the original sample. The major difference between results from the two samples can be seen in the factor intercorrelations. All three factors are moderately correlated in the heterogeneous sample, whereas the factor correlations are quite small in the homogeneous sample of college students.

As a result of this study, we decided to retain the four subtests (Capitals, Opposites, R scale, P scale) that provided the best factor definition for inclusion in the final version of the TBR used throughout the SLS.

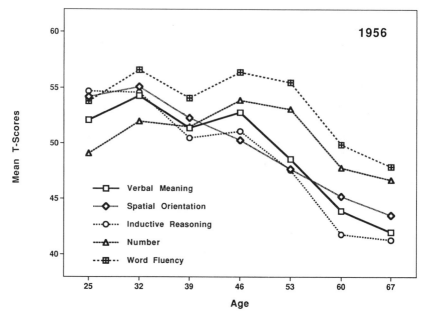

Figure 4.3. Age differences on the primary mental abilities for the 1956 base study. From Schaie, 1958c.

The 1956 baseline study

In our effort to determine the pattern of age differences, we sampled 500 individuals from our HMO population frame distributed evenly by gender and 5-year age interval from 21 to 70. For ease of comparison we standardized all variables across the entire sample to T-score format ($M = 50$, $SD = 10$). We have followed this procedure throughout, always restandardizing on the basis of the largest total sample of individuals' scores at first test (entry into the study). Age-difference findings from the baseline study are shown in Figure 4.3.

What is most noteworthy about the baseline study is that although negative age differences are found on all five abilities, peak ability ages occur generally later than had been observed in the previous literature (see Jones & Conrad, 1933; Wechsler, 1939), and that the differential ability patterns noted in our first pilot study could be confirmed in this reasonably representative and age-continuous investigation.

More specifically we noted that peak levels of the abilities were reached for Reasoning by the 21–25-year-old group, for Space by the 26–30-year-olds, and for Verbal Meaning and Word Fluency by the 31–35-year-olds, but for Number only at ages 46–50. Similarly, there are differences among abilities for the first occurrence of a significant age difference from performance at the peak age. Such significantly lower average performance levels are observed for Verbal Meaning, Space, Reasoning, and Word Fluency with respect to the 36–40-year-olds, but for Number only for the 56–60-year-olds. Differences were found also in the absolute magnitude of the age difference between the group at peak age and the oldest observed group (ages 66–70). This difference amounted to 1.5 standard deviations for Verbal Meaning, Space, and Reasoning but slightly less than 1 standard deviation for Number and Word Fluency. The absolute differences between the youngest and oldest age groups were greatest for Reasoning (1.5 *SD*), next largest for Space and Verbal Meaning (1.2 and 1 *SD* respectively), and smallest for Word Fluency and Number (0.6 and 0.2 *SD* respectively). These differences could be interpreted as being of substantial magnitude for Reasoning, Space, and Verbal Meaning, moderate for Word Fluency, and near trivial for Number.

Cross-sectional replications

This section will begin with the basic cognitive data collected throughout the study. I then turn to the expanded battery and consider the age-difference patterns within ability domains as well as the age-difference patterns in the factor scores for the latent ability constructs. Finally, cross-sectional results are provided for the measure of practical intelligence and the measures of cognitive style.

Basic cognitive data

Given the 7-year interval between our data cycles, all data were reorganized into 7-year age intervals. Thus, the baseline study for purposes of comparison with the subsequent replications contains seven age groups, with mean ages from 25 to 67. In the second cross-sectional sample (1963, $N = 997$), we included eight age groups with mean ages from 25 to 74. The third sample (1970, $N = 705$) and the remaining three cross-sectional samples (1977, $N = 609$; 1984, $N = 629$; and 1991, $N = 693$) include nine age groups with mean ages from 25 to 81.

Once again, for ease of comparison, all raw scores were converted to T-scores with means of 50 and standard deviations of 10, based on the entire set of 4,123 observations at first test.

Differential ability patterns. Mean scores by age and gender for the five PMA subtests and the two composite measures of Intellectual Ability and Educational Aptitude are presented in Table 4.3. For a more dramatic presentation of differences across abilities in age-difference pattern, we have graphed mean values by gender for the first (1956) and last (1991) cross-sectional comparisons (see Figure 4.4). Age-difference patterns for males have remained relatively constant over the course of the study, with the exception that peak ages for Verbal Meaning and Spatial Orientation shift to the late 30s. For the female study participants, much greater shifts can be observed. In young adulthood females now show markedly higher performance on Spatial Orientation than was the case some 35 years ago. For the women, age differences in Number ability have virtually disappeared, and the peak age for Verbal Meaning has moved to the early 50s.

Absolute age differences across the adult life span, observed at any given point, remain substantial for most abilities. But there has been a sharp reduction of age differences in performance observed until the late 60s are reached. For example, for Verbal Meaning the absolute difference between ages 25 and 81 currently amounts to 1.2 *SD* for both men and women. However, the absolute difference between ages 25 and 67 has been reduced from 0.8 *SD* to 0.2 *SD* for men and from 1.2 *SD* to 0.2 *SD* for women.

Age-difference patterns across abilities. Age-difference data are not directly relevant to testing propositions about ontogenetic change. Such data, however, when examined in the context of cross-sectional

Table 4.3. *Means and standard deviations for the basic ability battery, by sample and gender*

	1956			1963			1970			1977			1984			1991		
Age	M	F	T	M	F	T	M	F	T	M	F	T	M	F	T	M	F	T
Verbal Meaning																		
25	51.3 (9.3)	53.1 (7.3)	52.2 (8.3)	52.0 (8.5)	53.4 (8.4)	52.8 (8.4)	52.3 (8.2)	54.2 (7.7)	53.4 (8.0)	53.6 (7.6)	54.8 (9.7)	54.2 (8.6)	53.9 (8.1)	55.6 (7.4)	55.1 (7.6)	52.2 (8.0)	54.5 (6.9)	53.5 (7.4)
32	53.0 (9.2)	55.5 (7.0)	54.3 (8.1)	52.8 (8.1)	54.2 (7.7)	53.6 (8.0)	51.9 (9.0)	54.4 (8.2)	53.3 (8.5)	55.0 (7.1)	56.5 (6.9)	55.8 (7.0)	55.7 (8.8)	52.9 (8.5)	54.3 (7.5)	55.9 (6.6)	53.6 (8.5)	54.6 (7.8)
39	51.8 (10.0)	51.0 (10.6)	51.4 (10.2)	54.4 (7.9)	53.1 (7.6)	53.7 (7.7)	53.7 (7.6)	53.3 (7.7)	53.5 (7.6)	53.6 (9.9)	55.4 (8.1)	54.5 (9.0)	56.5 (6.0)	56.4 (6.5)	56.4 (6.4)	57.5 (6.4)	57.6 (6.1)	57.5 (6.2)
46	50.0 (9.9)	56.1 (7.4)	52.8 (9.3)	50.1 (9.1)	52.3 (8.4)	51.2 (8.8)	53.2 (9.4)	54.7 (8.1)	53.9 (8.8)	53.0 (9.1)	51.0 (10.2)	51.9 (9.7)	56.0 (6.2)	57.5 (6.2)	56.9 (6.2)	56.5 (6.2)	56.9 (6.5)	56.8 (6.4)
53	48.9 (9.8)	48.4 (8.9)	48.6 (9.3)	46.6 (10.0)	48.6 (9.4)	47.7 (9.7)	54.9 (7.2)	53.2 (7.5)	54.0 (7.4)	53.3 (9.6)	51.3 (9.8)	52.4 (9.7)	52.8 (8.2)	55.9 (6.7)	54.3 (7.6)	54.6 (8.5)	57.4 (6.6)	56.1 (7.1)
60	41.9 (9.5)	45.7 (8.5)	43.9 (9.2)	44.4 (9.3)	48.0 (10.3)	46.3 (10.0)	53.6 (9.4)	50.1 (8.3)	51.8 (9.0)	50.4 (10.1)	49.8 (8.9)	50.1 (9.4)	51.5 (8.0)	52.4 (7.8)	52.0 (7.9)	53.6 (8.8)	52.4 (7.1)	52.9 (8.3)
67	42.6 (8.2)	41.5 (8.2)	42.0 (8.1)	40.6 (9.2)	43.3 (8.6)	42.0 (9.0)	43.5 (7.5)	45.7 (8.6)	44.7 (8.1)	44.6 (8.8)	47.0 (8.8)	45.8 (8.8)	47.3 (8.5)	49.1 (8.2)	48.2 (8.4)	50.0 (9.1)	53.0 (8.2)	51.7 (8.7)
74	—	—	—	38.9 (9.4)	39.3 (8.9)	39.1 (9.1)	37.9 (7.5)	41.0 (5.9)	39.3 (6.9)	38.9 (9.0)	41.7 (10.2)	40.3 (9.6)	42.4 (6.0)	45.8 (7.9)	43.7 (7.5)	47.8 (8.5)	48.4 (9.2)	48.1 (8.7)
81	—	—	—	—	—	—	36.4 (8.5)	37.9 (7.8)	37.1 (8.1)	35.1 (7.0)	35.1 (6.9)	35.1 (6.8)	40.5 (9.4)	39.6 (7.7)	40.0 (8.4)	40.2 (7.1)	42.3 (9.8)	41.3 (8.7)
Spatial Orientation																		
25	57.2 (9.6)	51.2 (9.9)	54.2 (10.2)	59.4 (8.6)	56.5 (9.3)	57.7 (9.1)	61.3 (11.2)	55.7 (10.6)	58.2 (11.2)	58.8 (8.7)	52.1 (7.7)	55.5 (8.8)	59.0 (11.3)	54.4 (10.1)	55.9 (10.6)	60.7 (8.3)	59.2 (8.6)	59.9 (8.4)
32	56.5 (10.5)	53.8 (7.9)	55.1 (9.3)	56.8 (8.0)	52.6 (8.2)	54.4 (8.4)	60.2 (8.9)	56.0 (9.8)	57.6 (8.9)	56.4 (6.6)	56.3 (7.8)	56.4 (7.2)	54.8 (9.0)	54.2 (7.6)	54.5 (8.2)	57.6 (8.2)	54.7 (8.6)	56.0 (8.6)
39	54.7 (7.0)	49.9 (8.1)	52.3 (7.9)	56.7 (8.0)	50.2 (8.1)	53.3 (8.6)	57.5 (8.5)	50.9 (9.3)	53.6 (9.9)	57.7 (8.1)	52.7 (7.7)	55.2 (8.2)	56.9 (9.3)	51.2 (10.9)	53.6 (10.6)	60.4 (8.5)	53.6 (8.5)	56.9 (9.1)
46	52.6 (8.4)	47.7 (10.9)	50.3 (9.9)	54.2 (8.7)	48.7 (8.5)	51.5 (9.0)	56.5 (8.5)	51.8 (9.2)	54.1 (9.1)	54.6 (7.5)	50.9 (8.8)	52.6 (8.3)	54.6 (10.0)	54.2 (8.1)	54.4 (8.9)	57.3 (7.7)	52.3 (9.3)	54.3 (9.0)
53	49.8 (9.7)	45.5 (7.2)	47.7 (8.7)	51.0 (7.4)	46.9 (9.0)	48.7 (8.5)	53.3 (8.4)	48.9 (8.5)	50.9 (8.7)	53.8 (8.4)	48.3 (8.6)	51.2 (8.6)	51.7 (8.9)	48.7 (8.1)	50.2 (8.6)	55.2 (9.0)	50.4 (10.0)	52.8 (9.8)
60	48.1 (10.2)	42.4 (8.6)	45.2 (9.8)	49.2 (9.0)	45.1 (8.0)	47.0 (8.7)	52.1 (9.1)	47.0 (6.6)	49.4 (8.2)	50.0 (9.4)	45.8 (8.1)	47.8 (8.9)	51.9 (8.9)	46.4 (8.8)	48.9 (8.9)	51.8 (7.3)	47.4 (6.6)	49.3 (7.2)
67	45.9 (8.1)	41.2 (6.5)	43.5 (7.7)	45.0 (8.1)	41.4 (6.7)	43.2 (7.6)	46.9 (6.2)	40.9 (7.4)	43.7 (7.4)	48.3 (7.6)	47.4 (8.3)	47.8 (7.9)	46.5 (8.2)	43.6 (8.1)	45.0 (8.3)	49.4 (7.4)	44.3 (8.4)	46.4 (8.3)
74	—	—	—	42.9 (6.9)	39.6 (5.6)	41.0 (6.4)	42.3 (8.5)	39.6 (6.2)	41.1 (7.6)	43.8 (7.0)	41.1 (6.5)	42.5 (6.9)	43.8 (8.4)	41.6 (7.3)	42.8 (7.5)	46.4 (7.9)	41.7 (6.3)	44.0 (7.5)
81	—	—	—	—	—	—	42.6 (6.6)	37.0 (6.2)	39.9 (6.9)	41.7 (6.5)	37.7 (5.9)	39.6 (6.5)	42.2 (6.2)	39.9 (6.2)	41.0 (6.3)	41.1 (6.9)	39.3 (7.1)	40.2 (7.0)

Table 4.3. *(cont.)*

Inductive Reasoning

Age	1956 M	1956 F	1956 T	1963 M	1963 F	1963 T	1970 M	1970 F	1970 T	1977 M	1977 F	1977 T	1984 M	1984 F	1984 T	1991 M	1991 F	1991 T
25	53.4 (8.3)	55.9 (10.2)	54.7 (8.6)	57.4 (7.3)	58.7 (7.9)	58.2 (7.6)	59.7 (7.5)	59.2 (7.0)	59.4 (7.2)	56.5 (8.0)	60.5 (7.8)	59.4 (7.2)	59.1 (7.1)	59.7 (7.6)	59.5 (7.4)	59.3 (7.6)	61.6 (6.6)	60.6 (7.1)
32	53.3 (9.3)	55.6 (9.9)	54.6 (8.8)	53.7 (8.4)	56.8 (7.0)	55.5 (7.7)	67.1 (8.7)	58.2 (7.8)	57.7 (8.1)	56.6 (6.7)	57.8 (7.4)	57.7 (8.1)	58.4 (7.1)	58.3 (8.3)	58.4 (7.6)	58.8 (5.9)	59.4 (6.6)	59.1 (6.3)
39	49.4 (8.7)	51.7 (9.4)	50.5 (8.8)	53.6 (8.4)	52.9 (7.5)	53.3 (7.9)	54.1 (7.7)	53.3 (7.6)	53.6 (7.6)	55.6 (8.9)	56.5 (7.4)	56.1 (7.3)	58.4 (7.1)	58.3 (8.3)	57.3 (6.6)	58.2 (7.7)	59.1 (5.3)	58.7 (6.5)
46	50.3 (9.1)	51.1 (8.1)	51.1 (9.1)	48.3 (7.9)	50.8 (9.1)	49.5 (8.5)	52.3 (9.6)	53.2 (8.4)	52.8 (9.0)	51.3 (8.2)	52.8 (8.5)	52.8 (8.3)	57.1 (7.2)	57.5 (7.4)	55.7 (7.4)	56.7 (7.8)	58.5 (7.3)	57.7 (7.5)
53	47.3 (8.6)	48.0 (8.1)	47.6 (8.7)	45.4 (8.3)	46.2 (8.1)	45.9 (8.2)	49.7 (8.1)	50.7 (8.2)	50.3 (8.2)	52.1 (8.7)	49.8 (8.5)	51.3 (8.5)	53.5 (6.7)	55.5 (6.7)	52.6 (8.1)	53.3 (4.7)	55.8 (8.0)	54.6 (8.1)
60	40.1 (6.7)	43.3 (6.9)	41.8 (9.2)	42.7 (7.6)	45.2 (9.3)	44.0 (8.6)	50.2 (8.8)	47.7 (7.6)	48.9 (8.2)	48.3 (8.7)	47.2 (7.5)	47.7 (8.2)	49.7 (8.4)	50.4 (8.4)	50.4 (8.1)	50.1 (7.3)	50.7 (7.1)	50.4 (6.2)
67	41.3 (7.3)	41.3 (7.1)	41.3 (6.9)	39.5 (6.7)	40.4 (6.8)	40.0 (6.7)	41.3 (7.2)	42.2 (7.4)	41.8 (7.3)	43.3 (6.8)	45.4 (8.6)	44.4 (7.8)	44.3 (7.8)	48.4 (7.4)	46.4 (7.5)	47.5 (8.4)	50.8 (7.9)	49.4 (7.8)
74	—	—	—	40.6 (6.8)	37.6 (4.7)	39.1 (6.0)	38.4 (5.4)	39.2 (5.3)	38.8 (5.3)	40.0 (5.8)	40.2 (6.5)	40.1 (6.1)	42.8 (6.6)	45.5 (7.8)	44.1 (7.3)	45.1 (8.4)	47.0 (7.4)	46.1 (7.9)
81	—	—	—	—	—	—	37.8 (7.0)	38.0 (4.7)	37.9 (5.9)	37.2 (4.5)	38.9 (8.1)	38.1 (6.7)	39.0 (6.2)	37.9 (4.8)	38.4 (5.5)	40.3 (4.8)	40.2 (5.5)	40.3 (5.1)

Number

Age	1956 M	1956 F	1956 T	1963 M	1963 F	1963 T	1970 M	1970 F	1970 T	1977 M	1977 F	1977 T	1984 M	1984 F	1984 T	1991 M	1991 F	1991 T
25	47.9 (8.2)	50.3 (10.2)	49.1 (9.3)	50.8 (7.8)	51.1 (8.2)	51.0 (8.0)	52.6 (9.5)	50.7 (8.5)	51.5 (8.9)	49.2 (9.8)	49.8 (9.7)	49.5 (9.6)	50.4 (9.1)	47.6 (7.6)	48.3 (8.2)	47.7 (6.8)	47.5 (7.6)	47.6 (7.2)
32	53.6 (10.0)	50.5 (8.5)	52.0 (9.3)	55.5 (12.2)	53.0 (9.2)	54.1 (10.6)	58.4 (13.7)	50.2 (9.1)	53.8 (11.9)	49.5 (8.6)	52.4 (8.3)	51.0 (8.5)	53.2 (10.4)	48.5 (7.9)	50.8 (9.4)	49.0 (7.7)	47.7 (6.4)	48.3 (7.0)
39	52.8 (10.3)	50.1 (10.2)	51.5 (10.3)	56.9 (10.0)	52.6 (10.0)	54.7 (10.3)	54.2 (10.5)	51.6 (8.5)	52.6 (9.4)	51.6 (9.9)	51.3 (8.7)	51.5 (9.3)	48.3 (7.8)	49.6 (8.2)	49.1 (8.0)	51.1 (9.7)	50.0 (7.5)	50.5 (8.6)
46	56.3 (8.5)	51.1 (8.3)	53.9 (8.8)	53.2 (10.5)	53.4 (10.2)	53.3 (10.3)	56.1 (9.1)	54.2 (9.8)	55.2 (9.5)	48.8 (9.6)	47.9 (8.9)	48.3 (9.2)	51.6 (6.5)	51.9 (7.8)	51.8 (7.2)	53.3 (9.9)	50.6 (9.9)	51.7 (9.7)
53	53.4 (9.6)	52.7 (11.4)	53.1 (10.5)	51.2 (10.8)	48.9 (10.7)	49.9 (10.8)	55.1 (12.4)	54.4 (10.8)	54.7 (11.5)	54.7 (12.9)	48.7 (7.9)	51.8 (11.2)	48.4 (10.9)	50.0 (8.8)	49.2 (9.9)	51.8 (9.7)	50.0 (8.5)	50.8 (9.1)
60	48.0 (8.4)	47.6 (7.4)	47.8 (7.9)	49.7 (13.4)	48.8 (10.8)	49.2 (12.1)	56.3 (10.8)	54.7 (11.6)	55.5 (11.2)	51.6 (10.6)	49.9 (10.5)	50.7 (10.6)	52.4 (9.8)	47.5 (9.2)	49.7 (9.8)	48.9 (8.0)	49.3 (9.1)	49.1 (8.5)
67	47.4 (9.5)	46.1 (9.4)	46.7 (9.4)	47.0 (10.2)	44.3 (9.5)	45.7 (9.9)	48.8 (8.8)	47.3 (7.8)	48.0 (8.3)	50.7 (9.9)	49.7 (10.4)	50.2 (10.0)	48.2 (9.5)	49.4 (9.3)	48.8 (9.3)	50.7 (7.9)	48.9 (8.4)	49.7 (8.2)
74	—	—	—	46.6 (9.0)	42.2 (9.5)	44.3 (9.4)	44.2 (8.8)	44.6 (7.9)	44.4 (8.4)	44.7 (8.9)	45.0 (9.6)	44.8 (9.2)	48.2 (8.2)	46.1 (9.1)	47.2 (7.9)	48.3 (11.4)	49.8 (8.0)	49.1 (9.8)
81	—	—	—	—	—	—	43.8 (9.6)	38.1 (6.1)	41.1 (8.6)	42.1 (9.0)	42.0 (8.3)	42.1 (8.6)	43.9 (7.0)	39.6 (7.7)	41.7 (7.6)	44.8 (10.7)	47.6 (8.6)	46.2 (9.7)

Table 4.3. (cont.)

Word Fluency

Age	1956 M	1956 F	1956 T	1963 M	1963 F	1963 T	1970 M	1970 F	1970 T	1977 M	1977 F	1977 T	1984 M	1984 F	1984 T	1991 M	1991 F	1991 T
25	53.9 (9.7)	53.7 (10.6)	53.8 (10.1)	51.1 (8.3)	53.1 (8.0)	52.2 (8.2)	52.5 (8.1)	53.9 (8.3)	53.3 (8.2)	53.4 (8.3)	53.4 (11.1)	53.4 (9.7)	56.2 (13.9)	54.6 (9.6)	55.1 (11.2)	55.5 (9.4)	57.1 (10.0)	56.4 (9.7)
32	53.9 (9.9)	58.9 (10.9)	56.6 (10.7)	49.3 (9.2)	54.8 (8.9)	52.5 (9.4)	47.8 (9.1)	52.8 (9.3)	50.7 (9.5)	53.2 (8.3)	56.0 (7.0)	54.7 (7.7)	56.1 (6.9)	53.5 (10.5)	54.8 (9.0)	53.9 (9.1)	54.3 (10.3)	54.1 (9.8)
39	53.4 (10.3)	54.9 (10.3)	54.1 (10.7)	52.4 (9.0)	51.2 (8.9)	51.8 (9.4)	49.0 (8.1)	51.1 (9.1)	50.3 (8.8)	50.2 (8.6)	53.8 (8.1)	51.9 (7.7)	55.3 (10.4)	54.2 (9.3)	54.7 (9.0)	55.1 (10.0)	53.6 (10.3)	54.3 (9.8)
46	54.3 (9.1)	59.0 (10.3)	56.4 (9.7)	49.5 (9.0)	51.9 (7.5)	50.7 (8.3)	50.7 (8.1)	53.6 (9.1)	52.1 (8.7)	48.9 (9.9)	49.9 (8.4)	49.4 (9.1)	51.3 (10.0)	54.7 (10.3)	53.4 (10.3)	51.1 (10.0)	52.9 (8.7)	52.2 (9.3)
53	53.7 (10.7)	57.3 (9.5)	55.5 (10.4)	45.8 (9.7)	48.9 (9.4)	47.5 (9.6)	52.1 (10.5)	53.3 (7.2)	52.8 (8.7)	51.6 (11.5)	49.9 (8.7)	50.8 (10.3)	51.3 (10.2)	52.5 (8.9)	51.9 (9.5)	49.8 (8.8)	50.8 (10.4)	50.3 (9.7)
60	48.9 (11.5)	50.9 (10.3)	49.9 (11.0)	47.0 (9.5)	48.9 (8.4)	49.0 (9.0)	50.4 (10.1)	50.2 (7.0)	50.3 (8.7)	48.9 (8.0)	50.2 (9.2)	49.9 (8.3)	46.9 (7.1)	48.7 (8.9)	47.9 (9.4)	50.5 (8.9)	50.7 (9.2)	50.6 (9.0)
67	48.6 (11.0)	47.2 (10.5)	47.9 (10.0)	44.0 (7.6)	45.0 (10.6)	44.5 (9.5)	42.4 (10.1)	45.4 (6.4)	44.0 (8.3)	46.5 (8.6)	48.5 (7.4)	47.5 (8.5)	44.9 (7.1)	48.7 (11.0)	46.9 (9.4)	47.0 (9.4)	48.9 (9.1)	48.1 (9.2)
74	—	—	—	44.8 (8.3)	44.2 (8.1)	44.5 (8.2)	39.8 (8.2)	43.2 (8.2)	41.4 (8.3)	40.4 (8.0)	45.7 (9.9)	42.9 (9.3)	44.6 (8.3)	45.8 (8.8)	45.1 (8.5)	45.8 (9.2)	48.5 (7.3)	47.2 (8.2)
81	—	—	—	—	—	—	41.2 (9.7)	43.5 (7.1)	42.3 (8.6)	38.8 (6.8)	44.5 (8.7)	41.8 (8.3)	39.5 (7.4)	42.4 (7.1)	41.1 (7.3)	43.1 (8.6)	43.2 (8.3)	43.2 (8.4)

Index of Intellectual Ability

Age	1956 M	1956 F	1956 T	1963 M	1963 F	1963 T	1970 M	1970 F	1970 T	1977 M	1977 F	1977 T	1984 M	1984 F	1984 T	1991 M	1991 F	1991 T
25	52.6 (8.7)	53.4 (10.0)	53.0 (9.3)	54.8 (7.3)	55.5 (8.2)	55.2 (7.8)	56.9 (8.1)	55.7 (7.9)	56.2 (8.0)	54.7 (7.7)	55.0 (10.0)	54.8 (8.9)	56.6 (9.6)	54.8 (7.9)	55.4 (8.4)	55.5 (7.2)	56.6 (7.4)	56.1 (7.3)
32	55.2 (10.0)	55.8 (8.8)	55.5 (9.5)	55.0 (8.3)	55.5 (8.0)	55.3 (8.1)	57.1 (8.7)	54.9 (7.8)	55.9 (8.2)	54.6 (6.6)	56.9 (5.7)	55.6 (6.2)	57.3 (7.1)	54.0 (8.0)	55.6 (7.7)	55.6 (6.6)	54.2 (7.6)	54.8 (7.2)
39	55.2 (10.3)	51.9 (8.8)	52.5 (9.2)	56.6 (8.3)	52.8 (6.9)	54.6 (7.4)	54.8 (8.7)	52.6 (7.8)	53.5 (8.2)	54.5 (8.8)	54.8 (7.0)	54.6 (7.9)	55.3 (7.1)	54.4 (8.0)	54.8 (7.7)	57.5 (10.0)	55.6 (7.6)	56.5 (7.2)
46	53.2 (9.4)	53.9 (9.0)	54.0 (9.2)	51.6 (7.5)	52.3 (6.9)	51.9 (7.4)	55.7 (8.5)	54.7 (8.0)	55.2 (8.2)	51.2 (8.8)	50.3 (7.0)	50.7 (7.9)	53.9 (6.7)	56.2 (6.7)	55.3 (6.9)	56.1 (7.5)	55.0 (6.3)	55.5 (7.5)
53	51.2 (9.6)	51.0 (10.5)	51.1 (10.0)	47.8 (9.0)	47.5 (9.7)	47.6 (9.4)	54.1 (9.2)	53.2 (7.9)	53.6 (7.8)	54.2 (7.6)	49.4 (8.6)	51.9 (8.1)	50.6 (6.6)	53.0 (7.0)	51.8 (6.9)	53.5 (7.7)	53.4 (8.9)	53.4 (8.4)
60	44.3 (9.6)	45.1 (7.6)	44.7 (8.0)	46.0 (9.8)	47.0 (9.7)	46.5 (9.4)	53.8 (9.6)	50.7 (8.1)	52.2 (8.6)	50.0 (10.8)	48.6 (8.1)	49.8 (8.6)	51.1 (8.8)	48.6 (7.3)	49.7 (8.0)	50.9 (9.0)	50.0 (8.1)	50.4 (8.5)
67	44.1 (8.6)	41.9 (8.5)	43.0 (8.5)	41.7 (9.4)	41.0 (10.4)	41.3 (10.1)	43.4 (7.7)	43.0 (7.7)	43.2 (8.9)	46.3 (9.1)	47.2 (9.6)	46.8 (9.3)	45.3 (7.9)	47.6 (8.3)	46.5 (8.2)	48.9 (6.7)	49.1 (7.9)	49.0 (7.3)
74	—	—	—	41.2 (7.4)	38.0 (7.4)	39.5 (7.5)	38.1 (7.7)	39.4 (7.7)	38.7 (7.7)	39.4 (8.2)	40.9 (8.8)	40.1 (8.5)	43.6 (6.8)	43.6 (8.5)	43.6 (8.6)	45.9 (7.3)	46.8 (7.9)	46.3 (7.6)
81	—	—	—	—	—	—	37.9 (8.7)	35.4 (5.9)	36.7 (7.5)	36.4 (6.6)	37.0 (7.2)	36.7 (6.9)	39.1 (6.9)	36.7 (5.8)	37.9 (6.4)	40.0 (7.6)	41.2 (7.6)	40.6 (7.6)

Table 4.3. (cont.)

Index of Educational Aptitude

Age	1956 M	1956 F	1956 T	1963 M	1963 F	1963 T	1970 M	1970 F	1970 T	1977 M	1977 F	1977 T	1984 M	1984 F	1984 T	1991 M	1991 F	1991 T
25	51.8	54.0	52.9	53.5	54.9	54.3	54.4	55.7	55.1	54.5	56.5	55.5	55.3	56.9	56.4	54.3	56.5	55.5
	(8.6)	(7.5)	(8.1)	(8.0)	(8.3)	(8.1)	(7.7)	(7.4)	(7.5)	(7.8)	(9.2)	(8.5)	(7.8)	(7.1)	(7.3)	(8.0)	(6.6)	(7.3)
32	53.3	55.9	54.7	53.2	55.0	54.3	53.4	55.6	54.6	55.6	57.3	56.5	56.7	54.5	55.5	56.9	55.1	55.9
	(9.5)	(7.4)	(8.5)	(8.2)	(7.5)	(7.8)	(8.6)	(7.7)	(8.1)	(6.8)	(6.7)	(6.7)	(6.2)	(8.1)	(7.2)	(6.1)	(7.9)	(7.2)
39	51.4	51.2	51.3	54.4	53.3	53.8	54.1	53.4	53.7	54.3	56.0	55.1	56.9	57.0	57.0	58.0	58.5	58.3
	(9.3)	(10.3)	(9.7)	(7.6)	(7.0)	(7.3)	(7.4)	(7.5)	(7.4)	(9.6)	(7.4)	(8.5)	(5.9)	(6.1)	(6.0)	(6.4)	(5.6)	(6.0)
46	50.2	55.4	52.6	49.7	52.0	50.9	53.1	54.7	53.9	52.8	51.6	52.1	55.7	57.8	57.0	56.9	57.8	57.4
	(9.5)	(7.3)	(8.9)	(8.9)	(8.5)	(8.8)	(9.3)	(8.1)	(8.7)	(8.7)	(9.9)	(9.3)	(6.1)	(6.1)	(6.1)	(6.3)	(6.4)	(6.3)
53	48.4	48.2	48.3	46.1	48.0	47.2	53.9	52.7	53.2	53.2	51.0	52.1	52.1	56.1	51.8	54.5	57.4	56.0
	(9.9)	(9.1)	(9.4)	(9.7)	(9.2)	(9.5)	(7.2)	(7.5)	(7.3)	(9.5)	(9.7)	(9.6)	(8.0)	(6.3)	(7.4)	(7.4)	(6.7)	(7.2)
60	41.0	44.9	43.0	43.7	47.2	45.5	53.0	49.5	51.2	50.0	49.0	49.5	51.6	51.9	51.8	53.0	52.1	52.5
	(8.8)	(8.0)	(8.6)	(8.8)	(9.9)	(9.5)	(9.3)	(7.9)	(8.7)	(9.7)	(8.5)	(9.0)	(7.9)	(7.9)	(7.9)	(7.6)	(7.9)	(7.8)
67	41.8	40.9	41.4	39.7	42.2	41.0	42.5	44.5	43.6	44.0	46.5	45.3	46.6	48.9	47.8	49.3	52.6	51.2
	(7.9)	(7.7)	(7.7)	(8.7)	(8.1)	(8.5)	(7.3)	(8.3)	(7.9)	(8.0)	(8.8)	(8.4)	(8.0)	(8.0)	(8.0)	(8.2)	(8.0)	(8.2)
74	—	—	—	38.6	38.2	38.4	37.2	40.0	38.5	38.6	41.0	40.0	42.4	45.5	43.6	46.9	47.9	46.3
				(8.8)	(7.8)	(8.3)	(6.9)	(5.6)	(6.4)	(8.4)	(8.8)	(8.8)	(5.9)	(7.9)	(7.0)	(8.4)	(8.8)	(8.6)
81	—	—	—	—	—	—	36.1	37.1	36.8	34.9	35.3	36.7	39.6	38.5	37.7	40.2	41.4	40.7
							(8.3)	(6.8)	(7.5)	(6.5)	(6.6)	(6.5)	(8.6)	(6.8)	(7.7)	(6.4)	(8.8)	(7.7)

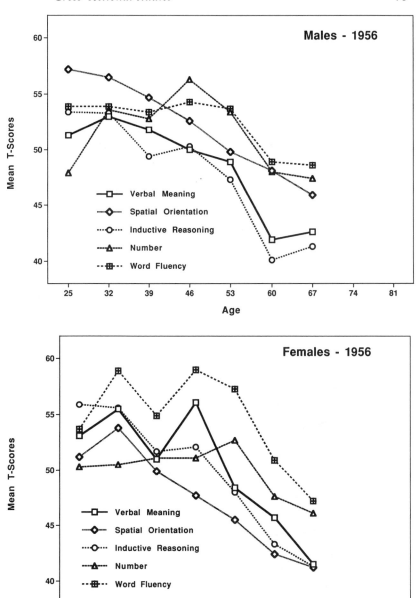

a

Figure 4.4. Age-difference patterns for the five primary mental abilities, by gender, for the first (1956) and last (1991) cross-sectional comparisons.

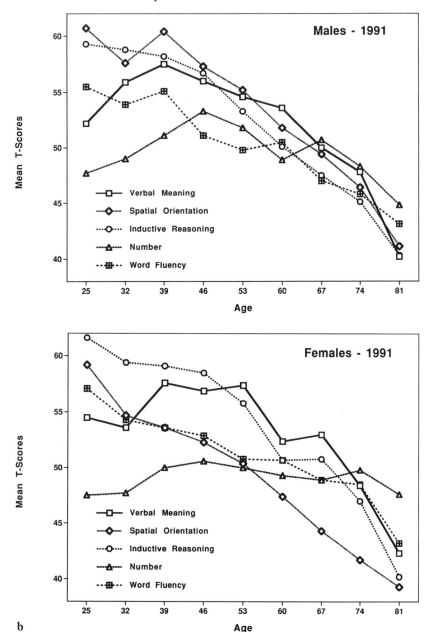

b

Figure 4.4. (*cont.*)

sequences, are most appropriate for testing the proposition of in-variance in age-difference patterns over time. Given certain as-sumptions, they are also the data of choice to evaluate the magnitude of cohort differences and time-of-measurement (period) effects.

Throughout our study we have questioned whether or not age-difference patterns remain invariant over time and have concluded that one can observe statistically significant shifts in such patterns. This conclusion is based in part on the findings of Age × Time interactions in time-sequential analyses and of Cohort × Time interactions in cross-sequential analyses (Schaie & Hertzog, 1983; Schaie, Labouvie, & Buech, 1973; Schaie & Strother, 1968c).

To examine shifts in age profiles as well as the peak ages across the six cross-sectional studies, mean values for each study across age for the five PMAs have been graphed in Figure 4.5. What seems most apparent is that until the 70s are reached, means observed at the same ages tend to fall at progressively higher levels for successive cohorts attaining a given age.

For *Verbal Meaning* there has been a general increase in per-formance level at all ages. Most noteworthy, however, are perfor-mance increases at the older ages. For ages 53 to 74 these increases amount to almost a full standard deviation. Even at age 81, perfor-mance has increased by almost 0.5 *SD* over the 21 years monitored for this age group. Somewhat smaller increases across time, averaging approximately 0.5 *SD*, were observed for *Spatial Orientation*. How-ever, there was little improvement for the two oldest age groups. Except for the oldest age group, *Inductive Reasoning* showed the largest rise in performance over time at comparable age, whereas *Number* and *Word Fluency* showed complex changes involving cur-vilinear patterns of age differences. For the summary indices of Intellectual Ability and Educational Aptitude, attention needs once again to be called to the reduction in age differences occurring until the late 60s and early 70s, which continued unabated into our most current period of observation. Changes in performance level are discussed in greater detail in chapter 6, where cohort and period effects are explicitly dealt with.

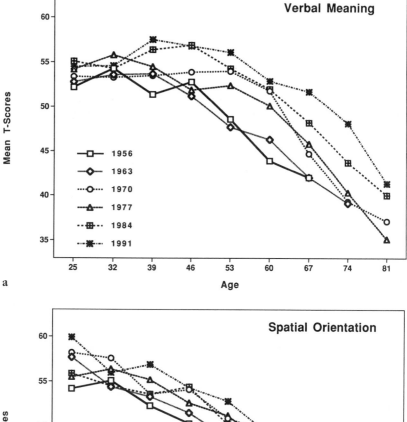

a

b

Figure 4.5. Comparison of mean scores for the primary mental abilities and the composite indices for the six cross-sectional studies.

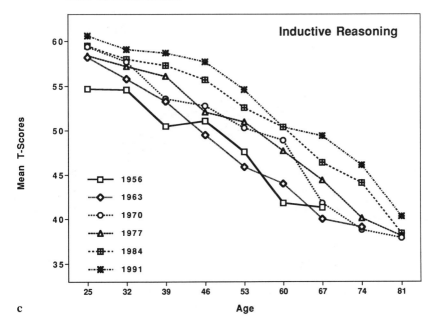

c

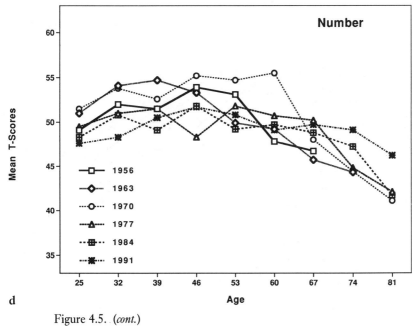

d

Figure 4.5. (*cont.*)

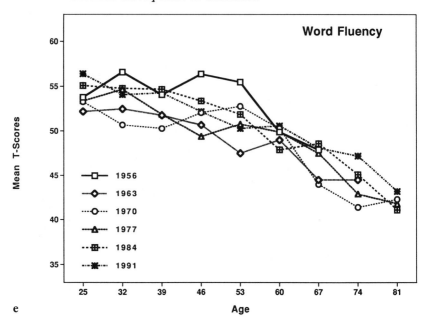

e

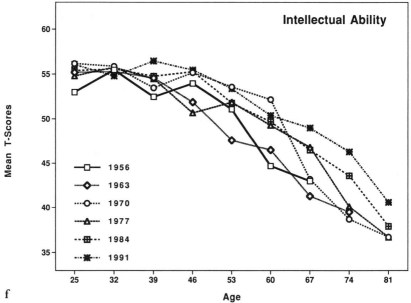

f

Figure 4.5. (*cont.*)

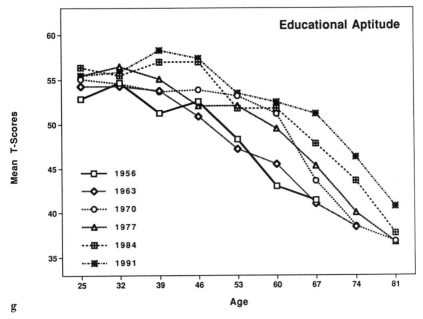

g

Figure 4.5. (*cont.*)

Expanded cognitive data

The expanded cognitive battery described in chapter 3 was administered in Cycles 5 and 6, except for the Perceptual Speed measures of Finding A's and Identical Pictures, which were introduced during the fourth cycle. Cross-sectional analyses for the fifth and sixth cycles were consequently done both at the level of individual measures and at the latent construct level to determine within-ability and across-ability age-difference patterns (see Schaie & Willis, 1993).

Most of the major longitudinal studies of adult development in the past collected only very limited data that speak to the issues of generalizability of findings within and across domains in the area of intellectual functioning (e.g., Busse, 1993; Costa & McCrae, 1993; Eichorn, Clausen, Haan, Honzik, & Mussen, 1981; Rott, 1990; Schaie, 1983b; Schmitz-Scherzer & Thomae, 1983; Shock et al., 1984; Siegler, 1983). Cross-sectional data may actually be quite instructive with respect to this issue, because such data allow us to draw *concurrent* comparisons of age-difference patterns within and across domains without requiring attention to the thorny methodological issues associated with comparisons across time (see chapter 2).

There are likely to be substantial life-stage differences in adulthood in the degree to which levels of performance for different ability markers are equivalent both within and across ability domains. I first examine the extent to which patterns of age differences are congruent within a particular ability domain by describing age difference patterns for six psychometric abilities (see Schaie & Willis, 1993). These abilities broadly sample higher-order constructs such as those espoused by Horn (1982). Thus, fluid intelligence is represented by the ability of Inductive Reasoning. Verbal Ability and Numeric Ability stand as representatives of crystallized intelligence, and mental rotation is represented by our Spatial Ability construct. Verbal Memory and Perceptual Speed are examined as ability samplers for the memory and speed domains, respectively. Next, consideration is given, therefore, to the age-difference patterns across the various ability domains.

What is at issue is the question of whether patterns of age differences in ability remain invariant for multiple markers of the primary mental abilities. The reader will find this issue addressed again in chapter 8, where a study is reported that examines invariance across age by means of structural analyses (see Schaie, Willis, Jay, & Chipuer, 1989), and where we show that configural invariance (i.e., number of factors and factor pattern) is preserved across widely differing age groups. Here we will examine shifts of different marker variables at different life stages, an effect observed a long time ago in cross-sectional studies of the WAIS (Cohen, 1957). The reasons for such shifts may be sought for in such contextual variables as shifts in educational exposure to the skills embodied in a particular marker variable or latent construct and the impact of slowing in perceptual and/or motor speed that may differentially affect various markers. For example, we know that conditions of instructions and speededness imposed by time limits differentially affect performance on the PMA and ETS vocabulary tests (Hertzog, 1989). Likewise, we know that there have been generational shifts in instruction in quantitative skills that should affect numerical performance for different cohorts. For other abilities, we would expect congruence across the entire life span until the 80s are reached. At that late stage, the differential memorization demands as well as the relative motor complexity of answer sheet as compared with disposable booklet formats might result in differential efficiency of a given marker.

Age-difference patterns appear generally invariant across sex within domains (albeit there is strong evidence for overall gender differences in level of performance), but it is not a foregone conclusion that such invariance holds for all abilities or for all markers of a given ability. Gender differences will therefore be examined, and results are reported separately by gender where warranted.

The issue of the generalizability of markers within domains is particularly important for age-comparative studies. For valid cross-sectional comparisons, we must show that an observed variable provides a reasonable representation of the developmental trajectory of the latent construct to be marked. If this is the case, then a single marker may suffice. But if there is wide discrepancy in developmental trajectories for multiple markers, we would then be forced to multiply mark the construct, providing differential weights for the markers at different life stages. The data to be presented here provide some guidance on these matters.

All scores on the observed variables were rescaled into T-score form ($M = 50$; $SD = 10$) using parameters for the total sample at first test ($N = 4,123$). Factor scores for the six intellectual abilities were computed using factor regression weights based on a previously determined best-fitting factor model (Schaie, Dutta, & Willis, 1991).

Age-difference patterns within ability domains

The age-difference patterns in the six primary ability factors (in standardized form) are reported in Table 4.4. Means and standard deviations are given separately by gender and for the total age/cohort groupings. The age-difference gradients are graphed in Figure 4.6, comparing the markers for each latent construct. Results with respect to congruence among the patterns for the different operations

Table 4.4. *Means and standard deviations for the expanded ability battery, by sample and gender*

Inductive Reasoning / Letter Series

Age	1984 M	1984 F	1984 T	1991 M	1991 F	1991 T
25	59.3 (9.3)	57.9 (7.7)	58.4 (8.3)	58.0 (9.3)	61.6 (8.7)	60.0 (9.1)
32	58.0 (7.7)	57.3 (9.0)	57.7 (8.3)	60.3 (6.8)	58.9 (7.9)	59.5 (7.5)
39	57.7 (8.2)	57.2 (7.8)	57.4 (8.0)	59.6 (7.4)	58.1 (7.9)	59.0 (6.7)
46	55.4 (7.4)	54.4 (7.7)	54.8 (7.6)	56.9 (7.0)	57.4 (9.5)	57.2 (8.6)
53	50.6 (9.8)	51.2 (8.1)	50.9 (7.9)	52.6 (8.4)	55.1 (7.4)	53.9 (8.0)
60	49.2 (9.5)	48.3 (8.5)	48.7 (8.5)	49.9 (6.3)	49.9 (7.7)	49.9 (7.0)
67	44.5 (8.2)	46.1 (7.6)	45.5 (7.7)	47.3 (8.4)	49.0 (8.8)	48.3 (8.6)
74	41.0 (5.9)	42.2 (6.6)	41.6 (9.4)	43.5 (8.5)	44.6 (7.0)	44.1 (7.5)
81	38.2 (5.4)	39.3 (6.3)	38.9 (6.0)	40.1 (6.2)	38.6 (7.0)	39.3 (6.6)

Spatial Orientation / Object Rotation

Age	1984 M	1984 F	1984 T	1991 M	1991 F	1991 T
25	60.2 (4.4)	53.3 (9.9)	55.9 (8.9)	58.2 (6.9)	57.9 (6.4)	58.0 (6.6)
32	58.0 (6.0)	55.6 (7.1)	56.6 (6.6)	57.9 (6.1)	55.6 (8.3)	56.6 (7.5)

Word Series

Age	1984 M	1984 F	1984 T	1991 M	1991 F	1991 T
25	57.9 (7.6)	57.9 (7.3)	57.9 (7.3)	57.1 (7.9)	60.5 (6.6)	59.0 (7.4)
32	57.0 (8.0)	57.2 (8.2)	57.1 (8.0)	57.9 (6.7)	59.3 (8.1)	58.7 (7.5)
39	56.2 (7.3)	58.0 (7.6)	57.3 (7.5)	56.1 (7.8)	58.5 (5.9)	57.3 (7.0)
46	54.8 (6.7)	55.8 (6.8)	55.3 (6.8)	56.7 (5.7)	57.2 (7.3)	57.0 (6.6)
53	50.6 (7.6)	53.1 (6.3)	51.8 (7.1)	52.0 (8.0)	56.0 (8.2)	54.1 (8.3)
60	49.0 (7.8)	50.1 (7.9)	49.5 (7.9)	50.7 (6.6)	49.9 (7.3)	50.2 (7.0)
67	44.0 (8.6)	46.8 (8.5)	45.6 (8.6)	47.0 (7.7)	49.4 (7.3)	48.4 (7.5)
74	40.2 (8.1)	43.9 (8.7)	42.2 (9.0)	42.7 (8.3)	46.5 (8.3)	44.7 (6.0)
81	35.7 (6.0)	37.2 (7.5)	36.6 (7.0)	36.7 (5.2)	40.2 (8.1)	38.5 (7.0)

Alphanumeric Rotation

Age	1984 M	1984 F	1984 T	1991 M	1991 F	1991 T
25	59.7 (2.5)	54.6 (7.8)	56.7 (6.6)	58.0 (4.6)	58.7 (4.6)	58.4 (4.6)
32	57.8 (4.3)	57.3 (5.3)	57.6 (4.7)	57.4 (5.7)	56.8 (6.0)	57.3 (5.8)

Number Series

Age	1984 M	1984 F	1984 T	1991 M	1991 F	1991 T
25	59.7 (8.4)	56.1 (8.8)	57.5 (8.8)	59.4 (8.9)	57.7 (8.5)	58.5 (8.7)
32	57.9 (9.7)	53.9 (7.1)	56.0 (8.8)	58.4 (8.1)	55.7 (7.6)	56.9 (7.9)
39	57.2 (8.0)	53.3 (8.6)	54.9 (8.5)	59.7 (9.5)	54.2 (6.6)	56.9 (8.5)
46	57.4 (8.0)	51.9 (9.9)	54.2 (9.5)	57.9 (9.5)	52.0 (8.4)	54.4 (8.7)
53	52.6 (8.0)	49.3 (8.3)	51.0 (8.6)	56.0 (9.5)	52.8 (8.5)	54.4 (9.1)
60	51.7 (8.5)	47.4 (9.8)	49.4 (9.5)	51.4 (7.3)	47.6 (7.9)	49.3 (9.3)
67	47.8 (8.5)	45.6 (8.9)	46.5 (9.2)	50.2 (8.6)	47.9 (10.0)	48.8 (9.5)
74	42.5 (7.9)	41.9 (6.8)	42.2 (7.4)	46.5 (9.6)	44.0 (6.8)	45.2 (9.5)
81	40.1 (6.5)	39.8 (6.7)	39.9 (6.6)	41.4 (6.1)	40.7 (6.2)	41.0 (6.1)

Cube Comparison

Age	1984 M	1984 F	1984 T	1991 M	1991 F	1991 T
25	60.3 (8.7)	56.3 (9.7)	58.0 (9.4)	61.8 (11.5)	58.4 (9.5)	59.9 (10.5)
32	58.0 (10.7)	53.1 (7.9)	55.8 (9.8)	60.7 (9.5)	55.8 (8.5)	57.8 (9.2)

39	57.8 (6.8)	54.2 (8.0)	55.7 (7.3)	58.7 (7.3)	51.8 (8.8)	55.2 (8.7)	57.2 (5.7)	55.6 (6.5)	56.3 (6.2)	58.0 (4.0)	56.6 (5.7)	57.3 (4.9)	60.4 (9.0)	53.2 (8.8)	56.2 (9.5)	63.6 (9.5)	56.2 (8.4)	59.9 (9.7)
46	56.3 (6.9)	55.1 (7.6)	55.5 (7.3)	56.6 (5.8)	54.6 (7.7)	55.4 (7.0)	55.9 (5.8)	55.2 (5.9)	55.5 (5.9)	57.8 (4.3)	56.2 (6.1)	56.9 (5.5)	57.7 (8.9)	51.3 (7.6)	53.8 (8.7)	59.1 (7.8)	54.3 (8.3)	56.2 (8.4)
53	54.1 (7.1)	51.4 (8.3)	52.7 (7.8)	55.4 (7.2)	52.4 (8.8)	53.8 (8.1)	54.4 (6.3)	52.3 (7.8)	53.4 (7.1)	55.3 (4.3)	54.6 (6.1)	54.9 (5.5)	53.4 (8.7)	48.2 (7.6)	50.9 (8.7)	55.8 (10.4)	51.3 (8.3)	53.5 (8.4)
60	54.1 (7.3)	49.6 (7.8)	51.8 (7.9)	55.4 (5.9)	49.8 (7.9)	52.3 (7.6)	52.5 (7.1)	50.7 (7.0)	51.5 (7.1)	53.5 (6.6)	50.4 (7.0)	51.8 (6.7)	51.9 (8.6)	46.4 (7.6)	49.0 (8.1)	52.4 (7.3)	46.7 (8.3)	49.3 (9.6)
67	48.1 (7.3)	46.5 (7.8)	47.2 (7.9)	50.0 (5.9)	45.4 (7.1)	47.2 (7.6)	48.2 (7.1)	48.7 (7.0)	48.5 (7.1)	49.5 (7.1)	49.2 (7.3)	49.3 (7.1)	45.9 (8.6)	44.2 (7.6)	44.9 (8.5)	47.4 (7.3)	47.1 (7.8)	47.2 (7.8)
74	44.2 (8.9)	42.4 (8.0)	43.2 (8.4)	46.2 (9.0)	42.1 (7.1)	44.1 (8.2)	45.0 (8.4)	45.0 (7.1)	45.0 (7.7)	47.0 (7.6)	46.4 (6.9)	46.7 (7.0)	43.7 (7.3)	43.1 (7.5)	43.4 (7.4)	46.5 (7.8)	42.8 (7.8)	44.6 (7.7)
81	41.5 (9.0)	38.3 (7.4)	39.5 (8.2)	41.3 (8.7)	39.0 (8.4)	40.1 (8.7)	41.4 (7.9)	42.5 (7.3)	42.0 (7.6)	43.0 (7.8)	41.2 (7.4)	42.1 (7.6)	42.0 (7.8)	40.9 (7.1)	41.4 (7.3)	39.9 (6.1)	42.0 (6.4)	41.0 (6.2)

	Perceptual Speed Identical Pictures						Number Comparison						Finding A's					
25	60.9 (6.8)	61.3 (4.7)	61.2 (5.5)	60.4 (6.5)	62.5 (3.9)	61.5 (5.3)	53.5 (10.0)	58.0 (7.4)	56.2 (8.7)	53.9 (8.6)	64.3 (8.2)	59.7 (9.8)	53.1 (14.2)	52.5 (10.4)	52.7 (11.7)	54.0 (10.0)	59.7 (11.0)	57.1 (10.9)
32	57.7 (6.3)	57.9 (9.2)	57.8 (6.7)	58.9 (6.9)	60.4 (6.9)	59.8 (6.2)	53.9 (8.3)	56.7 (10.5)	55.2 (9.4)	55.9 (8.9)	58.8 (8.0)	57.5 (8.5)	53.4 (9.7)	57.3 (11.6)	55.1 (10.6)	51.4 (11.2)	56.2 (10.5)	54.2 (11.0)
39	58.1 (6.3)	57.6 (7.3)	57.8 (6.9)	59.7 (5.8)	60.0 (4.9)	59.9 (5.3)	52.9 (8.9)	57.1 (8.5)	55.4 (8.9)	55.2 (10.5)	60.8 (8.4)	58.0 (9.8)	51.3 (8.7)	53.8 (10.8)	52.8 (10.0)	54.7 (9.3)	56.2 (9.7)	55.4 (9.5)
46	53.8 (6.6)	54.3 (7.4)	54.0 (7.1)	59.1 (6.1)	57.9 (4.9)	58.4 (6.4)	50.9 (8.1)	54.7 (9.9)	53.1 (9.4)	54.1 (7.3)	57.1 (8.4)	55.9 (9.8)	50.9 (9.1)	53.7 (10.3)	52.5 (10.0)	51.2 (8.6)	54.5 (9.7)	53.2 (9.1)
53	52.5 (7.0)	51.9 (7.4)	52.2 (7.1)	54.3 (7.6)	55.8 (6.6)	55.1 (6.4)	49.7 (8.1)	52.0 (9.9)	50.9 (9.4)	49.4 (7.3)	55.4 (9.0)	52.5 (8.4)	47.8 (9.6)	51.3 (8.7)	49.5 (9.9)	47.7 (9.6)	55.6 (9.3)	51.8 (9.1)
60	47.2 (6.1)	49.1 (6.8)	48.2 (6.7)	49.9 (7.6)	50.2 (6.9)	50.1 (7.2)	47.4 (7.6)	50.7 (9.2)	49.1 (7.6)	48.5 (9.1)	52.4 (9.6)	50.7 (10.0)	47.4 (8.9)	49.9 (9.6)	48.7 (9.4)	47.6 (7.4)	51.5 (9.5)	49.7 (10.3)
67	43.4 (7.9)	44.7 (7.1)	44.1 (7.4)	46.2 (7.4)	47.9 (5.7)	47.2 (5.9)	44.7 (8.3)	48.3 (8.0)	46.7 (8.3)	46.3 (6.6)	49.7 (8.3)	48.3 (8.6)	48.0 (10.2)	50.2 (8.1)	49.1 (9.8)	44.8 (8.2)	50.2 (9.4)	47.9 (9.3)
74	39.2 (6.5)	41.8 (7.4)	40.5 (7.1)	43.1 (7.0)	44.5 (5.9)	43.8 (6.4)	41.0 (7.7)	46.0 (8.5)	43.6 (8.5)	43.6 (6.2)	47.5 (7.9)	45.6 (7.6)	43.4 (7.3)	47.6 (8.1)	45.6 (7.9)	46.3 (6.7)	50.2 (9.4)	47.5 (8.2)
81	37.4 (7.1)	37.4 (7.1)	37.4 (7.4)	37.7 (6.9)	39.4 (7.4)	38.5 (7.1)	37.6 (7.6)	41.1 (7.4)	39.6 (7.6)	40.5 (7.6)	43.7 (7.5)	42.1 (7.6)	41.4 (8.5)	45.9 (7.5)	44.0 (8.2)	42.9 (6.8)	47.2 (9.7)	45.1 (8.6)

Table 4.4. *(cont.)*

	1984			1991				1984			1991		
Age	M	F	T	M	F	T		M	F	T	M	F	T
	Numeric Ability Addition							**Subtraction & Multiplication**					
25	48.9 (7.8)	48.3 (8.1)	48.5 (7.9)	46.1 (7.9)	49.4 (9.0)	47.9 (8.6)		47.7 (7.7)	46.6 (8.3)	46.9 (8.0)	47.7 (9.9)	51.0 (10.7)	49.6 (10.4)
32	52.9 (9.5)	50.4 (9.9)	51.7 (9.7)	48.7 (7.6)	49.0 (8.1)	48.9 (7.8)		54.4 (11.3)	50.3 (9.4)	52.5 (10.6)	50.2 (9.5)	50.0 (9.8)	50.1 (9.6)
39	51.0 (9.1)	52.3 (9.9)	51.8 (9.6)	52.2 (10.5)	51.5 (8.3)	51.9 (9.4)		53.2 (8.5)	53.7 (9.9)	53.5 (9.3)	54.0 (10.3)	52.8 (8.4)	53.4 (9.4)
46	53.2 (11.0)	52.9 (9.7)	53.0 (10.2)	53.0 (8.1)	52.2 (10.2)	52.5 (9.3)		54.9 (10.0)	53.0 (10.0)	53.7 (10.0)	55.2 (8.0)	54.8 (9.5)	55.0 (8.9)
53	50.3 (9.8)	51.7 (9.7)	51.0 (9.7)	48.9 (10.9)	51.0 (8.3)	50.0 (9.6)		51.1 (9.8)	51.9 (9.3)	51.5 (9.5)	49.8 (12.3)	52.2 (10.7)	51.0 (11.5)
60	51.5 (10.7)	51.0 (10.0)	51.3 (10.3)	48.2 (7.2)	48.9 (9.9)	48.6 (8.8)		51.6 (9.7)	50.7 (9.6)	51.1 (9.6)	49.3 (9.1)	47.6 (9.9)	48.4 (9.5)
67	49.6 (10.8)	51.1 (9.8)	50.4 (10.3)	49.2 (8.1)	49.0 (9.8)	49.1 (9.1)		49.0 (10.7)	49.7 (9.8)	49.4 (10.2)	49.5 (7.5)	48.7 (9.4)	49.0 (8.7)
74	48.8 (8.7)	47.9 (10.3)	48.4 (9.5)	48.2 (10.3)	50.7 (8.9)	49.5 (9.6)		46.2 (7.9)	45.9 (8.2)	46.1 (8.0)	47.2 (8.1)	49.3 (9.8)	48.3 (9.0)
81	43.1 (10.6)	43.8 (9.3)	43.4 (9.8)	44.9 (11.9)	47.8 (11.0)	46.4 (11.5)		42.3 (8.8)	42.4 (9.0)	42.3 (8.9)	43.7 (9.3)	47.3 (9.3)	45.5 (9.3)
	Verbal Ability ETS Vocabulary							**ETS Advanced Vocabulary**					
25	47.7 (9.0)	47.1 (10.6)	47.3 (9.8)	43.9 (8.1)	42.2 (8.9)	43.0 (8.5)		47.7 (9.0)	45.2 (9.5)	46.2 (9.3)	44.1 (8.5)	43.9 (8.0)	44.0 (8.4)
32	48.7 (7.1)	49.9 (9.8)	49.2 (8.4)	48.1 (7.8)	44.3 (11.7)	45.9 (10.3)		49.0 (8.4)	47.8 (9.6)	48.5 (8.9)	49.3 (9.1)	46.2 (10.0)	47.5 (9.7)

Continuation of normative table (rows by age). Column headings are not present on this page.

Age												
39	51.6 (9.3)	50.8 (8.6)	51.1 (8.9)	49.1 (8.7)	52.3 (6.1)	50.7 (7.6)	52.0 (9.9)	50.3 (8.9)	51.0 (9.4)	52.8 (8.8)	51.7 (8.4)	52.2 (8.6)
46	51.2 (8.6)	51.9 (8.0)	51.6 (8.2)	49.5 (8.9)	52.1 (7.9)	51.0 (8.4)	52.6 (8.6)	51.5 (9.2)	52.0 (8.9)	51.3 (9.4)	53.2 (10.2)	52.4 (9.9)
53	50.8 (9.4)	52.2 (8.2)	51.5 (8.8)	50.0 (9.2)	53.6 (6.5)	51.9 (8.1)	51.3 (9.5)	51.2 (9.6)	51.2 (9.5)	50.6 (9.2)	53.2 (8.8)	52.0 (9.0)
60	51.7 (9.7)	50.4 (10.0)	51.0 (9.8)	50.9 (8.7)	50.0 (9.5)	50.4 (9.1)	52.2 (9.2)	49.6 (10.2)	50.8 (9.8)	51.2 (9.4)	48.3 (9.0)	49.6 (9.2)
67	49.6 (11.9)	51.7 (9.4)	50.6 (10.7)	51.1 (9.4)	52.2 (8.3)	51.8 (8.7)	50.3 (10.8)	51.4 (9.9)	50.8 (10.3)	51.0 (9.5)	52.1 (9.5)	51.7 (9.5)
74	47.4 (13.1)	49.0 (10.6)	48.2 (11.9)	48.0 (11.6)	50.2 (10.1)	49.1 (10.8)	48.3 (11.3)	48.2 (11.1)	48.2 (11.2)	49.8 (12.1)	49.8 (11.9)	49.8 (11.9)
81	43.1 (15.0)	48.0 (11.9)	45.9 (13.5)	50.9 (11.2)	50.0 (9.7)	50.4 (10.4)	46.9 (13.0)	47.8 (10.4)	47.2 (11.6)	50.0 (11.7)	49.7 (10.8)	49.9 (11.2)

Verbal Memory

Immediate Recall

Age						
25	56.1 (9.0)	60.1 (6.5)	58.4 (7.8)	58.7 (5.8)	60.5 (6.0)	59.7 (6.0)
32	54.8 (7.6)	57.0 (8.3)	55.8 (7.9)	56.3 (8.5)	58.7 (5.5)	57.7 (7.0)
39	53.9 (8.6)	56.4 (7.6)	55.3 (8.1)	55.5 (8.5)	59.1 (6.7)	57.3 (7.8)
46	51.0 (8.3)	54.7 (8.1)	53.2 (8.4)	55.4 (8.5)	58.5 (5.3)	57.2 (6.9)
53	48.8 (8.8)	51.8 (8.4)	50.3 (8.7)	50.4 (10.0)	56.3 (7.6)	53.5 (9.2)
60	47.4 (8.8)	50.2 (8.9)	48.9 (8.9)	49.7 (7.8)	51.4 (9.7)	50.6 (8.9)
67	44.2 (9.7)	47.9 (9.6)	46.2 (9.8)	46.4 (8.5)	51.2 (7.8)	49.2 (8.4)
74	41.1 (8.2)	45.5 (7.9)	43.4 (8.3)	43.9 (10.1)	46.5 (8.1)	45.2 (9.1)
81	38.1 (7.6)	42.4 (9.1)	40.6 (8.8)	40.8 (7.4)	43.9 (8.5)	42.4 (8.0)

Delayed Recall

Age						
25	58.1 (9.4)	61.3 (6.5)	60.0 (7.9)	59.0 (6.2)	62.9 (6.2)	61.2 (6.4)
32	56.0 (7.7)	59.5 (8.3)	57.5 (8.1)	56.8 (9.2)	59.2 (6.0)	58.2 (7.6)
39	54.0 (8.6)	57.6 (8.0)	56.1 (8.4)	55.1 (8.1)	60.5 (6.8)	57.8 (7.9)
46	51.8 (8.1)	55.4 (8.3)	54.0 (8.3)	53.7 (9.1)	58.9 (8.0)	56.8 (8.8)
53	48.9 (8.8)	52.2 (9.0)	50.5 (9.0)	48.3 (9.6)	56.5 (8.8)	52.5 (10.0)
60	47.8 (8.2)	51.0 (8.6)	49.5 (8.5)	47.6 (7.6)	51.2 (9.3)	49.6 (8.7)
67	44.1 (8.4)	48.6 (9.0)	46.5 (9.0)	45.4 (7.0)	52.3 (8.2)	49.5 (8.4)
74	41.3 (7.4)	45.6 (7.3)	43.5 (7.6)	44.0 (9.1)	46.2 (7.5)	45.1 (8.3)
81	38.6 (6.2)	42.8 (7.5)	41.1 (7.3)	40.5 (7.4)	44.7 (7.3)	42.6 (7.6)

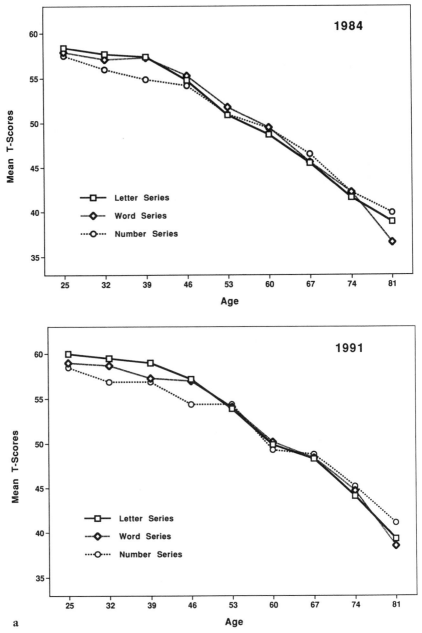

Figure 4.6. Age-difference patterns of the expanded battery, by test occasion.

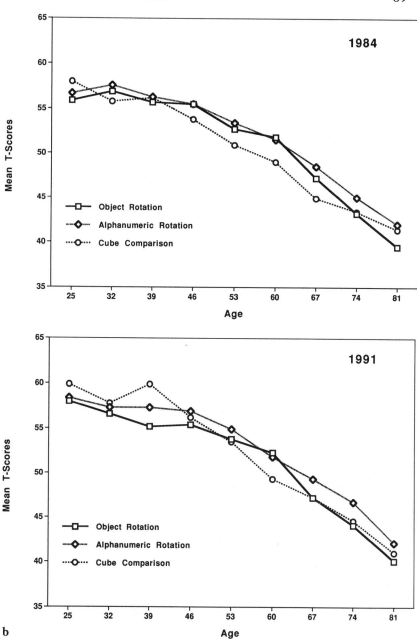

b

Figure 4.6. (*cont.*)

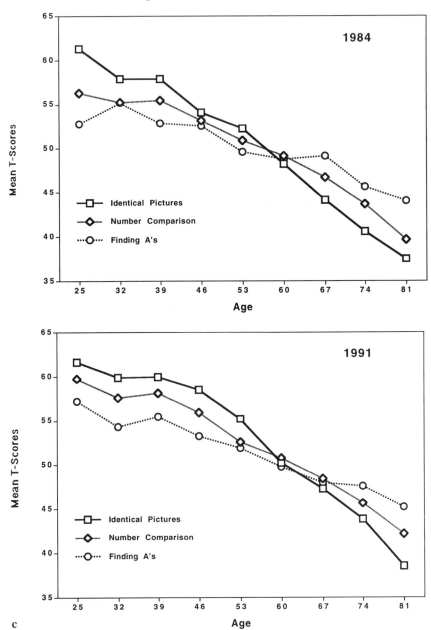

Figure 4.6. (*cont.*)

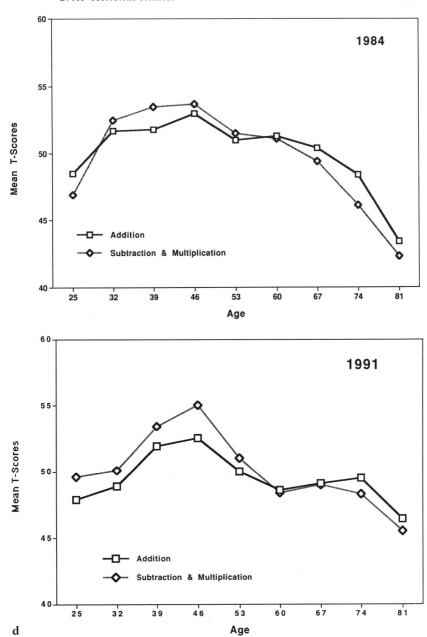

Figure 4.6. (*cont.*)

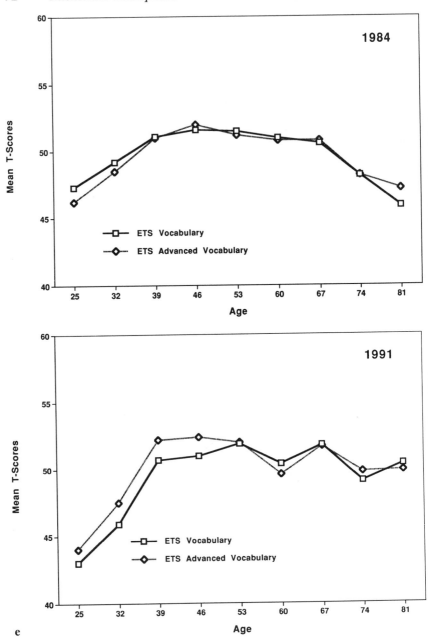

e

Figure 4.6. (*cont.*)

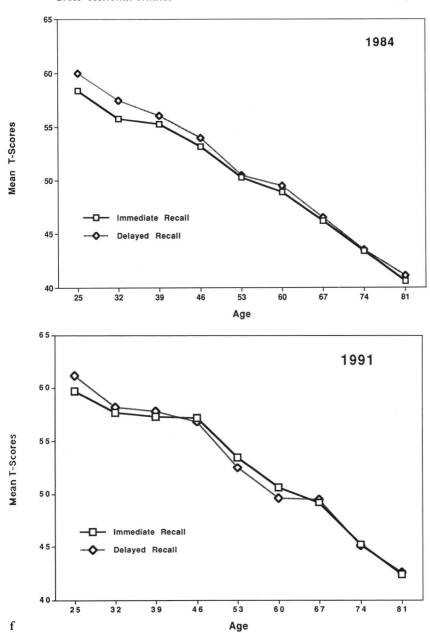

Figure 4.6. (*cont.*)

measuring the ability constructs are described in the following paragraphs.

The new markers of the *Inductive Reasoning* factor have very similar age profiles, with an overall age difference of about 2 *SD* from the youngest to the oldest age cohort. Significant age differences from the youngest (peak) age appear by age 53 for the Letter Series and Word Series tests, and by age 60 for the Number Series test. Gender differences were not significant for Letter Series, but favored women for Word Series ($F[df = 1, 1,670] = 18.96, p < .001$) and men for Number Series ($F[df = 1, 1,702] = 46.24, p < .001$). A significant overall increase in performance level across the two assessment times was found only for Letter Series ($F[df = 1, 1,667] = 6.42, p < .01$).

The ability profiles for the new markers of *Spatial Orientation* also showed a difference of approximately 2 *SD* from the youngest to the oldest group. Profiles differed somewhat more, with steepest age differences occurring for the Cube Comparison and shallowest for the Object Rotation tests. As for the original marker, there were significant gender differences favoring males for all three tests (Object Rotation, $F[df = 1, 1,721] = 59.84, p < .001$; Alphanumeric Rotation, $F[df = 1, 1,672] = 10.36, p < .001$; Cube Comparison, $F[df = 1, 1,669] = 63.59, p < .001$). Significant age differences from the youngest group were observed by age 53 for Object and Alphanumeric rotation, but already by age 46 for Cube Comparison. On the latter measure, there was also a significant gain across measurement occasions ($F[df = 1, 1,669] = 9.61, p < .01$), as well as a significant Sex × Age interaction ($F[df = 8, 1,669] = 4.45, p < .001$), which reflected the absence of sex differences in midlife (ages 39, 46, and 53).

The expanded battery contains three markers for the *Perceptual Speed* factor, which had not been measured earlier. Age differences from the youngest to the oldest group range from 1 *SD* for the Finding A's test to almost 2.5 *SD* for the Identical Pictures test. Interestingly, Identical Pictures appears to be the easiest measure for the young groups, whereas Finding A's is easier for the older groups. Gender differences favor women for all three tests (Identical Pictures, $F[df = 1, 1,746] = 5.76, p < .001$; Number Comparison, $F[df = 1, 1,719] = 55.47, p < .001$; Finding A's, $F[df = 1, 1,698] =$

43.86, $p < .001$). Significant differences from the youngest group were found by age 46 for Identical Pictures and by age 53 for Number Comparison and Finding A's. Significantly higher performance levels across the two assessment points were found for Identical Pictures ($F[df = 1, 1,746] = 17.08$, $p < .001$) and for Number Comparison ($F[df = 1, 1,716] = 14.21$, $p < .001$).

The new markers of *Numeric Ability* attain a peak at age 46 and then show a negative age difference of approximately 1 *SD* to the oldest age group. No significant gender differences were observed for either test, but there was a significant increase in performance level in 1991 for the Addition test ($F[df = 1, 1,720] = 7.09$, $p < .01$).

The new measures of *Verbal Ability* have rather different profiles from the original PMA marker because they are virtually unspeeded. The profile for the 1984 testing is slightly concave, with virtually no difference in level between the youngest and oldest sample and a peak plateau from age 39 to 67. By contrast, the 1991 profile shows positive age differences to age 39 followed by a virtual plateau to the oldest group measured. There were no significant gender differences on either test, but significantly higher overall performance levels were observed for the Advanced Vocabulary test in 1991 ($F[df = 1, 1,720] = 7.09$, $p < .01$).

Also newly included were two measures of the *Verbal Memory* factor. They have quite similar profiles, with an age difference of approximately 2 *SD* from the youngest to the oldest age/cohort. Significant gender differences on these measures favor women (Immediate Recall, $F[df = 1, 1,669] = 52.59$, $p < .001$; Delayed Recall, $F[df = 1, 1,668] = 70.47$, $p < .001$). Significant age differences from the level of the youngest group appear by age 39 for Delayed Recall and by age 46 for Immediate Recall. Significantly higher levels of performance on the second measurement occasion were also observed (Immediate Recall, $F[df = 1, 1,669] = 13.57$, $p < .001$; Delayed Recall, $F[df = 1, 1,666] = 5.38$, $p < .05$).

Cross-sectional differences on the latent constructs

Both the original markers and the new tests were combined as described above, and factor scores were computed for the resulting six latent constructs. Means and standard deviations separately by gender and for the total in each age group are given in Table 4.5 and are graphed across gender in Figure 4.7. For four of the six factors there are consistent negative age differences. They are statistically significant for Inductive Reasoning, Spatial Orientation, and Perceptual Speed at age 53 and for Verbal Memory at age 46. The magnitude of age differences from the youngest to the oldest group amounts to approximately 2 *SD* on average. The remaining two factors, Numeric and Verbal ability, have a very different profile. They both show positive age differences until midlife, with less than 0.5 *SD* negative difference thereafter, such that persons in advanced old age, on average, are at a higher level than the youngest age group. Gender differences on the latent construct measures were observed in favor of men on Spatial Orientation ($F[df = 1, 1,720] = 69.08$, $p < .001$) and in favor of women for Perceptual Speed ($F[df = 1, 1,717] = 25.61$, $p < .001$) and Verbal Memory ($F[df = 1, 1,666] = 65.72$, $p < .001$). A higher overall performance level in 1991 was shown for Inductive Reasoning ($F[df = 1, 1,717] = 4.60$, $p < .05$) and Verbal Memory ($F[df = 1, 1,666] = 9.73$, $p < .01$).

Practical intelligence data

The *Basic Skills – Reading* test developed by the Educational Testing Service (1977) simulates textual materials representing real-life tasks. This test was given in both the fifth and sixth cycles. An overall ANOVA of subjects at first test did not detect any significant gender differences but did result in a significant age/cohort main effect ($F[df = 8, 1,953] = 142.62$, $p < .001$). As shown in Table 4.6 and Figure 4.8, the age-difference profile is virtually flat until age 60; the first significant age difference occurs between ages 60 and 67. There was no significant Age × Gender interaction. Overall, there was a significantly higher level of performance in 1991 than in 1984 ($F[df = 1, 1,935] = 34.47$, $p < .001$) as well as a significant Age × Time interaction ($F[df = 1, 1,935] = 4.42$, $p < .001$). However, for a specific age group it was only the 81-year-old level that showed a statistically significant gain across cohorts in 1991.

Table 4.5. *Means and standard deviations for the latent construct scores, by sample and gender*

Inductive Reasoning

Age	1984 M	1984 F	1984 T	1991 M	1991 F	1991 T
25	59.8 (8.2)	58.6 (7.6)	59.0 (7.8)	59.1 (6.3)	61.4 (7.4)	60.4 (7.8)
32	58.3 (7.7)	57.2 (8.1)	57.8 (7.8)	59.1 (6.2)	59.0 (7.0)	59.0 (6.6)
39	57.4 (7.1)	57.3 (7.1)	57.4 (7.1)	58.7 (7.6)	58.0 (5.0)	58.4 (6.4)
46	55.6 (6.7)	55.2 (7.4)	55.3 (7.1)	57.3 (6.6)	57.0 (8.0)	57.1 (7.5)
53	51.1 (7.5)	52.0 (6.9)	51.6 (7.2)	53.3 (8.2)	55.2 (7.8)	54.3 (8.0)
60	49.8 (8.1)	48.9 (8.0)	49.3 (8.1)	50.6 (5.8)	49.4 (7.2)	49.9 (6.6)
67	44.2 (8.1)	45.9 (8.0)	45.2 (8.0)	47.3 (7.9)	49.0 (8.3)	48.3 (8.1)
74	40.3 (6.7)	42.0 (7.1)	41.2 (6.9)	43.3 (8.5)	45.0 (7.2)	44.1 (7.9)
81	36.6 (5.3)	36.9 (6.2)	36.8 (5.8)	38.1 (5.4)	38.5 (6.6)	38.3 (6.0)

Spatial Orientation

Age	1984 M	1984 F	1984 T	1991 M	1991 F	1991 T
25	61.4 (5.0)	54.8 (10.2)	57.3 (9.1)	60.5 (7.4)	59.6 (6.7)	60.0 (6.9)
32	58.3 (6.4)	55.4 (6.5)	56.9 (6.5)	58.8 (7.5)	56.4 (7.6)	57.4 (7.6)
39	59.2 (7.3)	54.4 (8.2)	56.4 (6.4)	60.9 (7.0)	54.4 (7.8)	57.6 (8.1)
46	57.0 (7.4)	54.5 (7.4)	55.5 (7.5)	58.5 (5.9)	54.8 (7.9)	56.3 (7.4)
53	54.2 (6.9)	50.3 (7.4)	52.2 (7.7)	55.8 (7.8)	52.0 (8.5)	53.8 (8.3)
60	53.1 (7.9)	48.0 (8.0)	50.5 (7.4)	53.6 (6.4)	48.2 (7.3)	50.6 (7.4)
67	46.4 (8.5)	45.1 (7.4)	45.7 (7.4)	48.6 (8.2)	45.1 (7.5)	46.5 (7.9)
74	42.8 (8.0)	40.9 (7.1)	41.8 (7.6)	45.3 (8.2)	41.4 (6.8)	43.3 (7.7)
81	39.5 (7.5)	37.4 (6.1)	38.2 (6.8)	39.2 (7.3)	37.8 (6.6)	38.5 (6.9)

Perceptual Speed

Age	1984 M	1984 F	1984 T	1991 M	1991 F	1991 T
25	57.0 (9.4)	61.2 (11.8)	59.6 (11.0)	54.8 (6.0)	59.2 (5.2)	57.3 (6.0)
32	55.5 (6.7)	58.8 (11.6)	57.1 (9.4)	57.1 (9.2)	56.2 (5.8)	56.6 (7.4)
39	56.5 (6.5)	57.6 (9.7)	57.1 (9.5)	56.1 (5.6)	58.3 (6.1)	57.2 (5.9)
46	55.4 (9.3)	54.9 (9.7)	55.1 (9.2)	54.7 (5.2)	55.5 (5.5)	55.1 (5.1)
53	52.4 (10.0)	53.9 (8.7)	53.1 (9.2)	50.8 (6.8)	54.7 (5.6)	52.8 (5.4)
60	48.1 (9.1)	49.2 (9.6)	48.7 (9.4)	48.9 (4.8)	50.9 (5.6)	50.0 (6.5)
67	44.6 (8.1)	46.6 (6.8)	45.7 (7.5)	45.7 (6.4)	48.6 (5.3)	47.4 (5.9)
74	40.7 (7.9)	43.6 (7.5)	42.2 (7.9)	43.5 (5.9)	45.6 (5.9)	44.6 (5.9)
81	39.7 (10.3)	40.5 (8.5)	40.2 (9.2)	38.6 (5.2)	41.2 (7.5)	39.9 (6.5)

Numeric Ability

Age	1984 M	1984 F	1984 T	1991 M	1991 F	1991 T
25	49.0 (7.7)	48.3 (8.5)	48.6 (8.1)	47.1 (8.2)	49.9 (9.2)	48.6 (8.8)
32	53.6 (10.3)	50.3 (9.2)	52.0 (9.9)	49.3 (8.4)	49.3 (8.3)	49.3 (8.3)
39	52.0 (8.8)	52.8 (9.9)	52.5 (9.5)	53.1 (10.5)	52.0 (8.0)	52.5 (9.3)
46	54.0 (10.7)	52.7 (9.5)	53.2 (10.0)	54.7 (8.6)	53.1 (10.0)	53.7 (9.4)
53	51.0 (9.9)	51.8 (9.5)	51.4 (9.6)	50.0 (11.6)	51.4 (9.3)	50.7 (10.4)
60	52.4 (10.6)	50.5 (9.6)	51.4 (10.1)	48.9 (8.0)	48.8 (9.8)	48.8 (9.0)
67	49.7 (10.8)	50.4 (9.8)	50.1 (10.3)	49.9 (7.9)	49.8 (9.7)	49.2 (9.2)
74	47.3 (8.4)	46.7 (9.5)	47.0 (8.9)	47.7 (9.9)	50.0 (9.1)	48.9 (9.5)
81	42.7 (9.5)	41.9 (9.1)	42.2 (9.2)	45.2 (10.3)	47.5 (9.9)	46.4 (10.1)

Verbal Ability

Age	1984 M	1984 F	1984 T	1991 M	1991 F	1991 T
25	47.8 (9.0)	46.6 (10.0)	47.1 (9.4)	44.1 (8.4)	43.5 (8.5)	43.8 (8.4)
32	49.3 (7.4)	49.2 (9.8)	49.3 (8.3)	49.2 (8.4)	49.6 (11.1)	47.1 (10.2)
39	52.3 (9.4)	51.1 (8.6)	51.6 (9.0)	51.4 (8.6)	52.6 (7.0)	52.0 (7.8)
46	52.4 (8.5)	52.2 (8.6)	52.3 (8.5)	51.0 (9.2)	53.2 (9.1)	52.3 (9.2)
53	51.1 (9.6)	52.0 (8.8)	51.5 (9.2)	50.6 (9.1)	54.0 (7.7)	52.4 (8.6)
60	52.0 (9.4)	50.1 (9.9)	51.0 (9.7)	51.3 (9.2)	49.2 (9.1)	50.1 (9.2)
67	49.5 (11.4)	51.2 (9.5)	50.5 (10.4)	50.9 (9.5)	52.2 (8.8)	51.7 (9.1)
74	46.8 (12.1)	48.0 (10.7)	47.4 (11.4)	48.5 (11.9)	49.8 (11.2)	49.1 (11.5)
81	43.9 (13.8)	46.7 (10.9)	45.7 (12.1)	49.2 (11.2)	49.0 (10.2)	49.1 (10.6)

Verbal Memory

Age	1984 M	1984 F	1984 T	1991 M	1991 F	1991 T
25	56.9 (9.2)	60.6 (6.4)	59.0 (7.9)	56.8 (5.6)	61.6 (6.0)	60.3 (5.9)
32	55.2 (7.4)	58.2 (8.2)	56.5 (7.8)	56.4 (7.8)	58.8 (5.4)	57.8 (6.9)
39	53.8 (8.5)	56.9 (7.5)	55.6 (8.1)	55.2 (7.9)	59.6 (6.4)	57.4 (7.5)
46	51.3 (8.1)	54.9 (8.0)	53.5 (8.2)	54.4 (8.4)	58.5 (6.1)	56.8 (6.8)
53	48.6 (8.7)	51.8 (8.5)	50.2 (8.7)	49.0 (9.5)	56.2 (6.2)	52.7 (7.4)
60	47.3 (8.5)	50.3 (8.7)	48.9 (8.7)	48.5 (7.6)	51.1 (8.1)	49.9 (9.5)
67	43.6 (9.0)	48.0 (9.2)	46.1 (9.4)	45.4 (7.6)	51.6 (7.9)	49.1 (8.3)
74	40.8 (7.6)	45.2 (7.4)	43.1 (7.8)	43.6 (9.5)	46.1 (7.9)	44.9 (8.8)
81	37.6 (6.8)	42.0 (8.2)	40.3 (8.0)	40.1 (7.5)	43.8 (7.8)	42.0 (7.9)

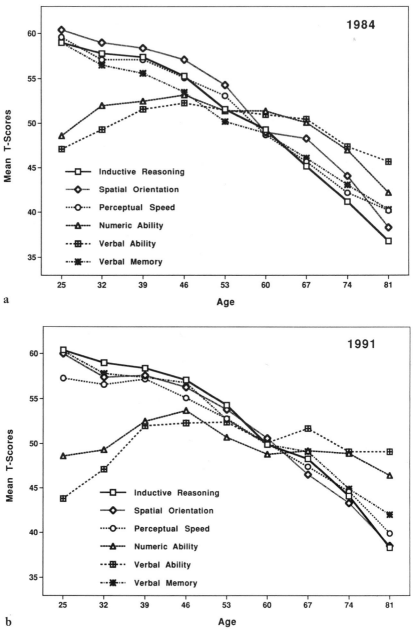

Figure 4.7. Age-difference patterns of the latent ability constructs, by test occasion.

Table 4.6. *Means and standard deviations for the Basic Skills test, by sample and gender*

	1984			1991		
Age	M	F	T	M	F	T
25	54.4	55.7	55.1	54.3	55.9	55.2
	(4.4)	(3.3)	(3.8)	(5.1)	(2.2)	(3.8)
32	55.8	54.3	55.0	56.3	54.3	55.2
	(2.1)	(6.5)	(5.0)	(2.1)	(4.2)	(3.6)
39	54.6	54.3	54.4	55.3	55.6	55.4
	(4.9)	(4.6)	(4.7)	(2.8)	(2.3)	(2.6)
46	54.2	54.0	54.1	54.8	55.0	54.9
	(3.4)	(3.9)	(3.7)	(3.0)	(3.2)	(3.1)
53	52.5	52.3	52.4	54.0	54.9	54.5
	(4.7)	(5.5)	(5.1)	(5.3)	(2.6)	(4.2)
60	52.1	51.1	51.6	52.7	51.8	52.2
	(6.2)	(6.5)	(6.4)	(7.3)	(6.4)	(6.8)
67	47.4	48.2	47.8	51.4	51.3	51.3
	(11.0)	(9.0)	(9.9)	(7.4)	(5.6)	(6.4)
74	41.2	43.2	42.2	47.8	46.9	47.3
	(12.1)	(11.0)	(11.6)	(8.4)	(8.0)	(8.1)
81	28.1	32.8	31.1	37.9	36.7	37.3
	(14.2)	(14.0)	(14.1)	(14.3)	(13.2)	(13.7)

Cognitive style data

Data on cognitive styles as measured by the Test of Behavioral Rigidity (TBR) were collected from the beginning of the SLS. A summary of cross-sectional data through the fourth cycle can be found in Schaie (1983b). Detailed data on the TBR subscores are provided by Schaie and Willis (1991b). In this section I will provide a summary of the cross-sectional data for the latent dimensions of Motor–Cognitive Flexibility (MCF), Attitudinal Flexibility (AF), and Psychomotor Speed (PS). The structural relationship between the primary mental abilities and the cognitive style constructs (see Dutta, 1992; Schaie, Dutta, & Willis, 1991) will be examined in chapter 9.

Cross-sectional data on the cognitive style variables were obtained for mean ages from 25 to 67 in Cycle 1, for mean ages from 25 to 74 in Cycle 2, and for mean ages from 25 to 81 in the remaining cycles. To provide appropriate comparisons with the ability data, the

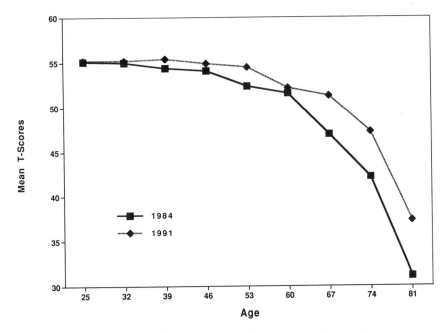

Figure 4.8. Age difference patterns of the measure of practical intelligence, by test occasion.

TBR factor scores were restandardized across all six cycles ($N = 4,123$). Table 4.7 presents means and standard deviations for the six test cycles separately by gender and for the total sample for each age level. Figure 4.9 provides a graphic representation of shifts in age differences over time combined across genders.

The cross-sectional data on cognitive style suggest that there is a decrease in Motor–Cognitive Flexibility and Psychomotor Speed for successive age/cohort groups. What is most noteworthy, however, is the fact that until the 80s are reached there has been an increase in flexibility and speed for successive cohorts at the same ages. This trend has led to successively later ages at which significant declines are observed. For the age groups represented on each test occasion (ages 25 to 67), there is a statistically significant Time × Age effect for both Motor–Cognitive Flexibility and Psychomotor Speed. Motor–Cognitive Flexibility seems to peak in young adulthood, with lower levels prevailing as early as age 39 in our 1956 sample but beginning only with the 60s in the most recent samples. A similar pattern is shown for Psychomotor Speed, which in the earliest sample peaked in young adulthood but now peaks in the mid-40s. However, significant age differences in flexibility are seen as early as age 53. Attitudinal Flexibility seems to be fairly level across age groups until the mid-40s, with decline below young-adult levels observable beginning with the 60s. Again, recent cohorts show average performance that is above earlier cohorts at the same ages.

Significant overall gender differences are found for all three cognitive style factors. Women exceed men on Psychomotor Speed, and men exceed women on Motor–Cognitive and Attitudinal flexibility. These gender differences generalize across age and measurement occasions.

Chapter summary

I begin this chapter by describing three pilot studies: The first two were designed to demonstrate the applicability of the PMA test to an older population, with respect to both its level of difficulty and to determine whether the low correlations among abilities observed in childhood would continue to prevail for adults. A third pilot study was concerned with the development of a set of psychometrically sound measurement instruments for the multiple dimensions of rigidity–flexibility that we wished to relate to cognitive abilities.

I next report findings from the 1956 baseline study, which found negative age differences on all five primary mental abilities but showed that peak ability ages occur later than had been observed in the previous literature and that the differential ability patterns noted in our first pilot study could be confirmed in this representative and age-continuous investigation. Cross-sectional findings are then reported for the six measurement occasions from 1956 to 1991, involving a total of 4,123 subjects. For these data sets I describe the differential ability patterns as they have changed in magnitude and pattern across time. Whereas there are increased performance levels at most ages in successive data sets, this shift is particularly note-worthy for women. Young-adult females now show markedly higher performance on Spatial Orientation than was the case 35 years earlier, age differences in Numeric Ability have virtually disappeared,

Table 4.7. *Means and standard deviations for the rigidity–flexibility factor scores by sample and gender*

Age	1956 M	1956 F	1956 T	1963 M	1963 F	1963 T	1970 M	1970 F	1970 T	1977 M	1977 F	1977 T	1984 M	1984 F	1984 T	1991 M	1991 F	1991 T
Motor–Cognitive Flexibility																		
25	53.7	56.0	54.9	57.8	55.8	56.6	55.0	55.8	55.4	58.5	56.4	57.4	59.5	56.6	57.6	56.4	56.3	56.3
	(6.7)	(6.1)	(6.5)	(5.6)	(7.1)	(6.6)	(6.6)	(7.3)	(7.0)	(5.5)	(6.4)	(6.0)	(4.5)	(6.1)	(5.7)	(8.1)	(9.7)	(8.9)
32	53.1	52.8	52.9	55.6	54.8	55.1	54.1	54.7	54.4	57.2	56.4	56.7	57.2	55.5	56.3	59.2	57.1	58.0
	(8.4)	(5.3)	(6.9)	(6.6)	(7.1)	(6.9)	(7.5)	(6.7)	(7.0)	(6.4)	(6.4)	(6.4)	(5.9)	(6.5)	(6.2)	(3.6)	(8.1)	(6.16)
39	49.6	46.8	48.2	53.5	53.0	53.2	52.7	50.1	51.1	55.9	55.7	55.8	56.5	55.5	55.9	58.9	57.0	57.9
	(6.8)	(10.4)	(8.8)	(7.2)	(6.6)	(6.8)	(11.2)	(8.2)	(9.6)	(6.7)	(4.7)	(5.8)	(6.5)	(7.8)	(7.3)	(6.2)	(5.9)	(6.1)
46	47.9	51.1	49.4	51.4	50.8	50.6	52.0	51.4	51.7	54.6	52.0	53.2	54.0	55.1	54.7	58.1	53.8	55.6
	(10.5)	(8.1)	(9.5)	(9.6)	(8.6)	(9.1)	(7.5)	(7.3)	(7.4)	(6.3)	(9.2)	(8.0)	(6.5)	(7.3)	(7.4)	(5.4)	(9.0)	(8.0)
53	48.4	45.6	47.0	48.3	48.5	48.4	51.6	48.1	49.7	52.6	50.2	51.5	53.3	54.2	53.8	55.9	53.8	54.8
	(9.3)	(9.6)	(9.5)	(9.8)	(7.9)	(8.7)	(9.4)	(8.5)	(9.0)	(9.1)	(7.7)	(8.5)	(8.6)	(7.3)	(7.9)	(5.0)	(9.7)	(7.8)
60	39.7	44.5	42.1	45.3	46.0	45.6	51.3	47.1	49.1	51.4	48.0	49.6	51.4	48.3	49.7	51.3	50.2	50.7
	(10.4)	(6.7)	(8.9)	(10.5)	(10.0)	(10.2)	(9.0)	(8.2)	(8.8)	(8.0)	(9.5)	(8.9)	(6.6)	(10.9)	(9.3)	(7.9)	(8.7)	(8.3)
67	41.4	39.9	40.7	42.5	42.8	42.6	41.9	40.8	41.3	44.9	45.6	45.3	48.5	49.4	49.0	49.9	48.3	49.0
	(10.6)	(10.9)	(10.7)	(10.7)	(9.5)	(10.1)	(8.5)	(10.4)	(9.6)	(11.4)	(9.6)	(10.5)	(6.5)	(7.9)	(7.2)	(8.9)	(8.5)	(8.6)
74	—	—	—	43.4	39.7	41.5	39.9	40.5	40.2	42.9	46.2	44.5	46.7	45.3	46.0	45.8	45.8	45.8
	—	—	—	(10.9)	(8.5)	(9.7)	(7.5)	(8.1)	(7.7)	(11.8)	(8.1)	(10.3)	(9.1)	(8.4)	(8.8)	(11.1)	(10.1)	(10.5)
81	—	—	—	—	—	—	42.5	36.5	39.6	42.2	40.6	41.3	40.0	39.1	39.6	47.4	40.2	43.9
	—	—	—	—	—	—	(11.0)	(7.4)	(9.9)	(9.0)	(11.5)	(10.3)	(9.4)	(11.6)	(10.5)	(10.0)	(9.9)	(10.5)
Attitudinal Flexibility																		
25	53.2	53.7	53.4	53.3	51.4	52.2	53.6	54.8	54.3	55.8	53.9	54.9	55.2	53.4	54.1	55.5	55.1	55.3
	(8.8)	(7.5)	(8.2)	(11.3)	(9.5)	(10.3)	(10.3)	(9.3)	(9.7)	(7.7)	(10.6)	(9.2)	(8.8)	(9.2)	(9.0)	(8.8)	(8.7)	(8.7)
32	51.8	52.5	52.2	52.9	50.7	51.7	56.0	53.6	54.6	56.7	51.7	54.1	55.6	53.1	54.3	52.6	54.5	53.7
	(8.1)	(8.6)	(8.3)	(8.4)	(9.1)	(8.9)	(8.8)	(10.2)	(9.6)	(7.9)	(9.4)	(9.0)	(9.4)	(9.4)	(9.4)	(10.2)	(9.1)	(9.5)
39	51.5	47.9	49.7	52.3	50.7	51.4	49.6	49.9	49.8	52.7	51.0	51.9	57.0	54.9	55.8	57.7	55.6	56.7
	(10.4)	(9.0)	(9.9)	(7.9)	(8.9)	(8.5)	(9.6)	(7.7)	(8.5)	(7.0)	(9.6)	(8.4)	(8.7)	(9.2)	(8.9)	(6.8)	(8.6)	(7.8)

46	50.4 (8.2)	50.7 (8.2)	50.6 (8.1)	47.2 (9.2)	50.3 (9.9)	49.7 (9.5)	55.1 (8.8)	52.7 (9.3)	53.9 (9.1)	54.8 (8.6)	50.4 (9.8)	52.4 (9.5)	55.1 (8.4)	57.8 (8.3)	56.8 (8.4)	53.7 (9.8)	55.4 (9.3)	54.7 (9.5)
53	48.2 (7.3)	49.2 (9.3)	48.7 (8.3)	47.3 (8.5)	48.0 (10.2)	47.7 (9.5)	52.2 (9.7)	50.5 (9.1)	51.2 (9.4)	50.7 (9.3)	49.2 (9.5)	49.9 (9.4)	55.3 (10.0)	49.7 (9.4)	52.5 (10.0)	54.4 (11.3)	56.5 (7.3)	55.5 (9.5)
60	46.0 (7.4)	46.5 (10.4)	46.3 (8.9)	46.0 (7.5)	47.2 (9.3)	46.6 (8.5)	49.3 (11.5)	46.8 (7.7)	48.0 (9.7)	52.5 (9.3)	49.7 (9.8)	51.1 (9.4)	53.0 (8.5)	51.7 (8.7)	52.2 (8.6)	51.3 (8.9)	53.5 (7.9)	52.5 (8.4)
67	44.3 (7.9)	43.2 (8.4)	43.7 (8.1)	42.5 (9.8)	43.5 (10.1)	43.0 (9.9)	46.1 (10.3)	46.6 (9.9)	46.4 (10.0)	43.2 (7.6)	48.3 (8.3)	45.9 (8.3)	47.6 (10.5)	49.7 (9.8)	48.7 (10.1)	51.0 (9.9)	52.9 (9.9)	52.0 (9.9)
74	—	—	—	39.7 (8.4)	40.0 (10.5)	39.8 (9.5)	41.4 (7.6)	44.0 (9.0)	42.6 (8.3)	45.7 (10.4)	45.3 (9.3)	45.5 (9.8)	45.0 (10.1)	46.6 (11.1)	45.8 (10.6)	47.7 (8.2)	48.4 (8.1)	48.1 (8.1)
81	—	—	—	—	—	—	43.9 (7.7)	43.8 (9.5)	43.9 (8.5)	40.5 (8.2)	43.6 (7.0)	42.2 (7.7)	41.1 (9.2)	45.6 (12.1)	43.6 (11.0)	46.0 (10.6)	48.0 (8.2)	47.0 (9.5)
Psychomotor Speed																		
25	50.2 (8.2)	55.4 (6.5)	52.8 (7.8)	49.2 (8.3)	52.8 (7.5)	51.3 (8.0)	52.7 (6.8)	56.9 (7.2)	55.1 (7.3)	51.8 (7.4)	54.8 (9.9)	53.3 (8.8)	54.6 (8.5)	57.7 (7.1)	56.6 (7.7)	61.0 (8.2)	65.6 (5.0)	63.6 (7.0)
32	48.6 (7.4)	54.9 (7.5)	52.0 (8.1)	47.9 (8.0)	52.3 (6.7)	50.5 (7.5)	54.1 (8.5)	55.2 (7.4)	54.7 (7.8)	55.7 (8.3)	57.9 (6.1)	56.9 (7.2)	55.3 (6.9)	56.9 (6.8)	56.1 (6.8)	60.3 (7.0)	63.1 (10.0)	61.9 (8.9)
39	50.1 (10.2)	52.0 (7.7)	51.0 (9.1)	48.4 (8.0)	50.5 (6.7)	49.5 (7.4)	51.2 (9.2)	52.2 (7.4)	51.8 (8.1)	51.6 (7.7)	56.5 (7.5)	54.0 (7.9)	55.4 (6.5)	58.6 (6.1)	57.2 (6.4)	61.8 (8.9)	64.6 (5.5)	63.2 (6.8)
46	50.3 (8.8)	52.5 (5.7)	51.3 (7.6)	44.9 (7.6)	50.3 (7.5)	47.5 (8.0)	51.7 (8.0)	54.9 (6.7)	53.3 (7.5)	49.3 (7.9)	51.0 (7.8)	50.2 (7.8)	56.4 (6.3)	57.4 (6.3)	57.0 (6.3)	59.9 (7.7)	63.4 (6.6)	61.9 (7.9)
53	47.6 (9.6)	51.9 (7.6)	49.7 (8.9)	43.3 (7.9)	46.9 (7.8)	45.3 (8.0)	51.8 (8.0)	53.8 (6.7)	52.9 (7.3)	49.2 (8.3)	48.3 (6.6)	48.7 (7.5)	51.1 (8.0)	56.1 (5.3)	53.6 (7.2)	57.8 (9.9)	60.5 (7.4)	59.2 (7.9)
60	43.6 (9.6)	49.1 (7.8)	46.4 (8.9)	42.1 (7.7)	44.9 (6.8)	43.5 (8.2)	48.2 (6.8)	49.5 (7.1)	48.9 (6.9)	45.6 (8.3)	48.5 (8.0)	47.1 (7.5)	50.2 (8.4)	52.6 (7.1)	51.5 (7.8)	54.5 (7.1)	55.0 (7.5)	54.8 (8.8)
67	42.7 (8.1)	44.6 (6.9)	43.6 (7.2)	39.6 (7.0)	42.6 (6.8)	41.1 (7.0)	41.3 (7.3)	45.6 (7.0)	43.6 (7.4)	44.1 (7.1)	46.7 (7.2)	45.5 (7.2)	46.0 (7.8)	49.9 (7.7)	48.0 (7.9)	51.5 (7.5)	53.8 (8.6)	52.8 (8.4)
74	—	—	—	40.6 (7.5)	40.8 (6.8)	40.7 (6.0)	38.3 (7.3)	43.6 (5.8)	40.8 (7.0)	36.2 (5.5)	42.1 (8.1)	39.0 (7.5)	45.3 (7.1)	48.5 (6.4)	46.9 (6.9)	48.3 (7.7)	51.6 (8.6)	50.0 (8.2)
81	—	—	—	—	—	—	37.7 (6.3)	40.7 (6.9)	39.1 (6.7)	36.8 (6.1)	39.3 (6.6)	38.1 (6.5)	40.0 (8.4)	41.0 (6.5)	40.5 (7.4)	43.0 (8.6)	45.2 (7.6)	44.1 (8.2)

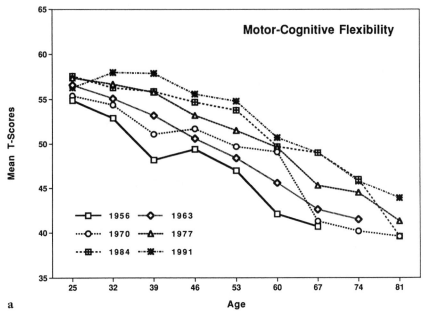

a

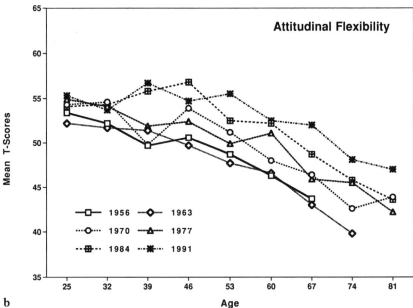

b

Figure 4.9. Age-difference patterns of the cognitive style variables for the total sample, by test occasion.

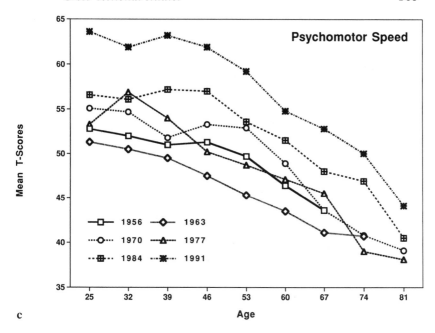

c

Figure 4.9. (*cont.*)

and Verbal Meaning now peaks in the early 50s. The magnitude of age differences at least until the mid-60s and early 70s has markedly decreased. The latter finding, of course, provides a strong rationale for the abandonment of mandatory retirement ages in all occupations.

Similar data are next provided for the expanded test battery given in 1984 and 1991, including the cross-sectional analysis of age differences on the latent constructs of Inductive Reasoning, Spatial Orientation, Verbal Ability, Numeric Ability, Perceptual Speed, and Verbal Memory. For four of these more broadly sampled constructs, the earliest evidence of reliable (though modest) negative age differences was found at somewhat earlier ages: Inductive Reasoning, Spatial Orientation, and Perceptual Speed at age 53, and Verbal Memory at age 46. The remaining two factors, Numeric and Verbal ability, showed positive age differences until midlife and even in advanced old age were at a higher level than for the youngest age group.

For the same two data points, cross-sectional data are also reported for the ETS Basic Skills test, our measure of practical intelligence. No significant age differences were found until age 60, but increasingly severe age differences occurred from then on.

Finally, cross-sectional data are presented for our measures of cognitive style for the latent constructs of Motor–Cognitive Flexibility, Attitudinal Flexibility, and Psychomotor Speed. Negative age differences in Attitudinal Flexibility were first observed at age 53, whereas such differences appear only at 60 for Motor–Cognitive Flexibility and Psychomotor Speed. Recent cohorts show average performance that is above earlier cohorts at the same ages. At all ages, women exceed men on Psychomotor Speed, whereas men exceed women on Motor–Cognitive and Attitudinal flexibility.

5

Longitudinal studies

This chapter reviews the central core of our study, the results from the longitudinal inquiries. As indicated in the description of the database, the longitudinal studies consist of five 7-year follow-ups, four 14-year follow-ups, three 21-year follow-ups, two 28-year follow-ups, and one 35-year follow-up. I shall not repeat the presentation of each individual segment of the longitudinal studies or the data and conclusions presented elsewhere (Hertzog & Schaie, 1986, 1988; Schaie, 1979, 1980a, 1980b, 1980c, 1983a, 1989a; Schaie & Hertzog, 1983, 1986; Schaie & Labouvie-Vief, 1974; Schaie & Parham, 1977; Schaie & Strother, 1968b). Instead I have tried to integrate the entire longitudinal database to provide estimates of age changes based on the largest available number of study participants for each age interval.

One of the major objectives of attempting to forecast ontogenetic change in individuals and of generating normative data on age changes in behavior is to be able to determine whether a particular individual change remains within the average range of interindividual differences in such change or whether the observed change is excessive and thus may provide a possible indicator of behavioral pathology. To obtain the requisite longitudinal estimates, it would seem best to average over as many cohorts and times of measurement as possible to yield data whose stability is maximized by being based on the largest possible number of observations. In the following sections, consequently, data are, whenever possible, aggregated across two or more samples observed at the same age.

To permit comparison with the cross-sectional findings (chapter 4), the base of our mean-level estimates was set to the observed values for the 53-year-old cohort tested in 1991 (the average age of our total sample). The average intraindividual age changes aggregated across all cohorts for which each age interval is available were then cumulated and added to or subtracted from these base values. In the following sections these predicted values are provided for the total sample as well as separately by gender.

Basic cognitive data

We will first consider the five primary mental abilities and their two composite indices for which data are available over the entire study.

Seven-year data

Intraindividual change estimates were computed by aggregating over all subjects with data for 7-year intervals from mean ages 25 to 88, based on 3,524 test records that were available for two points 7 years apart. Table 5.1 provides the resulting average within-subject age changes in T-score units, with positive values indicating gain from the age listed in the row to that listed in the column, and negative values indicating age-associated decrement. The values in the diagonals of this table represent the observed within-group age changes. The off diagonals are the cumulated changes obtained by summing the appropriate successive within-group values. These estimates are required in order to determine the ages at which decrement from some previously observed base age reaches statistical significance.

One can observe immediately that statistically significant cumulative age decrements from any previous age do not occur for any variable prior to age 60. Several variables were found to have modest increments in young adulthood and middle age. The increment above the performance level observed at age 25 remained significant for Verbal Meaning until age 67 and for Spatial Orientation and Inductive Reasoning until age 53. It was also found that cumulative age decrement, when taken from age 25, attained statistically significant magnitudes only at age 67, except for Number, where significant decline was found at age 60. The composite Index of Intellectual Aptitude showed early gain until age 46 and consistent

Table 5.1. *Cumulative age changes for 7-year longitudinal data, in T-score points*

	Mean age								
	32	39	46	53	60	67	74	81	88
Verbal Meaning									
25	1.58	2.90*	3.65*	3.96*	3.77*	2.41*	0.28	−2.82*	−8.94
32		1.32*	2.07*	2.38*	2.19*	0.83	−1.30	−4.40*	−10.52*
39			0.75	1.06	0.87	−0.49	−2.62*	−5.72*	−11.84*
46				0.31	0.12	−1.24	−3.37*	−6.47*	−12.59*
53					−0.19	−1.55*	−3.68*	−6.78*	−12.90*
60						−1.36*	−3.49*	−6.59*	−12.71*
67							−2.13*	−5.23*	−11.35*
74								−3.10*	−9.22*
81									−6.12*
Spatial Orientation									
25	1.23	1.99*	2.28*	2.06*	1.47	−0.43	−2.70*	−5.88*	−10.04*
32		0.76	1.05	0.83	0.24	−1.66	−3.93*	−7.11*	−11.27*
39			0.29	0.07	−0.52	−2.42*	−4.69*	−7.87*	−12.03*
46				−0.22	−0.81	−2.71*	−4.98*	−8.16*	−12.32*
53					−0.59	−2.49*	−4.76*	−7.94*	−12.10*
60						−1.90*	−4.17*	−7.35*	−11.51*
67							−2.27*	−5.45*	−9.61*
74								−3.18*	−7.34*
81									−4.16*

Table 5.1. (cont.)

	Mean age								
	32	39	46	53	60	67	74	81	88
Inductive Reasoning									
25	0.72	1.37	1.66*	1.72*	1.27	−0.33	−2.53*	−4.43*	−7.52*
32		0.65	0.94	1.00	0.55	−1.05	−3.25*	−5.15*	−8.24*
39			0.29	0.35	−0.10	−1.70*	−3.90*	−5.80*	−8.89*
46				0.06	−0.39	−1.99*	−4.19*	−6.09*	−9.18*
53					−0.45	−2.05*	−4.25*	−6.15*	−9.24*
60						−1.60*	−3.80*	−5.70*	−8.79*
67							−2.20*	−4.10*	−7.19*
74								−1.90*	−4.99*
81									−3.09*
Number									
25	0.92	0.76	0.54	−0.31	−0.92	−2.90*	−5.31*	−9.15*	−13.39*
32		−0.16	−0.38	−1.23	−1.84*	−3.82*	−6.23*	−10.07*	−15.31*
39			−0.22	−1.07	−1.68*	−3.66*	−6.07*	−9.91*	−15.15*
46				−0.85	−1.46*	−3.44*	−5.85*	−9.69*	−14.93*
53					−0.61	−2.59*	−5.00*	−8.84*	−14.08*
60						−1.98*	−4.39*	−8.23*	−13.47*
67							−2.41*	−6.25*	−11.49*
74								−3.84*	−8.08*
81									−4.24*

Word Fluency

	25	32	39	46	53	60	67	74	81
25	1.03								
32	0.77	-0.26							
39	1.12	0.09	0.35						
46	0.53	-0.50	-0.24	-0.59					
53	-0.83	-1.86*	-1.60*	-1.95*	-1.36*				
60	-2.63*	-3.66*	-3.40*	-3.75*	-3.16*	-1.80*			
67	-4.75*	-5.78*	-5.52*	-5.87*	-5.28*	-3.92*	-2.12*		
74	-7.63*	-8.66*	-8.40*	-8.75*	-8.16*	-6.80*	-5.00*	-2.88*	
81	-10.41*	-11.44*	-11.18*	-11.53*	-10.94*	-9.58*	-7.78*	-5.66*	-2.78

Intellectual ability

	25	32	39	46	53	60	67	74	81
25	1.38*								
32	1.80*	0.42							
39	1.54*	0.16	-0.26						
46	1.10	-0.28	-0.70	-0.44					
53	0.25	-1.13	-1.55*	-1.29	-0.85				
60	-2.02*	-3.40*	-3.82*	-3.56*	-3.12*	-2.27*			
67	-4.92*	-6.30*	-6.72*	-6.46*	-6.02*	-5.17*	-2.90*		
74	-8.73*	-10.11*	-10.53*	-10.27*	-9.83*	-8.98*	-6.71*	-3.81*	
81	-14.25*	-15.63*	-16.05*	-15.79*	-15.35*	-14.50*	-12.23*	-9.33*	-5.52*

Educational aptitude

	25	32	39	46	53	60	67	74	81
25	1.61*								
32	2.84*	1.23*							
39	3.52*	1.91*	0.68						
46	3.80*	2.19*	0.96	0.28					
53	3.55*	1.94*	0.71	0.03	-0.25				
60	2.05*	0.44	-0.79	-1.47*	-1.75*	-1.50*			
67	-0.03	-1.64*	-2.87*	-3.55*	-3.83*	-3.78*	-2.28*		
74	-2.85*	-4.46*	-5.59*	-6.27*	-6.55*	-6.30*	-4.80*	-2.85*	
81	-8.60*	-10.21*	-11.44*	-12.12*	-12.40*	-12.15*	-10.65*	-8.60*	-5.75*

* Difference is significant at or beyond the 1% level of confidence.

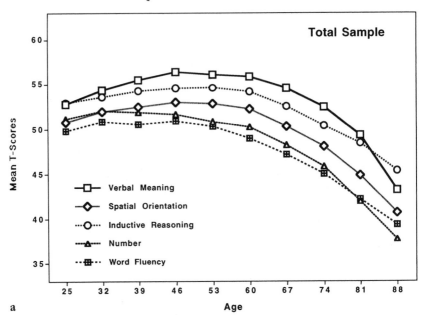

a

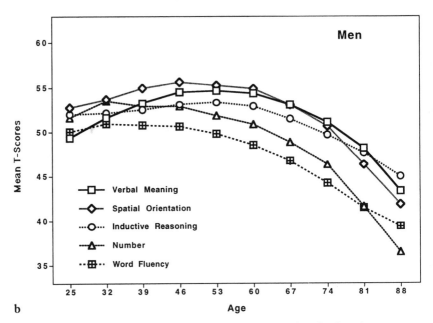

b

Figure 5.1. Estimated age changes from 7-year data for the primary mental abilities for the total sample and separately by gender.

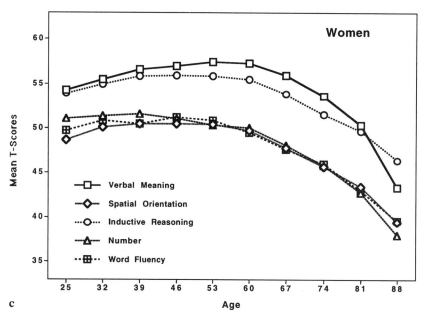

Figure 5.1. (*cont.*)

decline by age 67. The Index of Educational Aptitude showed gain until age 60. As compared with age 25, significant decline was not observed until age 81; however, from the peak performance at age 46 consistent decline was observed by age 67.

There are significant gender differences for all five abilities ($p <$ .01), with women excelling on Verbal Meaning, Inductive Reasoning, and Word Fluency and men doing better than women on Spatial Orientation and Number. There are no statistically significant gender differences in the shapes of the age gradients. However, because of the level differences, cumulative decline over the entire adult age range is somewhat greater for women than for men on Verbal Meaning and Inductive Reasoning.

A visual representation of the resultant longitudinal age gradients from age 25 to age 88 is provided in Figure 5.1 for the entire sample and separately for men and women. The gradients are centered on the latest actually observed mean values at age 53 (the average age of our sample) in 1991.

Fourteen-year data

We can also estimate longitudinal change in individuals using 14-year estimates. After aggregating age changes across the equivalent age ranges from the four 14-year data sets, we derive estimates similar to those given above for the 7-year data. The major difference here is that all data come from 1,287 individuals who were followed for at least 14 years over a given age range; hence they are somewhat less sensitive to possible changes in rates of aging across successive cohorts but have the disadvantage of being based on smaller samples. The resultant estimates of age changes are given in Table 5.2.

When we examine age changes over 14-year segments, such change becomes statistically significant for Number as early as age 46, for Word Fluency at age 60, and for the remaining three abilities at age 67. Fourteen-year changes were found to be significant for the Index of Intellectual Ability by age 53 and for the Index of Educational Aptitude by age 67.

The longitudinal age gradients resulting from these estimates are provided in Figure 5.2. Note that in contrast to Figure 5.1a, the 7-year segments represent a rolling average obtained from the within-subject 14-year age changes. As a consequence, the resultant age gradients show a somewhat later attainment of peak levels of performance (in late middle age), and, except for Number, decline does not become steep until the mid-70s are reached. Interestingly enough, in advanced old age decline is now steepest for Verbal Meaning and Number, the two crystallized abilities!

Twenty-one-year data

We next estimated longitudinal change over a 21-year period. Data used in these estimates are limited to those individuals who were followed for at least 21 years ($n = 602$). The individual age-change estimates are based on even smaller samples. On the other hand, now only three different samples are needed to cover the entire age range. The resultant estimates of age changes are given in Table 5.3.

Alhough we recognize that those subjects remaining in the study for as long as 21 years may be an increasingly select sample, it is still

Table 5.2. *Average 14-year longitudinal age changes, in T-score points*

Age range	n	Verbal Meaning	Spatial Orientation	Inductive Reasoning	Number	Word Fluency	Intellectual Ability	Educational Aptitude
25–39	69	2.20	0.81	0.39	0.79	1.74	1.44	1.85
32–46	159	0.45	0.04	0.09	−2.05**	0.78	−0.48	0.40
39–53	185	−0.08	−0.75	−0.52	−1.81**	−0.70	−1.18*	−0.20
46–60	199	−1.25	−1.19	−0.74	−2.58***	−1.66*	−2.13***	−1.25
53–67	267	−2.11***	−2.19***	−2.22***	−3.00***	−2.88***	−3.47***	−2.30***
60–74	225	−3.95***	−3.15***	−3.72***	−4.19***	−3.19***	−4.89***	−4.12***
67–81	150	−5.38***	−5.28***	−4.51***	−4.75***	−5.19***	−6.33***	−5.47***
74–88	33	−10.46***	−6.11***	−4.87***	−8.11***	−6.11***	−9.33***	−9.64***

$* p < 0.05$; $** p < 0.01$; $*** p < 0.001$.

interesting to point out that the rate of average decline is somewhat less for these persons. For the 21-year segments, modest but significant decrements are noted for Inductive Reasoning, Number, and the Index of Intellectual Ability by age 60 and for Spatial Orientation and Word Fluency by age 67, but for Verbal Meaning only by age 74. Cumulative decrements estimated from the three samples that cover the entire age range from 25 to 88 amount to 1.1 *SD* for Verbal Meaning, 0.8 *SD* for Spatial Orientation, 0.7 *SD* for Inductive Reasoning, 1.3 *SD* for Number, and 0.9 *SD* for Word Fluency.

The longitudinal age gradients resulting from these estimates, averaging across 7-year segments, are provided in Figure 5.3. Because of the longer within-cohort age ranges covered by the same subjects, these gradients are even smoother than for the 14-year data, the major difference being a somewhat less steep decrement for Verbal Meaning.

Twenty-eight-year data

Two data sets are available for subjects who were followed for 28 years (*n* = 323). Again data were aggregated for the comparable age ranges, and average longitudinal changes across the available 28-year ranges are given in Table 5.4. In this even more select group, significant decrements over the 28-year segments are first observed for Number, Inductive Reasoning and Word Fluency by age 67, and for Verbal Meaning and Spatial Orientation by age 74. The estimated longitudinal gradients are shown in Figure 5.4. For these subjects there is only modest average decline by age 74 (except for Number), with steep decline first observed by age 81.

Thirty-five-year data

Finally, we provide 35-year data on the small residual sample that has participated in our entire study (*n* = 71; see Table 5.5). Findings are quite similar to those for individuals followed for 28 years. However, data on the age of statistically significant onset of decline are more difficult to interpret because of the small sample size.

Table 5.3. *Average 21-year longitudinal age changes, in T-score points*

Age range	n	Verbal Meaning	Spatial Orientation	Inductive Reasoning	Number	Word Fluency	Intellectual Ability	Educational Aptitude
25–46	35	0.42	3.23	1.65	0.95	0.89	1.78	0.76
32–53	75	0.64	−0.76	−0.51	−1.65	−0.27	−0.87	0.38
39–60	88	−1.40	−1.51	−2.13*	−2.26*	−1.13	−2.33***	−1.69
46–67	118	−1.66	−2.50**	−2.07**	−4.15***	−3.17***	−3.94***	−1.87*
53–74	164	−4.04***	−3.66***	−3.60***	−4.85***	−4.52***	−5.55***	−4.19***
60–81	97	−6.38***	−5.03***	−5.51***	−6.12***	−6.35***	−7.74***	−6.82***
67–88	25	−9.66***	−7.59***	−6.59***	−10.38***	−7.00***	−11.07***	−9.43***

* $p < 0.05$; ** $p < 0.01$; *** $p < 0.001$.

Table 5.4. *Average 28-year longitudinal age changes, in T-score points*

Age range	n	Verbal Meaning	Spatial Orientation	Inductive Reasoning	Number	Word Fluency	Intellectual Ability	Educational Aptitude
25–53	31	2.95	−0.09	1.47	−0.76	1.42	1.02	2.74
32–60	73	0.65	−1.76	−1.74	−1.98*	−1.35	−1.79	0.12
39–67	72	−1.55	−1.53	−2.86**	−4.22***	−3.37**	−3.86***	−1.98
46–74	77	−2.95***	−3.25***	−2.85***	−4.66***	−6.77***	−5.49***	−3.10***
53–81	58	−6.94***	−5.73***	−6.32***	−6.80***	−8.27***	−8.87***	−7.17***
60–88	12	−12.23***	−7.65***	−9.93***	−10.84***	−7.48*	−12.75***	−12.34***

*$p < 0.05$; **$p < 0.01$; ***$p < 0.001$.

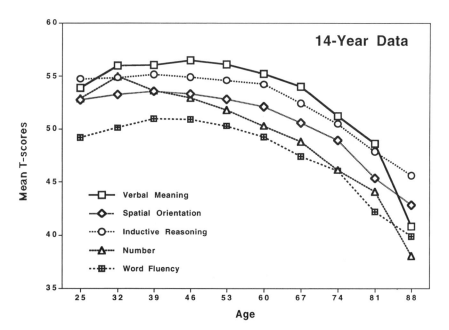

Figure 5.2. Estimated age changes from 14-year data for the primary mental abilities.

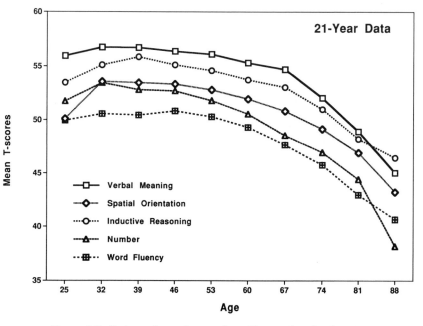

Figure 5.3. Estimated age changes from 21-year data for the primary mental abilities.

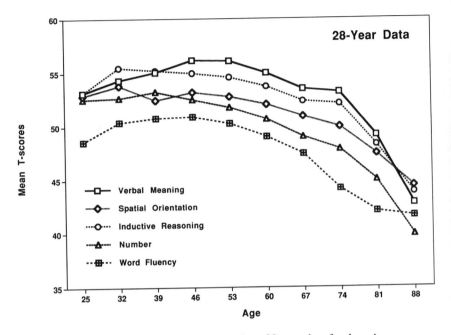

Figure 5.4. Estimated age changes from 28-year data for the primary mental abilities.

Expanded cognitive data

Longitudinal data are now available for the first time on the additional variables that entered the expanded test battery in 1984. In addition, this section contains the results for the longitudinal estimates of the latent ability constructs.

Observed variables

Intraindividual change estimates were computed for all variables added in the 1984 cycle. It should be noted that the longitudinal estimates provided in Table 5.6 and the resultant longitudinal gradients over the age range from 25 to 88 shown in Figure 5.5 are limited to two data points (1984 and 1991); that is, each age segment is based on a single sample followed over 7 years.

Table 5.5. *Average 35-year longitudinal age changes, in T-score points*

Age range	n	Verbal Meaning	Spatial Orientation	Inductive Reasoning	Number	Word Fluency	Intellectual Ability	Educational Aptitude
25–60	13	2.52	2.25	2.06	−0.42	−1.99	0.90	2.55
32–67	15	−0.86	−5.41	−3.12	−3.12	−5.43	−4.60*	−1.50
39–74	19	−3.77	−6.10**	−4.36*	−5.07*	−9.81***	−7.48***	−3.96
46–81	18	−2.30	−3.32	−5.21**	−4.78*	−9.47***	−6.55***	−3.18
53–88	5	−11.22**	−8.56	−10.98***	−13.93***	−16.59*	−16.36***	−11.81***

* $p < 0.05$; ** $p < 0.01$; *** $p < 0.001$.

Table 5.6. *Intraindividual age changes over 7 years for the extended cognitive test battery*

Variable	Age								
	25–32	32–39	39–46	46–53	53–60	60–67	67–74	74–81	81–88
Letter Series	2.33	1.40	0.80	-0.04	-0.06	-0.44	-1.60*	-2.15*	-1.93
Word Series	0.46	0.63	-0.05	-0.53	-0.96	-1.02	-2.16**	-4.17**	-2.84
Number Series	2.12	0.62	-0.42	-0.07	-0.44	-0.92	-2.27**	-1.28	-0.44
Object Rotation	1.64	0.24	-0.37	-0.23	-1.03	-1.83**	-2.59**	-3.66**	-5.11**
Alphanumeric Rotation	2.41	1.58	0.28	0.30	-0.88	-0.68	-2.13**	-3.18**	-3.00
Cube Comparison	3.73	1.58	0.67	0.03	-1.82*	-1.43	-1.30	-1.88	-1.08
Identical Pictures	1.27	0.50	-0.78	-0.07	-2.12**	-1.99**	-2.95**	-4.08**	-5.87**
Number Comparison	2.88	1.40	-0.47	-1.00	-1.85*	-2.21**	-2.02**	-3.33*	-4.39*
Finding A's	1.91	-0.40	0.15	-0.47	-0.14	0.63	-0.63	-1.75	-2.45
Addition	0.76	-0.58	-0.60	-1.43**	-1.37**	-2.15**	-3.44**	-4.88**	-6.25**
Subtraction & Multiplication	-6.20**	-3.77	-2.38	-2.15	-1.91	-0.52	-0.15	0.46	-1.92
ETS Vocabulary	2.82	0.95	0.06	0.43	-0.30	0.25	-1.47*	-0.79	-4.15**
ETS Advanced Vocabulary	3.34*	1.63	1.17	0.35	0.25	0.26	-0.96	-1.29	-3.30**
Immediate Recall	0.55	1.93	1.50	1.66	-0.46	-1.18	-2.54**	-2.53	-4.49
Delayed Recall	0.37	1.26	1.02	0.69	-0.06	-1.28	-2.00**	-1.98	-4.69*

Note: Positive values indicate increment over time.
$* p < 0.05; ** p < 0.01.$

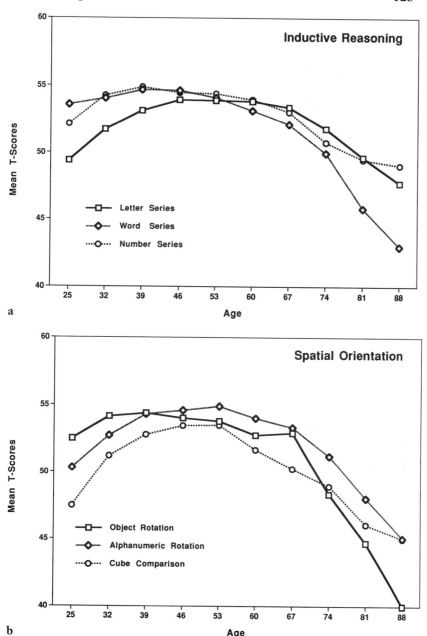

Figure 5.5. Estimated age changes from 7-year data for the expanded test battery.

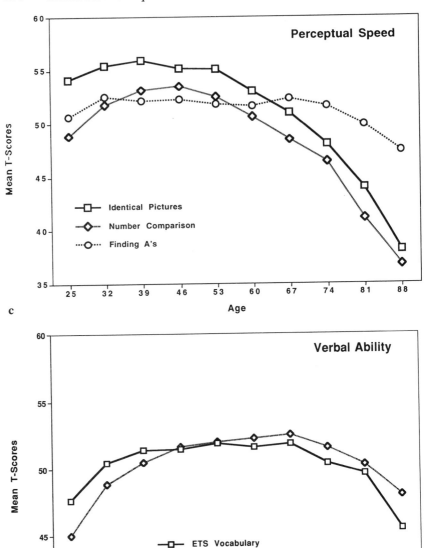

Figure 5.5. (*cont.*)

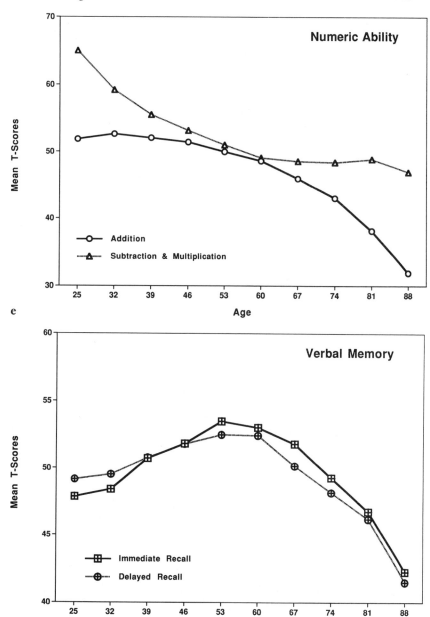

e

f

Figure 5.5. (*cont.*)

All three additional markers of Inductive Reasoning ability show significant 7-year decline only by age 74. For Spatial ability, the parallel form for PMA Space, Object Rotation, shows significant decline by age 67, and Alphanumeric Rotation shows decline by age 74. However, the three-dimensional rotation test, Cube Comparison, shows decline already by age 60. Of the new Perceptual Speed measures, Identical Pictures and Number Comparison decline by age 60, but Finding A's shows no significant 7-year decline at any age. With respect to the new Numeric markers, Addition shows relatively early decline by age 53. Subtraction and Multiplication, however, shows a significant decline only from age 25 to 32 and no significant 7-year change thereafter. The new unspeeded Verbal tests show even longer ability maintenance than our original marker. There is a significant decline for the easier test by age 67, but for the harder test there was a significant increment from age 25 to 32, and 7-year decrement is significant only by age 88. Finally, the new Verbal Memory markers show decline by age 74.

Latent constructs

Given the availability of multiple markers, 7-year longitudinal estimates of change within subjects were computed for the latent ability constructs. The resulting estimates are provided in Table 5.7, and longitudinal gradients separately by gender and for the total sample can be found in Figure 5.6. These gradients are centered on the last actually observed mean for the average age group in our sample (53 in 1991). With respect to these latent construct factor score estimates, earliest reliably observed decline over 7 years occurs for Spatial Orientation, Perceptual Speed, and Numeric Ability by age 60; for Inductive Reasoning by age 67; and for Verbal Ability and Verbal Memory by age 74.

The magnitude of decline for the longitudinal data is substantially lower for several latent abilities than would be suggested by cross-sectional data. Thus there is virtually no decline from young adulthood to advanced old age for Verbal Ability. For Inductive Reasoning and Verbal Memory, longitudinal change from age 25 to age 88 amounts to less than 0.6 *SD*; for Spatial Orientation it is approximately 0.75 *SD*. However, longitudinal estimates of change exceed

Table 5.7. *Intraindividual age changes over 7 years for the latent ability construct (factor) scores*

Variable	Age								
	25–32	32–39	39–46	46–53	53–60	60–67	67–74	74–81	81–88
Inductive Reasoning	1.88	1.25	0.35	−0.06	−0.54	−1.07*	−1.90**	−2.92**	−2.81*
Spatial Orientation	2.36	1.92	0.58	0.05	−1.17*	−1.70**	−2.40**	−3.58**	−3.92**
Perceptual Speed	−1.52	−1.34	−2.21	−1.97	−2.52**	−1.60**	−2.06**	−3.29**	−5.75**
Numeric Ability	0.36	0.14	−0.42	−1.92	−1.60**	−2.36**	−3.54**	−4.74**	−5.63**
Verbal Ability	3.18**	1.46	0.75	0.44	−0.04	0.25	−1.28**	−1.28*	−4.19**
Verbal Memory	0.45	1.55	1.29	1.17	−0.33	−1.28	−2.33**	−2.42*	−4.57*

* $p < 0.05$; ** $p < 0.01$.

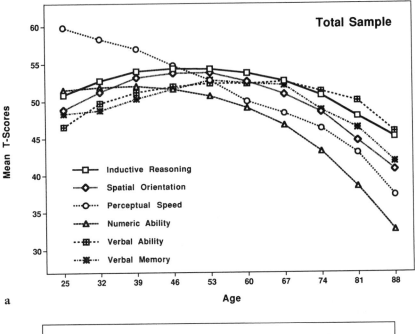

a

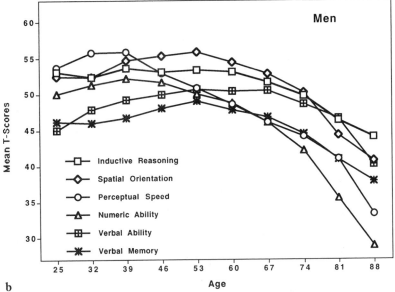

b

Figure 5.6. Estimated age changes from 7-year data for the latent ability constructs. From Schaie, 1994a, p. 308.

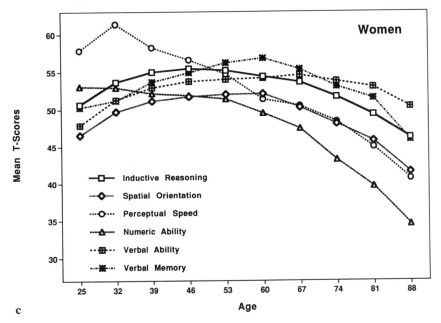

c

Figure 5.6. (*cont.*)

cross-sectional estimates for Perceptual Speed and Numeric Ability; they amount to roughly 2 *SD* for each of these abilities.

Practical intelligence data

In this section I report intraindividual change estimates for the *Basic Skills* measure of practical intelligence. As for the other variables added in the fifth cycle, these longitudinal estimates are based on only two data points. These estimates are reported in Table 5.8 and graphed in Figure 5.7. What is most noteworthy about these data is that peak performance for this measure is reached only by age 60 and that steep decline is noted only by age 81. Thereafter, decline in average performance is quite dramatic, amounting to approximately 2 *SD* from the 60s to the 80s. Note from the graphic presentation that there is virtually no difference in the shape of the age gradients by gender.

Table 5.8. *Cumulative age changes for the measure of practical intelligence, in T-score points*

	Mean age								
	32	39	46	53	60	67	74	81	88
25	0.00	0.65	0.61	0.98	1.11	−1.11	−2.67*	−9.64*	−19.80*
32		0.65	0.61	0.98	1.11	−1.11	−2.67*	−9.64*	−19.80*
39			−0.04	0.33	0.46	−0.76	−3.32*	−10.29*	−20.45*
46				0.37	0.50	−0.72	−3.28*	−10.25*	−20.41*
53					0.13	−1.09	−3.65*	−10.62*	−20.78*
60						−1.22*	−3.78*	−10.75*	−20.91*
67							−2.56*	−9.53*	−19.69*
74								−6.97*	−17.13*
81									−10.16*

*Difference is significant at or beyond the 1% level of confidence.

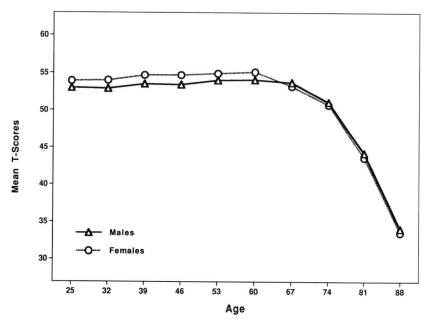

Figure 5.7. Estimated age changes from 7-year data, by gender, for the measure of practical intelligence.

Cognitive style data

The longitudinal estimates for the cognitive style data involve once again changes averaged over all five time periods and are based on all subjects for whom 7-year data were available. Table 5.9 provides the longitudinal estimates, and Figure 5.8 graphs the longitudinal gradients for the total sample and separately by gender. First examining the age gradients for the total sample, we note linear longitudinal increment (cumulatively about 0.5 *SD*) for Motor–Cognitive Flexibility to age 60 and stability thereafter. By contrast, a peak is reached for Attitudinal Flexibility by age 32, with stability until age 60 and decline (again about 0.5 *SD*) thereafter. Interestingly enough, Psychomotor Speed increases by almost 1 *SD* from age 25 to a peak attained in the 60s, again declining by about 1 *SD* by age 88.

Examining the longitudinal findings for the cognitive style data by gender, we noted continuing gain by males on Motor–Cognitive Flexibility until about age 60, with stability thereafter. Women, on the other hand, show a more modest gain until age 60, with equally modest decline thereafter. As for Attitudinal Flexibility, men seem to show early decline from age 32 to 46, then stability until about 60, with decline noticeable by age 67. For women, Attitudinal Flexibility remains virtually stable from 25 to 60, with modest decline (about 0.3 *SD*) thereafter. Finally, whereas women do not peak on Psychomotor Speed until age 67, men do so by age 53. Decline on this factor is equally steep for both sexes beginning at age 74.

Chapter summary

The presentation of our longitudinal findings begins with an examination of the within-subject estimates obtained from aggregating across subjects whose data are available over 7, 14, 21, 28, and 35 years. Next we consider 7-year longitudinal data for the additional marker variables added beginning with the 1984 data collection. For the same 7-year period we also provide longitudinal estimates for the latent ability construct factor scores and for the measure of practical intelligence. Similar longitudinal data are then presented for the measures of cognitive style.

Table 5.9. *Cumulative age changes for 7-year cognitive style data, in T-score points*

	Mean age								
	32	39	46	53	60	67	74	81	88
Motor–Cognitive Flexibility									
25	2.46*	3.11*	4.13*	4.52*	5.50*	5.49*	5.30*	4.66*	4.75*
32		0.65	1.67	2.06*	3.04*	3.03*	2.84*	2.20*	2.29*
39			1.02	1.41	2.39*	2.38*	2.19*	1.55	1.64
46				0.39	1.37	1.36	1.17	0.53	0.62
53					0.98	0.97	0.78	0.14	0.23
60						−0.01	−0.20	−0.84	−0.75
67							−0.19	−0.83	−0.74
74								−0.64	−0.55
81									0.09

Attitudinal Flexibility

25	2.45*	2.14*	2.24*	2.31*	2.39*	1.34	-0.14	-2.16*	-2.94*
32		-0.40	-0.30	-0.23	-0.15	-1.20	-2.68*	-4.70*	-5.48*
39			0.10	0.17	0.25	-0.80	-2.28*	-4.30*	-5.08*
46				0.07	0.15	-0.90	-2.38*	-4.40*	-5.18*
53					0.08	-0.97	-2.45*	-4.47*	-5.25*
60						-1.05	-2.53*	-4.55*	-5.33*
67							-1.48*	-3.50*	-4.28*
74								-2.02*	-2.80*
81									-0.78

Psychomotor Speed

25	1.91*	4.06*	5.26*	6.71*	7.13*	7.04*	5.84*	3.46*	-0.31
32		2.15*	3.35*	4.80*	5.22*	5.13*	3.93*	1.55	-2.22*
39			1.20	2.65*	3.07*	2.98*	1.78	-0.60	-4.37*
46				1.45	1.87	1.78	0.58	-1.80	-5.57*
53					0.42	0.33	-0.87	-3.25*	-7.02*
60						-0.09	-1.29	-3.67*	-7.44*
67							-1.20	-3.58*	-7.35*
74								-2.38*	-6.15*
81									-3.77*

* Difference is significant at or beyond the 1% level of confidence.

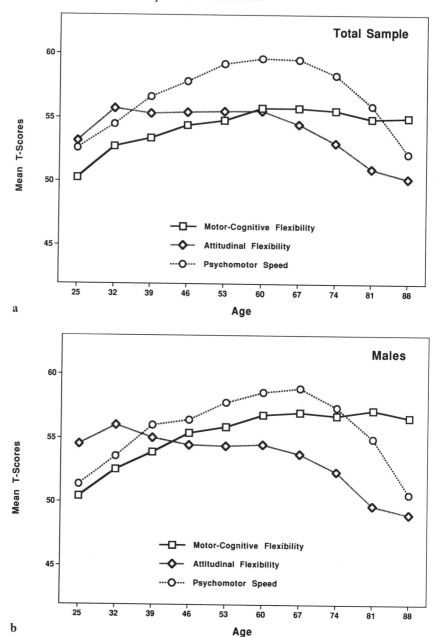

Figure 5.8. Estimated age changes from 7-year data for the cognitive style variables for the total sample and separately by gender.

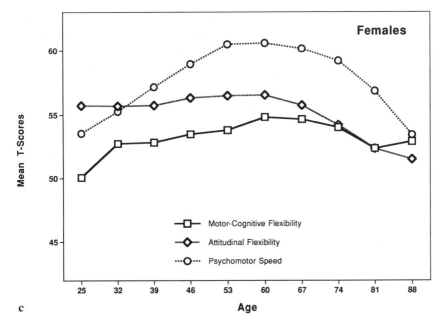

Figure 5.8. (*cont.*)

Longitudinal age changes are generally less pronounced than the cross-sectional data for most variables, with modest decline beginning in the early 60s and marked decline not occurring until the 80s are reached. The major exceptions to these findings occur for the Number ability, which begins to decline in the 50s. Cumulative decline is somewhat larger for men than for women on Verbal Meaning and Inductive Reasoning.

The 7-year data represent the most conservative estimates of within-subject change, since they are based on large samples. Data for the same individuals collected over a longer period of time (up to 35 years), who may be the select survivors of our study, show average maintenance of many abilities into the mid-70s.

For the more broadly marked ability constructs there is an even more dramatic difference between the cross-sectional and longitudinal findings. In the longitudinal data there is virtually no decline from young adulthood to advanced old age for Verbal Ability, and only modest declines are seen for Inductive Reasoning, Verbal

Memory, and Spatial Orientation until the 80s are reached. However, longitudinal estimates of change exceed cross-sectional estimates for Perceptual Speed and Numeric Ability. The profound age decline on Numeric Ability, in particular, seems hidden by negative cohort trends.

A peak is reached for our measure of practical intelligence by age 60, and steep decline again is not observed prior to the 80s.

Finally, on the measures of cognitive style, we noted increment for Motor–Cognitive Flexibility to age 60, with stability thereafter. Attitudinal Flexibility and Psychomotor Speed peak in young adulthood, remain stable until age 60, and decline thereafter. However, when examined by gender, women show moderate decline after age 60 on Motor–Cognitive Flexibility. Psychomotor Speed peaks for men at age 53 but for women at age 67, and decline on Attitudinal Flexibility is less for women then for men.

6

Studies of cohort and period differences

We discussed in chapter 2 the desirability of separate estimates of age, cohort, and period effects. In this chapter we will address our findings regarding cohort, and period differences in cognitive abilities as well as on the other variables included in our study. Data regarding these matters were previously reported through the fourth study cycle (Schaie, 1983a). Here we expand and update cumulative findings through the sixth study cycle.

Studies of cohort differences

In the absence of independent information, it is not possible to disaggregate cohort and period effects unambiguously. However, it is possible from data such as ours to estimate cohort differences over fixed time periods by comparing the performance of successive cohorts over the age ranges for which both cohorts have been observed. The cohort effects estimated in this manner will, of course, be confounded with period effects, but if series of cohort differences are computed across the same time period, each estimate will be equally affected. In our case it is possible to generate 11 cohort differences for twelve 7-year birth cohorts with mean birth years from 1889 to 1966.[1] It should be recognized that cohort differences reported here reflect the comparison of unrelated groups

---

1 Cohort comparisons for the seven oldest cohorts are based on five age levels, or a range of 28 years, except for cohorts born in 1945, 1952, 1959, and 1966, for which comparisons totaling only four, three, two, and one, respectively, are available.

of individuals. For estimates of intrafamily cohort effects, the reader is referred to chapter 13.

Cohort differences in cognitive abilities

The core battery. Table 6.1 gives mean differences in T-score points computed for all cohort combinations in our study. This table should be read as follows: A positive value indicates that the performance of the cohort identified by the column exceeds, on average, the performance of the cohort identified by the row. A negative value means that the performance of the row (earlier-born cohort) exceeds that of the column (later-born cohort).

Comparative cohort gradients for the five abilities and the composite indices are graphed in Figure 6.1. It is interesting to note that the composite Index of Intellectual Ability will tend to obscure cohort differences because of differential cohort trends in the subtests; for this composite index, only the five earliest-born cohorts differ significantly from any later-born cohort. On the other hand, when the abilities are considered separately it becomes clear from these data that there are systematic advances in cohort level for Verbal Meaning, Spatial Orientation, and Inductive Reasoning. A significant advantage of the later-born cohorts is apparent throughout for Spatial Orientation. However, the cohort gradients flatten out for Verbal Meaning beginning with the cohort born in 1952 and for Inductive Reasoning with the cohort born in 1945.

Very different findings, however, are seen for Number and Word Fluency. The former shows positive cohort differences up to about the 1910 cohort. Then there is a plateau and a shift to a successive lowering of performance level. Hence, the 1924 cohort is found to exceed both earlier- and later-born cohorts; both the youngest and oldest cohorts are currently at a disadvantage when compared with the middle cohorts. For Word Fluency, we find a successive lowering of cohort level up to the 1931 cohort but improvement for subsequent cohorts. Hence, for this ability earlier cohorts have an advantage over the later-born ones; but beginning with the cohort born in 1938 there are successive positive cohort differences for this variable also.

Perhaps of considerable significance in terms of policy implications

Table 6.1. *Mean advantage of later-born cohorts over earlier-born cohorts on the basic ability battery, in T-score points*

	Mean year of birth										
	1896	1903	1910	1917	1924	1931	1938	1945	1952	1959	1966
Verbal Meaning											
1889	-0.6	2.2	4.3*	6.2*	7.5*	7.5*	9.1*	10.3*	10.4*	11.0*	12.1*
1896		2.8*	4.9*	6.8*	8.1*	8.1*	9.7*	10.9*	11.0*	11.6*	12.7*
1903			2.1	4.0*	5.3*	5.3*	6.9*	8.1*	8.2*	8.8*	9.9*
1910				1.9	3.2*	3.2*	4.8*	6.0*	6.1*	6.7*	7.8*
1917					1.3	1.3	2.9*	4.1*	4.2*	4.8*	5.9*
1924						0.0	1.6	2.8*	2.9*	3.5*	4.6*
1931							1.6	2.8*	2.9*	3.5*	4.6*
1938								1.2	1.3	1.9	3.0*
1945									0.1	0.7	1.8
1952										0.6	1.7
1959											1.1
Spatial Orientation											
1889	0.0	1.3	2.7*	2.7*	3.5*	6.0*	5.4*	5.3*	6.3*	10.3*	14.3*
1896		1.3	2.7*	2.7*	4.0*	3.5*	6.0*	5.4*	5.3*	6.3*	10.3*
1903			1.4	1.4	2.7*	2.2	4.7*	4.1*	4.0*	5.0*	9.0*
1910				0.0	1.3	0.8	3.3*	2.7*	2.6*	3.6*	7.6*
1917					1.3	0.8	3.3*	2.7*	2.6*	3.6*	7.6*
1924						-0.5	2.0	1.4	1.3	2.3	6.3*
1931							2.5	1.9	1.8	2.8*	6.8*
1938								-0.6	-0.7	0.3	4.3*
1945									-0.1	0.9	4.9*
1952										1.0	5.0*
1959											4.0*

Table 6.1. (cont.)

	Mean year of birth										
	1896	1903	1910	1917	1924	1931	1938	1945	1952	1959	1966
Inductive Reasoning											
1889	-0.5	0.9	3.2*	4.4*	6.9*	7.3*	10.1*	11.1*	11.7*	12.6*	13.7*
1896		1.4	3.7*	4.9*	7.4*	7.8*	10.6*	11.6*	12.2*	13.1*	14.2*
1903			2.3	3.5*	6.0*	6.4*	9.2*	10.2*	10.7*	11.6*	12.7*
1910				1.2	3.7*	4.1*	6.9*	7.9*	8.4*	9.3*	10.4*
1917					2.5	2.9*	5.7*	6.7*	7.2*	8.1*	9.2*
1924						0.4	3.2*	4.2*	4.7*	5.6*	6.7*
1931							2.8*	3.8*	4.3*	5.2*	6.3*
1938								1.0	1.5	2.4	3.5*
1945									0.5	1.4	2.5
1952										0.9	2.0
1959											1.1
Number											
1889	0.0	0.7	3.1*	3.1*	3.5*	1.5	2.6*	1.4	1.1	-0.7	-1.4
1896		0.7	3.1*	3.1*	3.5*	1.5	2.6*	1.4	1.1	-0.7	-1.4
1903			2.4	2.4	2.8*	0.8	1.9	0.7	0.4	-1.4	-2.1
1910				0.0	0.4	-1.6	-0.5	-1.7	-2.0	-3.8*	-4.5*
1917					0.4	-1.6	-0.5	-1.7	-2.0	-3.8*	-4.5*
1924						-2.0	-0.9	-2.1	-2.4	-4.2*	-4.9*
1931							1.1	-0.1	-0.4	-2.2	-2.9*
1938								-1.2	-1.5	-3.3*	-4.0*
1945									-0.3	-2.1	-2.8*
1952										-1.8	-2.5
1959											-0.7

Word Fluency

Year											
1889	−2.3	−2.5	−2.3	−2.2	−4.1*	−5.0*	−4.9*	−3.2*	−3.2*	−2.8*	−1.6
1896		−0.2	0.0	0.1	−1.8	−2.7*	−2.6*	−0.9	−0.9	−0.5	0.7
1903			0.2	0.3	−1.6	−2.5	−2.4	−0.7	−0.7	−0.3	0.9
1910				0.1	−1.8	−2.7*	−2.6*	−0.9	−0.9	−0.5	0.7
1917					−1.9	−2.8*	−2.7*	−1.0	−1.0	−0.6	0.6
1924						−0.9	−0.8	0.9	0.9	1.3	2.5
1931							0.1	1.8	1.8	2.2	3.4*
1938								1.7	1.7	2.1	3.3*
1945									0.0	0.4	1.6
1952										0.4	1.6
1959											1.2

Index of Intellectual Ability

Year											
1889	−0.8	1.0	3.4*	4.3*	5.6*	4.6*	6.6*	6.9*	6.9*	6.8*	7.4*
1896		1.8	4.2*	5.1*	6.4*	5.4*	7.4*	7.7*	7.7*	7.6*	8.2*
1903			2.4	3.3*	4.6*	3.6*	5.6*	5.9*	5.9*	5.8*	6.4*
1910				0.9	2.2	1.2	3.2*	3.5*	3.5*	3.4*	4.0*
1917					1.3	0.3	2.3	2.6*	2.6*	2.5	3.1*
1924						−1.0	1.0	1.3	1.3	1.2	1.8
1931							2.0	2.3	2.3	2.2	2.8
1938								0.3	0.3	0.2	0.8
1945									0.0	−0.1	0.5
1952										−0.1	0.5
1959											0.6

Table 6.1. (*cont.*)

	Mean year of birth										
	1896	1903	1910	1917	1924	1931	1938	1945	1952	1959	1966
Index of Educational Aptitude											
1889	−0.1	2.3	4.9*	6.5*	8.5*	8.1*	10.0*	11.2*	11.2*	11.8*	10.9*
1896		2.4	5.0*	6.6*	8.6*	8.2*	10.1*	11.3*	11.3*	11.9*	11.0*
1903			2.6*	4.2*	6.2*	5.8*	8.7*	9.9*	9.9*	10.5*	9.6*
1910				1.6	3.6*	3.2*	5.1*	6.3*	6.3*	6.9*	6.0*
1917					2.0	1.6	3.5*	4.7*	4.7*	5.3*	4.4*
1924						−0.4	1.5	2.7*	2.7*	3.3*	2.4
1931							1.9	3.1*	3.1*	3.7*	2.8*
1938								1.2	1.2	1.8	0.9
1945									0.0	0.6	−0.3
1952										0.6	−0.3
1959											−0.9

Note: Negative values indicate that the later-born cohort is at a disadvantage compared with the earlier-born cohort.
* $p < 0.01$.

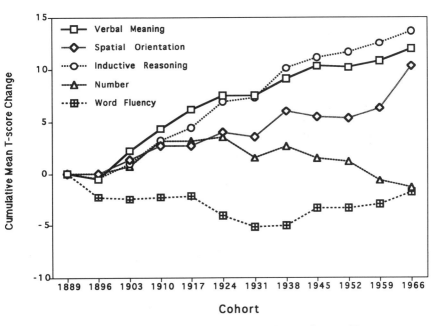

Figure 6.1. Cohort gradients for the basic ability test battery. From Schaie, 1994a, p. 308.

are the findings for cohort differences in the composite Index of Educational Aptitude. This index shows systematic positive cohort shifts, with a significant disadvantage for all cohorts born in 1931 or earlier. This finding would seem to be another convincing demonstration of the importance of taking generational differences into account when planning present and future adult education activities and programs.

The expanded battery. In this section I report cohort gradients for the additional ability markers used in the 1984 and 1991 testing cycles. The reader should be cautioned that, in contrast to the rather firm data provided above, the cohort estimates for the expanded battery provided in Table 6.2 and charted cumulatively in Figure 6.2 are based on only two estimates for each cohort from mean birth years 1903 to 1969.

Cohort differences for the added markers of the Inductive Reason-

Table 6.2. *Cohort differences for the expanded ability battery, in T-score points*

Inductive Reasoning

Birth cohort	Letter Series Cohort difference	Letter Series Cumulative difference	Word Series Cohort difference	Word Series Cumulative difference	Number Series Cohort difference	Number Series Cumulative difference
1910–1903	0.4	0.4	1.9	1.9	1.1	1.1
1917–1910	2.5	2.9	2.5	4.4	3.0	4.1
1924–1917	2.9	5.8	2.8	7.2	2.3	6.4
1931–1924	1.2	7.0	0.7	7.9	-0.1	6.3
1938–1931	3.0	10.0	2.3	10.2	3.4	9.7
1945–1938	2.4	12.4	1.7	11.9	0.2	9.9
1952–1945	1.6	14.0	0.0	11.9	2.0	11.9
1959–1952	1.8	15.8	1.6	13.5	0.9	12.8
1966–1959	1.6	17.4	1.1	14.6	1.0	13.8

Spatial Orientation

Birth cohort	Object Rotation Cohort difference	Object Rotation Cumulative difference	Alphanumeric Rotation Cohort difference	Alphanumeric Rotation Cumulative difference	Cube Comparison Cohort difference	Cube Comparison Cumulative difference
1910–1903	0.6	0.6	0.1	0.1	-0.4	-0.4
1917–1910	0.9	1.5	1.7	1.8	1.3	0.9
1924–1917	0.0	1.5	0.8	2.6	2.3	3.2
1931–1924	0.5	2.0	0.3	2.9	0.3	3.5
1938–1931	1.1	3.1	1.6	4.5	2.6	6.1
1945–1938	-0.1	3.0	1.4	5.9	2.4	8.5
1952–1945	-0.5	2.5	1.0	6.9	3.7	12.2
1959–1952	-0.3	2.2	-0.3	6.6	2.0	14.2
1966–1959	2.1	4.3	1.7	8.3	1.9	16.1

Perceptual speed

Birth cohort	Identical Pictures		Number Comparison		Finding A's	
	Cohort difference	Cumulative difference	Cohort difference	Cumulative difference	Cohort difference	Cumulative difference
1910–1903	1.1	1.1	2.5	2.5	1.1	1.1
1917–1910	3.3	4.4	2.0	4.5	0.9	2.0
1924–1917	3.1	7.5	1.6	6.1	-1.2	0.8
1931–1924	1.9	9.4	1.6	7.7	1.0	1.8
1938–1931	2.9	12.3	1.6	9.3	1.3	3.1
1945–1938	4.4	16.7	2.8	12.1	0.7	3.8
1952–1945	2.1	18.8	2.6	14.7	2.6	6.4
1959–1952	2.0	20.8	2.3	17.0	-0.9	5.9
1966–1959	0.3	21.1	2.5	20.5	4.4	10.3

Numeric Ability

Birth cohort	Addition		Subtraction & Multiplication	
	Cohort difference	Cumulative difference	Cohort difference	Cumulative difference
1910–1903	2.0	2.0	3.2	3.2
1917–1910	1.1	3.1	2.2	5.4
1924–1917	-1.3	1.8	-0.4	5.0
1931–1924	-2.7	-0.9	-2.7	2.3
1938–1931	-1.0	-1.9	-0.5	1.8
1945–1938	-0.5	-2.4	1.3	3.1
1952–1945	-0.1	-2.5	-0.1	3.0
1959–1952	-2.8	-5.3	-2.4	0.6
1966–1959	-0.6	-3.9	2.7	3.3

Table 6.2. *Continued*

Birth cohort	Cohort difference	Cumulative difference	Cohort difference	Cumulative difference
Verbal Ability	ETS Vocabulary		ETS Advanced Vocabulary	
1910–1903	4.5	4.5	2.7	2.7
1917–1910	0.9	5.4	0.6	3.3
1924–1917	1.2	6.6	0.9	4.2
1931–1924	-0.6	6.0	-1.2	3.0
1938–1931	0.4	6.4	0.8	3.8
1945–1938	-0.6	5.8	0.4	4.2
1952–1945	-0.4	5.4	1.2	5.4
1959–1952	-3.3	2.1	-1.0	4.4
1966–1959	-4.3	-2.2	-2.2	2.2
Verbal Memory	Immediate Recall		Delayed Recall	
1910–1903	1.8	1.8	1.5	1.5
1917–1910	1.8	3.6	1.6	3.1
1924–1917	3.0	6.6	3.0	6.1
1931–1924	1.7	8.3	0.1	6.2
1938–1931	3.2	11.5	2.0	8.2
1945–1938	4.0	15.5	2.8	11.0
1952–1945	2.0	17.5	1.7	12.7
1959–1952	1.9	19.4	0.7	13.4
1966–1959	1.3	20.7	1.2	14.6

Note: Negative values indicate that the later-born cohort is at disadvantage compared with the earlier-born cohort. Cumulative difference equals birth cohort in left column minus 1903 cohort.

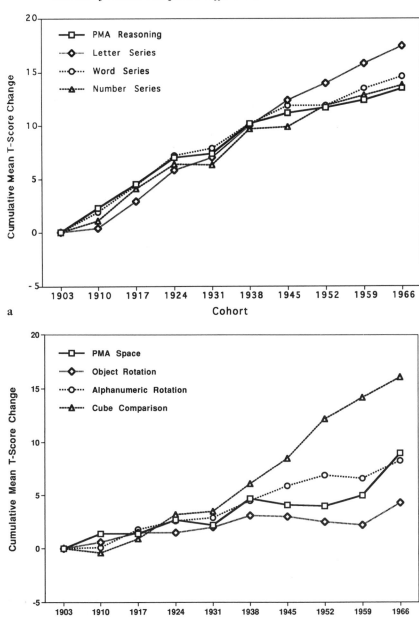

Figure 6.2. Cohort gradients within ability domains from the expanded test battery.

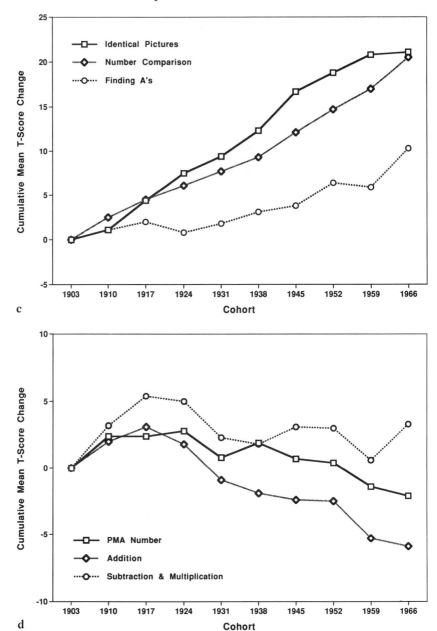

Figure 6.2. (*cont.*)

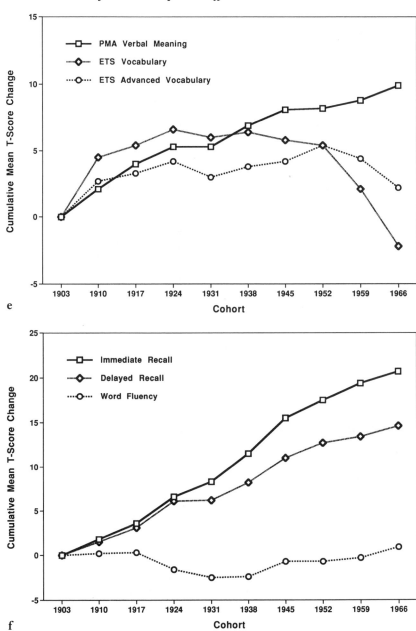

Figure 6.2. (*cont.*)

ing factor show the same positive linear shape observed for the original marker test. Over the cohort range from 1903 to 1966 there is a gain of from 1.3 to 1.7 *SD*, the largest being for the ADEPT Letter Series test and the least for the Number Series test.

Two of the new markers for the Spatial Orientation factor show significantly lower cohort differences than the original marker. Perhaps because of the more concrete nature of the stimulus material, cumulative cohort differences amount to only 0.4 *SD* for the Object Rotation test and to 0.8 *SD* for the Alphanumeric Rotation test. However, the new marker introducing three-dimensional rotation, the Cube Comparison test, does show a cumulative cohort difference of approximately 1.5 *SD*, which is of a magnitude similar to the cohort effect shown for the original marker.

The cohort differences for the markers of the Perceptual Speed factor show a positive and accelerating profile. The cumulative cohort difference for Finding A's, the most concrete measure, is only half the magnitude of cohort differences for the more abstract measures: 1 *SD* as compared with 2 *SD*.

The new markers for the Numeric Ability factor also attain a peak for the early cohorts, with modest decline thereafter. Differences, however, are less pronounced than for the original marker, and there is an uptrend for the most recently born cohort on Subtraction and Multiplication.

After an initial rise from the oldest to the second-oldest cohort, there seems to be a plateau for the new vocabulary tests until the most recent – baby boom – cohorts, for whom a negative trend can be noted.

Finally, for the measures of Verbal Memory we observed pronounced positive cohort trends amounting to 2 *SD* for the Immediate Recall and 1.5 *SD* for the Delayed Recall of the word list memorized in this test.

The latent constructs. Having considered differences among alternative markers of mental abilities, we are now ready to consider cohort differences at the latent construct level. Differences between adjacent cohorts were computed for the factor scores for the six latent constructs for which cross-sectional and longitudinal age differences were reported in chapters 4 and 5. The cohort difference

Table 6.3. *Cohort differences for the latent construct factor scores, in T-score points*

Birth cohort	Inductive Reasoning		Spatial Orientation		Perceptual Speed	
	Cohort difference	Cumulative difference	Cohort difference	Cumulative difference	Cohort difference	Cumulative difference
1910–1903	1.5	1.5	0.3	0.3	−0.3	−0.3
1917–1910	2.9	4.4	1.5	1.8	2.3	2.0
1924–1917	3.1	7.5	0.8	2.6	1.7	3.7
1931–1924	0.6	8.1	0.1	2.7	1.3	5.0
1938–1931	2.7	10.8	1.6	4.3	−0.3	4.7
1945–1938	1.8	12.6	0.8	5.1	0.0	4.7
1952–1945	1.0	13.6	1.2	6.3	0.1	4.8
1959–1952	1.2	14.8	0.5	6.8	−0.5	4.3
1966–1959	1.4	16.2	2.7	10.5	−2.3	2.0

Birth cohort	Numeric Ability		Verbal Ability		Verbal Memory	
	Cohort difference	Cumulative difference	Cohort difference	Cumulative difference	Cohort difference	Cumulative difference
1910–1903	4.2	4.2	3.4	3.4	1.7	1.7
1917–1910	1.8	6.1	1.7	5.1	1.8	3.5
1924–1917	−0.9	5.2	1.2	6.3	3.0	6.5
1931–1924	−2.8	2.4	−0.9	5.4	1.0	7.5
1938–1931	−0.7	1.7	0.9	6.3	2.5	10.0
1945–1938	0.5	2.2	0.0	6.3	3.3	13.3
1952–1945	0.0	2.2	0.4	6.7	0.8	14.1
1959–1952	−2.3	−0.1	−2.2	4.5	1.3	15.4
1966–1959	0.0	−0.1	−3.4	1.1	1.3	16.7

Note: Negative values indicate that the later-born cohort is at disadvantage compared with the earlier-born cohort. Cumulative difference equals birth cohort in left column minus 1903 cohort.

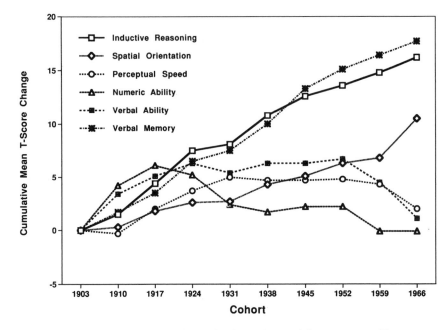

Figure 6.3. Cohort gradients for the six latent ability constructs. From Schaie, 1994a, p. 309.

estimates at the latent construct level are provided in Table 6.3 and graphed cumulatively in Figure 6.3.

For the factor scores describing the latent constructs, substantial positive and linear cohort differences were observed for the Inductive Reasoning and Verbal Memory factors (approximately 1.5 *SD*). A similar although less steep difference pattern occurred for Spatial Orientation (1 *SD*), a modest negative gradient (approximately 0.5 *SD*) was found for Numeric Ability, and there were modest concave gradients with recent declines for Perceptual Speed and Verbal Ability.

Cohort differences for the measure of practical intelligence

Our measure of practical intelligence, the ETS Basic Skills test, is an expression of combinations and permutations of the basic abilities in particular practical situations. It is therefore not surprising that

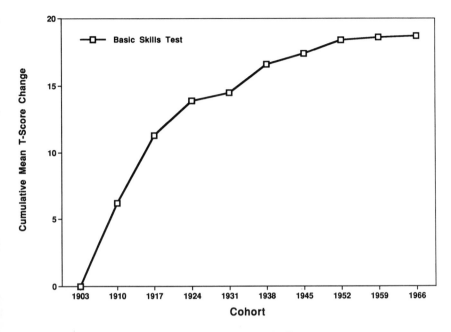

Figure 6.4. Cohort gradient for the Basic Skills test.

the cohort pattern for this ability (estimated over a single 7-year interval) is rather similar to that observed for the measures of Inductive Reasoning. Indeed, Inductive Reasoning is the ability that seems to correlate most with the practical intelligence measure (see Willis & Schaie, 1986a). Figure 6.4 shows substantial increments in performance level from our earlier-born cohorts up to the cohort born in 1938; thereafter the cohort gradient for practical intelligence reaches a virtual asymptote.

Cohort differences in cognitive styles

We have also updated the cohort gradients for the measures of cognitive style last reported in Schaie (1983a). Table 6.4 provides the cumulative cohort difference estimates, which are graphed in Figure 6.5. All of these measures show positive cohort effects. Those for the Motor–Cognitive and Attitudinal flexibility factors

Table 6.4. *Mean advantage of later-born cohorts over earlier-born cohorts in the measures of cognitive style, in T-score points*

	Mean year of birth										
	1896	1903	1910	1917	1924	1931	1938	1945	1952	1959	1966
Motor–Cognitive Flexibility											
1889	0.8	2.0	4.9*	6.2*	7.8*	8.8*	10.4*	11.7*	12.2*	12.9*	11.6*
1896		1.2	4.1*	5.4*	7.0*	8.0*	9.8*	10.2*	11.4*	12.1*	10.8*
1903			2.9*	4.2*	5.8*	6.8*	8.6*	9.0*	10.2*	10.9*	9.6*
1910				1.3	2.9*	3.9*	5.7*	6.1*	7.3*	8.0*	6.7*
1917					1.6	2.6*	4.4*	4.8*	6.0*	6.7*	5.4*
1924						1.0	2.8*	3.2*	4.4*	5.1*	3.8*
1931							1.6	2.2	3.4*	4.1*	2.8*
1938								0.5	1.8	2.5	1.2
1945									1.2	2.0	1.7
1952										1.0	0.5
1959											-1.3
Attitudinal Flexibility											
1889	0.1	2.1	2.1	4.3*	6.1*	6.0*	8.2*	9.1*	9.6*	8.9*	10.1*
1896		2.0	2.6*	4.2*	6.0*	5.9*	8.1*	9.0*	9.5*	8.8*	10.0*
1903			0.0	2.2	4.0*	3.9*	6.1*	7.0*	7.5*	6.8*	8.0*
1910				2.2	4.0*	3.9*	6.1*	7.0*	7.5*	6.8*	8.0*

1917	1.8	1.7	3.9*	4.8*	5.3*	4.6*	5.8*
1924		-0.1	1.1	3.0*	3.5*	2.8*	4.0*
1931			2.2	3.1*	3.6*	2.9*	4.1*
1938				0.8	1.4	0.7	1.9
1945					0.6	-0.1	1.1
1952						-0.7	0.5
1959							1.2

Psychomotor Speed

1889	-1.1	-1.0	2.6*	3.6*	5.5*	6.9*	10.4*	13.9*	15.0*	19.6*	26.6*
1896		0.1	3.7*	4.7*	6.6*	8.0*	11.5*	15.0*	16.1*	20.7*	27.7*
1903			3.6*	4.6*	6.5*	7.9*	11.4*	14.9*	16.0*	20.6*	27.6*
1910				1.0	2.9*	4.3*	7.8*	11.3*	12.4*	17.0*	24.0*
1917					1.9	3.1*	6.6*	10.2*	11.3*	15.8*	22.8*
1924						1.4	4.9*	8.4*	9.5*	14.2*	21.1*
1931							3.5*	7.0*	8.1*	12.5*	19.7*
1938								3.5*	4.6*	9.2*	16.2*
1945									1.1	5.7*	12.7*
1952										4.6*	11.6*
1959											7.0*

Note: Negative values indicate that the later-born cohort is at a disadvantage compared with the earlier-born cohort.
*p < 0.01.

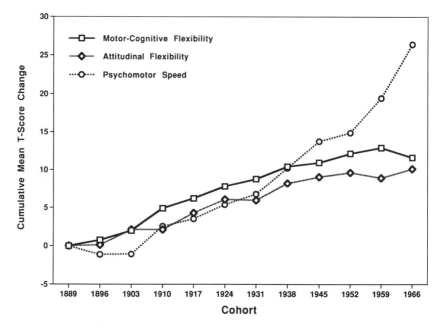

Figure 6.5. Cohort gradients for the rigidity–flexibility factor scores.

parallel each other and cumulatively amount to almost 1 *SD*. The cohort gradient for Psychomotor Speed shows some modest decline from the first to the third-oldest cohort; after that it parallels the cohort gradients for the other cognitive style measures, but beginning with the 1938 cohort shows much steeper positive increment. Indeed, for this measure, cumulative increment from the oldest to the youngest cohorts is in excess of 2.5 *SD*.

Cohort differences in demographic characteristics

Data have also been accumulated in the SLS on cohort shifts in the demographic characteristics of our sample. Of particular interest are data on educational level, age at first marriage, and age when the study participants' first child was born (see Table 6.5 and Figure 6.6). For these variables we report both cohort differences for the entire group and separately by gender. Over the cohort range repre-

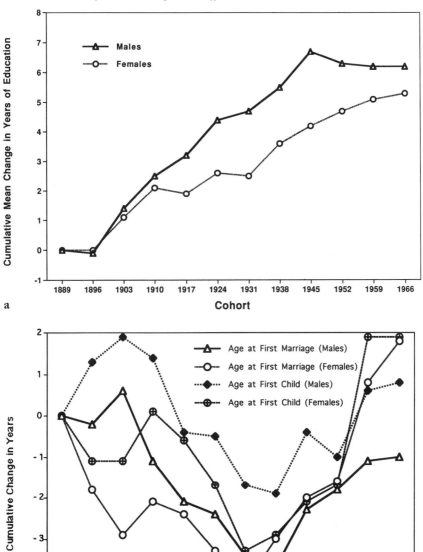

Figure 6.6. Cohort gradients for the demographic variables of education, age at first marriage, and age at birth of first child.

Table 6.5. *Cohort differences for years of education, Age at first marriage, and Age at birth of first child, for total sample and by gender*

Birth cohort	Males		Females		Total	
	Cohort difference	Cumulative difference	Cohort difference	Cumulative difference	Cohort difference	Cumulative difference
Years of education						
1896–1889	-0.1	-0.1	0.0	0.0	0.0	0.0
1903–1896	1.5	1.4	1.1	1.1	1.1	1.1
1910–1903	1.1	2.5	1.0	2.1	0.8	1.9
1917–1910	0.7	3.2	-0.2	1.9	1.0	2.9
1924–1917	1.2	4.4	0.7	2.6	1.1	4.0
1931–1924	0.3	4.7	-0.1	2.5	0.4	4.4
1938–1931	0.8	5.5	1.1	3.6	1.0	5.4
1945–1938	1.2	6.7	0.6	4.2	0.9	6.3
1952–1945	-0.4	6.3	0.5	4.7	0.2	6.5
1959–1952	-0.1	6.2	0.4	5.1	0.1	6.6
1966–1959	0.0	6.2	0.2	5.3	0.1	6.7
Age at first marriage						
1896–1889	-0.2	-0.2	-1.8	-1.8	-1.0	-1.0
1903–1896	0.8	0.6	-1.1	-2.9	-0.1	-1.1
1910–1903	-1.7	-1.1	0.8	-2.1	-1.0	-2.1
1917–1910	-1.0	-2.1	-0.3	-2.4	-0.8	-2.9
1924–1917	-0.4	-2.4	-0.9	-3.3	-0.8	-3.7

	Males		Females		Total	
1931–1924	−1.0	−3.4	−0.8	−4.1	−1.5	−5.2
1938–1931	−0.3	−3.7	1.1	−3.0	0.3	−4.9
1945–1938	1.4	−2.3	1.0	−2.0	1.1	−3.8
1952–1945	0.5	−1.8	0.4	−1.6	0.8	−3.0
1959–1952	0.7	−1.1	2.8	0.8	1.2	−1.8
1966–1959	0.1	−1.0	1.0	1.8	0.9	−0.9

Age at birth of first child

	Males		Females		Total	
1896–1889	1.3	1.3	−1.1	−1.1	0.7	0.7
1903–1896	0.6	1.9	0.0	−1.1	0.2	0.9
1910–1903	−0.5	1.4	1.2	0.1	0.5	1.4
1917–1910	−1.8	−0.4	−0.7	−0.6	−1.4	0.0
1924–1917	−0.1	−0.5	−1.1	−1.7	−1.0	−1.0
1931–1924	−1.2	−1.7	−1.6	−3.3	−1.3	−2.3
1938–1931	−0.2	−1.9	0.4	−2.9	0.2	−2.1
1945–1938	1.5	−0.4	0.8	−2.1	1.1	−1.0
1952–1945	−0.6	−1.0	0.4	−1.7	0.2	−0.8
1959–1952	1.6	0.6	3.6	1.9	2.8	2.0
1966–1959	0.2	0.8	0.0	1.9	0.0	2.0

Note: Negative values indicate that the level of the later-born cohort is lower than that of the earlier-born cohort. Cumulative difference equals birth cohort in left column minus 1889 cohort.

sented in our study there has been a steady increase in years of education, amounting to a difference in education of about 5 years between the earliest and latest cohorts studied. The increase has been approximately 1 year greater for men than for women.

Age at first marriage declined by approximately 4 years from our earliest cohort to those born in the 1930s (the lowest level was reached by men for the 1931 cohort and by women for the 1938 cohort). From then on there has been a steady rise, which is most pronounced for women. As for the age when our subjects' first child was born, there has been a steady increment that leveled off for males with the 1952 cohort but has continued to rise for women. On average, parental age at birth of the first child occurs approximately 5 years later for the most recently born than for the earliest cohort.

Other demographic characteristics that may be important in understanding cohort differences in the cognitive variables include our measures of mobility (changes in the location of one's home, changes of job, and changes in occupation). Average data over the 5 years preceding each reporting date are employed for these measures, which are reported across gender (Table 6.6 and Figure 6.7). Note that there is some very modest drop in residential and job mobility from the oldest cohort to that born in 1931; over the same cohort range there are virtually no cohort differences in occupational mobility. Mobility characteristics increase sharply with the baby-boomer cohorts for all three measures, residential and job mobility changes being the most pronounced.

Studies of period (time-of-measurement) differences

Just as we were able to estimate cohort differences by matching across age and assuming equivalence of period effects across cohorts, so we can use our data to estimate period (time-of-measurement) effects by matching across age and assuming equivalence of cohort effects across periods. This computation has been done by considering the six sets of first-time tests summed across the range of mean ages from 25 to 67 (for which all ages are represented six times).

Table 6.6. *Cohort differences for the mobility measures of change in home, job, and occupational pursuit over the preceding 5 years*

Birth cohort	Cohort difference	Cumulative difference	Cohort difference	Cumulative difference	Cohort difference	Cumulative difference
	Change of home		Change of job		Change of occupation	
1896–1889	-0.10	-0.10	0.02	0.02	-0.23	-0.23
1903–1896	-0.08	-0.08	0.02	0.04	-0.09	-0.32
1910–1903	0.08	-0.10	-0.01	0.03	0.09	-0.23
1917–1910	-0.17	-0.27	-0.01	0.02	-0.08	-0.31
1924–1917	0.05	-0.22	-0.06	-0.04	-0.03	-0.34
1931–1924	-0.09	-0.31	-0.05	-0.09	0.00	-0.34
1938–1931	0.07	-0.24	0.18	0.09	0.22	-0.12
1945–1938	0.65	0.41	0.16	0.25	0.08	-0.04
1952–1945	0.29	0.70	0.39	0.64	0.18	0.14
1959–1952	0.60	1.30	0.31	0.94	0.05	0.19
1966–1959	-0.23	1.07	0.29	0.65	-0.11	0.08

Note: Negative values indicate that the level of the later-born cohort is lower than that of the earlier-born cohort. Cumulative difference equals birth cohort in left column minus 1889 cohort.

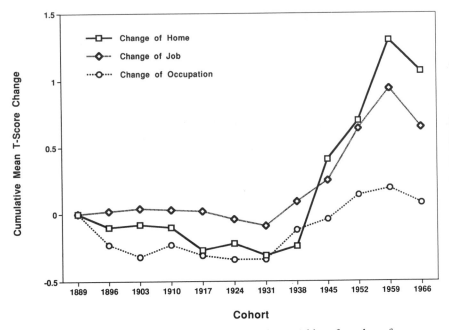

Figure 6.7. Cohort gradients for the mobility variables of number of changes in job, occupation, and place of residence.

Period effects for the cognitive abilities

The five period effects for the primary mental abilities are shown in Table 6.7 for the total sample, since no significant Period × Gender interactions were found. Significant positive period trends were observed from 1956 to 1991 for Verbal Meaning, Spatial Orientation, and Inductive Reasoning. For Number there was a positive trend from 1956 to 1970 but a negative trend from 1970 through 1991. For Word Fluency a significant negative period trend occurred from 1956 to 1977, reversing to a positive trend from 1977 to 1991.

Period effects for the cognitive styles

Similar to the period effects for the ability data, significant period effects were also observed for the measures of cognitive style. These effects are shown in Table 6.8. Significant positive period effects were found for Motor–Cognitive Flexibility from 1956 to 1963 and

Table 6.7. *Period (time-of-measurement) effects for the primary mental abilities, in T-score points*

Verbal Meaning

	1963	1970	1977	1984	1991
1956	0.37	2.78*	2.74*	4.49*	5.45*
1963		2.41*	2.37*	4.12*	5.08*
1970			-0.04	1.71	2.67*
1977				1.75	2.71*
1984					0.96

Inductive Reasoning

	1963	1970	1977	1984	1991
1956	0.45	2.88*	3.38*	5.25*	6.65*
1963		2.43*	2.93*	4.80*	6.20*
1970			0.50	2.37*	3.77*
1977				1.87	3.27*
1984					1.40

Word Fluency

	1963	1970	1977	1984	1991
1956	-3.64*	-2.93*	-2.32*	-1.43	-1.28
1963		0.71	1.32	2.21*	2.36*
1970			0.61	1.50	1.65
1977				0.89	1.04
1984					0.15

Intellectual Ability

	1963	1970	1977	1984	1991
1956	-0.12	2.17*	1.39	2.06*	3.08*
1963		2.29*	1.51	2.18*	3.20*
1970			-0.78	-0.11	0.91
1977				0.67	1.69
1984					1.02

Spatial Orientation

	1963	1970	1977	1984	1991
1956	1.00	2.51*	2.37*	1.96*	3.69*
1963		1.51	1.37	0.96	2.69*
1970			-0.14	-0.55	1.18
1977				-0.41	1.32
1984					1.73

Number

	1963	1970	1977	1984	1991
1956	0.83	2.63*	1.02	0.17	0.37
1963		1.80	0.19	-0.66	-0.46
1970			-1.61	-2.46*	-2.26*
1977				-0.85	-0.65
1984					0.20

Educational Aptitude

	1963	1970	1977	1984	1991
1956	0.39	1.95*	2.05*	3.85*	5.04*
1963		1.56*	1.66*	3.46*	5.65*
1970			0.10	1.90*	3.09*
1977				1.80	2.99*
1984					1.19

* $p < 0.01$.

Table 6.8. *Period (time-of-measurement) effects for the measures of cognitive style, in T-score points*

Motor–Cognitive Flexibility

	1963	1970	1977	1984	1991
1956	2.34*	2.26*	4.72*	5.76*	6.59*
1963		−0.08	2.38*	3.42*	4.26*
1970			2.46*	3.50*	4.33*
1977				1.04	1.87
1984					0.83

Attitudinal Flexibility

	1963	1970	1977	1984	1991
1956	−0.31	−1.81	2.08*	4.12*	5.03*
1963		2.12*	2.39*	4.43*	5.34*
1970			0.26	2.31*	3.22*
1977				2.04*	2.96*
1984					0.91

Psychomotor Speed

	1963	1970	1977	1984	1991
1956	−2.74*	1.60	1.07	4.26*	9.71*
1963		4.35*	3.79*	7.01*	12.45*
1970			−0.53	2.66*	8.10*
1977				3.19*	8.64*
1984					5.44*

* $p < 0.01$.

again from 1970 to 1977. Beyond that time small (albeit not statistically significant) positive trends continue.

For Attitudinal Flexibility, positive period effects also occurred that were statistically significant for effects from 1963 to 1970 and from 1977 to 1984. For the Psychomotor Speed factor, a negative period difference was found from 1956 to 1963, but statistically significant positive period effects occurred from 1963 to 1970 and again from 1977 through 1991.

Period effects in demographic characteristics

Finally, I provide data on period effects for the demographic variables for which cohort data were given above. Significant period effects were found for all, except for the variable of age at birth of first child. Table 6.9 provides the estimates for educational level and age at first marriage. Statistically significant period effects (in a positive direction) are found throughout except between the 1956 and 1963 and between the 1984 and 1991 data collections. Period effects for age at first marriage, however, reach statistical significance only for the difference between the 1956 and 1963 data collections and between the 1956 and the 1977 and 1984 data collections. In all these instances there is a negative period effect from our first to the later assessment points.

Statistically significant period effects were also found for the mobility measures. A shift toward lower residential and occupational mobility occurred between 1956 and 1963. However, period effects in the direction of greater mobility occurred for residential change between the 1963 and 1970 data collections and those from 1977 to 1991. Greater job mobility was observed between 1956 and 1991 as well as between 1963 and 1970 with respect to the 1977-to-1991 data collections. Greater occupational mobility was also seen between the 1963 and 1970 and all later data collections. (see Table 6.10).

Interpretation and application of period effect estimates

Several alternative explanations can be offered for the observed period effects. They may simply represent testing effects; that is,

Table 6.9. *Period (time-of-measurement) effects for the demographic variables*

	Years of education				
	1963	1970	1977	1984	1991
1956	−0.18	0.66*	1.43*	2.17*	2.67*
1963		0.84*	1.61*	2.35*	2.85*
1970			0.77*	1.51*	2.01*
1977				0.74*	1.24*
1984					0.49
	Age at first marriage				
	1963	1970	1977	1984	1991
1956	−1.10*	−0.87	−1.30*	−1.28*	−0.78
1963		0.23	−0.20	−0.18	0.25
1970			0.43	0.41	−0.09
1977				0.02	0.52
1984					0.50

*$p < 0.01$.

inadvertent small but systematic changes in test administration and scoring procedures that, even with the best documentation, can easily slip into long-term longitudinal studies. Although it is unlikely for large samples, it is nevertheless possible that these differences represent systematic sampling errors attributable to changes in the composition of the pool from which the successive samples were drawn. Another explanation would be a systematic cohort trend, although cohort differences should only minimally affect the period estimates, since for each period difference estimate, five of the seven cohorts used are identical. Finally, of course, these findings might represent true period effects caused by systematic positive environmental impacts such as the improvement of media, increased utilization of adult education opportunities, improved nutrition, and increased participation in preventive health care programs, or, in the case of negative period effects, the neglect of drill in number skills or writing exercises in educational practice.

Table 6.10. *Period (time-of-measurement) effects for the mobility variables*

Residential change

	1963	1970	1977	1984	1991
1956	-0.40*	-0.32	0.30	0.24	0.23
1963		0.08	0.60*	0.64*	0.63*
1970			0.52*	0.56*	0.55*
1977				0.04	0.03
1984					-0.01

Job change

	1963	1970	1977	1984	1991
1956	-0.21	-0.10	0.24	0.28	0.28*
1963		0.11	0.45*	0.49*	0.49*
1970			0.24*	0.28*	0.28*
1977				0.04	0.04
1984					0.00

Occupational change

	1963	1970	1977	1984	1991
1956	-0.33*	-0.26*	0.01	0.19	0.15
1963		0.07	0.34*	0.52*	0.48*
1970			0.28*	0.45*	0.41*
1977				0.18	0.14
1984					-0.04

$*p < 0.01.$

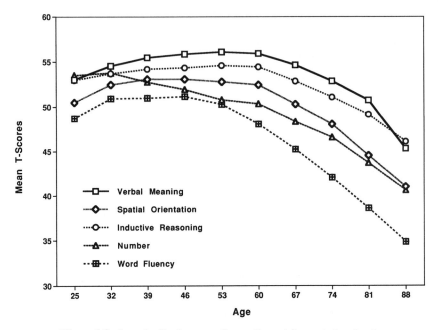

Figure 6.8. Longitudinal age gradient adjusted for period and cohort effects.

These matters are far from trivial, because longitudinal data must be adjusted for period effects if one wishes to obtain age functions that can be generalized across time. In particular, the matter of period effects becomes an important problem when age functions are constructed from short-term longitudinal studies that apply sequential data-gathering strategies. Fortunately, however, data from cross-sectional sequences allow us to consider certain adjustments to these short-term longitudinal age functions. If one assumes that cohort differences are trivial, then it is possible to adjust longitudinal change estimates by means of values such those presented in Table 6.7. If cohort differences are presumed to exist, then more complicated corrections are needed. In that case, one would compute age/time-specific time lags from the cross-sectional data in Table 4.1, subtract the appropriate cohort differences given in Table 6.1, and use the resultant age/cohort-specific estimates of period effects to adjust the longitudinal age-change estimates. The first correction would be most appropriate for use in dealing with testing effects or true period effects occurring across all age/cohort levels. The second correction is appropriate for dealing with age/cohort-specific sampling fluctuations.

As an example, I have recomputed the 7-year longitudinal estimates graphed for the total sample in Figure 5.1, and I present the revised estimates in Figure 6.8. These graphs generally look very similar. However, the adjustments have the effect of increasing the separation between the five abilities, and they tend to reduce the slope of the age gradients during early old age but increase them in advanced old age. Detailed numeric examples of the adjustment procedure can be found in Schaie (1988d).

Chapter summary

This chapter reports findings on systematic cohort trends, which generally favor later-born cohorts for variables such as Verbal Meaning, Spatial Orientation, and Inductive Reasoning. But different cohort patterns do occur, including a convex pattern favoring the middle cohorts for Number, with a currently negative trend favoring the earlier-born cohorts, and a concave trend for Word Fluency, which attains a low point for the middle generations, with a recent favorable reversal.

The implication of the positive cohort differences is that when older persons are compared with their younger peers they will, on average, show lower performance even if they have experienced little or no age decrement. On the other hand, where negative cohort differences occur, such as on Number, older persons may compare favorably with younger persons even though they may actually have declined from previous performance levels. Whether or not older persons are at a disadvantage in occupations requiring certain basic skills will therefore depend markedly on their relative position in the cohort succession.

At the latent construct level, positive cohort gradients (favoring more recently born cohorts) were found for Inductive Reasoning, Verbal Memory, and Spatial Orientation. Perceptual Speed as well as Verbal and Numeric abilities had concave cohort gradients, showing lower levels for the baby-boomer cohorts. Positive cohort gradients were also observed for our measure of practical intelligence, the measures of cognitive style, level of education, and measures of mobility. These findings are important, because they suggest that as future cohorts age they will be better positioned to respond to an increasingly complex environment, given their greater education and ability to respond in a more flexible manner.

Estimates of period effects are also provided. These effects were found to show a positive time trend for Verbal Meaning, Spatial Orientation, and Inductive Reasoning. Such secular trends imply that performance levels over time have improved for persons at all adult stages.

Finally, possible applications of the period effect estimates are considered. An example was provided of how corrections for cohort and period effects can be applied to adjust longitudinal estimates.

7

Intervention studies

When an investigation has led to a reasonably complete description of the phenomenon under study and one has begun to understand some of the antecedent conditions that might lead to differential outcomes, it then becomes interesting to design interventions that might modify such outcomes. In collaboration with Sherry Willis, who had previously designed and carried out a number of cognitive interventions as part of the Adult Development and Enrichment Project at Penn State (ADEPT; Baltes & Willis, 1982), we explored how one might best take advantage of a longitudinal study to advance the methodology of cognitive interventions in older adults (see also Willis 1987, 1990a, 1990b; Willis & Schaie, 1994b).

Remediation versus new learning

Over the past two decades, increased attention has been given in the study of adult intelligence to the question of modifiability of intellectual performance by means of cognitive training procedures (see Baltes & Lindenberger, 1988; Denney & Heidrich, 1990: Giambra & Arenberg, 1980; Willis, 1985, 1987; Willis & Schaie, 1993). There has always been great interest in determining whether and how well old dogs can be taught new tricks. However, from the point of view of developmental theory, as well as to determine whether such interventions might have societal benefit, it may be even more important to ask the question whether cognitive interventions would result in the remediation of reliably documented age-related decline. The theoretical importance of this question relates to the fact that if it is possible to show that such decline can be reversed, then grave doubt is cast on the tenability of an irreversible decrement model of aging that assumes the inevitability of normative patterns of intellectual decline for all. Irreversible decrement models of cognitive aging also generally imply that observed behavioral deficits should be isomorphic with underlying adverse physiological age changes (cf. Botwinick, 1977; Kausler, 1982; Salthouse, 1982). A demonstration of the reversal of cognitive decline, on the contrary, would lend greater plausibility to the hypothesis that behavioral deficit occurring with age is more likely to be caused by specific patterns of disuse. The remediation of cognitive decline in at least some individuals would also provide support for a hypothesis postulating behavioral plasticity through life (see Baltes, 1987; Baltes & Willis, 1977).

Important practical implications would follow the demonstration of successful remediation of cognitive decline. Older individuals are often institutionalized because their intellectual competence no longer suffices for them to function independently. Cognitive interventions, if shown to be effective in the laboratory, could then lead to the development of both generalized and specific educational intervention programs that might help restore the intellectual competence of many older individuals to levels that would maintain or prolong their ability to engage at an adequate level in tasks of daily living and thus to function independently in the community (see Willis, 1992, 1995).

Earlier cognitive training research strongly suggested that older adults' performance could be modified on a number of cognitive dimensions, such as memory span, inductive reasoning, cognitive problem solving, spatial egocentrism, and so on (for reviews see Baltes & Lindenberger, 1988; Denney, 1982; Poon, Walsh-Sweeney, & Fozard, 1980; Sterns & Sanders, 1980; Willis, 1985, 1987, 1989b; Willis & Schaie, 1994b). Training effects have also previously been shown to generalize to multiple measures of the cognitive dimension on which training occurred (Baltes & Willis, 1982). However, all of the training studies prior to the interventions conducted in the context of the SLS were cross-sectional. These studies therefore could not reach any conclusions on whether the training gains represented remediation of prior cognitive decline or might represent the attainment of new performance levels (perhaps closer to the limits of their reserve capacities; see Baltes, 1993; Baltes, Dittmann-Kohli, & Kliegl, 1986) in individuals who had not experienced any cognitive decline. Obviously, addressing this distinction requires that the subjects' preintervention level of functioning must be compared with prior data. Given the availability of subjects in the SLS who had been followed over time, it seemed desirable to approach this question directly.

The 1983–1984 cognitive training study

In order to obtain sufficiently large samples of subjects for whom we could reliably document decline, we decided to restrict the training study to those subjects for whom we had at least two previous data points (i.e., who at the time of the intervention had been followed over a minimum of 14 years) and who in 1983 were at least 64 years old (SLS Cohorts 1 to 5). We also decided to train on the abilities of Inductive Reasoning and Spatial Orientation, for which average decline had been documented to occur by the early 60s (see chapter 5). Including younger study participants or attempting to train on abilities such as Verbal Meaning, for which modal decline occurs at later ages, would have resulted in an insufficient number of subjects who had reliably declined. Conversely, setting an older age cutoff would have reduced the number of stable individuals needed to contrast the effects of remediation of cognitive decline with improvement from a prior stable level of functioning (Schaie & Willis, 1986b; Willis & Schaie, 1986b, 1988).

Method

Subjects. The 1983–84 training phase of the SLS included 229 participants (132 women, 97 men) who were born in 1920 or earlier and who had been SLS participants at least since 1970. Their mean age was 72.8 (*SD* = 6.41; range 64 to 95). Mean educational level was 13.9 years (*SD* = 2.98; range = 6–20). There were no sex differences in age or educational level. Mean income level was $19,879 (*SD* = $8,520; range = $1,000–$33,000). All of the subjects were community-dwelling, and most were Caucasian. Prior to initiating the study, each participant's family physician was contacted and asked to indicate whether the subject suffered any known physical or mental disabilities that would interfere with study participation.

Classification procedure. Subjects' test performances on the Thurstone (1949) Primary Mental Abilities (PMA) Inductive Reasoning and Spatial Orientation measures were classified as having remained stable or as having declined over the 14-year interval from 1970 to pretest. The statistical criterion for the definition of decline was 1 standard error of measurement (*SEM*) or greater over the entire 14-year period (Reasoning = 4 points, Space = 6 points).[1] Subjects were classified by defining a 1 *SEM* confidence interval about their observed 1970 score (see Dudek, 1979). Subjects who in 1984 were within the confidence interval about their 1970 score were classified as stables. Those who fell below the interval were classified as decliners.

There were 107 subjects (46.7% of the sample) classified as having remained stable on both ability measures; 35 subjects (15%) had declined on Reasoning but not on Space; 37 subjects (16%) had declined on Space but not on Reasoning; and 50 subjects (21.8%) had declined on both measures. As would be expected, stable subjects (*M* = 70.9 years; *SD* = 5.35) were somewhat younger than decline subjects (*M* = 74.4 years; *SD* = 6.84). Although the mean age differed significantly (*p* < .001), it is noteworthy that a wide age range occurred for both stables (range = 64–85 years) and decliners (64–95 years). Decline and stable subjects did not differ significantly on educational level or income.

Effects of regression on subject classification. At the base point used for classification (1970), there was no significant difference between subjects who had been classified as stables or decliners on Space performance. However, those classified as declining on Reasoning performed, at base, significantly better (*p* < .02) than those who remained stable. Regression to the mean might therefore be a

1   Setting the classification criterion at 1 *SEM* produces an expected misclassification rate of 16% in identifying persons as having declined when they have actually remained stable. This was adopted as a rather conservative criterion. Consequences of other intervals were reported in Schaie (1989c).

possible threat to the validity of the training study with respect to the Inductive Reasoning variable. However, the Reasoning measure has high internal consistency (Thurstone & Thurstone reported an r of .90 in their original studies [1949]) and long-term test–retest reliability of .80 or higher (Schaie, 1983a, 1985). As an independent check of the plausibility of regression effects, we conducted a time-reversed control analysis (see Baltes, Nesselroade, Schaie, & Labouvie, 1972; Campbell & Stanley, 1963; Schaie & Willis, 1986b). Trace lines observed in this analysis were incompatible with the presence of substantial repression effects, and classification errors as specified by our ± 1 *SEM* criterion are therefore not significantly inflated.

Subject assignment. Subjects were assigned to either Inductive Reasoning or Spatial Orientation training programs, based on their performance status. Those who had declined on Reasoning but not on Space, or vice versa, were assigned to the training program for the ability exhibiting decline. Subjects who had remained stable on both abilities or had shown decline on both abilities were randomly assigned to one of the training programs. Spatial Orientation training subjects included 51 stables (28 women, 23 men) and 67 decliners (38 women, 29 men). Inductive Reasoning training subjects included 56 stables (31 women, 25 men) and 55 decliners (35 women, 20 men).

Procedure. The study involved a pretest–treatment–posttest control group design. The Inductive Reasoning training group served as a treatment control for the Spatial Orientation training group, and vice versa. Subjects were administered the expanded battery described in chapter 3. Training began within 1 week of pretest and involved five 1-hour individually conducted training sessions. The training sessions were conducted within a 2-week period. The majority of subjects were trained in their homes. Middle-aged persons with prior educational experience involving adults served as trainers. Subjects were randomly assigned to the trainers within pragmatic constraints such that each trainer worked with approximately equal numbers of stable and decline subjects in each training program. Upon completion of training, subjects were assessed within 1 week on the same measures that were administered at pretest. They were paid $150 for participating in the study.

Training programs

The focus of the training was on facilitating the subject's use of effective cognitive strategies identified in previous research on the respective abilities. A content task analysis was conducted on the two PMA measures representing these abilities, in order to identify relevant cognitive strategies.

Inductive Reasoning. For each item of the PMA Reasoning test, the pattern-description rule(s) used in problem solution was identified. Four major types of pattern-description rules (identity, next, skips, and backward next) were identified and focused on in training. These pattern-description rules are similar to those discussed previously in the literature (Holzman, Pellegrino, & Glaser, 1982; Kotovsky & Simon, 1973; Simon & Kotovsky, 1963). Practice problems and exercises were developed based on these pattern-description rules. Practice problems often involved content other than letters, so that the applicability of these rules to other content areas could be explored. For example, patterns of musical notes and travel schedules were devised based on these rules, and subjects were asked to identify the next note or destination in the series. No training problems were identical in content to test items. Subjects were taught through modeling, feedback, and practice procedures to identify these pattern-description rules. Three strategies for identifying the patterns were emphasized in training: visual scanning of the series, saying the series aloud in order to hear the letter pattern, and underlining repeated letters occurring throughout the series. Once a hypothesis regarding the pattern type was generated, subjects were taught to mark repetitions of the pattern within the series and thus to determine the next item required to fit the pattern rule.

Spatial Orientation. A content task analysis of the PMA Space test was conducted to identify the angle of rotation for each answer choice. Practice problems were developed to represent the angle of rotation identified in the task analysis (45°, 90°, 135°, and 180°).

Cognitive strategies to facilitate mental rotation that were focused on in training included (a) development of concrete terms for various angles, (b) practice with manual rotation of figures prior to mental rotation, (c) practice with rotation of drawings of concrete familiar objects prior to the introduction of abstract figures, (d) subject-generated names for abstract figures, and (e) having the subject focus on two or more features of the figure during rotation. These cognitive strategies had been identified in prior descriptive research on mental rotation ability (Cooper, 1975; Cooper & Shepard, 1973; Egan, 1981; Kail, Pellegrino, & Carter, 1980).

Results of the 1983–1984 training study

We will consider first training effects at the raw score level for the PMA Reasoning and Space tests, because these are the measures for which longitudinal data were available and which served as the basis of subject classification. Second, training effects are examined at the latent construct level; that is, for the multiply marked ability factors on which training was conducted. Third, we will note the proportion of subjects whose decline was remediated, as well as the proportion of stable subjects who experienced significant improvement in functioning on the trained abilities. Fourth, we will deal with the specificity of the training; that is, the question whether the training effects were indeed directed to the target abilities or whether far transfer to other abilities would occur (see Thorndike & Woodworth, 1901). And fifth, we will examine the question of whether training resulted in the remediation of losses in speed and/ or accuracy. The question of whether or not training results in shifts in ability factor structure will be further examined in chapter 8.

Raw score analyses: PMA Reasoning and Space. Training effects for the two measures with longitudinal data were analyzed with repeated measurement ANOVAs, using a Training Condition (Reasoning, Space) × Status (Stable, Decline) × Gender × Occasion (Pretest, Posttest) design separately for the two tests (Table 7.1). For *PMA Reasoning* there were significant main effects for status ($p < .001$), gender ($p < .01$), and occasion ($p < .001$). The status and gender main effects reflect the lower scores on the target measure for

Table 7.1. *Summary of analyses of variance: primary mental ability raw scores*

Source	MS	df	F
Reasoning			
Training	41.03	1	0.61
Status	1,471.25	1	21.89***
Training × Status	1.34	1	0.02
Gender	483.58	1	7.20**
Training × Gender	113.73	1	1.69
Status × Gender	54.51	1	0.81
Training × Status × Gender	5.77	1	0.09
Error	67.20	221	
Occasion	857.25	1	150.24***
Training × Occasion	231.02	1	40.47***
Status × Occasion	12.24	1	2.14
Training × Status × Occasion	12.71	1	2.23
Gender × Occasion	2.77	1	0.48
Training × Gender × Occasion	0.75	1	0.13
Status × Gender × Occasion	7.24	1	1.27
Training × Status × Gender × Occasion	16.16	1	2.83
Error	5.71	221	
Space			
Training	470.12	1	2.91
Status	4,228.33	1	26.14***
Training × Status	177.70	1	1.10
Gender	922.39	1	5.70*
Training × Gender	359.65	1	2.22
Status × Gender	388.56	1	2.40
Training × Status × Gender	0.66	1	0.00
Error	161.74	221	
Occasion	2,044.16	1	90.68***
Training × Occasion	301.64	1	13.38***
Status × Occasion	49.23	1	2.18
Training × Status × Occasion	106.56	1	4.73*
Gender × Occasion	85.12	1	3.78*
Training × Gender × Occasion	55.47	1	2.46
Status × Gender × Occasion	46.55	1	2.06
Training × Status × Gender × Occasion	0.53	1	0.02
Error	22.54	221	

$*p < 0.05$; $**p < 0.01$; $***p < 0.001$.

decliners and men, respectively. The occasion main effect represents the retest effects occurring for both groups. With respect to the training effects of central concern, there was a significant Training × Occasion interaction ($p < .001$), indicating higher performance at posttest of those trained on Reasoning. There was a trend toward a significant fourfold interaction ($p < .09$). Post hoc tests on PMA Reasoning gain scores indicated that decliners showed greater gain than did stables. Gender and Gender × Status effects were not significant. When the Reasoning and Space training groups were compared, there were significantly greater Reasoning training effects for the target training group for stables ($p < .001$), decliners ($p < .001$), stable women ($p < .002$), and male and female decliners ($p < .001$).

For *PMA Space* there were significant main effects for status ($p < .001$), gender ($p < .02$), and occasion ($p < .001$). The status and gender main effects reflect the lower scores of the decliners and women, respectively, across occasions. The occasion main effect indicates the retest effects occurring for both the Reasoning and Space training groups. As for the crucial results with respect to the training paradigm, there were significant interactions for Training × Occasion ($p < .004$) and for Training × Status × Occasion ($p < .05$). The Training × Occasion interaction indicated a significantly higher performance for the Space training group at posttest. The triple interaction with Status reflects greater training gain for the decliners at posttest. A significant Gender × Occasion interaction ($p < .05$) suggests the occurrence of larger retest effects for women. Post hoc tests on PMA Space gain scores indicated that there were significantly greater ($p < .01$) gains for decliners than for stables.

Figure 7.1 depicts the pretest–posttest gain computed from the standardized scores for the PMA Reasoning and Space tests for the four training subgroups (stable or decline on Reasoning, stable or decline on Space). Each set of bars in Figure 7.1 compares the two subgroups trained on Reasoning with the two trained on Space; that is, each training group serves as a control for the other training condition.

Analyses at the latent construct level. The factor structure of the pretest ability battery was examined via confirmatory factor analyses. An

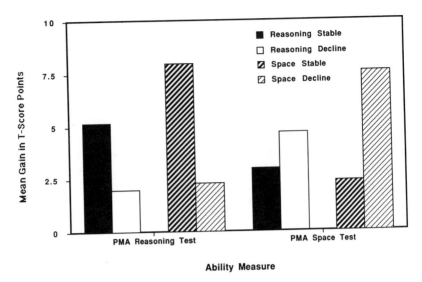

Figure 7.1. Mean factor score gains, by training program and stability status (in T-score units). Adapted from Schaie & Willis, 1986b, p. 227.

acceptable five-factor model ($\chi^2[243, N = 401] = 463.17, p < .01$) was obtained that represented the hypothesized primary mental ability factors of Inductive Reasoning, Spatial Orientation, Perceptual Speed, Verbal Ability, and Numeric Ability. All marker measures for Inductive Reasoning and Spatial Orientation, as predicted, had significant loadings on their respective factors. Regression weights (after orthonormal transformation) for tests loading on the Inductive Reasoning factor were: PMA Reasoning = .378; ADEPT Letter Series = .213; Word Series = .298; Number Series = .111. Regression weights of tests loading on the Spatial Orientation factor were: PMA Space = .260; Object Rotation = .393; Alphanumeric Rotation = .287; Cube Comparison = .060. Although the Number Series and Cube Comparison measures contribute relatively little variance to their respective factors, they were retained because they helped to obtain better definition of the factors within the broader ability space in which they were embedded. Factor scores were computed for the Inductive Reasoning and Spatial Orientation factors by standardizing ($M = 50$; $SD = 10$) the raw scores to the pretest base and then multiplying the standardized scores by their normalized regression weights.

Repeated measures ANOVAs were again performed separately on the Inductive Reasoning and Spatial Orientation factor scores, using the same design applied to the PMA raw scores; that is, Training Condition (Reasoning, Space) × Status (Stable, Decline) × Gender × Occasion (Pretest, Posttest), as shown in Table 7.2. For *Inductive Reasoning*, there were significant main effects for status ($p < .001$) and occasion ($p < .001$). The status and gender main effects reflect the lower scores of decliners and men, respectively. The occasion main effects represent the retest effects occurring for both training groups. Specifically relevant with regard to the effects of training was the significant Training × Occasion interaction ($p < .001$), indicating a significant training effect at posttest. No status, gender, or Gender × Status comparisons within the Reasoning training group were significant; hence, the training effect was general and not specific to status and/or gender.

For *Spatial Orientation*, there were significant main effects for status ($p < .001$), gender ($p < .01$), and occasion ($p < .001$). The status and gender main effects reflect the lower scores of the decliners and women, respectively, across occasions. The occasion main effect indicates the retest effects occurring for both Reasoning and Space training groups. There were significant interactions for Training × Occasion ($p < .02$) and Training × Gender ($p < .04$). The Training × Occasion interaction indicated a significant training effect at posttest. The Training × Gender interaction indicates that overall performance on Space was higher for the target training group than for the controls for women only.

Distinguishing between regression and training effects. In order to exclude the possibility that regression effects might confound the results of the training study, we first of all examined the stability of our instruments over the interval between pretest and posttest by administering the measures over the same interval to a group of 172 subjects of comparable age and socioeconomic status who did not receive any training. Stability coefficients obtained in this study were found to be .917 for the Space factor score and .939 for the Reasoning factor score. Stabilities for the two PMA measures were

Table 7.2. *Summary of analyses of variance: factor scores*

Source	MS	df	F
Inductive Reasoning			
Training	336.58	1	2.18
Status	3,038.35	1	19.66***
Training × Status	25.71	1	0.17
Gender	733.10	1	4.74*
Training × Gender	362.67	1	2.35
Status × Gender	30.31	1	0.20
Training × Status × Gender	0.08	1	0.00
Error	154.59	221	
Occasion	1,649.15	1	303.15***
Training × Occasion	205.99	1	37.86***
Status × Occasion	1.76	1	0.34
Training × Status × Occasion	7.76	1	1.43
Gender × Occasion	0.58	1	0.11
Training × Gender × Occasion	1.18	1	0.22
Status × Gender × Occasion	0.07	1	0.01
Training × Status × Gender × Occasion	1.08	1	0.20
Error	5.44	221	
Spatial Orientation			
Training	84.19	1	0.56
Status	3,884.11	1	30.10***
Training × Status	26.33	1	0.20
Gender	852.04	1	6.60**
Training × Gender	521.31	1	4.04*
Status × Gender	423.18	1	3.28
Training × Status × Gender	79.17	1	0.61
Error	129.06	221	
Occasion	1,556.41	1	195.48***
Training × Occasion	41.82	1	5.25*
Status × Occasion	9.49	1	1.19
Training × Status × Occasion	18.14	1	2.28
Gender × Occasion	4.14	1	0.52
Training × Gender × Occasion	16.27	1	2.04
Status × Gender × Occasion	0.75	1	0.09
Training × Status × Gender × Occasion	4.83	1	0.61
Error	7.96	221	

*$p < 0.05$; **$p < 0.01$; ***$p < 0.001$.

found to be .838 for Space and .886 for Reasoning. These estimates were next used to compute regressed deviation scores for our experimental subjects (see Nunnally, 1982). The ANOVAs described above were then repeated on the adjusted scores. As would be expected in light of the high stabilities, resulting F ratios differed only trivially, and none of the previously reported findings were significantly affected.

Effects of age, education, and income. Because of slight differences between subgroups in terms of demographic characteristics, we also repeated the ANOVAs, covarying on age, education, and income. Again, effects of the covariance adjustments were trivial, and none of the findings reported above were changed significantly.

What is the benefit of cognitive training?

The effects of cognitive training must be assessed in several ways. First of all, we need to know what proportion of participants showed significant gain from the intervention procedure. Next, we would like to know how successful the intervention was in remediating decline to an earlier – higher – level of functioning. Questions arise also as to whether training effects are specific to the targeted abilities or generalize to other abilities. Finally, one needs to ask whether the training resulted in qualitative cognitive change.

Pretest–posttest training improvement. The proportion of subjects showing statistically reliable pretest–posttest training improvement on the PMA Reasoning or Space measure was computed. The statistical criterion for significant improvement was defined as a gain ± 1 *SEM* from pretest to posttest. The proportion of subjects at the individual level with reliable training gain is shown in Table 7.3. Approximately half the subjects in each training group showed significant pretest–posttest improvement. Although there was a trend for a greater proportion of decline subjects to show improvement in both training conditions, the difference between proportions was statistically significant only for the Space training group ($p < .01$).

Remediation of decline. The question arises next as to what proportion of subjects benefited from training sufficiently to result in a 14-year

Table 7.3. *Proportion of subjects attaining significant pretest-to-posttest training gain*

	Reasoning			Space		
Status	Men	Women	Total	Men	Women	Total
Stable	52.0	54.8	53.6	34.8	42.9	39.2
Decline	60.0	60.0	60.0	51.7	57.9	55.2
Total	55.6	57.6	56.8	44.2	51.5	48.3

Note: Significant training gain was defined as a pretest-to-posttest gain of ≥ 1 *SEM* on the PMA Reasoning or Space test.

remediation to their 1970 base performance level. Two criterion levels were used to define remediation. The first level deemed remediation as having occurred when the difference between the subject's PMA posttest score and the 1970 score was ≤ 1 *SEM*. This is the same statistical definition that was used in the first place to classify subjects with respect to their 14-year decline. The second criterion level was even more conservative; it defined remediation as the attainment of a PMA posttest score that was equal to or greater than the 1970 base score. Figure 7.2 presents the proportion of decline subjects attaining these remediation criteria. Sixty-two percent of the decline subjects were remediated to their predecline level if the ≤ 1 *SEM* criterion is used. In both training groups, more women were returned to their 1970 score level than were men. Using the more stringent criterion of return to the 1970 base level, approximately 40% of the decline sample were returned to the performance level they had exhibited 14 years earlier. Again, the proportion of subjects whose decline was fully remediated was greater for women on Space and for men on Reasoning.

Transfer-of-training issues. The question arises next as to whether the training effects generalize across alternative measures of the same ability dimension (near transfer) or whether the intervention is so general that it affects performance on abilities not specifically targeted for training (far transfer). Near transfer is desirable, since it offers evidence of convergent validity; far transfer is to be eschewed

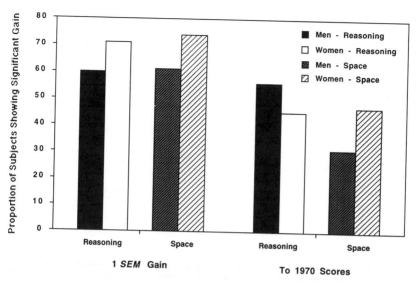

Figure 7.2. Proportion of decline subjects remediated to within 1 *SEM* of 1970 base scores, and to or beyond their 1970 base score. Adapted from Schaie & Willis, 1986b, p. 230.

if we wish to modify ability-specific behaviors rather than obtaining a Hawthorne effect that could be attributed simply to the intensive contact with our study participants.

Strong near transfer was observed for those measures most similar to the longitudinal marker (Object and Alphanumeric rotation for the Spatial Orientation factor; Letter Series and Word Series for the Inductive Reasoning factor). With respect to far transfer, we examined pretest–posttest gains for the two target abilities as well as the dimensions of Perceptual Speed, Numeric Ability, and Verbal Ability, which had not been targets for training. Figure 7.3 shows the far-transfer pattern, which confirms our training specificity hypotheses. When factor score gains are averaged for two training groups on each of the five ability dimensions, we find that each training group has significantly greater gain on the ability on which it was trained and that there are no differences on the abilities not targeted for training. Gains for the latter abilities represent retest effects and/or small generalized training effects.

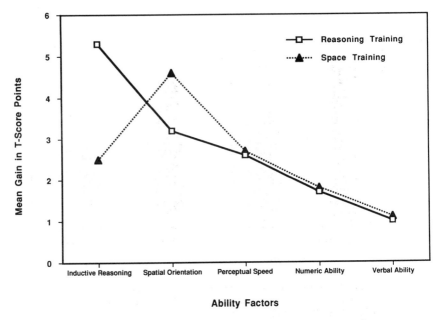

Figure 7.3. Far-transfer pattern confirming the training specificity hypotheses. From Willis & Schaie, 1986b, p. 244.

Decomposing training effects into gains in accuracy and speed

Performance change over time and as the effect of training can be disaggregated into separate components that are due to subjects' accuracy and speed. During the longitudinal preintervention phase, decline in accuracy may occur through disuse, and gain in accuracy during training may result from the reactivation of appropriate problem-solving strategies. We would expect a reduction in speed of performance with increasing age, but the intensive practice during the training phase might help to speed up subjects' response.

Change in accuracy for the preintervention and the pretest–posttest comparisons was obtained by the following procedures. An accuracy score was computed as the proportion of the attempted answer choices marked correctly (e.g., 1970 baseline rights/1970 items attempted). The expected accuracy score for the next test occasion was then computed, assuming that level of accuracy

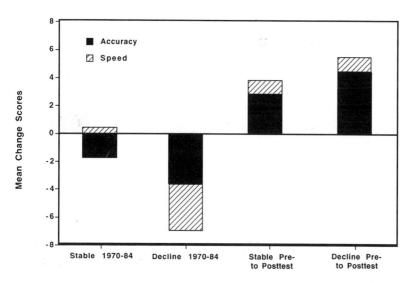

Figure 7.4. Changes in speed and accuracy from 1970 to 1984 and for the training gain for Inductive Reasoning, by stability condition. From Willis, 1990a, p. 34.

remained constant over the two occasions. For example, the 1984 expected score was computed as the proportion of 1970 correct responses multiplied by the 1984 number attempted. The change in accuracy then becomes the observed 1984 rights less the expected 1984 score. Subtracting the change in accuracy from the total observed score then yields the change in speed. The same procedure was used to decompose training gain, using the 1984 observed rights score to estimate the expected posttest accuracy score (see Willis & Schaie, 1988).

Longitudinal change in accuracy and speed. The average change in speed and accuracy from 1970 to 1984 is depicted on the left-hand side of Figures 7.4 and 7.5 for Inductive Reasoning and Spatial Orientation, respectively. Since there were no significant gender differences in patterns of accuracy and speed, Figure 7.4 shows change for the stable and decline subjects. On Spatial Orientation there was a significant Gender × Stability condition interaction.

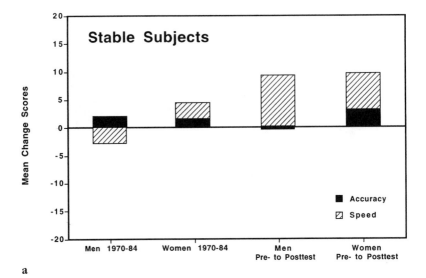

a

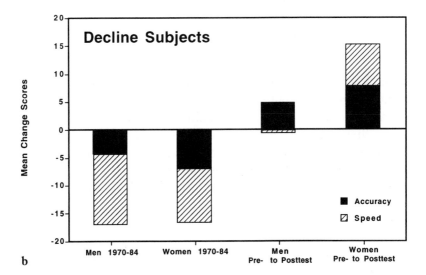

b

Figure 7.5. Changes in speed and accuracy from 1970 to 1984 and for the training gain for Spatial Orientation, by stability condition and gender. From Willis & Schaie, 1988, p. 198.

Data are therefore presented separately by gender and stability condition.

The 14-year decline on *Inductive Reasoning* can be apportioned about equally to speed and accuracy. For the stable group, a small loss in accuracy is partially compensated for by a gain in speed. No gender difference in composition of change was observed.

On *Spatial Orientation*, there was no significant gender difference for the entire group in the magnitude of total decline. However, a significant gender difference was found for the speed change score ($p < .03$). A greater proportion of the total decline of the men was attributable to a decrease in problem-solving speed. For the stable subjects, men remained stable by compensating for a slight loss in speed by a commensurate increase in accuracy. Stable women showed a slight gain in both speed and accuracy. For the decline subjects, men lost primarily in speed, whereas women declined approximately equally in both speed and accuracy.

Training gain in accuracy and speed. The right-hand side of Figures 7.4 and 7.5 shows training gain decomposed into speed and accuracy in the same manner as for the longitudinal change. For *Inductive Reasoning* most of the training gain was accounted for by increased accuracy; only minimal gain in speed was found. This pattern was equally true for those who had declined and those who had remained stable. Note, however, that the decliners recovered virtually all their loss in accuracy. No gender difference in training gain pattern was found.

On *Spatial Orientation*, by contrast, there was a significant gender difference in favor of women for total training gain ($p < .03$). Gain for the stable subgroup was primarily due to an increase in problem-solving speed, and there was no gender difference for this subgroup. The gender difference appeared only in the decline group. Here men showed gain in accuracy but not in speed, whereas gain for the women was approximately equal for speed and accuracy.

Seven-year follow-up studies

The question remains whether the effects of cognitive intervention such as ours do provide benefits that last over extended periods of time and whether it is possible to remediate further losses that occur as study participants move into advanced old age. To address these questions, the 1991 cycle included a 7-year follow-up of the original training study (see Willis & Schaie, 1992, 1994b). This section presents data that bear directly on the question of maintaining and sustaining cognitive training effects. Specifically, we address the question whether or not persons receiving brief cognitive training remain at an advantage compared with those not so trained. Second, we consider the effects of booster training to determine the benefits of further reactivation of the abilities trained earlier.

Method

Subjects. All subjects who participated in the 1983–84 training and who were known to be alive in 1990 were contacted. One hundred forty-eight trained subjects agreed to participate in the follow-up study. Of these, a total of 141 were able to complete the follow-up testing, and 132 subjects received booster training. Their ages in 1990–91 averaged 77.74 ($SD = 4.98$; range 71 to 92).

Subject classification. All participants were assigned to the same classification they had had in 1983–84. The surviving participants consisted of 67 Spatial Orientation training subjects, including 33 stables (15 men, 18 women) and 35 decliners (10 men, 25 women), as well as 74 Inductive Reasoning training subjects, including 44 stables (17 men, 27 women) and 29 decliners (11 men, 18 women).

Study design. The pretest–posttest design of the original training study was replicated as exactly as possible. The booster training was given on the same ability (Inductive Reasoning or Spatial Orientation) that subjects had originally been trained on. Subjects were assessed within 1 week of training on the same measures that were administered at pretest. They were paid $150 for participating in the study.

Results of the follow-up study

Results of the follow-up study are reported in three parts. First, we describe the magnitude of the initial training for the surviving sample

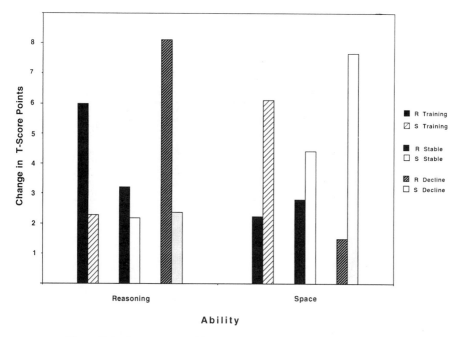

Figure 7.6. Gain at initial 1983–84 training for the group returning for follow-up training.

and the nature of attrition effects. Second, we consider the maintenance of training over 7 years; that is, the question whether or not persons receiving brief cognitive training remain at a long-term advantage over those not so trained. And third, we report the effects of sustaining training effects by means of booster training in order to determine the benefits of further reactivation of the abilities trained earlier. For simplicity in presentation, we emphasize the longitudinal markers that were applied throughout the SLS.

Magnitude of initial training. During the 1983–84 training study, significant training effects were obtained for both abilities trained. Because of attrition of approximately 40% in the follow-up studies, we recomputed training effects for the surviving sample. Overall, there was a gain of approximately 0.5 *SD* in each training program. These effects continue to be significantly greater than those for the comparison control group. However, contrary to findings in the

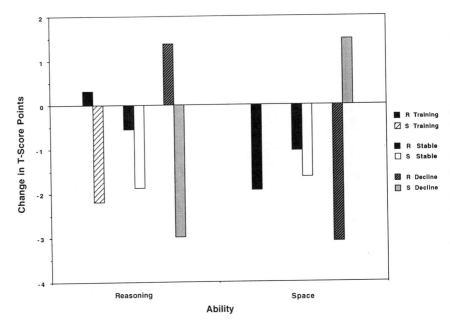

Figure 7.7. Maintenance of training effects over 7 years.

unattrited sample, there was significantly greater effect for those subjects who had been identified as decliners (see Figure 7.6). These results reflect greater retention of those of the decline subjects who showed significant training gain in the initial training. There was an interaction effect in retention for the stable subjects. Those with greater training gain on Space also showed higher retention, but those with greater training gain on Reasoning showed lower retention.

Maintenance of training effects. We next consider the extent to which training gains are retained after 7 years. In 1990–91 subjects trained in 1983–84 were functioning, on average, at their 1983–84 pretest level on the trained ability. In contrast, the comparison group (those trained on the other ability) were functioning significantly below their 1983–84 pretest level. As shown in Figure 7.7, there was a significant maintenance of function on the trained ability even after a 7-year interval. For the total group, this was a modest effect, amounting to approximately 0.3 *SD*. Once again, however, this effect was most pronounced for those subjects who had been classified as decliners for purposes of the initial training. For both abilities these individuals, on average, still performed above their 1983–84 pretest level, whereas their comparisons had declined further. The trained groups of decliners in 1990–91 had an advantage of approximately 0.4 *SD* over their comparison groups. By contrast, those who had been stable in 1983–84 were at an advantage of approximately 0.15 *SD* over their comparisons on Reasoning. The difference between the stable experimental and control groups on Space was not statistically significant.

Sustaining training effects through booster training. When the previously trained subjects were once again put through the same training regimen they had experienced earlier, significant ability-specific training effects were obtained for both training conditions as well as for the subsets of subjects who had been classified as having declined or remained stable at initial training. That is, in all instances gains from pretest to posttest were significantly larger than for the untrained comparison groups. However, the effects of the 1990–91 booster training were of a somewhat lower magnitude in these subjects, who are now 7 years older.

Of particular interest is the question of cumulative magnitude of initial and booster training when subjects are compared with control groups who had the same amount of attention (by being trained on another ability). As shown in Figure 7.8, there is a clear advantage for those subjects who were originally identified as experiencing decline. After booster training, they are at a better than 0.5 *SD* advantage over their comparison groups. The training advantage for those subjects described as stable at initial training is more equivocal. It is still highly significant for Reasoning, although their advantage is more modest, but there is no significant cumulative advantage for stable subjects who were trained on Space.

To show the generality of the follow-up findings beyond the prime longitudinal marker, we also computed factor scores across each set of four markers of the abilities on which we trained. Figure 7.9 shows the cumulative training effects at the latent construct

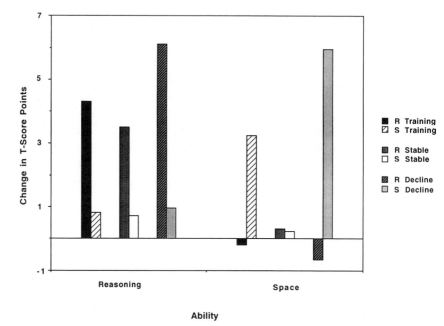

Figure 7.8. Cumulative training effects over two training periods for the principal marker variables.

level, which were quite similar to those shown in the preceding figure.

Replication of cognitive training effects

In order to assess the replicability of our training effects with another sample, we also trained an additional 179 subjects who met the original selection criteria in 1990–91 but who had not been trained previously. Preliminary analyses of the replication (first-time training) suggest that significant training effects and near transfer to alternate operational forms of the target tests can again be demonstrated, and suggest that significant effects of training in excess of pretest–posttest practice can be demonstrated as well at the latent variable level. We also replicate stronger training effects for the Inductive Reasoning than for the Spatial Orientation ability. Figure 7.10 com-

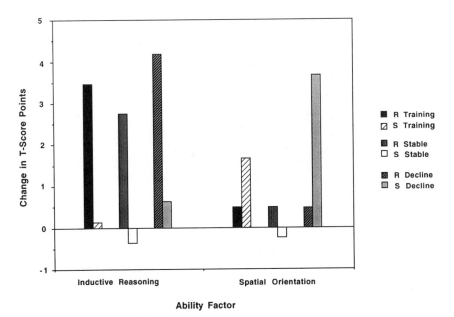

Figure 7.9. Cumulative training effects over two training periods for the latent abilities.

pares training gains at the factor level for initial training in 1983–84 and 1990–91 and effects of booster training (1990–91) for Induction and Space training. The lower average level of gain in the booster training could be due to the fact that subjects on average are now in the old-old range, or that the residual of the earlier training brought them closer to their personal asymptote. Further analyses and additional data collections will be needed to answer this question.

Chapter summary

Our cognitive intervention studies have made it clear that, for many older persons, cognitive decline in old age may be a function of disuse rather than deterioration of the physiological substrates of cognitive behavior. A brief 5-hour training program involving individual tutorials was designed to improve the performance of subjects above the age of 64 on the abilities of Inductive Reasoning and

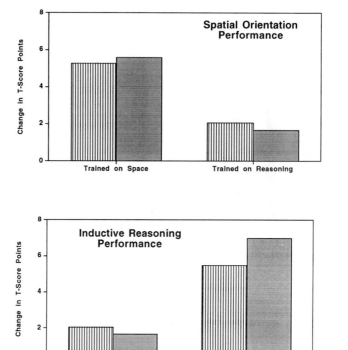

Figure 7.10. Comparative magnitude of initial training, booster training, and replicated initial training.

Spatial Orientation. Subjects were assigned either to training on the ability on which they had declined or randomly to one of the two training conditions if they had declined or remained stable on both abilities.

The training program succeeded in improving the performance of about two thirds of the participants. More important, of those participants for whom significant decrement had been documented, roughly 40% were returned to the level at which they had functioned 14 years earlier. Training effects were shown for the single marker for which longitudinal data were available, as well as near transfer to additional markers, indicating training improvement to be at the latent construct level. No far transfer was observed, demonstrating both convergent and divergent validity for the training procedures.

Follow-up studies of cognitive training after a 7-year interval furthermore demonstrated that those subjects who at initial training had shown significant decline remained at substantial advantage over untrained comparison groups. Booster training increased the advantage of these groups further. Long-term effects for those who had remained stable at initial training differed by ability. More modest, but significant, effects were shown to prevail on Inductive Reasoning but not on Space training. In addition, replication of initial training with a new sample confirmed the magnitudes of training effects obtained in the initial study.

Findings from the training study suggest that targeted cognitive intervention programs can reverse the modest age-related decline that is likely to be related to disuse of certain cognitive skills. Wider applications of similar interventions may well be useful in retaining independent living status for older persons who might otherwise be institutionalized because of marginal cognitive competence.

8

Methodological studies

In this chapter I will describe some of the methodological studies that were conducted either by means of collateral data collections or by secondary analyses of the core data archives. I begin with a concern that arose after our third cycle: that we needed to shift from a sampling-without-replacement paradigm to one that involved sampling with replacement if we were to be able to continue drawing new samples not previously tested (1974 collateral study). I then discuss the issue of the aging of tests, and report results from an investigation designed to determine whether or not switching to more recently constructed tests would be appropriate in the context of the longitudinal study (1975 collateral study). Next I deal with the question of the effects upon subject self-selection when we shifted to the current trend of offering monetary incentives to prospective study participants.

A number of secondary analyses will be described that deal with the topic of experimental mortality (subject attrition) and the consequent adjustments that might be needed in our substantive findings. Next I consider the possible effect of repeated-measurement designs in understating cognitive decline, and present analyses that adjust for practice effects. Finally, I examine the issue of structural equivalence across cohorts, age, and time to determine whether or not we can validly compare our findings. Here I describe a number of relevant studies employing restricted (confirmatory) factor analysis designed to determine the degree of invariance of the regression of our observed variables on the latent constructs that are of interest in this study.

Changing from sampling without replacement to sampling with replacement (1974 collateral study)

The process of maintaining longitudinal panels and supplementing them from random samples of an equivalent population base raises special problems. It has become evident, for example, that over time a sample that is representative of a given population at a study's inception will become successively less representative. This shift is due to the effects of nonrandom experimental mortality (subject attrition) as well as reactivity to repeated testing (practice). I will discuss the measurement of these effects and possible adjustment for them later in this chapter. First, however, I want to consider the effects of circumventing the inherent shortcomings of longitudinal studies by means of appropriate control groups.

One such possible control is to draw independent samples from the same population at different measurement points, thus obtaining measures of performance changes that are not confounded by attrition and practice factors. Such an approach, however, requires adoption of a sampling model that, depending on the size and mobility characteristics of the population sampled, involves sampling either with or without replacement. Sampling without replacement assumes that the population is fixed and large enough so that successive samples will be reasonably equivalent. Sampling with replacement assumes a dynamic population, but one where on average the characteristics of individuals leaving the population are equivalent to those of individuals replacing them.

Although the independent random sampling approach is a useful tool for controlling effects of experimental mortality, practice, and reactivity, it requires the assumption that the characteristics of the parent population from which sampling over time is to occur will remain relatively stable. Riegel and Riegel (1972) argued that such an assumption might be flawed. They argued that "because of selective death of less able persons (especially at younger age levels) the population from which consecutive age samples are drawn is not homogeneous but, increasingly with age, becomes positively biased." This argument is indeed relevant for repeated sampling from the same cohorts, but not necessarily for the same age levels measured from successive cohorts. Moreover, successive samples are necessarily measured at different points in time, thus introducing additional time-of-measurement confounds.

Another problem occurs when successive samples are drawn from a population without replacement. Unless the parent population is very large, it will eventually become exhausted. That is, either all members of that population may already be included in the study, or the remainder of the population is either unable or unwilling to participate. In addition, the residue of a limited population, because of nonrandom attrition, may eventually become less and less representative of the originally defined population. As a consequence, at some point in a longitudinal inquiry it may become necessary to switch from a model of sampling without replacement to one of sampling with replacement.

Subsequent to the third SLS cycle, it became clear that a further random sample drawn from the remainder of the 1956 HMO population might be fraught with the problems mentioned above. It therefore became necessary to conduct a special collateral study that would determine the effects of switching to a model of sampling with replacement. We decided to draw a random sample from the redefined population and compare the characteristics of this sample and its performance on our major dependent variables with those of the samples drawn from the original fixed population. This approach would enable us, first, to test whether there would be significant effects; and if so, secondly, to estimate the magnitude of the differences, which could then be used for appropriate adjustments in comparisons of the later with the earlier data collections (see Gribbin, Schaie, & Stone, 1976).

Method

Subjects. The original population of the HMO (in 1956) had consisted of approximately 18,000 adults over the age of 22. Of these, 2,201 persons had been included in our study through the third SLS cycle. The redefined population base in 1974 consisted of all of the approximately 186,000 adult members, regardless of the date of entry into the medical plan (except for those individuals already included in our study). Sampling procedures similar to those described for the main study (see chapter 3) were used to obtain a sample of 591 participants, ranging in age from 22 to 88 (in 1974).

The membership of the HMO, as of 1956, had been somewhat skewed toward the upper economic levels, because many well-educated persons were early HMO joiners for principled rather than economic reasons. The membership was limited at the lower economic levels and almost devoid of minorities. Given these exceptions, the HMO membership did provide a wide range of educational, occupational, and income levels and was a reasonable match of the 1960 and 1970 census figures for the service area. By 1974, however, with the membership grown to ten times that of the original population, there was a far greater proportion of minorities, as well as a somewhat broader range of socioeconomic levels.

Measurement variables. Variables in the collateral study were those included in the first three SLS cycles: the primary mental abilities of Verbal Meaning (V), Spatial Orientation (S), Inductive Reasoning (R), Number (N), and Word Fluency (W) and their composites (Intellectual Ability [IQ] and Educational Aptitude [EQ]); the factor scores from the Test of Behavioral Rigidity (TBR): Motor–Cognitive Flexibility (MCF), Attitudinal Flexibility (AF), and Psychomotor Speed (PS); as well as the attitude scale of Social Responsibility (SR). (See chapter 3 for detailed descriptions.)

Design and data analysis. The data collected in the 1974 collateral study can be analyzed by means of two of the designs derived from the general developmental model (Schaie, 1965, 1977; chapter 2). Assuming that a major proportion of variance is accounted for by cohort-related (year-of-birth) differences, data may be organized into a cross-sequential format – in this instance, comparing individuals from the same birth cohorts but drawn from two different populations. Alternatively, assuming that age-related differences are of significance, the data can be grouped according to age levels in the form of a time-sequential design – comparing individuals at the same age but drawn not only from different birth cohorts but also from different populations. Both designs were used in this study.

Scores for all subjects were first transformed into T-scores ($M = 50$, $SD = 10$), based on all samples at first test occasion from the first three SLS cycles. For the analyses by cohort, subjects in both populations were grouped into 7-year birth cohorts, with mean year of birth ranging from 1889 to 1945. Since the sample from the redefined population was tested in 1974, 4 years subsequent to the last measurement point for the original samples, subject groupings were reorganized and mean year of birth for the new sample shifted by 4 years to maintain equivalent mean ages for the analyses by age levels. Data were thus available for seven cohorts (mean birth years = 1889 to 1945) at all times of measurement. Similarly, data were available for seven age levels (mean ages = 25 to 67) from all occasions; specifically, observations from Cohorts 1 to 7 in 1956, Cohorts 2 to 8 in 1963, and Cohorts 3 to 9 in 1970 were compared with the reorganized groupings of the participants in the 1974 testing.

Previous analyses of data from the original population samples had suggested a significant time-of-measurement (period) effect (Schaie & Labouvie-Vief, 1974; Schaie, Labouvie, & Buech, 1973). To estimate and control for these effects, trend line analyses were conducted over the first three measurement occasions, and the expected time-of-measurement effect for the 1974 sample was estimated. The coefficients of determination (degree of fit of the linear equation) ranged from .74 to .92 in both cohort and age analyses. Psychomotor Speed and Attitudinal Flexibility in the cohort analysis did not adequately fit a linear model but could be fitted with a logarithmic function. Estimated values for these variables were therefore obtained subsequent to such transformation. The null hypothesis with respect to the difference between observed scores from the 1974 sample and estimated scores was evaluated by means of independent t-tests.

Findings from the sampling equivalence study

Summary results for the comparison of data from the original and redefined populations can be found in Tables 8.1 and 8.2. Significant overall differences ($p < .01$) between samples from the two populations for both cohort and age analyses were observed on a number of variables – Verbal Meaning, Spatial Orientation, Number, Word Fluency, and the Index of Educational Aptitude. The sample from the redefined population scored somewhat lower than that from the original population, with the exception of Word

Table 8.1. *Cohort analysis of differences between estimated and observed scores*

Variable	Estimated mean	Observed mean	*t*-ratio
Verbal Meaning (V)	48.96	45.55	4.94***
Spatial Orientation (S)	47.73	45.81	3.01**
Inductive Reasoning (R)	47.31	46.63	—
Number (N)	50.03	47.09	4.53***
Word Fluency (W)	45.75	47.40	—
Intellectual Ability (IQ)	47.71	46.06	—
Educational Aptitude (EQ)	48.47	45.90	3.77**
Motor–Cognitive Flexibility (MCF)	47.03	46.44	—
Attitudinal Flexibility (AF)	48.74	48.83	—
Psychomotor Speed (PS)	48.08	48.86	—
Social Responsibility (SR)	49.95	49.25	—

Note: Means are in T-scores with population mean of 50 and standard deviation of 10. *t*-ratios are given only for values significant at or beyond the 5% level of confidence.
*$p < 0.05$; **$p < 0.01$; ***$p < 0.001$.

Table 8.2. *Age analysis of differences between estimated and observed scores*

Variable	Estimated mean	Observed mean	*t*-ratio
Verbal Meaning (V)	53.36	51.02	3.74***
Spatial Orientation (S)	52.76	50.80	3.08**
Inductive Reasoning (R)	53.30	52.79	—
Number (N)	52.64	49.70	4.83***
Word Fluency (W)	48.78	51.00	3.46***
Intellectual Ability (IQ)	52.88	51.35	—
Educational Aptitude (EQ)	53.56	51.64	3.09**
Motor–Cognitive Flexibility (MCF)	52.41	51.35	—
Attitudinal Flexibility (AF)	52.26	52.73	—
Psychomotor Speed (PS)	52.98	53.87	—
Social Responsibility (SR)	49.75	48.52	—

Note: Means are in T-scores with population mean of 50 and standard deviation of 10. *t*-ratios are given only for values significant at or beyond the 5% level of confidence.
*$p < 0.05$; **$p < 0.01$; ***$p < 0.001$.

Fluency, for which it scored higher. No differences were observed for the measures from the Test of Behavioral Rigidity, the Social Responsibility scale, or the composite IQ score.

Having established that differences in level between the two populations did exist on certain variables, the question next arises whether these differences prevail across the board for all cohort/age groups or are localized at specific age levels. This is a critical issue: If there is an overall difference, then future analyses would require systematic adjustments; if the differences were confined to specific age and cohort levels, then we simply need to take note of this in interpreting local blips in our overall data analyses. Results of the age- and cohort-specific analyses suggest that the differences are indeed local: They affect primarily members of Cohorts 4 and 5 (mean birth years = 1910 and 1917, respectively), who in 1974 would have been in their late 50s and early 60s. Comparisons for none of the other age/cohort levels reached statistical significance ($p < .01$).

The major conclusion of this study echoes for the investigation of developmental problems the caution first raised by Campbell and Stanley (1963) that there is always a trade-off between internal and external validity. In our case, we find that designs that maximize internal validity may indeed impair the generalizability of the phenomena studied (see also Schaie, 1978). Fortunately, the results of the 1974 collateral study suggest that such threat to the external validity of developmental designs is not equally serious for all variables or for all ages and cohorts. Hence, I do not necessarily advocate that all studies must include analyses such as the one presented in this section, but would caution the initiator of long-range studies to design data collections in a manner permitting similar analyses for those variables where the literature does not provide appropriate evidence of external validity.

The aging of tests (1975 study)

Although longitudinal designs are the most powerful approach for determining changes that occur with increasing age, they are associated with a number of serious limitations (see chapter 2; Baltes & Nesselroade, 1979; Schaie, 1973b, 1977, 1988d, 1994b).

One of these limitations is the fact that outmoded measurement instruments must usually continue to be employed, even though newer (and possibly better) instruments may become available, in order to allow orderly comparisons of the measurement variables over time.

However, if the primary interest is at the level of psychological constructs, then specific measurement operations may be seen as no more than arbitrary samples of observable behaviors designed to measure the latent constructs (Baltes, Nesselroade, Schaie, & Labouvie, 1972; Schaie, 1973b, 1988d). In that case it might well be possible to convert from one set of measures to another if the appropriate linkage studies are undertaken. These linkage studies must be designed to give an indication of the common factor structure for both old and new measures. Designing such linkage studies requires considerable attention to a number of issues. New instruments must be chosen that, on either theoretical or empirical grounds, may be expected to measure the same constructs as the old instruments. Thus it is necessary to include a variety of tasks thought to measure the same constructs. It is then possible to determine empirically which of the new measures best describe information that was gained from the older measures, so that scores obtained from the new test battery will closely reproduce the information gathered by means of the original measures.

The sample of participants for the linkage study must be drawn from the same parent population and should comprise individuals of the same gender and age range as those in the longitudinal study. Only in this manner can we be sure that comparable information will be gathered on the range of performance, reliability, and construct validity for both old and new measures. Given information for the same participants on both the old and new measurement variables, regression techniques can then be employed, the results of which will allow judgment whether to convert to new measures and, if so, which measures must be included in the new battery. Alternatively, study results may suggest that switching to the new measures will result in significant information loss, an outcome that would argue for retention of one or more of the old measures.

Because of the cohort effects described earlier (see chapter 6), we began to worry as we prepared for the fourth (1977) cycle that a ceiling effect might be reached by some of the younger participants on some of the measures in the 1948 PMA battery. Although these tests had been found to be appropriate for older people (Schaie, Rosenthal, & Perlman, 1953), the question was now raised as to whether the tests had "aged" over the time period they had been used. In other words, we were concerned whether or not measures retained appropriate construct validity for the more recent cohorts introduced into our study. On the other hand, we were also concerned about the possibility that although the test might have restricted validity for the younger cohorts, switching to a newer test might raise construct validity problems for the older cohorts. For example, Gardner and Monge (1975) found that whereas 20- and 30-year-olds performed significantly better on items entering the language after 1960, 40- and 60-year-olds performed significantly better on items entering the language in the late 1920s.

We consequently decided that it would be prudent to examine the continuing utility of the 1948 PMA version by administering this test together with a more recent PMA revision (T. G. Thurstone, 1962) and selected measures from the *Kit of Referenced Tests for Cognitive Factors* published by the Educational Testing Service (French, Ekstrom, & Price, 1963). The 1962 PMA was chosen because it was felt that this test would be most similar to the 1948 PMA version; the ETS tests were included with the expectation that they might account for additional variance that would reduce the information loss caused by a decision to switch the PMA test for future test occasions (see Gribbin & Schaie, 1977).

Method

Subjects. The approximately 128,000 members of our HMO over the age range from 22 to 82 (in 1975) were stratified by age and gender, and a balanced random sample in these strata was drawn. Data were collected on 242 men and women.

Measurement Variables. The test battery for this study included the five subtests of the PMA 1948 version (Thurstone & Thurstone, 1949): Verbal Meaning (V48), Spatial Orientation (S48), Inductive Reasoning (R48), Number (N48), and Word Fluency (W48). The

1962 version (T. G. Thurstone, 1962) differs from the earlier format by omitting Word Fluency; by having Number (N62) include subtraction, multiplication, and division instead of just addition; and by having Inductive Reasoning (R62) include number series and word groupings as well as the letter series that make up N48. The number of items is also increased in the Verbal Meaning (V62) test. Eight tests were added from the ETS test kit (French et al., 1963): *Hidden Patterns*, a measure of flexibility of closure; *Letter Sets*, a measure of inductive reasoning; *Length Estimation*, the ability to judge and compare visually perceived distances; *Finding A's* and *Identical Pictures*, measures of perceptual speed; *Nonsense Syllogisms*, a measure of syllogistic reasoning; *Maze Tracing*, which requires spatial scanning; and *Paper Folding*, which requires transforming the image of spatial patterns into other visual arrangements. All of the ETS tests have two parts of similar form.

Procedure. Tests were administered in a modified counterbalanced order; that is, one order presented the 1948 PMA first, followed by the ETS tests, with the 1962 PMA last. The second order presented the 1962 PMA first, followed by the ETS tests in reverse order and ending with the 1948 PMA. A 20-min break, with refreshments, was given after half the ETS tests had been administered.

"Aging of tests" study findings

Regression analyses were employed to determine the relationship between the tests. For each subtest score to be predicted (that is, subtests from both versions of the PMA), scores on all subtests from the alternative version plus each part of the eight ETS tests were used as predictor variables across all subjects. Since we are also concerned about the relationships among our variables by age level, similar analyses were conducted by dividing the sample into two age groups (22 to 51 and 52 to 82) in order to determine whether predictability of the tests differed by age groupings. Table 8.3 presents the R^2 (proportion of variance accounted for) for each subtest of the 1948 PMA, as well as the beta weights (βs: standardized regression coefficients) for each predictor variable, for the younger,

Table 8.3. *Regression equations predicting the 1948 PMA*

	Verbal Meaning			Spatial Orientation			Inductive Reasoning			Number			Word Fluency		
	Y	O	T	Y	O	T	Y	O	T	Y	O	T	Y	O	T
Verbal 62	0.59	0.28	0.50	-0.17	—	—	0.09	-0.12	—	0.21	0.26	0.26	0.27	—	0.24
Space 62	-0.11	0.14	—	0.64	—	0.46	0.58	-0.13	—	—	—	—	—	—	-0.11
Letter Series 62	0.19	-0.26	-0.18	0.42	—	0.47	0.43	0.18	0.18	—	0.12	—	—	—	—
Number Series 62	0.39	—	0.24	0.22	-0.17	0.14	0.24	0.14	—	—	—	—	—	0.18	0.18
Word Groupings 62	-0.23	-0.18	-0.24	—	0.17	0.17	-0.21	—	—	—	—	0.12	-0.13	—	—
Number 62	0.18	—	0.13	0.27	—	—	—	—	—	0.18	0.31	0.33	—	—	—
Hidden Patterns 1	-0.14	0.27	—	—	—	—	—	0.17	—	—	—	—	—	—	—
Hidden Patterns 2	0.22	-0.14	0.11	—	—	—	0.20	—	0.10	—	—	—	—	—	—
Finding A's 1	-0.15	—	—	0.15	0.10	—	0.09	—	0.14	0.10	0.11	—	-0.17	—	—
Finding A's 2	0.19	0.05	—	—	—	—	—	0.04	—	—	—	-0.11	0.27	0.14	0.18
Maze Tracing 1	-0.22	-0.15	-0.08	—	—	-0.10	—	—	—	-0.18	-0.33	—	0.18	0.16	—
Maze Tracing 2	—	—	—	—	—	0.08	-0.09	0.25	—	0.16	-0.24	-0.23	—	—	—
Paper Folding 1	—	—	—	—	0.14	—	—	—	-0.13	—	—	—	—	—	—
Paper Folding 2	—	—	0.06	—	0.12	—	—	—	—	—	-0.08	—	—	—	—
Identical Pictures 1	0.16	—	—	—	—	0.26	—	—	—	0.11	—	—	0.18	—	—
Identical Pictures 2	0.23	0.14	0.15	—	0.09	-0.16	—	0.12	—	—	—	—	—	0.09	—
Letter Sets 1	0.10	—	—	0.15	—	0.28	0.10	0.15	-0.26	0.14	0.25	0.15	0.27	0.37	0.25
Letter Sets 2	-0.09	—	0.11	0.11	—	0.07	—	0.19	0.14	—	—	—	—	—	—
Line Estimation 1	—	—	—	—	—	—	—	0.11	0.04	—	-0.11	-0.11	—	—	—
Line Estimation 2	—	—	—	—	—	—	—	-0.07	—	—	—	0.15	0.06	—	—
Nonsense Syllogisms 1	—	—	—	-0.11	—	0.11	0.06	—	-0.10	-0.06	—	—	—	—	—
Nonsence Syllogisms 2	—	—	—	-0.08	-0.04	—	—	—	—	—	—	—	—	—	—
R^2	0.65	0.68	0.69	0.61	0.72	0.70	0.72	0.85	0.84	0.37	0.52	0.43	0.45	0.34	0.40

older, and total data sets. Similar information is provided in Table 8.4 for the 1962 PMA.

As can be seen by comparing the R^2 of the comparable subtests from each PMA version, it turns out that the 1962 version is better predicted than is the 1948 version. Of the 1948 PMA tests, Verbal Meaning, Spatial Orientation, and Inductive Reasoning can be reasonably well predicted from their 1962 counterparts. However, this is not the case for Number and Word Fluency. For these subtests, only 43% and 40% of the variance, respectively, can be accounted for, suggesting that it would not have been prudent to replace these tests.

When examining findings by age level, it becomes clear that N48 and W48 are even less well predicted for the younger half of the sample. However, it is worth noting that W48 is better predicted for older than younger subjects, and that the reverse is true for N48.

These results suggest that by adding certain of the ETS tests it would have been practicable to replace V48 with V62, S48 with S62, and R48 with R62 and sustain relatively little information loss. For N48 and W48, however, it is clear that replacement was not justified. By contrast, it was found that a combination of the 1948 PMA and certain of the ETS tests would allow substantial prediction of most of the reliable variance in the 1962 PMA.

In sum, it appeared that shifting to the newer version of the PMA, even with the addition of several other tests, would lead to serious problems in maintaining linkage across test occasions. Moreover, since it was possible to predict performance on the 1962 PMA well with the addition of certain ETS tests, it did not seem that any advantage was to be gained in shifting to the newer test version. We thus concluded that continued use of the 1948 PMA was justified, but we augmented the fourth-cycle battery by adding the ETS Identical Pictures and Finding A's tests in order to be able to define an additional Perceptual Speed factor.

Effects of monetary incentives

Over the course of the SLS there have been a number of subtle changes in the nature of volunteering behavior by prospective subjects. In particular, our original solicitation was directed toward

Table 8.4. *Regression equations predicting the 1962 PMA*

	Verbal Meaning			Spatial Orientation			Inductive Reasoning			Number		
	Y	O	T	Y	O	T	Y	O	T	Y	O	T
Verbal 48	0.50	0.25	0.41	-0.10	0.13	—	0.17	0.20	0.10	0.24	—	0.12
Space 48	—	—	—	0.59	0.51	0.54	0.38	0.35	0.39	0.16	0.04	0.18
Reasoning 48	0.08	0.22	0.13	0.13	—	—	0.10	0.14	0.10	-0.16	0.24	-0.07
Number 48	0.11	—	0.10	—	—	—	0.12	—	0.06	0.11	0.08	0.20
Word Fluency 48	0.13	—	—	—	—	0.12	—	—	—	—	0.18	—
Hidden Patterns 1	—	—	—	—	0.29	—	0.11	—	—	—	—	—
Hidden Patterns 2	—	—	—	0.21	0.13	—	—	—	-0.10	—	—	—
Finding A's 1	0.16	0.18	0.13	—	-0.14	-0.10	—	—	—	—	—	—
Finding A's 2	—	—	—	—	0.08	0.10	—	—	—	—	—	0.12
Maze Tracing 1	—	—	—	—	—	—	0.19	—	0.14	—	—	0.16
Maze Tracing 2	0.13	0.14	—	0.16	-0.20	—	—	-0.07	—	0.36	0.18	0.09
Paper Folding 1	—	—	—	—	—	—	—	0.11	—	—	—	—
Paper Folding 2	—	—	—	0.20	—	0.13	-0.10	—	—	—	—	—
Identical Pictures 1	0.12	0.11	—	—	—	—	—	0.09	—	—	—	—
Identical Pictures 2	—	—	0.11	—	—	—	0.22	0.22	0.22	0.37	0.15	0.23
Letter Sets 1	—	—	—	—	—	—	—	—	—	—	—	—
Letter Sets 2	-0.13	-0.13	-0.12	—	—	—	0.09	—	—	0.10	0.10	—
Line Estimation 1	0.14	—	—	—	—	—	—	0.14	0.09	0.26	0.13	0.16
Line Estimation 2	—	0.21	0.12	-0.08	—	0.06	—	—	0.05	—	—	—
Nonsence Syllogisms 1	—	—	—	0.13	0.08	0.07	0.18	0.08	—	—	—	—
Nonsence Syllogisms 2	0.19	0.09	0.15	—	—	—	—	—	—	—	—	—
R_2	0.67	0.67	0.72	0.62	0.68	0.73	0.76	0.87	0.87	0.63	0.72	0.72

encouraging participation by appealing to the prospective subjects' interest in helping to generate new knowledge as well as in assisting their health plan in acquiring information on its membership that might help in program planning activities. As the study progressed, payments to participants in psychological studies became more frequent, and it is now virtually the rule for study participants beyond college age.

It has been well known for some time that rate of volunteering differs by age. Typically, adult volunteers tend to be younger, and when older people do volunteer they tend to do so more often for survey research than for laboratory studies (Rosenthal & Rosnow, 1975). Indeed, in our very first effort we found a curvilinear age pattern, with middle-aged persons being most likely to volunteer (Schaie, 1958c).

The increased employment of monetary incentives may have a substantial effect upon the self-selection of volunteer study participants. In a study with young adult subjects, MacDonald (1972) utilized three incentive conditions: (1) for pay, (2) for extra class credit, and (3) for love of science. He found that participants high in need of approval on the Marlowe–Crowne scale were more willing to volunteer than subjects low in need of approval on the pay condition but not on the other two conditions.

Since we could not find a comparable study using older adults, as part of the 1974 collateral study we attempted to determine the effects of a monetary incentive on self-selection of volunteer subjects across the adult age range. Specifically, we were interested in determining whether those participants who had been promised payment differed on certain cognitive and personality factors from those who had been told that they would not be paid (see Gribbin & Schaie, 1976).

Method

Sampling and procedures for this investigation were described in the section on the 1974 collateral study. However, certain additional information relating to the monetary incentive aspects needs to be added. As part of the subject recruitment letter, half of the potential participants were informed that they would be paid $10 for their participation; no mention of payment was made in the letter to the other half. After completion of the assessment procedures, both groups were paid the subject fee. Data evaluated for the effects of monetary incentives include the five primary mental abilities, the Test of Behavioral Rigidity, and the 16 PF (Cattell, Eber, & Tatsuoka, 1970).

"Monetary incentives" study findings

Of the 1,233 potential subjects in each incentive category, 34% of the pay condition (P) and 32% of the no-pay condition (NP) subjects volunteered to participate in the study. In both conditions women (P = 37%; NP = 35%) were more willing to participate then men (P = 30%; NP = 29%). Peak participation occurred for subjects in the age range from 40 to 68, with participation decreasing linearly for both those older and younger. Nonsignificant chi squares were obtained for age, gender, and their interaction.

No significant differences for the pay conditions were found for any of the primary mental abilities or any of the dimensions of the Test of Behavioral Rigidity. Neither did we observe any significant pay condition by gender interactions. The effect of incentive conditions on personality traits was next considered via MANOVAs of both primary source traits and the secondary stratum factors of the 16 PF. Again, none of the multivariate tests of Trait × Pay Condition, or Trait × Pay Condition × Gender were found to be statistically significant.

It thus seems clear that offering a monetary incentive does not seem to result in biased self-selection, at least as far as measures of cognitive abilities, cognitive styles, and self-reported personality traits are concerned. In addition, it does not seem that offering a monetary incentive has any effect on recruitment rate for a relatively brief (2-hour) laboratory experiment. Of course we do not know whether similar findings would hold for more extensive protocols, such as those employed in our training studies (see chapter 7). Nevertheless, it seems safe to argue from these results that findings from studies using monetary incentives may legitimately be generalized to those that do not offer such incentives without fear that the samples will differ with regard to characteristics that might be attributed to extraneous incentive conditions.

Effects of experimental mortality: the problem of subject attrition

One of the major threats to the internal validity of a longitudinal study is the occurrence of subject attrition (experimental mortality) such that not all subjects tested at T_1 are available for retest at T_2 or subsequently. In studies of cognitive aging, subject attrition may be due to death, disability, disappearance, or failure to cooperate with the researcher on a subsequent test occasion. Substantial differences in base performance have been observed between those who return and those who fail to be retrieved for the second or subsequent test. Typically dropouts score lower at base on ability variables or describe themselves as possessing less socially desirable traits than do those who return (see Riegel, Riegel, & Meyer, 1967; Schaie, 1988d). Hence, the argument has been advanced that longitudinal studies represent increasingly more elite subsets of the general population and may eventually produce data that are not sufficiently generalizable (see Botwinick, 1977). This proposition can and should be tested empirically, of course. In the SLS we have assessed experimental mortality subsequent to each cycle (for Cycle 2, see Baltes, Schaie, & Nardi, 1971; Cycle 3, Schaie, Labouvie, & Barrett, 1973; Cycle 4, Gribbin & Schaie, 1979; Cycle 5, Cooney, Schaie, & Willis, 1988). Below I will summarize a comprehensive analysis of attrition effects across all six cycles (see also Schaie, 1988d).

We have examined the magnitude of attrition effects for several longitudinal sequences in order to contrast base performance of those individuals for whom longitudinal data are available with those who dropped out after the initial assessment. In addition, we consider shifts in direction and magnitude of attrition after multiple assessment occasions. In Table 8.5 I report attrition data as the difference in average performance between dropouts and returnees. It will be seen that attrition effects vary across samples entering the study at different points in time. However, between T_1 and T_2 they generally range from 0.3 to 0.6 *SD* and must therefore be considered of a magnitude that represents at least a moderate-size effect (see Cohen & Cohen, 1975). Although attrition effects become somewhat less pronounced as test occasions multiply, they do remain of a statistically significant magnitude.

Before the reader is overly impressed by the substantial dif-

Table 8.5. *Difference in average performance at base assessment between dropouts and returnees, in T-score points*

	Sample 1 N = 500	Sample 2 N = 997	Sample 3 N = 705	Sample 4 N = 612	Sample 5 N = 628
After Test 1					
Verbal Meaning	4.07**	6.38**	6.27**	6.12**	2.85**
Spatial Orientation	2.52**	4.00**	4.08**	4.25**	2.44**
Inductive Reasoning	3.06**	5.28**	5.70**	6.70**	2.58**
Number	1.97*	3.95**	5.16**	4.45**	1.91
Word Fluency	3.06**	3.66**	4.84**	3.68**	2.28**
After Test 2					
Verbal Meaning	1.51**	1.97**	3.71**	3.33**	
Spatial Orientation	2.16**	1.35	5.09**	3.44**	
Inductive Reasoning	5.14**	2.54**	5.81**	2.71**	
Number	2.13*	1.65*	2.87**	2.05**	
Word Fluency	2.41*	1.01	2.67**	3.43**	
After Test 3					
Verbal Meaning	4.10**	2.30*	3.78**		
Spatial Orientation	4.85**	0.48*	4.50**		
Inductive Reasoning	4.35**	4.73**	4.30**		
Number	0.58*	1.89	2.53**		
Word Fluency	3.96**	1.16	2.48		
After Test 4					
Verbal Meaning	4.72**	6.75**			
Spatial Orientation	3.45*	2.38			
Inductive Reasoning	4.45*	3.15**			
Number	1.35	1.79			
Word Fluency	4.25**	2.20			
After Test 5					
Verbal Meaning	5.04**				
Spatial Orientation	5.67**				
Inductive Reasoning	3.36				
Number	2.44				
Word Fluency	2.09				

Note: All differences are in favor of the returnees.
*$p < 0.05$; **$p < 0.01$.

ferences between dropouts and returnees, a caution must be raised. Bias in longitudinal studies due to experimental mortality depends solely on the proportion of dropouts to the total sample. Hence, if attrition is modest experimental mortality effects will be quite small, but if attrition is large, the effects can be as substantial as noted above. Table 8.6 therefore presents the actual net attrition effects (in T-score points) for our samples, showing the different attrition patterns. It is apparent from these data that experimental mortality is largest for those test occasions at which the greatest proportion of dropouts occurs (normally at T_2) and becomes smaller as panels stabilize and the remaining attrition occurs primarily as a consequence of the subjects' death or disability.

We can infer from these data that parameter estimates of levels of cognitive function from longitudinal studies, when experimental mortality is appreciable, could be substantially higher in many instances than would be true if the entire original sample could have been followed over time. Nevertheless, it does not follow that rates of change will also be overestimated unless it can be shown that there is a substantial positive correlation between base-level performance and age change. Because of the favorable attrition (i.e., excess attrition of low-performing subjects), the regression should result in modest negative correlations between base and age-change measures. This is indeed what was found (see Schaie, 1988d). Hence, contrary to Botwinick's (1977) inference, experimental mortality may actually result in the overestimation of rates of cognitive aging in longitudinal studies.

Effects of practice in repeated testing

Longitudinal studies have been thought to reflect overly optimistic results also because age-related declines in behavior may be obscured by the consequences of practice on the measurement instruments used to detect such decline. In addition, practice effects may differ by age. We have studied the effects of practice by comparing individuals who return for follow-up with the performance of individuals assessed at the same age for the first time (Schaie, 1988d). Practice effects estimated in this manner appear, at first glance, to be impressively large between T_1 and T_2 (up to approxi-

Table 8.6. *Attrition effects calculated as difference between base means for total sample and returnees, in T-score points*

	Sample 1 $N = 500$	Sample 2 $N = 997$	Sample 3 $N = 705$	Sample 4 $N = 612$	Sample 5 $N = 629$
Attrition after Test 1	*38.2%*	*53.5%*	*51.9%*	*52.3%*	*32.0%*
Verbal Meaning	1.52*	3.41**	2.97**	3.20**	2.85**
Spatial Orientation	0.96	2.14**	2.12**	1.40*	2.44**
Inductive Reasoning	1.17	2.82**	2.96**	2.22**	2.58**
Number	0.76	2.11**	2.68**	2.46**	1.91
Word Fluency	1.17	1.95**	2.51**	2.33**	2.28**
Attrition after Test 2	*25.0%*	*16.0%*	*16.5%*	*15.4%*	
Verbal Meaning	1.59	0.70	1.54	3.33**	
Spatial Orientation	1.02	0.48	1.40	3.44**	
Inductive Reasoning	2.33**	0.91	1.99	2.71**	
Number	0.93	0.59	0.98	2.05	
Word Fluency	1.09	0.36	0.74	3.43**	
Attrition after Test 3	*8.0%*	*7.4%*	*6.8%*		
Verbal Meaning	0.97	0.57	3.78**		
Spatial Orientation	1.12	0.12	4.50**		
Inductive Reasoning	1.03	1.14	4.30**		
Number	0.16	0.47	2.53		
Word Fluency	0.94	0.29	2.48		
Attrition after Test 4	*6.4%*	*6.4%*			
Verbal Meaning	1.21	6.75**			
Spatial Orientation	0.86	2.38			
Inductive Reasoning	1.14	3.15**			
Number	0.35	1.79			
Word Fluency	1.09	2.20			
Attrition after Test 5	*5.0%*				
Verbal Meaning	5.04**				
Spatial Orientation	5.67**				
Inductive Reasoning	3.36				
Number	2.44				
Word Fluency	2.09				

Note: All differences are in favor of the returnees.
* $p < 0.05$; ** $p < 0.01$.

mately 0.3 *SD*), although they become increasingly smaller over subsequent time intervals (see Table 8.7). Note, however, that practice effects estimated in this manner of necessity involve the comparison of attrited and random samples. The mean values for the longitudinal samples must therefore be adjusted for experimental mortality to permit valid comparison. The appropriate adjustment is based on the values in Table 8.6 (i.e., the differences between returnees and the entire sample). Since practice effects are assumed to be positive, all significance tests in Table 8.7 are one-tailed. Although the raw practice effects appear to be statistically significant for virtually all variables and samples, none of the adjusted effects reach significance except for Verbal Meaning in Sample 1. We conclude therefore that practice effects do not tend to produce favorably biased results in the longitudinal findings of our study.

We have also examined the joint effects of attrition and history, attrition and cohort, history and practice, cohort and practice, and the joint effects of all these four potential threats to the internal validity of longitudinal studies. Designs for these analyses are given in Schaie (1977), with worked-out examples in Schaie (1988d). In a data set involving two age cohorts aged 46 and 53 at the first assessment and comparing their performance 7 years later, these effects were all significant and accounted for roughly 7% of the total variance (see Schaie, 1988d, for further details).

Structural equivalence

As I suggested in chapter 2, all of the comparisons across age and time as well as the gains reported for cognitive interventions depend on the assumption that structural invariance is maintained across these conditions. Very few studies have the requisite data to investigate this assumption empirically. In this section I describe three methodological investigations that apply restricted (confirmatory) factor analysis (Mulaik, 1972) to investigate these issues. All of the analyses use the LISREL paradigm (Jöreskog & Sörbom, 1988).

Factorial invariance across samples differing in age

In a study employing the entire set of 1,621 subjects tested in 1984, we investigated the validity of the assumption that the measurement

Table 8.7. Raw and attrition-adjusted effects of practice, by sample and test occasion, in T-score points

	Sample 1		Sample 2		Sample 3		Sample 4	
	Raw	Adjusted	Raw	Adjusted	Raw	Adjusted	Raw	Adjusted
From Test 1 to Test 2								
Verbal Meaning	2.81**	1.31*	4.02**	0.61	3.25***	0.28	1.21*	−1.99
Spatial Orientation	1.02	0.06	3.00***	0.86	2.28***	0.28	2.06**	0.14
Inductive Reasoning	2.03**	0.86	3.43**	0.61	2.77***	−0.19	1.33*	−0.69
Number	1.02	0.26	1.29*	−0.82	3.09***	0.41	1.60*	−0.86
Word Fluency	1.71*	0.54	2.94***	0.99	2.97***	0.87	1.10	−1.23
From Test 2 to Test 3								
Verbal Meaning	−3.07	−2.77	3.11**	1.97*	−3.15	−4.46		
Spatial Orientation	−0.03	0.13	2.05**	0.65	1.68*	−0.06		
Inductive Reasoning	1.16	0.48	2.71***	1.34	1.93*	−0.80		
Number	−0.50	−0.08	1.84*	1.82*	1.13	−0.07		
Word Fluency	0.22	−0.09	0.41	0.61	2.15**	1.23		
From Test 3 to Test 4								
Verbal Meaning	0.20	0.20	−0.78	0.79				
Spatial Orientation	0.14	−0.34	0.30	0.63				
Inductive Reasoning	−0.17	−0.97	0.04	0.09				
Number	−1.03	−0.18	0.10	0.59				
Word Fluency	0.10	−0.80	−0.99	−0.34				
From Test 4 to Test 5								
Verbal Meaning	0.90	0.29						
Spatial Orientation	0.81	−0.41						
Inductive Reasoning	−0.09	−0.86						
Number	−1.83	−1.66						
Word Fluency	−1.74	0.05						

*$p \leq 0.05$; **$p \leq 0.01$

operations employed in the study are comparable across age groups (Schaie, Willis, Jay, & Chipuer, 1989). The basic assumption to be tested was that each observed marker variable measures the same latent construct equally well regardless of the age of the subjects assessed.

Three levels of stringency of measurement equivalence were defined: complete metric invariance, incomplete metric invariance, and configural invariance (see also Horn, 1991; Horn & McArdle, 1992). The most stringent level of invariance, *complete metric invariance*, implies not only that the measurement operations remain relevant to the same latent construct but also that the regressions of the latent constructs on the observed measures remain invariant across age and, further, that the interrelationships among the different constructs representing a domain (factor intercorrelations) also remain invariant. If invariance can be accepted at this level, it then follows that inferences can be validly drawn from age-comparative studies both for the comparison of directly observed mean levels and for the comparison of derived factor score means for the latent ability constructs.

A somewhat less stringent equivalence requirement, *incomplete metric invariance*, allows the unique variances and factor intercorrelations to vary across groups while requiring the regressions of the latent constructs on the observed variables to remain invariant. Given the acceptability of this relaxed requirement, it is still possible to claim that observations remain invariant across age. However, comparison of factor scores now requires that changes in the factor space (unequal factor variances and covariances) need to be adequately modeled in the algorithm employed for the computation of factor scores.

For the least stringent requirement, *configural invariance*, we expect that observables remain relevant to the same latent construct across age (i.e., across age groups the same variables have statistically significant loadings, and the same variables have zero loadings). However, we do not insist that the relationships among the latent constructs retain the same magnitude, nor do we require that the regression of the latent constructs on the observed variables remain invariant. If we must accept the least restrictive model, we must then conclude that our test battery does not measure the latent constructs equally well over the entire age range studied, and we must estimate factor scores using differential weights by age group.

Method. In this analysis we tested the hypothesis of invariance under the three assumptions outlined above for the domain of psychometric intelligence as defined by 17 tests representing multiple markers of the latent constructs of Inductive Reasoning, Spatial Orientation, Perceptual Speed, Numeric Ability, and Verbal Ability (see description of the expanded battery in chapter 3). An initial factor structure (suggested by earlier work described below [see also Schaie, Willis, Hertzog, & Schulenberg, 1987]) was confirmed on the entire sample's 1,621 study participants, yielding a satisfactory fit ($\chi^2[107, N = 1,621] = 946.62, p < .001$ [*GFI* = .936]). Table 8.8 shows the factor loadings and factor intercorrelations that entered subsequent analyses. In this model, each ability is marked by at least three operationally distinct observed markers. Each test marks only one ability, except for Number Comparison, which splits between Perceptual Speed and Number, and the PMA Verbal Meaning test, which splits between Perceptual Speed and Verbal Ability.

The total sample was then subdivided by age into nine nonoverlapping subsets with mean ages 90 ($n = 39$), 81 ($n = 136$), 74 ($n = 260$), 67 ($n = 291$), 60 ($n = 260$), 53 ($n = 193$), 46 ($n = 154$), 39 ($n = 124$), and 29 ($n = 164$). The variance–covariance matrix for each set was then modeled with respect to each of the three invariance levels specified for the overall model.

Results. As indicated above, model testing then proceeded at the three levels of stringency listed for determining factorial invariance:

1. *Complete metric invariance.* Model fits for the subsets are, of course, somewhat lower than for the total set but, except for ages 81 and 90 (the oldest cohorts), are still quite acceptable. The oldest cohort, perhaps because of the small sample size, had the lowest GFI (.596), and the 67-year-olds had the highest (.893).

2. *Incomplete metric invariance.* When unique variances and the factor variance–covariance matrices are freely estimated across groups, statistically significant improvements of model fit occur for all age groups. As in the complete metric invariance models, the

Factor loadings

Variable	Inductive Reasoning	Spatial Orientation	Perceptual Speed	Numeric Ability	Verbal Ability	Unique variance
PMA Reasoning	0.893					0.199
ADEPT Letter Series	0.884					0.219
Word Series	0.891					0.207
Number Series	0.787					0.381
PMA Space		0.831				0.309
Object Rotation		0.877				0.231
Alphanumeric Rotation		0.831				0.309
Cube Comparison		0.594				0.647
Finding A's			0.524			0.725
Number Comparison			0.576	0.270		0.424
Identical pictures			0.832			0.308
PMA Number				0.838		0.297
Addition				0.938		0.121
Subtraction & Multiplication				0.865		0.252
PMA Verbal Meaning			0.660		0.386	0.254
ETS Vocabulary					0.897	0.195
ETS Advanced Vocabulary					0.893	0.203

Factor Intercorrelations

Factor	Inductive Reasoning	Spatial Orientation	Perceptual Speed	Numeric Ability	Verbal Ability
Inductive Reasoning	—				
Spatial Orientation	0.675	—			
Perceptual Speed	0.777	0.736	—		
Numeric Ability	0.687	0.584	0.689	—	
Verbal Ability	0.631	0.298	0.381	0.552	—

Note: All factor loadings are significant at or beyond the 1% level of confidence. $\chi^2(107, N = 1,621) = 946.62$. Goodness-of-fit index = 0.936.

poorest fit is again found for the oldest age group (.669), with the best fit occurring for the 74-year-olds (.913). Substantial differences in factor variances were found across the age groups. Variances increase systematically until the 60s and then decrease. Covariances also show substantial increment with increasing age.

3. *Configural invariance.* In the final set of analyses, factor patterns as specified in Table 8.8 were maintained, but the factor patterns were freely estimated. Again, significant improvement in fit was obtained for all age groups, with the goodness-of-fit indices ranging from a low of .697 for the oldest group to a high of .930 for the 74-year-olds. Hence, the configural invariance model must be accepted as the most plausible description of the structure of this data set.

Conclusions. The demonstration of configural (factor pattern) invariance is initially reassuring to developmentalists in that it confirms the hope that it is realistic to track the same basic constructs across age and cohorts in adulthood. Nevertheless, these findings give rise to serious cautions with respect to the adequacy of the construct equivalence of an age-comparative study. Given the fact that we could not accept a total-population-based measurement model at either metric or incomplete metric invariance level for any age/cohort, we must now consider the use of *single* estimators of latent constructs as problematic in age-comparative studies.

How serious is the divergence from complete metric equivalence? In the past, shifts in the interrelation among ability constructs have been associated with a differentiation–dedifferentiation theory of intelligence (see Reinert, 1970). This theory predicts that factor covariances should be lowest for the young and should increase with advancing age. As predicted by theory, we found factor covariances to be lowest for our youngest age groups and increasing with advancing age. Factor variances also increase until the 70s, when the disproportionate dropout of those at greatest risk once again increases sample homogeneity and reduces factor variances. Since our data set for the test of complete metric invariance was centered in late midlife, it does not surprise us that discrepancies in factor covariances are confined primarily to the extremes of the age range studied (see Schaie, Willis, Jay, & Chipuer, 1989). Consequently, these shifts will not seriously impair the validity of age comparisons using factor scores except at the age extremes.

Since we accept the configural invariance model as the most plausible description of our data, we must be concerned about the relative efficiency of the observed variables as markers of the latent variables at different age levels. The shift in efficiency may be a function of the influence of extreme outliers in small samples or a consequence of the attainment of floor effects in the older age groups and ceiling effects in the younger age groups, when a common measurement battery is used over the entire adult life course. In this study, across age groups, for example, the Cube Comparison test becomes a less efficient marker of Spatial Orientation, whereas the PMA Space test becomes a better marker with increasing age. Likewise, the Number Comparison test (a marker of Perceptual Speed), which has a secondary loading on Numerical Ability in the general factor model, loses that secondary loading with increasing age.

These findings suggest that age comparisons in performance level on certain single markers of an ability may be confounded by the changing efficiency of the marker in making the desired assessment. Fortunately, in our case the divergences are typically quite local in nature. That is, for a particular ability, the optimal regression weights of observable measures on their latent factors may shift slightly, but since there is no shift in the primary loading to another factor, structural relationships are well maintained across the entire age range sampled in the study.

Factorial invariance across experimental interventions

We have also investigated the stability of the expanded battery's ability structure across the cognitive training intervention described in chapter 7 (Schaie, Willis, Hertzog, & Schulenberg, 1987). This study was designed to show that the structure of abilities remains invariant across a brief time period for a nonintervention group (experimental control), and to show that the two intervention programs (Inductive Reasoning, Spatial Orientation) employed in the cognitive intervention study did not result in shifts of factor structure, a possible outcome for training studies suggested by Donaldson (1981; but see Willis & Baltes, 1981).

Method. The subset of subjects used for this study included 401 persons (224 women and 177 men) who were tested twice in 1983–84. Of these, 111 subjects received Inductive Reasoning training, 118 were trained on Spatial Orientation, and 172 were pre- and posttested but did not receive any training. Mean age of the total sample in these analyses was 72.5 (SD = 6.41, range = 64 to 95). Mean educational level was 13.9 years (SD = 2.98, range = 6 to 20). The test battery consisted of 16 tests representing multiple markers of the latent constructs of Inductive Reasoning, Spatial Orientation, Perceptual Speed, Numeric Ability, and Verbal Ability (see description of the expanded battery in chapter 3).

We first used the pretest data for the entire sample to select an appropriate factor model. Given that the training analysis classified groups by prior developmental history, we next evaluated the metric invariance of the ability factor structure across the stable and decline groups (see chapter 7). Both groups were found to have equivalent factor loadings and factor intercorrelations (χ^2[243, N = 401] = 463.17; *GFI* stable = .847, *GFI* unstable = .892). A similar analysis confirmed the acceptability of metric invariance across gender (χ^2[243, N = 401] = 466.22; *GFI* men = .851, *GFI* women = .904). Finally, metric invariance could be accepted also across the three training conditions (χ^2[243, N = 401] = 511.55; *GFI* Inductive Reasoning = .871, *GFI* Spatial Orientation = .783, *GFI* controls = .902).

In the main analysis, separate longitudinal factor analyses of the pretest–posttest data were run for each of the training groups. The basic model extended the five-factor model for the pretest data to a repeated measures factor model for the pretest–posttest data. The model also specified correlated residuals to allow test-specific relations across times to provide unbiased estimates of individual differences in the factors (see Hertzog & Schaie, 1986; Sörbom, 1975).

Results. Examination of the pretest–posttest factor analysis results for the *control* group led to the acceptance of metric invariance with an adequate model fit (χ^2[412, $N = 172$] = 574.84; *GFI* = .833). Freeing parameters across test occasions did not lead to a significant improvement in fit, thus indicating short-term stability of factor structure and providing a benchmark for the pretest–posttest comparisons of the experimental intervention groups.

The fit of the basic longitudinal factor model for the *Inductive Reasoning training* group was almost as good as for the controls (χ^2[412, $N = 111$] = 599.00; *GFI* = .767). It appeared that most of the difference in model fit could be attributed to subtle shifts in the relative value of factor loadings among the Inductive Reasoning markers; specifically, after training, the Word Series test received a significantly lower loading, whereas the letter and number series test received higher loadings.

The *Spatial Orientation training* group had a somewhat lower model fit across occasions (χ^2[411, $N = 118$] = 700.84; *GFI* = .742). Again the reduction in fit was found to be a function of slight changes in factor loading for the markers of the trained ability, with increases in loadings for PMA Space and Alphanumeric Rotation and decrease in the loading for Object Rotation.

In both training groups the integrity of the trained factor with respect to the other (nontrained) factors remained undisturbed. Indeed, the stability of individual differences on the latent constructs remained extremely high, with the correlations of latent variables from pretest to posttest in excess of .93.

Conclusions. In this study we first of all demonstrated that our measurement model for assessing psychometric ability in older adults remained invariant across gender and across subsets of individuals who had remained stable or declined over time. We next demonstrated short-term stability of factor structure (that is, impermeability to practice effects) by demonstrating metric invariance of factor structure for a control group. We also demonstrated high stability of the estimates of the latent constructs across test occasions.

The hypothesis of factorial integrity across experimental interventions was next tested separately for the two training groups. In each case configural invariance was readily demonstrated. However, in each case some improvement of model fit could be obtained by allowing for shifts in the factor loadings for one of the markers of the trained ability. Nevertheless, the stability of the latent constructs also remained above .93 for the trained constructs. Perturbations in the projection of the observed variables on the latent ability factors induced by training were specific to the ability trained, were of small magnitude, and had no significant effect with respect to the relationship between the latent constructs and observed measures for the nontrained abilities. Hence, we provide support to the construct validity for both observed markers and estimates of latent variables in the training studies reported in chapter 7.

Factorial invariance within samples across time

Our most recent data collection provides us with complete repeated measurement data on the expanded battery for 984 study participants. These data can be used to conduct longitudinal factor analyses within samples across time. We consequently present initial data on the issue of longitudinal invariance over 7 years for the total sample as well as for six age/cohort groups (see also Schaie, Maitland, & Willis, 1994).

Preliminary results. We began with the factor model estimated for the entire 1984 data set (see Schaie, Dutta, & Willis, 1991). In addition to the battery used in the cross-sectional factor analyses shown in Table 8.8, we included a latent construct for Verbal Memory, which meant adding the variables of Word Fluency, Immediate Recall, and Delayed Recall to the battery.

In the longitudinal analysis we first fitted the model above to both test occasions for the entire sample, allowing salient factor loading and factor variance–covariance matrices to be freely estimated but constraining all values across time (1984 and 1991). In addition we allowed errors (theta epsilon) to be correlated across occasion for the same markers. Using this approach, we found the initial model to have an acceptable fit ($\chi^2[685, N = 984] = 1,902.58$; $GFI = .913$, $RMSR = 5.94$). However, when the factor variance–covariance matrices were allowed to be freely estimated for both occasions, a significant improvement in fit was observed ($\chi^2[664, N = 984] = 1,689.62$; $GFI = .922$, $RMSR = 4.28$). The difference in fit was significant at the .01 level of confidence ($\Delta\chi^2[21] = 212.96$). We next relaxed the constraints over time on the factor loading matrices ($\chi^2[646, N = 984] = 1,676.42$; *GFI* = .922, *RMSR* = 4.21). This time the improvement in fit was not statistically significant ($\Delta\chi^2[18] = 13.20$). We therefore accepted the second model, implying stability of factor regressions over time but allowing for shifts in the variance–covariance matrix (see Table 8.9).

We next tested the fit to the common model across the six subsamples that were observed from mean ages 32 to 39 ($n = 170$), 46 to 53 ($n = 128$), 53 to 60 ($n = 147$), 60 to 67 ($n = 183$), 67 to 74 ($n = 194$), and 76 to 83 ($n = 162$), respectively. The initial model tests complete metric invariance; that is, it constrains both factor loading and psi matrices across groups and time. The fit statistics for this model are $\chi^2[4,320, N = 984] = 6,051.06$. We next relaxed the constraints across groups ($\chi^2[4,230, N = 984] = 5,713.45$) and obtained a significant improvement in fit ($\Delta\chi^2[90] = 354.77$, $p < .001$). Having rejected invariance across age/cohort groups, confirming the earlier cross-sectional analyses, we next tested for invariance across time within groups by allowing factor variances and covariances to be freely estimated across the 7-year period ($\chi^2[4,098, N = 984] = 5,529.55$). This model fit significantly better ($\Delta\chi^2[132] = 184.06$, $p < .001$), and we concluded that the factor variances and covariances also change across time within groups. However, relaxing the constraints over time for the factor loadings ($\chi^2[3,996, N = 984] = 5,409.83$) does not result in any significant improvement in fit. The six-group analysis therefore further supports the finding of semimetric invariance of factor regressions on the observed variables.

When differences in chi squares for the three models are examined separately by age group, we find far greater within-group stability. Complete metric invariance across time can be accepted for all but the oldest group. Hence, we conclude that our longitudinal comparisons of both observable and latent mean scores reported in chapter 5 utilizing within-group 7-year changes represent valid comparisons.

The question now remains as to what abilities (and observable measures) are particularly susceptible to cohort differences. In Table 8.10 I present the factor loading coefficients by cohort group. There are minor shifts in magnitude for all observed variables, and

Table 8.9. *Measurement model for the longitudinal factor analysis*

Variable	Factor loadings						Unique variance	
	Inductive Reasoning	Spatial Orientation	Perceptual Speed	Numeric Ability	Verbal Ability	Verbal Memory	1984	1991
PMA Reasoning	0.919						0.180	0.133
ADEPT Letter Series	0.892						0.232	0.181
Word Series	0.884						0.244	0.195
Number Series	0.755						0.461	0.400
PMA Space		0.842					0.328	0.257
Object Rotation		0.871					0.258	0.227
Alphanumeric Rotation		0.836					0.337	0.269
Cube Comparison		0.645					0.607	0.560
Finding A's			0.536				0.758	0.670
Number Comparison			0.544	0.233			0.540	0.383
Identical Pictures			0.821				0.394	0.271
PMA Number				0.846			0.299	0.270
Addition				0.950			0.111	0.085
Subtraction & Multiplication				0.860			0.266	0.255
PMA Verbal Meaning			0.565		0.473		0.331	0.254

	Inductive Reasoning	Spatial Orientation	Perceptual Speed	Numeric Ability	Verbal Ability	Verbal Memory		
ETS Vocabulary					0.881		0.231	0.218
ETS Advanced Vocabulary					0.914		0.176	0.153
PMA Word Fluency			0.374		0.331	0.093	0.664	0.581
Immediate Recall						0.947	0.102	0.010
Delayed Recall						0.934	0.132	0.124

Factor intercorrelations[a]

Factor	Inductive Reasoning	Spatial Orientation	Perceptual Speed	Numeric Ability	Verbal Ability	Verbal Memory
Inductive Reasoning	0.963	0.760	0.858	0.517	0.448	0.641
Spatial Orientation	0.686	0.921	0.788	0.407	0.232	0.483
Perceptual Speed	0.829	0.687	0.978	0.556	0.258	0.679
Numeric Ability	0.425	0.265	0.423	0.940	0.264	0.318
Verbal Ability	0.413	0.173	0.177	0.229	0.960	0.397
Verbal Memory	0.536	0.329	0.559	0.185	0.329	0.799

Note: All factor loadings are significant at or beyond the 1% level of confidence. $\chi^2(644, N = 984) = 1,868.62$; $GFI = 0.922$; $RMSR = 4.28$.

[a] Factor intercorrelations for 1984 are below the diagonal and those for 1991 above the diagonal, and stability coefficents are the underlined values in the diagonal.

Table 8.10. *Factor loadings for the six cohort groups*

	Factor loadings					
Variable	Cohort 1	Cohort 2	Cohort 3	Cohort 4	Cohort 5	Cohort 6
Inductive Reasoning						
PMA Reasoning	0.895	0.890	0.893	0.882	0.856	0.838
ADEPT Letter Series	0.797	0.844	0.864	0.831	0.826	0.843
Word Series	0.864	0.864	0.802	0.794	0.814	0.786
Number Series	0.643	0.720	0.751	0.695	0.617	0.644
Spatial Orientation						
PMA Space	0.812	0.784	0.811	0.797	0.809	0.840
Object Rotation	0.878	0.825	0.816	0.848	0.837	0.799
Alphanumeric Rotation	0.827	0.767	0.776	0.744	0.755	0.629
Cube Comparison	0.305	0.527	0.415	0.450	0.527	0.633
Verbal Ability						
PMA Verbal Meaning	0.329	0.462	0.519	0.582	0.626	0.593
ETS Vocabulary	0.899	0.902	0.867	0.872	0.875	0.868
ETS Advanced Voc	0.929	0.908	0.910	0.901	0.907	0.923
Word Fluency	0.300	0.359	0.341	0.335	0.347	0.368
Numeric Ability						
PMA Number	0.832	0.857	0.871	0.838	0.804	0.839
Addition	0.944	0.951	0.952	0.946	0.955	0.942
Subtraction & Mult	0.854	0.862	0.858	0.818	0.863	0.858
Number Comparison	0.332	0.159	0.157	0.205	0.232	0.087
Perceptual Speed						
Identical Pictures	0.681	0.626	0.615	0.597	0.591	0.456
Number Comparison	0.438	0.575	0.556	0.457	0.522	0.582
Finding A's	0.554	0.498	0.543	0.490	0.639	0.536
Word Fluency	0.228	0.310	0.308	0.245	0.381	0.312
PMA Verbal Meaning	0.645	0.530	0.494	0.385	0.278	0.244
Verbal Memory						
Word Fluency	0.131	0.049	0.139	0.080	0.042	0.020
Immediate Recall	0.954	0.947	0.942	0.930	0.887	0.939
Delayed Recall	0.880	0.917	0.910	0.904	0.959	0.877

some are so substantial as to call into question the direct comparability of some markers across cohorts. These differences are particularly noteworthy for the Cube Comparison test, which virtually loses its role as an important marker of Spatial Orientation in old age. The PMA Verbal Meaning test also becomes a less efficient marker of Verbal Ability in old age, while becoming a stronger marker of Perceptual Speed. Finally, the secondary loading for Number Comparison on Numeric Ability, trivial in young adulthood, becomes significant at older ages.

Gender differences. The analyses above were repeated in order to determine whether our structural longitudinal findings held equally across gender. The accepted model of semimetric invariance across time fits reasonably well for both genders ($\chi^2[1,428] = 2,694.40$, $p < .001$; males: *GFI* = .875, *RMSR* = 7.62; females: *GFI* = .888, *RMSR* = 5.24). However, statistically significant improvement can be obtained when both regression weights and factor intercorrelations are freed across gender ($\chi^2[1,366] = 2,414.11$, $p < .001$; males: *GFI* = .890, *RMSR* = 5.27; females: *GFI* = .896, *RMSR* = 3.70).

The significant gender differences in regression coefficients affect two of the markers of Spatial Orientation and one marker each for Inductive Reasoning, Numeric Ability, and Perceptual Speed. Regression coefficients are significantly lower for women on the Number Series (N), PMA Space (S), and Cube Comparison tests (S). They are higher for women on Number Comparison (N) and on the Finding A's test (P). Two findings emerged at the factor level: First, women's factor structure is slightly less differentiated, with significantly higher factor intercorrelations between Verbal and Numeric ability, Spatial and Numeric ability, and Verbal Ability and Verbal Memory. Second, factor stability coefficients are significantly lower for women for the latent constructs of Spatial Orientation and Verbal Memory.

Finally, we considered the question of cohort specificity of gender differences in structure; that is, that such differences could be localized at particular developmental stages. Multiple-group analyses by gender were conducted for each of the six cohort groupings. Significant gender differences could be rejected for the factor loading patterns for the three youngest groups and the second-oldest group (ages 32, 46, 53, and 67 at first measurement point). However, for both Cohorts 1 and 3 (ages 60 and 76, respectively, at Time 1), it was necessary to free both factor loadings and factor intercorrelations across gender. Factor intercorrelations had to be freed also across gender for Cohort 2 (age 67 at Time 1).

Implications for the differentiation–dedifferentiation hypothesis. An interesting question long debated in the developmental psychology literature (see Reinert, 1970; Werner, 1948) is whether differentia-

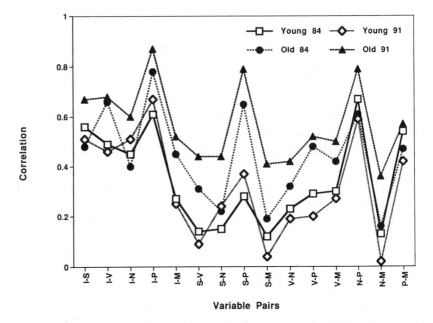

Figure 8.1. Correlations among the latent ability constructs across time for the youngest and oldest cohorts. I = Inductive Reasoning, S = Spatial Orientation, V = Verbal Ability, N = Numeric Ability, P = Perceptual Speed, M = Verbal Memory.

tion of ability structure occurs in childhood and adolescence and is followed by dedifferentiation of that structure in old age. Our findings on changes in covariance structures from young adulthood to old age lend support to the differentiation–dedifferentiation theory. I show magnitudes of intercorrelations for the 1984 and 1991 test occasions for a young adult cohort at ages 29 and 36 and an old adult cohort at ages 76 and 84, respectively. Note that factor intercorrelations decrease slightly for 11 out of 15 correlations for the young cohort but increase for all correlations for the old cohort.

Conclusions. As we expected from the earlier cross-sectional analyses, we can accept invariance of factor patterns but not of the regression coefficients across age/cohort groups or across gender. Within groups, we obtain improvement in model fit if we allow the factor variances and covariances to vary over time, but we can accept the stability of the regression weights across time in the individual groups as well. These findings strongly suggest greater stability of individual differences within cohorts than across cohorts or gender, and they provide further arguments for the superiority of longitudinal data.

Chapter summary

This chapter describes some of the methodological studies that were conducted by means of secondary analyses of the core data archives or through collateral data collections. The first study examines the consequences of shifting from a sampling-without-replacement paradigm to one that involved sampling with replacement. I conclude that no substantial differences in findings result; hence, the first three data collections using the sampling-without-replacement approach are directly comparable to later studies using the sampling-with-replacement paradigm. The second study investigated the "aging" of tests by comparing the 1948 and 1962 PMA tests. It concluded that there was advantage in retaining the original measures. The third study considered the question of shifts in subject self-selection when changing from a nonpaid to a paid volunteer sample. No selection effects related to subject fees were observed.

A set of secondary analyses is described that deals with the topic of experimental mortality (subject attrition) and the consequent adjustments needed for our substantive findings. Such adjustments primarily affect level of performance but not the rate of cognitive aging. Analyses of the effect of repeated measurement in under-stating cognitive decline showed only slight effects, but methods are presented for adjusting for the observed practice effects.

Finally, I consider the issue of structural invariance of the psychometric abilities across cohorts, age, and time. Findings are presented from analyses using restricted (confirmatory) factor analysis in order to determine the degree of invariance of the regression of the observed variables on the latent constructs of interest in this study. Cross-sectional factor analyses resulted in a demonstration of configural (pattern) invariance but not of complete metric invariance. These findings imply that factor regressions for young adults and the very old may require differential weighting in age-comparative studies. Another study demonstrated factorial invariance across a cognitive training intervention, confirming that cognitive training results in quantitative change in performance without qualitative shifts in factor structure. And last I report preliminary data on longitudinal factor analyses that suggest significant shifts in the variance–covariance matrices but stability of regression coefficients linking the observed variables and latent constructs over a 7-year period. This study also examines gender equivalence in structure, which is confirmed through middle adulthood; but the findings also show that regressions of the latent constructs on the observed variables differ by gender in old age.

9

The relationship between cognitive styles and intellectual functioning

The base study that led to the SLS had as its primary objective the test of the hypothesis that differential age changes in abilities might be related to initial status on the dimensions of flexibility–rigidity (see chapter 1). Although we had to reject the viability of this proposition on the basis of the initial crosssectional data, we have since returned to the question, utilizing the longitudinal data base for a more appropriate set of inquiries than was possible with the original 1956 data (see Schaie, 1958c). Before returning to a further examination of this issue, we first need to examine the data on whether our ability measures and the flexibility–rigidity factors defined by the TBR do indeed represent independent constructs. After confirming this important assumption, we turn to the effect of flexible behavior at earlier ages in predicting maintenance of cognitive functioning in old age.

Does flexibility–rigidity represent an independent domain?

The original multiple group factor analyses that led to the development of the Test of Behavioral Rigidity (TBR; Schaie, 1955; see also chapter 4) identified the independence of three latent constructs to account for the individual differences variance in the flexibility–rigidity measures. These measures were then correlated with the five PMAs in our core battery, and, given the moderate positive correlations between the flexibility–rigidity factor scores and the cognitive measures, we assumed that their independence had been empirically demonstrated (Schaie, 1958c). Given the state of the art at the time of these studies, this assumption seemed reasonable. However, modern research practice requires more formal tests. The results of such formal tests were reported by Schaie, Dutta, and Willis (1991; see also Dutta, 1992) and are summarized here.

Confirmation of the TBR factor structure

The TBR factor structure was reexamined, using the data on 1,628 subjects (743 men and 885 women) who were examined in the fifth (1984) SLS cycle. The initial model tested was based on the original factor analyses (Schaie, 1955) and was examined using the LISREL procedure (for a description of the TBR subtests, see section on measurement variables in chapter 3). Seven measures were modeled to map on three cognitive style factors: Psychomotor Speed, Motor–Cognitive Flexibility, and Attitudinal Flexibility. Several of the TBR measures represent scores derived from the same subtests; hence, their errors would be expected to correlate. For example, the Capitals test yields a speed score (Cap-NR) and a flexibility score (Cap-R). Similarly, two flexibility scores are derived from the Opposites test, using different scoring approaches. The four elements in the error matrix corresponding to the correlation among the measures originating from the same source data were freed. The model was first tested on a random half of the total sample and then confirmed on the second random half as well as on the total sample. This model was accepted as having an excellent fit ($\chi^2[7, N = 1,628] = 14.47$, $p < .04$; $GFI = .997$, $RMSR = 1.64$). The measurement model for the flexibility–rigidity domain can be found in Figure 9.1.

Confirmation of the cognitive factor structure

In a similar manner, we also confirmed the factor structure for our expanded battery on the same sample used for the TBR analysis. Here the initial model was based on prior analyses but with the addition of a Memory factor (see Schaie, Willis, Hertzog, & Schulenberg, 1987; Schaie, Willis, Jay, & Chipuer, 1989; see also chapter 8). The 20 cognitive measures were modeled as indicators of six oblique factors: Inductive Reasoning, Spatial Orientation, Verbal Ability, Numeric Ability, Perceptual Speed, and Verbal

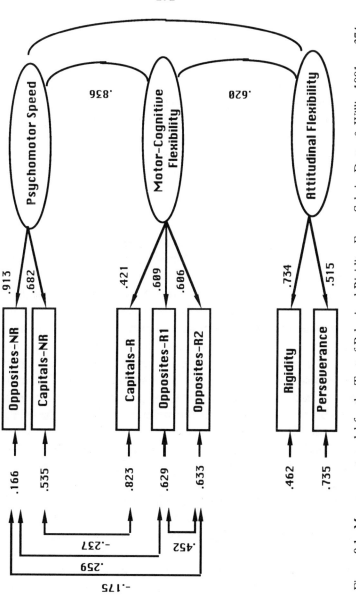

Figure 9.1. Measurement model for the Test of Behavioral Rigidity. From Schaie, Dutta, & Willis, 1991, p. 374.

Memory. The original model had good overall fit, but for this particular sample showed stress in the specification of the word fluency measure. In addition to its placement on the Memory factor, this measure was therefore allowed to load as well on the Perceptual Speed and Verbal Ability factors. The model was again tested on a random half of the sample, confirmed on the second half, and then reestimated on the total sample (χ^2[151, $N = 1,628$] $= 1,144.26$, $p < .001$; $GFI = .934$, $RMSR = 4.09$). The accepted model was characterized by high and statistically significant loadings of all variables on their associated primary ability factors, as well as high communalities (see Figure 9.2 for the resulting measurement model).

Confirmation of distinct domains

In order to test the hypothesis of distinct cognitive and cognitive style domains, we analyzed the combined covariance matrix of the 27 cognitive and flexibility–rigidity measures. An exploratory factor analysis of this matrix suggested that from 8 to 10 factors would be required to explain the total reliable variance. Hence, our first model hypothesized the 9 factors resulting from the separate domain analyses. This model essentially specifies maintenance of the original factor structures when the two batteries are combined. We again estimated this model on a random half, with subsequent confirmation on the second half. The initial estimate suggested a good fit, with comparable parameter estimates to the separate analyses. The initial indices of model fit were χ^2(280, $N = 814$) $= 979.33$, $p < .001$; $GFI = .918$, $RMSR = 5.10$, for Sample 1, and χ^2(280, $N = 814$) $= 1,095.73$, $p < .001$; $GFI = .909$, $RMSR = 5.66$ for Sample 2.

Cross-battery interfactor correlations were then examined, and three high correlations were identified. The Psychomotor Speed and Motor–Cognitive Flexibility factors correlated highly with Inductive Reasoning, and Perceptual Speed correlated highly with Psychomotor Speed. As our exploratory analyses had suggested the plausibility of an eight-factor solution, and since the highest interfactor correlations were found between the two speed factors, we next examined a model combining the latter into a second factor. However, this model resulted in a significantly worse fit ($\Delta\chi^2$[8, $N = 814$] $= 137.29$, $p < .01$ in Sample 1, and $\Delta\chi^2$[8, $N = 814$] $=$

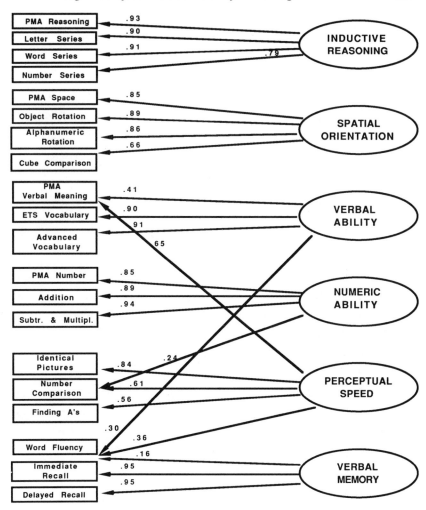

Figure 9.2. Measurement model for the expanded cognitive ability battery. From Schaie, Dutta, & Willis, 1991, p. 377.

121.41, $p < .01$ in Sample 2) and was therefore rejected. The accepted total model has a good fit ($\chi^2[280, N = 814] = 1,116.62$, $p < .001$; *GFI* = .924, *RMSR* = 5.08); it is shown in Table 9.1.

As a result of these studies, we conclude that rigidity–flexibility does indeed represent a domain of cognitive styles that can be

Table 9.1. *Accepted solution for cognitive styles and cognitive abilities combined*

Variable	Inductive Reasoning	Spatial Orientation	Verbal Ability	Numeric Ability	Perceptual Speed	Verbal Memory	Psychomotor Speed	Motor– Cognitive Flexibility	Attitudinal Flexibility	Unique variance
Factor loadings										
PMA Reasoning	0.933									0.130
Letter Series	0.900									0.190
Word Series	0.914									0.164
Number Series	0.791									0.375
PMA Space		0.848								0.281
Object Rotation		0.893								0.202
Alphanumeric Rotation		0.860								0.261
Cube Comparison		0.663								0.560
PMA Verbal Meaning			0.413							0.244
ETS Vocabulary			0.903							0.185
ETS Advanced Vocabulary			0.907							0.177
PMA Number				0.853						0.273
Addition				0.944						0.109
Subtraction & Multiplication				0.794						0.200

	Spatial Orientation	Verbal Ability	Numeric Ability	Perceptual Speed	Verbal Memory	Psychomotor Speed	Motor–Cognitive Flexibility	Attitudinal Flexibility
Identical Pictures				0.291				
Number Comparison				0.405				
Finding A's			0.251	0.707				
Word Fluency	0.305	0.400		0.553	0.131	0.852		
Immediate Recall				0.097	0.950	0.601		
Delayed Recall				0.105	0.946	0.542		
Opposites		0.872		0.239				
Capitals		0.721		0.481				
Capitals-R							0.391	0.847
Opposites-R1							0.626	0.608
Opposites-R2							0.634	0.598
R Scale							0.761	0.421
P Scale							0.496	0.754

Factor intercorrelations

	Spatial Orientation	Verbal Ability	Numeric Ability	Perceptual Speed	Verbal Memory	Psychomotor Speed	Motor–Cognitive Flexibility	Attitudinal Flexibility
Spatial Orientation	0.769							
Verbal Ability	0.470	0.253						
Numeric Ability	0.560	0.417	0.368					
Perceptual Speed	0.875	0.774	0.313	0.563				
Verbal Memory	0.645	0.472	0.370	0.355	0.672			
Psychomotor Speed	0.863	0.665	0.557	0.667	0.913	0.663		
Motor–Cognitive Flexibility	0.906	0.811	0.507	0.499	0.866	0.637	0.840	
Attitudinal Flexibility	0.546	0.418	0.423	0.255	0.531	0.454	0.553	0.597

distinguished from the cognitive abilities domain. The question of the reciprocal influence of these two domains first raised at the inception of the SLS (Schaie, 1958c) therefore continues to be of interest and is examined below.

Does rigidity–flexibility affect the maintenance of intellectual abilities into old age?

To answer this question, we first consider the concurrent relationship between rigidity–flexibility and core ability measures. We then examine the cross-lagged correlations between the two domains in order to generate hypotheses about the possible causal path between the domains. These relationships were examined earlier for the first four study cycles (Schaie, 1983a, 1984b). Data presented here include all six cycles.

Concurrent relationships

To obtain the largest possible sample sizes, we aggregated all subjects at first test for the measures in the core battery. Table 9.2 lists correlations for all available ages. It should be noted that there are moderate to substantial correlations between Psychomotor Speed and all ability measures. Motor–Cognitive Flexibility correlates moderately with all ability measures, with the highest relationship found with Verbal Meaning and Reasoning. Somewhat lower correlations, mostly during midlife, were found between Attitudinal Flexibility and Verbal Meaning, Reasoning, and Word Fluency. Of considerable interest is the finding that, for all three correlates, values of the concurrent correlations typically increase from young adulthood to early old age but decline somewhat thereafter. These findings suggest that the reciprocal relationship is particularly salient in midlife.

Predictors of future ability level

From the longitudinal data on the rigidity–flexibility and cognitive ability measures, it is possible to compute cross-lagged correlations that can be used in a cautious test of the time-dependent causal

Table 9.2. *Concurrent correlations between the cognitive style and intellectual ability measures at first test*

Mean age	n	Verbal Meaning	Space	Reasoning	Number	Word Fluency
Motor–Cognitive Flexibility						
25	446	0.22**	0.30**	0.30**	0.17**	0.16**
32	446	0.32**	0.28**	0.39**	0.22**	0.15**
39	527	0.39**	0.30**	0.45**	0.17**	0.21**
46	524	0.53**	0.36**	0.51**	0.28**	0.34**
53	523	0.48**	0.34**	0.53**	0.37**	0.25**
60	499	0.47**	0.31**	0.48**	0.36**	0.33**
67	545	0.49**	0.33**	0.52**	0.31**	0.34**
74	394	0.42**	0.26**	0.42**	0.32**	0.35**
81	222	0.34**	0.26**	0.34**	0.29**	0.10
Attitudinal Flexibility						
25	430	0.25**	0.09	0.20**	0.07	0.26**
32	441	0.26**	0.09	0.21**	0.06	0.10
39	520	0.28**	0.12*	0.21**	0.01	0.11*
46	520	0.40**	0.05	0.29**	0.06	0.18**
53	521	0.33**	0.22**	0.31**	0.14*	0.25**
60	494	0.31**	0.15**	0.31**	0.15*	0.25**
67	545	0.35**	0.17**	0.36**	0.19**	0.22**
74	390	0.31**	0.14*	0.32**	0.23**	0.22**
81	220	0.22**	0.11	0.10	0.10	0.09
Psychomotor Speed						
25	445	0.57**	0.20**	0.56**	0.36**	0.51**
32	446	0.48**	0.16**	0.49**	0.19**	0.36**
39	527	0.53**	0.13*	0.55**	0.22**	0.41**
46	524	0.62**	0.21**	0.58**	0.28**	0.40**
53	523	0.66**	0.25**	0.64**	0.37**	0.50**
60	499	0.65**	0.23**	0.58**	0.44**	0.46**
67	546	0.68**	0.28**	0.65**	0.48**	0.53**
74	391	0.67**	0.23**	0.59**	0.45**	0.51**
81	222	0.59**	0.18*	0.46**	0.48**	0.52**

*$p < 0.01$; **$p < 0.001$.

relationships between the two domains. For this purpose we use the sample first tested in 1956, for which cross-lags are available over 7, 14, 21, 28, and 35 years. The average age of the sample was 43 at the initial test, and their ages at the endpoint of each comparison were 53, 60, 67, 74, and 81, respectively ($N = 303$, 162, 120, 96, and 68). Again, the measures used are the five primary mental abilities of the core battery and the three cognitive style factor scores. For each of the five time intervals, cross-lags were corrected for changes in reliability using Kenny's (1975, 1979) method, and significant differences between cross-lags were computed by means of the Pearson–Filon test. Table 9.3 shows the corrected cross-lagged correlations for each of the five time periods.

In this sample we find a number of predictive relationships that differ somewhat, depending on the length of time between the measurement of the predictor and criterion variables. For the 7-year interval, the causal path is from both Motor–Cognitive and Attitudinal flexibility to the T_2 measure of Verbal Meaning. However, there is also a causal path from Reasoning at T_1 to Psychomotor Speed at T_2. These paths are not found for the 14-year interval. Instead all cognitive style variables have causal paths to the T_3 measure of the Number ability. Over the 21-year interval, the causal path from Psychomotor Speed to Number is also shown. In addition, all three cognitive style variables now have a significant causal path to Word Fluency at T_4. None of these relationships appear over 28 years, from T_1 to T_5. Here the only significant path is from Verbal Meaning at T_1 to Psychomotor Speed at T_5. Finally, across the 35-year interval we find causal paths from Motor-Cognitive Flexibility to Number and Word Fluency, and from Attitudinal Flexibility to Verbal Meaning and Word Fluency. In addition there are significant paths from Reasoning to Motor–Cognitive Flexibility and from Space to Psychomotor Speed.

One of the difficulties in interpreting these analyses is the successive attrition of the long-term sample, so that sample sizes may be too small to maintain stable cross-lags. However, most of the causal paths clearly lead from the cognitive style measures to the intellectual abilities.

Relationships between the latent ability constructs and the cognitive style measures

Of interest also is a repetition of these analyses for the relationship of the cognitive styles and the latent cognitive ability measures. The latter data are available only for the 1984 and 1991 cycles.

Table 9.3. *Cross-lagged correlations between the cognitive style and intellectual ability variables after correction for changes in reliability*

	Motor–Cognitive Flexibility	Attitudinal Flexibility	Psychomotor Speed
	Over 7 years (1956–1963), $N = 303$		
	1956	1956	1956
Verbal Meaning 1963	0.48*	0.47*	0.57
Space 1963	0.41	0.27	0.26
Reasoning 1963	0.55	0.32	0.57
Number 1963	0.31	0.19	0.44
Word Fluency 1963	0.38	0.33	0.48
	1963	1963	1963
Verbal Meaning 1956	0.38	0.38	0.66
Space 1956	0.36	0.22	0.34
Reasoning 1956	0.45	0.42	0.63*
Number 1956	0.27	0.15	0.43
Word Fluency 1956	0.27	0.31	0.53
	Over 14 years (1956–1970), $N = 162$		
	1956	1956	1956
Verbal Meaning 1970	0.40	0.31	0.52
Space 1970	0.38	0.19	0.22
Reasoning 1970	0.42	0.26	0.53
Number 1970	0.33*	0.23*	0.59*
Word Fluency 1970	0.27	0.30	0.45
	1970	1970	1970
Verbal Meaning 1956	0.47	0.38	0.64
Space 1956	0.34	0.15	0.28
Reasoning 1956	0.49	0.40	0.61
Number 1956	0.18	0.12	0.35
Word Fluency 1956	0.33	0.28	0.42
	Over 21 years (1956–1977), $N = 120$		
	1956	1956	1956
Verbal Meaning 1977	0.35	0.31	0.56
Space 1977	0.35	0.20	0.24
Reasoning 1977	0.38	0.33	0.47
Number 1977	0.26	0.16	0.58*
Word Fluency 1977	0.32*	0.41*	0.53*

Table 9.3. *continued*

	Motor–Cognitive Flexibility	Attitudinal Flexibility	Psychomotor Speed
	1977	1977	1977
Verbal Meaning 1956	0.32	0.38	0.69
Space 1956	0.26	0.22	0.28
Reasoning 1956	0.44	0.35	0.59
Number 1956	0.23	0.13	0.40
Word Fluency 1956	0.13	0.24	0.40
	Over 28 years (1956–1984), $N = 96$		
	1956	1956	1956
Verbal Meaning 1984	0.32	0.42	0.40
Space 1984	0.39	0.32	0.19
Reasoning 1984	0.34	0.33	0.32
Number 1984	0.29	0.14	0.36
Word Fluency 1984	0.18	0.34	0.36
	1984	1984	1984
Verbal Meaning 1956	0.32	0.38	0.55*
Space 1956	0.45	0.16	0.34
Reasoning 1956	0.42	0.36	0.53
Number 1956	0.22	0.15	0.49
Word Fluency 1956	0.18	0.29	0.38
	Over 35 years (1956–1991), $N = 68$		
	1956	1956	1956
Verbal Meaning 1991	0.34	0.50*	0.42
Space 1991	0.43	0.15	0.04
Reasoning 1991	0.31	0.30	0.32
Number 1991	0.30*	0.14	0.46
Word Fluency 1991	0.12*	0.42*	0.23
	1991	1991	1991
Verbal Meaning 1956	0.27	0.30	0.46
Space 1956	0.42	0.23	0.28*
Reasoning 1956	0.54*	0.42	0.45
Number 1956	0.09	0.06	0.27
Word Fluency 1956	−0.12	0.15	0.27

Note: Cross-lags followed by asterisks are significantly greater than their falsifications.
*$p < 0.05$.

Table 9.4. *Concurrent correlations between the cognitive style and intellectual ability latent construct measures*

Mean age	n	Inductive Reasoning	Spatial Orientation	Perceptual Speed	Numeric Ability	Verbal Ability	Verbal Memory
Motor–Cognitive Flexibility							
25	83	0.26*	0.19	0.05	0.05	0.14	0.27*
32	126	0.28**	0.24*	−0.14	0.17	0.10	0.11
39	212	0.29**	0.32**	0.05	0.21*	0.08	0.04
46	241	0.51**	0.32**	0.17*	0.30**	0.38**	0.23**
53	234	0.47**	0.30**	0.23**	0.19*	0.35**	0.20*
60	263	0.43**	0.28**	0.35**	0.23**	0.35**	0.22**
67	277	0.50**	0.34**	0.34**	0.23**	0.37**	0.18*
74	170	0.44**	0.29**	0.33**	0.22*	0.37**	0.30**
81	93	0.29**	0.05	0.04	0.12	0.38**	0.17
Attitudinal Flexibility							
25	83	0.21	0.08	0.10	0.10	0.06	0.14
32	124	0.14	−0.07	0.09	0.03	0.22*	0.14
39	213	0.14	0.03	0.16	−0.01	0.19*	0.06
46	241	0.16*	0.01	0.05	0.08	0.25**	0.18*
53	234	0.24**	0.14	0.16*	0.11	0.23**	0.14
60	260	0.08	0.09	0.08	0.05	0.26**	0.29**
67	275	0.28**	0.19*	0.22**	0.09	0.31**	0.22**
74	170	0.33**	0.08	0.16	0.13	0.30**	0.25*
81	92	0.10	0.06	0.18	0.05	0.38**	0.19
Psychomotor Speed							
25	82	0.45**	0.31*	0.39**	0.36**	0.34*	0.50**
32	126	0.43**	0.15	0.28**	0.30**	0.31**	0.29**
39	212	0.31**	0.09	0.20*	0.31**	0.34**	0.31**
46	241	0.44**	0.13	0.24**	0.43**	0.43**	0.37**
53	234	0.58**	0.26**	0.47**	0.38**	0.45**	0.39**
60	263	0.52**	0.22**	0.47**	0.45**	0.47**	0.31**
67	276	0.65**	0.43**	0.62**	0.50**	0.50**	0.41**
74	170	0.60**	0.27**	0.60**	0.43**	0.58**	0.52**
81	93	0.45**	0.44**	0.56**	0.62**	0.43**	0.42**

*$p < 0.01$; **$p < 0.001$.

Concurrent relationships

The relevant correlations are provided in Table 9.4. For Motor–Cognitive Flexibility the strongest concurrent relationships are shown with Inductive Reasoning. Concurrent correlations for the

Table 9.5. *Cross-lagged correlations between the cognitive style and intellectual ability latent factor scores after correction for changes in reliability*

	Motor–Cognitive Flexibility	Attitudinal Flexibility	Psychomotor Speed
	1984	1984	1984
Inductive Reasoning 1991	0.58	0.35	0.62
Spatial Orientation 1991	0.37	0.22	0.37
Perceptual Speed 1991	0.61	0.30	0.62
Numeric Ability 1991	0.49*	0.19*	0.49*
Verbal Ability 1991	0.48*	0.28*	0.48*
Verbal Memory 1991	0.49	0.33	0.49
	1991	1991	1991
Inductive Reasoning 1984	0.63	0.32	0.64
Spatial Orientation 1984	0.52*	0.31	0.52*
Perceptual Speed 1984	0.63	0.28	0.63
Numeric Ability 1984	0.42	0.09	0.42
Verbal Ability 1984	0.36	0.21	0.36
Verbal Memory 1984	0.53	0.30	0.53

*$p < 0.05$.

factor scores follow the age pattern described above. They are quite weak in young adulthood, increase until early old age, and are lowered again for the oldest group.

Predictors of future ability level

Seven-year cross-lags are available for a set of 1,011 subjects for whom latent ability construct scores are available in both 1984 and 1991. These cross-lags are shown in Table 9.5. Crosslag differences significant at or beyond the 1% level of confidence occur for all three cognitive style measures from T_1 to the latent construct measures of Verbal and Numeric ability in 1991. However, we also found significantly larger cross-lags from the Spatial Orientation factor score at T_1 to Motor–Cognitive Flexibility and Psychomotor Speed in 1991.

The causal analyses described above need to be taken with caution even though we correct for differences in stability and syncronicity coefficients. In future work we intend to examine the directionality issues in further analyses modeling the relationships between cognitive style and cognitive ability variables within the LISREL paradigm.

Chapter summary

In this chapter we first present evidence on the distinctiveness of the cognitive styles of Motor–Cognitive Flexibility, Attitudinal Flexibility, and Psychomotor Speed from the domain of psychometric intelligence as measured in the SLS. Results of separate and joint factor analyses for the three cognitive style and six psychometric ability constructs leads us to conclude that these domains are indeed separate. We next consider the concurrent and predictive relationships for the two domains, utilizing the cognitive style and core battery PMA variables over 7, 14, 21, 28, and 35 years. We conclude that the concurrent relationships increase into young old age and then decline again. We also examine similar data for the latent ability constructs over a 7-year period. The predictive direction was identified to lead from the cognitive style measures to the ability measures of Verbal Meaning, Number, and Word Fluency in the core battery, and to the latent construct measures of Verbal and Numeric ability. However, we found occasional paths in the core battery from Verbal Meaning to Psychomotor Speed and from Reasoning to Motor–Cognitive Flexibility. Likewise a significant causal path was shown for the latent construct of Spatial Orientation to both Motor–Cognitive Flexibility and Psychomotor Speed.

10

Health and maintenance of intellectual functioning

When one is searching for the antecedents of individual differences in the maintenance or decline of intellectual functioning, one of the first domains that seems worthy of inquiry is the impact of health on cognition. As will be seen, however, it does not necessarily follow that the relationship between health and intellectual functioning is a unidirectional one. Recent reviews of the literature (see Elias, Elias, & Elias, 1990; Siegler, 1988) suggest that the relationship may, indeed, be a reciprocal one: a healthy body facilitating intellectual competence, and competent behavior facilitating the maintenance of health. In this chapter we will consider both. I will first report our efforts to assess health histories in a manner suitable for relating them to behavioral development. Second, I will consider the diseases that seem to affect the maintenance of cognitive functions, and finally I will return to the role of intellectual functioning as a predictor of physical health.

The analysis of health histories

One of the interesting aspects of our panel of study participants is the fact that all panel members, during their time of participation in our study, received all of their health care (with the rare exception of emergency procedures while away from home) from the HMO that forms the base of our sampling frame. Virtually complete records are therefore available on the frequency and kinds of illnesses requiring medical care, as well as anecdotal records of treatment history. Subsequent to the third study cycle, we were finally able to obtain the necessary resources to take advantage of the existence of these records for our study participants (Schaie, 1973a). We have worked intensively with the medical and research staff of the HMO to develop procedures designed to quantify the health records of our panel in such a way that it is possible to index them both in terms of the age of the individual and the points in time when incidents of ill health occurred.

We soon discovered that though most physicians generate voluminous medical histories, only a few have any experience or interest in retrieving data from such histories, particularly in a form that lends itself to research. At the time we became interested in this problem, a number of formal ways existed to code medical data. We elected to use the American version of the international system sponsored by the World Health Organization (U.S. Public Health Service, 1968). Unfortunately, as others interested in abstracting from medical records (e.g., Hurtado & Greenlick, 1971) have found, it is quite difficult to relate descriptive disease categories to individual outcome parameters. To do so requires the specialized services of medical record librarians, who must detect and decipher the information required for such coding.

Incidents and episodes

If one is interested in relating medical histories to outcomes of a nonmedical nature, moreover, one must be concerned also with the issue of incidents and episodes of medical care, in addition to simply recording diagnostic entries. Such an approach was first used by Solon and his associates (Solon, Feeney, Jones, Rigg, & Sheps, 1967; Solon et al., 1969). For our purposes we decided to code data for our panel members with respect to incidents of a given disease condition, as well as to apply the episode or "spell of illness" approach.

Severity ratings

If we are concerned with the impact of disease on behavior, we must deal with the relative significance of a particular diagnostic condition as it affects the life of the person experiencing that condition. That is, we would like to assign a "severity" weight to particular diagnostic entities. A special study was therefore conducted to obtain such weights (Parham, Gribbin, Hertzog, & Schaie, 1975).

In this study the health records for 150 participants were coded for a 14-year period. Although the International Classification of Diseases (ICDA; U.S. Public Health Service, 1968) contains over 8,000 disease classifications, only about 820 were actually encountered in our sample. By collapsing and overlapping categories, we further reduced this number to 448 of the most frequently occurring classifications. These were then Q-sorted by twelve physicians on an 11-point severity scale ranging from *benign* to *extremely severe*. The physicians were asked to rate severity according to the long-range impact of the particular disease on the general health and well-being of the patient. The 448 categories were divided into four decks of 112 cards each, upon which the disease name and a brief description were typed. Each physician Q-sorted two of these decks; a total of four physicians sorted each deck. Interrater reliabilities for the disease severity ratings ranged from .82 to .90. Average weights were then computed, and these severity weights were used in some of the analyses described below.

Age and health histories

Before we can begin to discuss our data, I first must consider how a disease model can be related to the study of cognitive aging. A model will then be explicated that might explain the complex relationship between health breakdown and decline in cognitive functioning.

How meaningful is the disease model?

I begin by raising the question: Ought there to be a direct relationship between raw indices of disease diagnoses (or incidence of medical care) and behavioral outcomes (e.g., Wilkie & Eisdorfer, 1973)? I follow here the work of Aaron Antonovsky and his associates, who have addressed this question in some detail. These investigators hold that the social or behavioral scientist dealing with the consequences of physical illness should not be concerned with the particular physiological dimensions involved in a disease but should rather address the behavioral and social consequences embedded in the concept of "breakdown."

More specifically, Antonovsky (1972) argues that there are basically four dimensions of breakdown that deserve attention. First, a disease may or may not be directly painful to the individual; second, it may or may not handicap individuals in the exercise of their faculties or performance of social roles; third, it can be characterized along the dimension of acuteness – chronicity with respect to its possible threat to life; and fourth, it is or is not recognized by society's medical institutions as requiring care under the direction of such institutions.

A very similar system of classification can be suggested with respect to the impact a particular disease may have on cognitive functions, particularly if we were to reclassify medical histories in terms of the degree of breakdown presented therein rather than in terms of the specific disease represented by the history.

Although we must pursue the impact of specific diseases on behavior, we should also be conscious of the possibility that it may not be fruitful to insist on a direct connection between specific diseases and behavior. It would therefore be better to organize information on illness and the utilization of medical care in terms of more psychologically meaningful organizing principles, such as the concept of breakdown. Such an approach would reduce the conceptual dilemma of having to distinguish between the contribution of the actual disease process and the manner in which the individual responds to the disease condition. It is often the latter that may be the more direct mediator of the behavioral consequences, at least at the macro level most easily accessible to observation and analysis.

Health breakdown and cognitive functioning

Given the methods of coding described earlier in this chapter, we can first of all study the impact of specific diseases in relation to cognitive change. But we can also chart the cumulative impact of health trauma in at least two ways. First we can assign a cumulative index of physical health breakdown that is simply the summation of all incidents observed as weighted by their impact on the life of each study participant. Second, we can also graph the average level of breakdown at each measurement point for which behavioral data are available and relate the slope of physical health states to the slope of observed cognitive change.

Throughout these analyses, it will be just as necessary as it was with the cognitive data to be concerned with the effects of cohort differences in the utilization of medical care, as well as with the tendency of previous episodes of ill health to elicit different patterns of subsequent ill health than would be true if the occurrence of health breakdown were the first. Fortunately, our system of data acquisition permits a reasonable modicum of controls.

Diseases that affect maintenance of cognitive functioning

The first two analyses bearing on this question involved relatively small data sets. The first focused on the relation of cardiovascular disease and maintenance of intellectual functioning; the second attempted to include a somewhat broader spectrum of diseases.

Cardiovascular disease and intelligence

In our first effort to chart the relationship between cardiovascular disease (CVD) and maintenance of cognitive functioning systematically (Hertzog, Schaie, & Gribbin, 1978), we studied the health records of 156 subjects who were tested in 1956 and 1963, of whom 86 also participated in the 1970 testing. For this study, subjects were classified as having the diagnoses of hypertension, atherosclerosis (constriction of arterial pathways by fatty deposits), hypertension and atherosclerosis, cerebrovascular disease, miscellaneous CVD, and benign CVD, or as having no evidence of CVD. After exclusion of subjects who had only hypertension and those with benign CVD, the remaining CVD subjects were then compared with those without CVD. It was first noted that there was an excess of persons with CVD among the dropouts at the 1970 test occasions, thus making CVD a major factor in experimental mortality (see chapter 8). The CVD dichotomy was then related by means of ANOVAs to the maintenance of intellectual performance over time. Significant main effects favoring the subjects without cardiovascular disease were found for Verbal Meaning, Inductive Reasoning, Number, and the composite indices, as well as Motor–Cognitive Flexibility. However, an increase in the additional risk over time was found only for Psychomotor Speed. Breaking down CVD into subgroups, greater risk for those affected over time occurred for those with atherosclerosis and cerebrovascular disease for the Space and Number tests as well as for the composite IQ and the Psychomotor Speed measure. However, those with hypertension without other manifestations of CVD actually improved over time.

Application of structural equations methods to the study of relationships between disease and cognition

The next set of analyses of the health data was conducted in a doctoral dissertation by Stone (1980). She examined a sample of 253 subjects for whom psychological and health data were available at three time points: 1963, 1970, and 1977. Disease codes were aggregated into 16 systemic categories, of which 11 were sufficiently well represented to warrant investigation. These were (1) diseases of the blood and blood-forming organs; (2) diseases of the circulatory system; (3) endocrine, nutritional, and metabolic disorders; (4) diseases of the digestive system; (5) diseases of the genitourinary system; (6) infectious diseases; (7) diseases of the musculoskeletal system and of connective tissues; (8) diseases of the skin and subcutaneous tissues; (9) neoplasms; (10) diseases of the nervous system; and (11) diseases of the respiratory system.

Structural models were examined to link illness variables to PMA performance. Since there was little covariation among disease entities, separate structural models were tested for those categories that were well represented for all three time periods. Three of the concatenated disease categories listed above appeared to be significant predictors of time-related change in intellectual functioning – circulatory disorders, neoplasms, and musculoskeletal disorders. However, when the sample was divided by age into two halves (35 to 58 and 59 to 87 at T_3), the relationship held for both age groups only for circulatory disease, and the other two variables were significant only in the older group. Interestingly enough, there was an unexpected positive relationship between diagnosed neoplasms at T_2 and intelligence at

T_3. It might be speculated that the more able persons were more likely to seek earlier diagnosis and had better opportunities for effective treatment, thus increasing their survival rate. Another possible problem with the findings was the failure to disaggregate diagnoses of neoplasms into malignant and benign types (see below).

More comprehensive recent analyses

Our most complete analysis of the prevalence of disease and its impact on cognitive functioning was conducted as part of the dissertation research of Ann Gruber-Baldini (1991a) for a sample of 845 subjects on whom data were available through the completion of the fifth cycle (1984). These subjects entered and departed the SLS at various measurement points (1956, 1963, 1970, 1977), but all had at least two points of measurement. Analyses either organized data by age at testing or utilized the 1970–77 period, for which most of the subjects had complete data.

Disease occurrence

One goal of this analysis was to utilize the data from the HMO medical records to assess patterns of disease occurrence, prevalence and incidence of diseases, comorbidity of chronic disease conditions, and the progression and complications of disease categories (Gruber-Baldini, 1991b). Findings from HMO records were comparable to rates in other studies using self-report methods. Diseases increased in prevalence, incidence (except for neoplasms), and comorbidity with age. Arthritis was the most prevalent condition, followed by vision problems, neoplasms, and hypertension. Differences were found in rates of disease occurrence for men and women and in rates across time periods. Women had higher rates of arthritis, benign cardiovascular disease (CVD), benign neoplasms, essential hypertension, osteoporosis and hip fractures, and depression. Males had higher frequency of more serious conditions (in terms of risk of mortality), such as atherosclerosis, cerebrovascular disease, and malignant neoplasms. The number of physician contacts and hospital days was more frequent in the latest measurement period, whereas the average number of chronic conditions in the sample peaked during the period from 1964 to 1970.

Rates of chronic conditions varied by time of measurement as well as age. Overall, arthritis, benign CVD, neoplasms, and osteoporosis peaked from 1957 to 1963 (the first measurement period), but from 1970 to 1977 for all others. Rates from 1977 to 1984 appear to be lower than for other periods for arthritis, vision problems, and benign CVD. This period had lower rates of conditions even when rates were examined only for the 60–67 age range. However, subjects with data from 1977 to 1984 were members of a training study in the SLS and may have been a more select sample, since they were able to undergo five 1-hour sessions of cognitive training. Also, differences due to cohort effects in risk factors associated with medical utilization were confounded with time of measurement.

Average age of disease onset occurred after 50 for all chronic conditions. Rheumatoid arthritis, benign CVD, and nonmalignant neoplasms have earlier disease onset; osteoarthritis, atherosclerosis, cerebrovascular disease, and malignant neoplasms have average onset after age 60.

Impact of disease on cognitive functioning

The impact of diseases on cognitive functioning was examined longitudinally by three sets of analyses (Gruber-Baldini, 1991a). The first included logistic regression and event history analyses of predictors for the occurrence of and age at onset of significant cognitive decline. The second used latent growth curve models (LGM; McArdle & Anderson, 1990; McArdle & Hamagami, 1991) to examine longitudinal patterns of PMA functioning from ages 53 to 60. The third examined a LISREL path model for the direct effects of diseases on cognitive level and change, and for indirect effects on level and change through measures of inactive lifestyle (leisure activities and an obesity measure).

Overall health. Prior research has suggested that ratings of poor overall health predict lowered cognitive functioning. In the current study, measures of the number of chronic conditions, total number of physician visits, and number of hospital days were examined. The number of chronic conditions had negative influences on cognitive level for Verbal Meaning, Number, and Word Fluency and predicted greater decline on Verbal Meaning and Number. However, the age of experiencing significant decline occurred later for persons with more chronic conditions on Number and Word Fluency. A greater number of physician visits predicted an increased hazard of cognitive decline for Reasoning and a later age of onset of decline for Number. Physician visits were positively correlated with arthritis episodes, and arthritis was predictive of lower cognitive level on a number of the PMA measures. Hospitalization had no significant impact on PMA functioning, except that it was positively correlated with number of physician visits, number of chronic conditions, and number of episodes for some chronic diseases (especially arthritis), all of which were predictive of PMA performance.

Cardiovascular disease. Research on the relation of specific diseases and cognitive functioning has focused mostly on cardiovascular disease (CVD), and in particular on hypertension. This research has found mixed results with respect to the direction of influence of hypertension on cognition. Most studies in the literature suggest that more severe CVD (atherosclerosis, cerebrovascular disease, etc.) has a negative impact on cognitive functioning. However, much of the prior research was cross-sectional. Longitudinal studies in this area have often involved small samples, have included a limited number of testing occasions (i.e., fewer than three points), have failed to compare hypertension groups with groups with more severe CVD, and did not have information on cognitive functioning prior to disease onset.

In the analyses summarized here, multiple CVD groups were examined for the influence of the disease on cognitive functioning. Results suggest that atherosclerosis is associated with lower cognitive functioning and greater decline on Space and Number. LGM results suggest, however, that less decline occurred for Verbal Meaning in people with atherosclerosis; the decline occurred after age 60 and resulted in little level difference at age 81 in groups with and without atherosclerosis. Cerebrovascular disease was also negatively associated with cognitive level and increased the risk of and amount of cognitive decline (although the age of onset of significant decline was later than average for Spatial Orientation in the event history analyses).

The LGM results suggested that hypertensives with other CVD complications performed worse over time than uncomplicated hypertensives and normotensives. Noncomplicated hypertensives had higher performances and less decline than complicated hypertensives and normotensives. The total number of hypertension episodes predicted increased hazard of significant decline and overall level on Word Fluency but significantly later decline onset for Spatial Orientation and Reasoning. Also, hypertension was the only significant disease predictor for people under age 60 in the path models (again predicting lower performance and negative change over time for Word Fluency). Miscellaneous CVD predicted earlier decline on Word Fluency. Results from logistic and event history models suggest that miscellaneous CVD predicted less decline and later onset on Spatial Orientation. However, miscellaneous CVD also indirectly predicted (through leisure activities involving phone calls, game playing, and daydreaming) decreased Spatial Orientation level and change over time. Persons with miscellaneous CVD also performed at lower levels on Reasoning from ages 53 to 81, although their onset of decline was later than for people free of miscellaneous CVD. Benign CVD was associated with a lower rate of cognitive decline. Thus, the more serious CVD conditions (atherosclerosis and cerebrovascular disease) have generally negative influences, and benign CVD has more positive influences on cognition. Miscellaneous CVD and hypertension appear to fall between serious and benign CVD, with uncomplicated hypertensives maintaining higher cognitive functioning. Studies are needed to confirm the differences between CVD groups on a different longitudinal sample.

Diabetes. Few other chronic conditions have been investigated in the prior literature. Studies on the influence of diabetes have shown a negative impact of diabetes on functioning. However, these studies have also been cross-sectional and did not screen subjects for complications from other chronic diseases. We had available only a limited number of diabetics ($n = 51$) and thus were not able to examine the longitudinal pattern of functioning for this group by means of LGM analyses. However, other types of analysis showed that diabetes had an indirect positive effect on Inductive Reasoning level and longitudinal change (mediated via the measure of Body Mass Index). It is conceivable again that long-term survivors like those included in our study who are functioning at high intellectual levels may be able to manage their chronic conditions more adequately. These findings contradict prior findings and need to be replicated.

Arthritis. Only a few prior studies have examined the influence of arthritis on cognitive functioning, despite the high prevalence of this disease among the aged. Results from the LGM analyses suggest that arthritics have lower functioni ig and greater decline on Verbal Meaning, Spatial Orientation, and Inductive Reasoning. Logistic regression results, however, found that arthritis presented a lower proportional hazard of decline for Spatial Orientation and later average onset of significant decline on Verbal Meaning, Spatial Orientation, and Reasoning. Also, LISREL path models showed that arthritis had a direct negative effect on Spatial Orientation level and change from 1970 to 1977 and an indirect negative effect (through diversity of leisure activities) on Number and Word Fluency level and change (less decline). Dividing arthritics by age of occurrence, LGM results indicate that persons who developed arthritis after age 60 had lower levels and experienced greater decline on Verbal Meaning. However, persons with arthritis before age 60 had lower levels and greater decline on Inductive Reasoning. A mixed pattern resulted for Spatial Orientation, with pre-60 arthritics experiencing greater decline, whereas the post-60 group had lower overall levels of functioning by age 81. Future studies may need to examine longitudinally the separate effects of rheumatoid arthritis and osteoarthritis – subdiagnoses of arthritis that differ by age of diagnosis – on cognition to clarify the results of arthritis influences on cognitive level and cognitive change.

Neoplasms. In prior research on neoplasms, Stone (1980) found positive effects of neoplasms on cognitive performance in the SLS, but used a global measure of neoplasms (the entire ICDA category). The analyses described here employed more specific categories, considering differences between malignant and benign neoplasms and between skin (the most frequent neoplasms) and other neoplasms. Results suggest that the positive effects found by Stone might be due to the large frequency of benign neoplasms in the neoplasms category. Benign neoplasms (not skin) were found to produce earlier onset of decline but less overall decline. Malignant neoplasms and benign skin neoplasms had indirect (through activity factors) negative influences on performance. Results of the influence of neoplasms on cognition might be specific to combinations of type (malignant versus nonmalignant) and location (skin, bone, etc.). Small subsample sizes again limit detailed examination of these effects.

Other chronic conditions. Other conditions found to be related to cognitive functioning included osteoporosis and hip fractures and sensory problems. Osteoporosis and hip fractures were predictive of earlier decline on Word Fluency. Hearing impairment was associated with an increased risk of experiencing Verbal Meaning decline but was associated with better performance and later decline on Space. Vision difficulties predicted later age at onset of decline for Verbal Meaning and Space.

Intellectual functioning as a predictor of physical health

We have also investigated the reverse side of the coin: more specifically, whether we can demonstrate that our measures of cognitive abilities and cognitive style might be useful in predicting the occurrence and onset of physical disease (Maitland, 1993).

Our first analysis (Maitland & Schaie, 1991) involved a sample of 370 subjects (M = 169; F = 201; mean age = 66.5) who were studied between 1970 and 1984. Two logistic regression models were tested. In the first model all subjects diagnosed as having CVD were contrasted with normal controls. Age, gender, education, Attitudinal Flexibility, and decline in Spatial Ability were identified as significant predictors of the CVD condition ($\chi^2[13] = 80.96, p < .001$). When examined separately by gender, age and Attitudinal Flexibility were significant for the females ($\chi^2[12] = 39.02, p <$

.001); whereas age, Attitudinal Flexibility, and education were significant predictors of CVD for males ($\chi^2[12] = 44.67$, $p < .001$).

The second model included only those subjects who developed a CVD condition after the second data point. The prediction model for recent occurrence of conditions implicated age, Attitudinal Flexibility, decline in Psychomotor Speed, Spatial Ability decline, and decline in Reasoning Ability as significant ($\chi^2[13] = 43.14$, $p < .001$). Separately by gender, age, decline of Reasoning Ability, and decline in Word Fluency were significant for males ($\chi^2[12] = 29.13$, $p < .01$); whereas Attitudinal Flexibility was the only significant predictor for females. Lifestyle predictors of change in activity level and smoking, surprisingly, did not contribute to the prediction of recent CVD in this particular sample.

The most interesting finding from this analysis is the establishment of an association between the cognitive style measure of Attitudinal Flexibility and the presence of CVD, regardless of time of onset of the disease. Explanations of these findings would be that very rigid subjects may already have dropped out of the study prior to the onset of CVD or, alternatively, that rigid individuals might be more attentive to their health behaviors, thus being more likely to avoid disease outcomes.

In a second analysis, as part of a master's thesis Maitland (1993) extended the findings above to the possible effects of behaviors on the occurrence of arthritic disease, as well as applying survival analysis to the prediction of the occurrence of both cardiovascular and arthritic disease. In this sample, women were more likely than men to have arthritis, but measures of social status, obesity, and smoking were not significant predictors. Greater Attitudinal Flexibility and decline of Psychomotor Speed were found to be associated with preexisting arthritis, whereas declines in Spatial and Reasoning abilities were predictive of the occurrence of arthritis.

Life table and survival analysis methods were used to predict age of onset of cardiovascular and arthritic disease. Declines in Verbal and Reasoning abilities were found to predict later occurrence of first diagnosis of CVD; high levels of Spatial Ability were associated with earlier onset. For the arthritic subjects, greater declines in Verbal and Spatial ability, as well as higher level of education and Psychomotor Speed base levels, were associated with later ages of disease onset; decline in Psychomotor Speed and low baseline function on Spatial Ability predicted earlier onset.

Chapter summary

This chapter discusses the manner in which physical disease may affect the maintenance of function, as well as how disease onset might be affected by behavioral antecedents and concomitants. A series of studies are described that relate the role of disease and intellectual functioning in the SLS. The first study implicated cardiovascular disease as being associated with earlier onset of decline of intellectual functioning. Decline in Psychomotor Speed was also identified as a risk factor for the occurrence of CVD. However, when hypertensives were disaggregated, they did not show any increased risk of cognitive decline.

The second study, concerned with the structural relationship between disease processes and maintenance of intellectual functioning, also implicated cardiovascular and musculoskeletal conditions as leading to excess risk for cognitive decline. Surprisingly, the diagnosis of neoplasms was negatively correlated with cognitive decline.

A more comprehensive analysis has extended these findings to the disease categories of diabetes, neoplasms, and arthritis as well as to a measure of overall health. Overall health status as measured by number of chronic disease diagnoses was found to have a negative effect on the abilities of Verbal Meaning, Number, and Word Fluency. The more serious CVD conditions (atherosclerosis and cerebrovascular disease) have generally negative influences, whereas benign CVD (including uncomplicated hypertension) has a slightly positive influence on cognition. Diabetes was correlated positively with intellectual functioning, perhaps reflecting the survival of those who can manage this condition more intelligently. The onset of arthritis was associated with timing of cognitive decline on Inductive Reasoning and Spatial abilities. When neoplasms were disaggregated into benign and malignant forms, the malignant cases were associated with cognitive decline.

Finally, we considered the impact of our behavioral measures as predictors of the occurrence of and the age of onset of cardiovascular disease and arthritis. As expected, higher levels of cognitive functioning and of education were generally found to be associated with later disease onset, but the picture is complex, not uniform across all abilities.

11

Lifestyle variables that affect intellectual functioning

Although we collected data on some limited demographic characteristics of our subjects from the beginning of our study, it was not until 1974 that we began to engage systematically in an exploration of what we then termed our subjects' microenvironment as a possible source of influences that might help us understand individual differences in cognitive aging (Gribbin, Schaie, & Parham, 1980; Schaie & Gribbin, 1975; Schaie & O'Hanlon, 1990).

We constructed a survey instrument called the Life Complexity Inventory (LCI) that was designed to measure various aspects of our subjects' immediate environment. This questionnaire was originally administered in the spring of 1974 as a structured interview in home visits to 140 of the subjects who had taken part in the first three study cycles. The data from this interview were then clustered, and eight distinct dimensions were identified (Gribbin, Schaie, & Parham, 1980). Variables comprising these item clusters are shown in Table 11.1. Subsequent to the analyses described below, we made minor changes in the interview scheme and converted it to a survey instrument that has been used systematically, beginning with the 1977 data collection.

The term *disengaged* used in the following discussion refers to the tendency of many older persons to reduce environmental stress and perhaps compensate for perceived losses in competence by reducing their interaction with other persons as well as reducing their active participation in the community and their social participation (see Cumming & Henry, 1961; Havighurst, Neugarten, & Tobin, 1968).

In the initial analysis of the LCI, significant gender differences were found for two clusters. As expected, women had higher scores

Table 11.1. *Variables comprising the LCI item clusters*

Social status
High level of education
High present and previous income
High present and previous occupational
    status
Perceived time pressure
Reads many magazines
Large number of rooms in home

Subjective dissatisfaction with life status
High present and retrospective
    dissatisfaction with life
High present and retrospective
    dissatisfaction with job success
Few friends

Noisy environment
Living now and previously close to
    freeways or airports
Living in a noisy environment and being
    bothered by it
Present and past environment filled with
    traffic noise

Family dissolution
High number of changes in residence in
    past 5 years
Spouse lost by death
Living in multiple-unit dwelling
Living in neighborhood with large
    elderly population
Widowed or not married

*Semipassive engagement with the
environment*
Retrospective upper-middle-class
    lifestyle
Many home-related activities
Many friends with diverse interests

*Disengagement from interaction with
the environment*
High number of passive activities
Few changes of occupation
More advanced age
Many solitary activities
Few past and present hours spent
    reading
Low involvement in people-related
    activities
Low present and past involvement in
    work activities

Maintenance of acculturation
High number of fiction and nonfiction
    books read
High number of college or adult
    education courses taken
High number of weeks spent in
    educational activities

Female homemaker role
Younger than spouse
Widowed or not married
Much time spent in homemaking
    activities
Much time spent in solitary activities
Much time spent in working with hands
Never in military service
High on unnecessary conversation

on the homemaker role cluster, and, surprisingly, they were also higher on the disengagement cluster than the men. With respect to age differences, we found the younger subjects to be higher on social status, whereas older subjects were more disengaged and were more likely to be high on the family dissolution cluster.

Lifestyle characteristics and cognitive functioning: initial analyses

We have examined the relationship between lifestyle characteristics and maintenance of cognitive function in several ways. We began by clustering individuals in terms of their cluster scores on the LCI variables and were able to identify four types of persons with distinct lifestyle characteristics who differed markedly in maintaining high levels of cognitive performance (Gribbin, Schaie, & Parham, 1980; Schaie, 1984b). Over both 7- and 14-year periods, we found that there was least decline for those persons who had high socioeconomic status and who were fully engaged in interaction with their environment. Next were those fully engaged persons who had average socioeconomic status. Substantial decline was shown by persons who were relatively passive in their interaction (those whom we called semiengaged). And finally, it was the widowed women who had never had a career of their own and who showed a disengaged lifestyle who were most likely to show excess decline. These differences in maintenance of cognitive ability level of the lifestyle types were statistically significant for all abilities except Number; they were also significant for the factor measures of cognitive style. In particular, high social status has positive predictive value, whereas disengagement has negative predictive value for the abilities. Maintenance of acculturation is a positive predictor of Word Fluency, Attitudinal Flexibility, and Psychomotor Speed, and family dissolution predicts negatively to future performance on most variables. Finally, centrality of the homemaker role predicts positively to Psychomotor Speed but negatively to Spatial Orientation.

Lifestyle characteristics and cognitive functioning: more recent analyses

The relationship between environmental factors and intellectual aging in the SLS data set was also examined in greater detail in two doctoral dissertations conducted in my laboratory. The first (Stone,

1980) was concerned primarily with the structural relations between environmental factors, health, and cognition and was therefore referred to in chapter 10. The second (O'Hanlon, 1993) is of particular current interest, as it focused primarily on the environmental factors. O'Hanlon's analysis included data for 1,376 subjects who completed the Life Complexity Inventory (LCI) as part of the 1977 data collection. It also included a subset of 779 persons on whom LCI data were available both in 1977 and in 1984. Findings from this work will therefore be summarized below.

Dimensions of leisure activities

In the O'Hanlon study, initial analyses focused on developing empirical dimensions for the 30 leisure activities included in the LCI (see also Maitland, O'Hanlon, & Schaie, 1990). An initial series of exploratory and confirmatory factor analyses determined that 17 of these activities had sufficient commonalities to permit the development of a six-factor model. The resulting factors were labeled Household Activities, Social Activities, Educational–Cultural Activities, Fitness Activities, Solitary Activities, and Communicative Activities. The model was estimated on a random half of the 1977 subjects and confirmed on the other random half, maintaining excellent fit ($\chi^2[df = 100] = 155.56$, $p < .001$; $GFI = .974$, $AGFI = .965$, $RMSR = .03$). Maximum likelihood factor loading estimates and factor intercorrelations for the accepted model are given in Table 11.2.

Factor scores were then calculated and a 2 (gender) × 9 (cohort) MANOVA was run to determine whether there were significant differences by age/cohort and gender. Women were found to have significantly higher means on the Social, Solitary, and Household activities factors; men had higher scores on the Fitness factor. No significant gender differences occurred for the Social and Communicative activities factors. Age differences were significant between the most extreme age groups for all factors except Solitary Activities. The youngest cohorts had generally higher mean levels of participation in leisure activities than did the oldest cohorts.

Table 11.2. *Measurement model for the LSA factor structure*

Variable	Household	Social	Educational–Cultural	Fitness	Solitary	Communicative	Unique variance
Factor loadings							
Cooking	0.807						0.348
Household chores	0.733						0.463
Shopping	0.427	0.261					0.654
Being visited		0.682					0.535
Visiting others		0.696					0.516
Social life & parties		0.363	0.288				0.701
Educational activities			0.625				0.609
Cultural activities			0.565				0.681
Self-improvement			0.504				0.745
Participant sports				0.386			0.851
Physical fitness				0.618			0.618
Outdoor hobbies				0.301	0.194		0.848
Solitary games or hobbies					0.487		0.763
Handicrafts					0.603		0.637
Discussion and talking						0.749	0.440
Daydreaming and reminiscing						0.533	0.715
Writing correspondence	0.296					0.356	0.710
Factor intercorrelations							
Household							
Social	0.431						
Educational–Cultural	0.199	0.400					
Fitness	−0.022	0.375	0.485				
Solitary	0.406	0.478	0.300	0.200			
Communicative	0.360	0.709	0.588	0.452	0.380		

Note: All factor loadings are significant at or beyond the 1% level of confidence.
Source: From *Inter-individual patterns of intellectual aging: The influence of environmental factors* by A. M. O'Hanlon, 1993. Unpublished doctoral dissertation, Pennsylvania State University, University Park.

Relationship between leisure activities and cognitive functioning

Correlations between the activity factors and the PMA core variables were low to modest. The highest significant correlations found were those of Verbal Meaning with Educational–Cultural ($r = .37$) and Communications ($r = .25$); Spatial Orientation with Communications ($r = .19$); Reasoning with Educational–Cultural ($r = .26$) and Communications ($r = .27$); and Word Fluency with Educational–Cultural ($r = .27$) and Communications ($r = .24$).

Dimensions of the Life Complexity Inventory

Another series of factor analyses was conducted to determine the latent dimensions of the Life Complexity Inventory. The variables included a broad spectrum of environmental dimensions as well as the factor scores derived from the leisure activity analyses described above. Again the basic analyses were run on a random half of the 1977 samples, with verification of the best-fitting factor model on the remaining half. The model that was finally accepted includes 30 variables and eight factors ($\chi^2[df = 373] = 986.09$, $p < .001$; *GFI* $= .912$, *AGFI* $= .890$, *RMSR* $= .05$). The environmental factors identified were: Prestige, Social Status, Leisure Activities, Physical Environment, Mobility, Intellectual Environment, Social Network, and Work Characteristics. Maximum likelihood factor loading estimates and factor intercorrelations for the accepted model are given in Table 11.3.

Factor scores were calculated for the eight latent lifestyle dimensions, and again a 2 (gender) × 9 (cohort) MANOVA was run to determine gender and age/cohort differences. It was found that men had significantly higher scores than women on the Prestige, Social Status, and Work factors. Women had significantly higher scores on the Leisure Activities factor, but no significant sex differences were found for Physical Environment, Mobility, Intellectual Environment, and Social Network. Age/cohort differences were significant for all factors except for the Physical Environment factor.

In general, age differences were in favor of the younger cohorts. For the Social Status factor, there was a significant difference between the youngest cohort (mean age 25) and the three oldest cohorts (mean ages 67 and above); none of the other cohorts differed significantly. With respect to the Leisure Activities factor, all other cohorts were significantly above the level of the oldest cohort (mean age 81). On the Intellectual Environment factor, the middle-aged cohorts (mean ages 39 to 53) were significantly above the two oldest cohorts. The youngest cohort was also above the level of the oldest cohort. With respect to the Mobility factor, the youngest cohort (mean age 25) was significantly above all other cohorts. The early-middle-aged cohorts (mean ages 32 and 39) were also significantly more mobile than all cohorts above a mean age of 60.

Considering the Prestige factor, it is interesting to note that the early-middle-aged cohort (mean age 32) exceeded the level of persons who were in their 60s or older. In addition, the middle-aged exceeded the oldest cohorts. Not surprisingly, all cohorts exceeded the two oldest cohorts on the Work factor. The Social Status factor, however, showed a rather different pattern. Here the highest level was shown by the cohort with a mean age of 46 years, which was significantly higher than all but the two adjacent cohorts.

Finally, we observed a significant Gender × Cohort interaction for the Mobility factor. Women had lower means for all cohorts except one of the middle-aged cohorts (mean age 46). For this cohort, women exceeded men in Mobility level.

Correlation of lifestyle factors and intellectual abilities

Once again, the lifestyle factor scores were correlated with the core mental abilities. Three factors showed strong ability correlates. These factors were Prestige, Social Status, and Work Characteristics; all were positively correlated with the ability scores, with correlations ranging from .27 to .51. Lower, but still significant, correlations were found for the Leisure, Intellectual Environment, and Physical Environment factors. There were no significant correlations with the extent of the subjects' Social Network.

As an alternative approach, O'Hanlon (1993) also investigated the characterization of our subjects in terms of their lifestyle profiles. Using cluster analysis, she identified 11 clusters of persons who had similar profiles but differed from other cluster types in certain

Table 11.3. *Measurement model for the LCI lifestyle dimensions*

Variable	Prestige	Social Status	Leisure	Physical Environment	Mobility	Intellectual Environment	Social Network	Work Characteristics	Unique variance
Factor loadings									
Education	0.781								0.390
Occupation	0.757								0.426
Marital status		0.485							0.765
Home ownership		0.467							0.782
Income		0.798							0.362
Number of rooms		0.626							0.608
Fitness Activities			0.401						0.839
Educational–cultural activities			0.616						0.621
Communicative activities			0.698						0.512
Social activities			0.577						0.667
Solitary activities			0.335						0.888
Household activities			0.442						0.805
Air quality				0.695					0.516
Trees in neighborhood				0.688					0.526
Noise level				−0.373					0.861
Changes in jobs					0.744				0.447
Changes in homes					0.584				0.659
Changes in occupations						0.476			0.774
Books in home						0.544			0.704

Art objects in home	0.492			0.758
Magazines read	0.360			0.871
Educational course taken	0.385			0.852
Confidants		0.378		0.857
Meetings attended		0.524		0.726
Visits outside neighborhood		0.374		0.860
Reading (proportion of work)			0.489	0.761
Work status (working/retired)			0.811	0.342
Work under pressure			0.541	0.707
Workplace (indoors/out)			-0.728	0.470
Working with people			0.407	0.834

Factor intercorrelations

	Prestige	Social Status	Leisure Activities	Physical Environment	Mobility	Intellectual Environment	Social Network
Prestige							
Social Status	0.431						
Leisure Activities	0.339	0.204					
Physical Environment	0.359	0.343	0.164				
Mobility	0.131	-0.083	0.195	-0.072			
Intellectual Environment	0.577	0.451	0.573	0.367	-0.001		
Social Network	0.007	-0.150	0.210	0.110	-0.341	0.173	
Work Charcteristics	0.460	0.539	0.077	0.150	0.264	0.323	-0.340

Note: All factor loadings are significant at or beyond the 1% level of confidence.
Source: From *Inter-individual patterns of intellectual aging: The influence of environmental factors* by A. M. O'Hanlon, 1993. Unpublished doctoral dissertation, Pennsylvania State University, University Park.

salient characteristics. Subject type was then entered as an independent variable in the MANOVA of cognitive abilities.

This analysis identified three clusters whose members performed significantly worse on the mental abilities than did member of other clusters. These were the same cluster types that also scored lower than other clusters on various permutations of environmental factors. The adverse factors typically represented low scores on the Prestige, Social Status, and Work Characteristics or on the Intellectual and Physical environment factors. By contrast, the subject cluster that was characterized by above-average scores on the Prestige, Social Status, Intellectual Environment, and Work Characteristics factors also performed significantly better than other cluster types on Verbal Meaning, Space, Reasoning, and Word Fluency. In addition, the cluster that exhibited moderately high Mobility and Intellectual Environment scores scored significantly above average on Verbal Meaning, Space, and Reasoning abilities.

Longitudinal analyses of the lifestyle variables

A series of confirmatory factor analyses determined whether the LCI dimensions developed on the basis of the 1977 sample would be maintained longitudinally over a 7-year period. Confirmatory models constraining factor loading across time, for the subjects still available in 1984, were tested for both the leisure activities data and for the lifestyle factors described above. The structure of the leisure activities remained invariant by the most stringent criteria (invariance of patterns, loadings, and error variances across time). The lifestyle latent variable structure was somewhat less stable. However, it was possible to accept the equivalence of factor patterns across times (configural invariance).

A 2 (gender) × 9 (cohort) repeated measurement MANOVA was next run to determine whether there was longitudinal stability in mean levels. No statistically significant changes in mean level were found over the 7-year period for any of the leisure activities factors for any of the gender or age/cohort groupings.

When a similar analysis was conducted for the eight LCI lifestyle factors, however, several significant findings emerged. A significant Gender × Time effect was found only for the Work Characteristics factor, with women showing an increase at the second time of measurement. Significant Time × Age/Cohort interactions were found for Social Status, with the two youngest cohorts gaining significantly on this factor over the 7 years, all other cohorts remaining stable. With respect to the Mobility factor, there was a significant increase in mobility over time for the four youngest cohorts, and reduced mobility for all other cohorts. The youngest four cohorts also showed a significant increase on the Work factor, whereas the cohort whose mean age was 53 at base measurement decreased significantly over the 7 years.

Effects of retirement on the lifestyle variables

A final series of analyses examined the question whether stability in the lifestyle variables might be influenced by the marked lifestyle changes brought about by retirement. The longitudinal sample was divided into three groups: those who reported that they were working in both 1977 and 1984, those who were working in 1977 but were retired in 1984, and those who had retired prior to 1977. Repeated measurement MANOVAs were then run crossing gender, work status, and time of measurement.

The effects of greatest interest with respect to the leisure activities are those concerned with the question of whether retirement significantly affects participation in leisure activities. The Retirement Status × Time interaction was indeed significant. For those recently retired, there was a significant increase in Social Activities, Solitary Activities, and Household Activities. On the other hand, both the long-term retired and working groups showed decline over time in Social Activities, and the working group declined in Household Activities.

Similar analyses were conducted for the LCI lifestyle factors. There was an overall increase over time for the Work factor, as well as several significant Retirement Status × Time interactions. On the Prestige factor, the working group showed an increase over time, and the retired groups showed a decrease. Consistent with the analyses of the leisure activities, the Leisure factor showed a significant increase for the recently retired but decreases for those working and for the long-term retirees. With respect to Mobility, those working showed an increase, those recently retired remained stable, and the long-term retirees decreased. Finally, on the Work factor, as expected, the recently retired showed a significant decrease, whereas those still working showed an increase.

Chapter summary

The Life Complexity Inventory (LCI) has been used since 1974 to characterize the microenvironment of participants in the SLS. Early analyses of this instrument identified eight lifestyle factors that were related to our measures of intellectual abilities. Four subject types were identified: the affluent fully engaged, those of average socioeconomic status who were fully engaged, the semiengaged, and widowed homemakers. The first two groups maintained their levels of intellectual functioning or even showed modest improvement over 7 and 14 years; the other two groups showed significant decline – substantial for the widowed homemakers.

More recent analyses utilized larger samples to establish six dimensions of the leisure activities contained in the LCI: Household Activities, Social Activities, Educational–Cultural Activities, Fitness Activities, Solitary Activities, and Communicative Activities. Factor scores for these dimensions were included in the analysis of the remaining LCI variables, with an eight-factor lifestyle dimensions structure emerging: Prestige, Social Status, Leisure Activities, Physical Environment, Mobility, Intellectual Environment, Social Network, and Work Characteristics. Women exceeded men on the Social, Solitary, and Household activities factors; men were higher on the Fitness factor. The youngest age group exceeded the oldest group on all factors except Solitary Activities. The younger cohorts were higher in Leisure Activities. Men exceeded women on the Prestige, Social Status, and Work lifestyle factors; women were higher on Leisure Activities.

Low to modest positive correlations were found between amount of leisure activity and levels of cognitive functioning. Positive lifestyle characteristics were also correlated with high levels of cognitive functioning, the dimensions of Prestige, Social Status, and Work Characteristics showing the highest correlations.

Longitudinal stability was demonstrated at the metric invariance level for the leisure activities factors and at the configural invariance level for the lifestyle dimensions.

No significant level changes occurred over 7 years for the Leisure Activities. However, there was an increase over time for women on Work Characteristics. The two youngest cohorts gained significantly on Prestige, and there was an increase in Mobility and Work Characteristics for the four youngest cohorts, with reduced Mobility for all others.

Finally, retirement increased Leisure Activities for the recently retired, with a reduction of activities for those working or retired for a substantial time. As expected, the retired showed a decrease in Work and Prestige; the opposite pattern prevailed for those still working after 7 years.

12

The sequential study of personality traits and attitudes

Although not the central focus in the SLS, a large body of data on a limited number of personality traits and attitudes has been acquired almost incidentally. These data come primarily from the Test of Behavioral Rigidity (TBR; Schaie, 1955, 1960; Schaie & Parham, 1975). As mentioned in chapter 3, when I constructed the TBR questionnaire that provided the base for our latent construct of Attitudinal Flexibility, I included as masking items a set of 44 items from the Social Responsibility scale of the California Psychological Inventory (Gough, 1957; Gough, McCloskey, & Meehl, 1952). The sequential data (cross-sectional and longitudinal) on this scale are, of course, of interest in their own right in chronicling stability and change on this trait over the adult age range and time period covered by our study.

I soon realized, moreover, that personality and/or attitudinal true-or-false questionnaire items are likely to carry information on other personality characteristics than the particular traits for which they were originally selected. Hence, we began to engage in item factor analyses of the entire set of 75 items contained in the TBR questionnaire (see Schaie & Parham, 1976).

Social Responsibility

Initial cross-sectional findings for the Social Responsibility scale were reported on the base-level study (Schaie, 1959b), and sequential models have been applied to this scale on data from the first three cycles (Schaie & Parham, 1974). In the following sections I report data over all six study occasions, using the format employed earlier for the cognitive data.

Cross-sectional findings

Means and standard deviations by gender for the total sample are reported by test occasion in Table 12.1. As can be seen from Figure 12.1, there is a tendency for the cross-sectional data to suggest relatively lower responsibility levels until early midlife and from then on what seem to be occasion-specific age differences. That is, for the early cohorts lower levels are shown into old age, whereas for the more recent cohorts there seem to be favorable trends for the oldest groups.

Longitudinal findings

The longitudinal data reported here are averaged across all subjects within each 7-year age segment over all periods for which appropriate 7-year data are available. By contrast to the cross-sectional data, the longitudinal estimates provided in Table 12.2 and graphed in Figure 12.2 separately by gender suggest that there is within-subject stability in reported Social Responsibility throughout young adulthood and middle age. A modest gender difference in favor of women is found to occur until age 60. However, a marked within-subject decline in Social Responsibility was observed beginning at age 67 for women and at age 74 for men. This was followed, for men only, by an abrupt rise at age 81.

Cohort and period effects

When examined over all six waves, *cohort effects* for the Social Responsibility scale do not seem very pronounced. There is a modest concave pattern, but it is only the 1938 cohort that displays a significantly higher level of Social Responsibility than the remaining cohorts (see Table 12.3). With respect to secular trends, it appears that Social Responsibility was at a nadir on the 1977 measurement occasion. Significant overall decline in reported Social Responsibility

Table 12.1. *Means and standard deviations for the Social Responsibility scale, by sample and gender*

Mean age	1956			1963			1970			1977			1984			1991		
	M	F	T	M	F	T	M	F	T	M	F	T	M	F	T	M	F	T
25	46.3 (11.0)	49.9 (10.0)	48.1 (10.6)	49.2 (10.3)	50.1 (9.2)	49.7 (9.6)	46.4 (10.6)	46.8 (9.8)	46.6 (10.1)	42.6 (11.1)	45.2 (10.0)	43.9 (10.5)	44.2 (10.8)	47.2 (10.8)	46.0 (10.8)	45.3 (10.7)	44.9 (10.5)	45.1 (10.5)
32	48.7 (8.4)	52.7 (8.7)	50.8 (8.7)	49.1 (11.9)	50.7 (10.4)	50.0 (11.0)	51.5 (6.6)	51.0 (7.7)	51.2 (7.2)	45.9 (7.5)	45.7 (11.0)	45.8 (9.4)	46.6 (9.7)	46.3 (8.6)	46.4 (9.0)	44.6 (12.4)	48.8 (11.1)	47.1 (11.7)
39	51.9 (9.2)	51.9 (10.1)	51.9 (9.6)	48.8 (10.2)	52.5 (8.3)	50.8 (9.4)	49.0 (11.1)	51.2 (9.1)	50.3 (9.9)	49.7 (9.3)	49.8 (8.7)	49.7 (8.9)	52.1 (8.9)	48.2 (11.2)	50.0 (10.4)	52.2 (9.9)	50.0 (10.9)	51.1 (10.4)
46	49.6 (8.8)	53.5 (10.3)	51.4 (9.7)	49.4 (9.9)	50.8 (9.2)	50.1 (9.6)	51.2 (8.0)	51.7 (7.9)	51.4 (7.9)	45.3 (10.3)	47.6 (12.0)	46.5 (11.2)	51.4 (10.9)	52.7 (8.0)	52.2 (9.2)	51.6 (9.6)	53.4 (7.5)	52.7 (8.4)
53	54.2 (8.7)	54.0 (9.3)	54.1 (8.9)	47.3 (11.8)	51.2 (8.1)	49.5 (10.0)	51.4 (8.6)	51.9 (10.1)	51.7 (9.4)	50.1 (7.8)	49.2 (9.0)	49.6 (8.3)	49.3 (12.4)	49.2 (8.0)	49.2 (10.4)	51.7 (10.6)	51.8 (7.8)	51.7 (9.2)
60	48.9 (11.0)	53.0 (8.6)	51.0 (10.0)	48.7 (10.6)	50.5 (10.4)	49.7 (10.5)	51.6 (8.0)	52.8 (9.5)	52.3 (8.8)	47.4 (9.3)	49.7 (9.6)	48.6 (9.5)	50.7 (9.3)	52.3 (8.8)	51.6 (9.0)	51.5 (9.4)	52.8 (10.1)	52.2 (9.7)
67	53.0 (8.6)	49.6 (9.1)	51.3 (9.0)	46.4 (10.4)	51.1 (11.0)	48.7 (10.9)	48.1 (9.3)	51.1 (8.8)	49.7 (9.1)	49.3 (8.0)	48.4 (12.8)	48.9 (10.5)	48.9 (10.8)	50.5 (11.6)	49.7 (11.2)	54.6 (8.7)	55.2 (10.8)	54.9 (9.9)
74	—	—	—	48.8 (11.2)	46.0 (8.2)	47.3 (9.8)	49.0 (8.6)	52.0 (9.7)	50.4 (9.2)	47.8 (10.7)	47.1 (11.0)	47.4 (10.7)	47.7 (11.6)	48.0 (9.3)	47.8 (10.5)	52.8 (12.0)	53.7 (8.6)	53.3 (10.3)
81	—	—	—	—	—	—	48.9 (7.5)	49.1 (11.6)	49.0 (9.6)	44.5 (9.8)	49.5 (11.4)	47.2 (10.9)	48.7 (9.5)	52.6 (8.0)	50.9 (8.9)	54.0 (8.1)	53.7 (7.4)	53.8 (7.7)

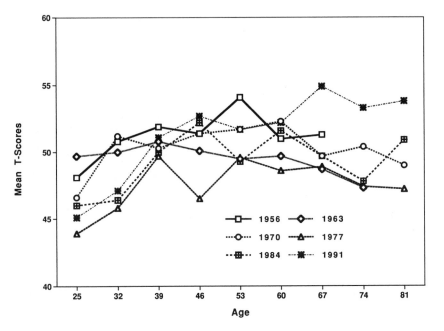

Figure 12.1. Age-difference patterns for the scale of Social Responsibility for the total sample, by test occasion.

was found from 1956 to 1977, whereas a significant increase occurred from 1977 to 1991 (see Table 12.4).

The cohort and period data suggest that the trait of Social Responsibility is much more affected by secular (period) than by cohort trends. Recent positive secular trends, moreover, tend to camouflage the systematic decline in Social Responsibility in advanced old age that is seen, at least in women, in the within-subject data.

Other personality traits

An item factor analysis of the 75 TBR questionnaire items using all available data from the 1963 and 1970 data collections resulted in the acceptance of a 19-factor structure. The resultant factors were matched by content to Cattell's (1957) personality taxonomy.

Table 12.2. *Cumulative age changes for the scale of Social Responsibility, in T-score points*

Mean age	32	39	46	53	60	67	74	81	88
25	4.59*	4.69*	6.85*	6.71*	7.62*	9.00*	9.72*	9.50*	11.18*
32		0.10	2.26	2.12	3.03*	4.41*	5.13*	4.91*	6.59*
39			2.16	2.02	2.93	4.31*	5.03*	4.81*	6.49*
46				−0.14	0.77	2.15	2.87	2.65*	4.33*
53					0.91	2.29	3.01*	2.79	4.47*
60						1.38	2.10	1.88	3.56*
67							0.72	0.50	2.18
74								−0.22	1.44
81									1.68

*Difference is significant at or beyond the 1% level of confidence.

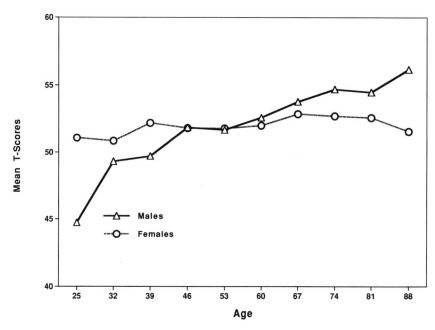

Figure 12.2. Estimated age changes from 7-year data, by gender, for the scale of Social Responsibility.

Table 12.3. *Mean advantage of later-born cohorts over earlier-born cohorts on the Social Responsibility scale, in T-score points*

	Mean year of birth										
	1896	1903	1910	1917	1924	1931	1938	1945	1952	1959	1966
1889	−0.4	−0.3	−0.2	0.3	1.6	0.4	2.5*	0.5	0.2	1.6	0.7
1896		0.1	0.2	0.7	2.0	0.8	2.9*	0.9	0.6	2.0	1.1
1903			0.1	0.6	1.9	0.7	2.8*	0.8	0.5	1.9	1.0
1910				0.5	1.8	0.6	2.7*	0.7	0.4	1.8	0.9
1917					1.3	0.1	2.2	0.2	−0.1	1.3	0.4
1924						−1.2	0.9	−1.1	−1.4	0.1	−0.9
1931							2.1	0.1	−0.2	1.3	0.3
1938								−2.0	−2.3	−0.7	−1.6
1945									−0.3	1.1	0.2
1952										1.4	0.5
1959											−0.9

Note: Negative values indicate that the later-born cohort is at a disadvantage relative to the earlier-born cohort.
*$p < 0.01$.

Table 12.4. *Period (time-of-measurement) effects for the scale of Social Responsibility, in T-score points*

	1963	1970	1977	1984	1991
1956	−1.46	−0.72	−3.44*	−1.76	−0.13
1963		0.74	−1.98	−0.30	1.33
1970			−2.72*	−1.04	0.59
1977				1.68	3.48*
1984					1.62

*$p < 0.01$.

Thirteen of the factors appeared to me to be substantively similar to one of the trait ends of the Cattell taxonomy; the remaining factors appeared to be primarily attitudinal in nature (see Table 12.5). The factor scores estimated for these factors were then subjected to ANOVAs, utilizing sequential strategies. Given the availability of two points in time, these analyses had to use the cross-sequential

Table 12.5. *Nineteen personality traits from the TBR questionnaire*

A + Affectothymia	Q1 − Conservatism of Temperament
D + Excitability	Q2 − Group Dependency
E + Dominance	Q3 − Low Self-Sentiment
G + Superego Strength	Honesty
H + Threctia	Interest in Science
I + Premsia	Flexibility
J + Coasthenia	Financial Support of Society
L + Protension	Humanitarian Concern
M − Praxernia	Community Involvement
O − Untroubled Adequacy	

Note: Signs represent the unidimensional pole of the Cattell factor represented by these scales.

and time-sequential strategies. By comparing results from these alternative analyses, it was possible to identify three types of developmental pattern for the personality traits: biostable, acculturated, and biocultural (see Schaie & Parham, 1976).

A classification model for personality traits

Biostable traits represent a class of behaviors that may be genetically determined or constrained by environmental influences that occur early in life, perhaps during a critical imprinting period. These traits typically show systematic gender differences at all age levels but are rather stable across age, whether examined in cross-sectional or longitudinal data. *Acculturated* traits, conversely, appear to be over-determined by environmental events occurring at different life stages and tend to be subject to rather rapid modification by sociocultural change. These traits usually display no systematic gender differences. Their age differences rarely form systematic patterns and can usually be resolved into generational shifts and/or secular trend components upon sequential analysis. *Biocultural* traits display ontogenetic trends whose expression is modified either by generational shifts or by sociocultural events that affect all age levels in a similar fashion. Cross-sectional data for such traits would typically show Age × Gender interactions.

Four subtypes are possible for the *biostable* traits:

(1) *Gender differences only*. Such traits seem to be overdetermined by genetic variance, probably located on the sex chromosome. The only trait that fits this paradigm in our study was that of premsia (tender-mindedness, which was higher for women), but even that gender difference was barely significant and thus should be treated with caution. We suggest that it is probably unreasonable to expect personality traits that fit the purely inherited category without ambiguity.

(2) *Period differences only*. Such traits also appear to be overdetermined by genetic variance, but they are modified in their expression by secular sociocultural shifts. In our analysis, this type of trait was represented by untroubled adequacy, which showed a decrease over the 7 years monitored.

(3) *Cohort differences only*. These traits are not subject to transient environmental influences, but seem to reflect generation-specific patterns in early training or socialization procedures. This would seem to be the modal pattern for those traits that are indeed determined by early socialization. The traits matching this category observed in our study were those of threat reactivity, coasthenia, expressed honesty, interest in sciences, and community involvement.

(4) *Period and cohort differences*. A final subtype involves development of a trait in response to early socialization as well as to transient sociocultural impact. Both praxernia and group dependence followed that pattern in our study.

It is the *acculturated* traits that display no gender difference but that may show a variety of combinations of age changes, and/or period and cohort differences. Six possible subtypes can be identified:

(1) *Age changes only*. This type of trait reflects social roles that are determined by universals that underlie stage models of human development (see Piaget, 1972; Schaie, 1977–1978) and that are rather impermeable to cohort differences or secular trends. The only trait that met these criteria was humanitarian concern, which showed increase with age.

(2) *Age changes and cohort differences*. Such traits are mediated by life-stage changes in universally determined life roles that in turn are modified by generational shifts in early socialization practices. Identification of traits of this type was not possible in this study,

because a cohort-sequential data matrix would have been required for their identification.

(3) *Age changes and period differences*. Such traits are determined by universally prescribed life roles that are impermeable to early socialization practices but are subject to transient secular impacts for persons of all ages. It is difficult to imagine that a trait could have such attributes, and none of those included in our study fit this pattern.

(4) *Cohort differences only*. Such traits are not subject to ontogenetic change, but instead their development is mediated by generation-specific patterns of early socialization practices. This pattern prevailed for affectothymia, superego strength, protension, and low self-sentiment. Except for superego strength, it is conceivable, however, that these traits could also have fit subtype 2 above had we had the appropriate data to test for the presence of both age and cohort differences.

(5) *Period differences only*. Such traits are non-age-related and independent of shifts in early socialization practices. However, they are affected by sociocultural impact for all age levels. Dominance and financial support of society fit this pattern.

(6) *Cohort and period, differences*. Non-age-related traits may be modified both by specific patterns of early socialization and by transient sociocultural changes that affect individuals at all ages. In our study it was the Flexibility factor that showed these characteristics, displaying a general pattern toward greater flexibility across cohorts, accompanied by additional increase in flexibility across the periods monitored.

The *biocultural* traits are those that are overdetermined by genetic variance and consequently show significant gender differences but are also modified in their expression because of universally experienced life-stage expectancies or the effects of early socialization experiences. Three subtypes were identified:

(1) *Age changes only*. Such traits are characterized by clear onto-genetic "programs" that seem to be impermeable to cohort differences or sociocultural change. Our only example of this type was excitability, which systematically increased with age.

(2) *Age changes and cohort differences*. Such traits in addition to systematic ontogenetic shifts are also modified in level by generation-

specific socialization practices. Again, our data set did not permit clear identification of such traits; it is probably unlikely that they exist.

(3) *Age changes and period differences.* Such traits have clear ontogenetic "programs" but are amenable to modification due to specific environmental interventions that affect persons at all ages. The only trait that fit this criterion in our study was premsia.

Our principal conclusion from this study was that age-related change in personality traits was quite rare but that cohort and period differences were common and would lead to the spurious reporting of lack of stability for personality traits when reliance is had primarily on cross-sectional data.

Recent analyses of the personality data

Although we continued to collect the personality items data, if only to be able to measure the cognitive style of Attitudinal Flexibility, we did not go beyond the work summarized above until quite recently.

The original work on the personality items had been conducted by means of then state-of-the-art methods of exploratory factor analysis that did not allow adequate tests of the number of nonrandom factors represented in the item pool or allow formal tests confirming the invariance of factor structures over time.

We shall now summarize results of new item factor analyses over the data set stretching from 1963 to 1984 and consider some preliminary longitudinal findings on the relationship of the derived scales to other constructs investigated in the SLS (see Maitland, Dutta, Schaie, & Willis, 1992; Maitland & Schaie, 1991; Maitland, Willis, & Schaie, 1993; Willis, Schaie, & Maitland, 1992).

Reassessment of item factor structure. Contemporary analysis techniques (using LISREL 7) were used to confirm the factor structure identified in the earlier work (Schaie & Parham, 1976). The database for this analysis included the 2,515 test records used in the original study, as well as an additional 2,811 tests accumulated in the 1977 and 1984 cycles. When confirmatory factor analysis was used to assess the fit for the 19-factor model determined in the exploratory analyses, it was decided that the data had been overfitted, resulting in several factors with extremely high factor intercorrelations. Further consideration of the number of factors unambiguously represented in the data resulted in an acceptable 13-factor model with good fit ($\chi^2[df = 1,191] = 3,548.16, p < .001$; *GFI* = .945, *RMSR* = .007). The 13-factor model was then tested on the subjects assessed in 1977 and 1984, and it continued to show an acceptable fit ($\chi^2[df = 1,191] = 4,302.98, p < .001$; *GFI* = .941, *RMSR* = .007). A two-group analysis further investigated factorial invariance across time by constraining factor loadings and factor variance–covariance matrices to be equal across the two data sets. This analysis also yielded an acceptable fit ($\chi^2[df = 2,512] = 6,910.00, p < .001$; *GFI* = .945, *RMSR* = .007).

The 13-factor model includes 8 factors that can be mapped upon the Cattell (1957; Cattell, Eber, & Tatsuoka, 1970) taxonomy of personality dimensions: Affectothymia, Superego Strength, Threctia, Premsia, Untroubled Adequacy, Conservatism of Temperament, Group Dependency, and Low Self-Sentiment. The remaining five factors are best described as attitudinal traits and were labeled Honesty, Interest in Science, Inflexibility, Political Concern, and Community Involvement.

The factors that were mapped on one end of the trait continuum described by Cattell have been described as follows (Cattell, Eber, & Tatsuoka, 1970):

> *Affectothymia* – Outgoing, warmhearted, easygoing, participating tendencies
> *Superego Strength* – Conscientious, persistent, moralistic, staid
> *Threctia* – Shy, timid, restrained, threat-sensitive
> *Premsia* – Tender-minded, sensitive, clinging, overprotected
> *Untroubled Adequacy* – Self-assured, placid, secure, complacent, serene
> *Conservatism of Temperament* – Respecting traditional ideas, tolerant of traditional difficulties
> *Group Dependency* – A "joiner" and sound follower, group adherence
> *Low Self-Sentiment* – Uncontrolled, lax, follows own urge, careless of social rules

The additional five attitudinal traits may be described as follows:

> *Honesty* – Endorsement of items that reflect personal beliefs of honesty

Interest in Science – Endorsement of an item couplet that reflects interest in science

Inflexibility – Endorsement of items that reflect lack of tolerance for disruption of routines

Political Concern – Reflects attitudes toward other countries

Community Involvement – Endorsement of positive attitudes about citizenship and civic responsibilities

Age, gender, and cohort differences in personality traits and attitudes

Cross-sectional data were available across the age range from mean age 25 to mean age 81 from 3,539 subjects at first test in Study Cycles 1 through 6. The overall MANOVA yielded overall gender (Raos's $R(13, 3,509) = 57.43$, $p < .001$) and age (Raos's $R(104, 24,174) = 9.88$, $p < .001$) effects. The interaction between age and gender was not significant.

Gender differences. Univariate follow-up tests found gender differences significant at or beyond the .001 level of confidence, with higher overall scores for women on Group Dependency, Interest in Science, Inflexibility, and Political Concern. Overall means for men were higher on Affectothymia, Threctia, Untroubled Adequacy, and Honesty.

Age differences. All univariate follow-up tests found significant age differences at or beyond the .001 level of confidence. The cross-sectional age differences are shown in Figure 12.3. Because of the absence of an overall Age × Gender interaction, they are shown only for the total group without regard to gender. Eight of the factors show negative age differences, which are most pronounced for Conservatism of Temperament and smallest for Group Dependency and Political Concern. Five factors show positive age differences, most pronounced for Premsia (tender-mindedness) and Untroubled Adequacy. Interest in Science remains almost flat until the 50s and than shows some rise, albeit falling again to base level at the oldest age.

Cohort differences. As for our ability measures, these age differences confound cohort and maturational changes. We therefore computed

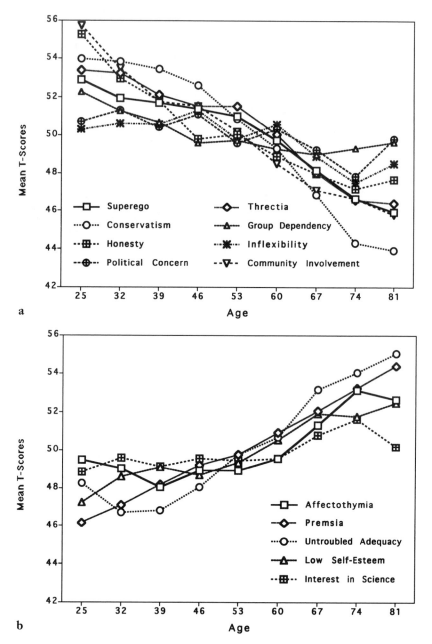

Figure 12.3. Age-difference patterns on the 13 personality factor scores.

cohort differences in the manner described earlier and chart the resulting cohort gradients in Figure 12.4. The upper portion of that figure shows the six traits that are characterized by negative cohort differences until the turn of the century. Thereafter, the cohort gradients for Low Self-Sentiment and Interest in Science remain virtually flat. Affectothymia, Untroubled Adequacy, and Premsia continue to decline, but they rise again for the baby boomers. On the other hand, Honesty shows a continuous rise after the initial downturn, except for a temporary decline from the 1952 to the 1959 cohort.

The lower part of Figure 12.4 shows the seven traits that show systematic increment for the older cohorts until at least 1924. Threctia continues to rise throughout the entire period, except for a dip for the 1924 cohort. Community Involvement reaches a peak with the 1945 cohort, with some decline thereafter. Conservatism of Temperament peaks for the 1924 cohort but shows a sharper downturn for the baby boomers. Downturns for the latter group are also seen for Group Dependency and Superego Strength. Political Concern reaches a peak for the 1938 cohort, with decline thereafter, but an upturn for the two most recently born cohorts. Finally, Inflexibility also reaches a peak in the 1938 cohort, with an upturn seen only in the most recent cohort.

Age changes in personality traits

When we aggregate within-subject age changes over each 7-year period in our study, we can obtain direct estimates of average age changes. For the personality data, we were able to base our estimates on all subjects entering the study in 1963, 1970, 1977, and 1984 who were followed up at least once. This resulted in 2,892 observations covering the age range from 25 to 88. Given the large number of observations, we did obtain overall within-subject change over 7 years on all variables except for Interest in Science.

Longitudinal age patterns on the personality variables are, of course, generally quite stable. However, there were significant occasion effects for four of the personality traits and two of the attitudinal measures. In addition, there were significant Occasion × Age group interactions for four of the personality traits and for three

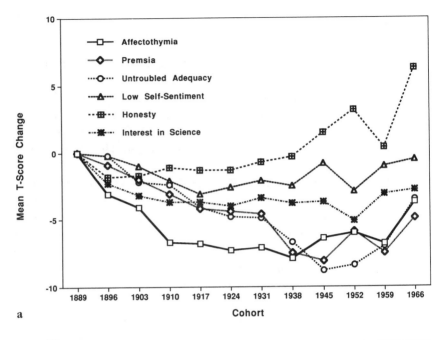

a

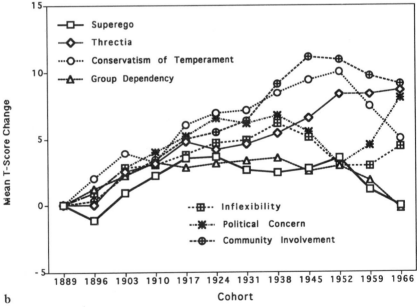

b

Figure 12.4. Cohort gradients for the 13 personality factor scores.

of the attitudinal measures. Figure 12.5 charts the estimates of longitudinal changes in personality traits obtained from these data, anchoring all age gradients on the observed values at age 53. For ease of inspection, I have grouped separately the traits that show decline over age and time in the top part of the figure and those that show an incremental trend in the bottom part.

Most noteworthy are modest within-subject decreases with age in Superego Strength and Threctia (threat reactivity). Even more dramatic is the systematic decline in reported Honesty; but note the upturn at age 88. The very slight downward trends for Conservatism of Temperament and Interest in Science are not statistically significant. With respect to Untroubled Adequacy, there is a slight downtrend until midlife, followed by slight increment until age 81 and then a sharp decline.

Affectothymia decreases from young adulthood to middle age but increases significantly into old age. Community Involvement increases systematically with age, as does Political Concern. Group Dependency is level through most of life but moves up sharply in the 80s. Inflexibility, Low Self-Sentiment, and Premsia (tender-mindedness) show a slight positive trend that does not reach statistical significance. The apparent decline in Inflexibility in advanced old age is also not statistically significant.

Chapter summary

Although the primary objectives of the SLS did not address the study of personality per se, we have collected a substantial corpus of data on the adult development of personality and attitudinal traits. We explicitly studied the attitudinal trait of Social Responsibility. Cross-sectional data suggested the presence of an Age × Cohort interaction that suggested lower Social Responsibility in old age in the earlier cohorts but a reversal in the younger cohorts. When aggregate longitudinal data are examined, however, we conclude that there is stability throughout young adulthood and middle age, with a marked decline in Social Responsibility occurring in men by age 74 and in women by age 67. Only modest cohort differences were found, with the highest Social Responsibility level shown by the 1938 cohort. However, there were significant secular trends

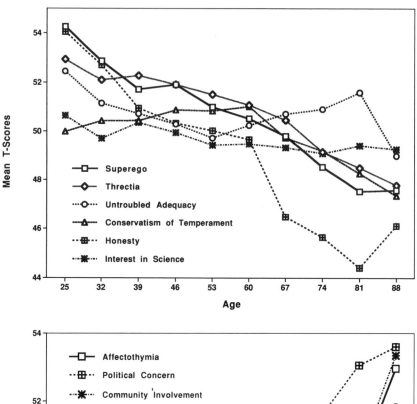

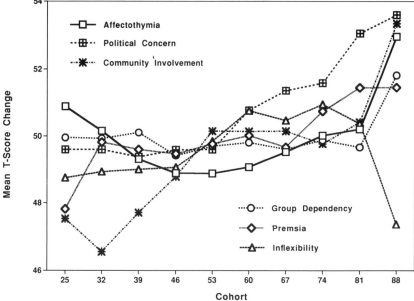

Figure 12.5. Estimated age changes from 7-year data for the 13 personality factor scores.

displaying an overall decline in Social Responsibility from 1956 to 1977 and a significant rise thereafter.

Item factor analyses of the 75-item TBR questionnaire originally resulted in the identification of 19 personality factors (based on data from the first three cycles) that were assigned to a personality trait taxonomy of biostable, biocultural, and acculturated traits. A more recent confirmatory factor analysis of our entire data set found a 13-factor solution to be more parsimonious. The factors identified were Affectothymia, Superego Strength, Threctia, Premsia, Untroubled Adequacy, Conservatism of Temperament, Group Dependency, Low Self-Sentiment, Honesty, Interest in Science, Inflexibility, Political Concern, and Community Involvement. Significant cross-sectional age differences were found for all personality factors. However, these differences can largely be explained by a pattern of positive and negative cohort differences. Far fewer significant within-subject age changes were found. Most noteworthy were modest within-subject decreases with age in Superego Strength and Threctia (threat reactivity) and a dramatic decline in Honesty. Affectothymia decreases from young adulthood to middle age but increases significantly into old age. Both Community Involvement and Political Concern increase with age.

13

Family studies of intellectual abilities in adulthood

Our interest in studying intrafamily relationships began serendipitously because of the fact that membership in an HMO is usually on a family rather than an individual basis. Our sampling procedures therefore yielded subsamples of married couples. More recently, exposure to the behavior genetics literature suggested that the SLS would be a natural vehicle for studying family similarity in the general (nontwin) population, and we began to gather data systematically on many adult children and siblings of our longitudinal panel members.[1]

Married couples

Similarity between married couples has usually been examined in the context of marital assortativity. Previous researchers have found significant correlations between spouses on a number of cognitive abilities and personality dimensions (see Murstein, 1980; Zonderman, Vandenberg, Spuhler, & Fain, 1977). The observed similarity was typically explained as being based either on initial couple similarity, the convergence of abilities over the marriage, the divorce of couples who are dissimilar, or confounds due to age-related trends (Price &

---

1 As indicated in chapter 3, we have also collected data on the perceptions of longitudinal study members and their relatives of the environment in their families of origin and their current families as well as their perceived work environment. I do not include this material here, because it has not yet been linked to our cognitive data. A first report on the topic of family environment perceptions can be found in Schaie and Willis (1995).

Vandenberg, 1980). Cross-sectional research designs have dominated research in this field, and findings are thus based on comparisons of similarity within couples of different marriage duration. By contrast, we were able to examine a longitudinal sample of married couples for whom we could investigate change in couple similarity over time on our measures of cognitive abilities and cognitive styles (Gruber-Baldini & Schaie, 1986; Gruber-Baldini, Schaie, & Willis, 1995).

This study addresses four questions. First, we asked to what degree couples' scores are similar on cognitive and cognitive style measures and whether spousal similarity varies across abilities. Second, we raised the question whether further convergence occurs as couples remain married for long periods of time. Third, we inquired whether the observed level of similarity is attributable to spousal similarity on background variables such as age and education. Fourth, we examined whether convergence is a product of both spouses changing, or whether one spouse is more likely to move closer to the other's level of functioning over time.

Method

Subjects. We were able to identify 169 married couples where both partners participated in at least two SLS waves. Couples entered the study in either 1956, 1963, or 1970. Data are available over 7 years for 150 couples, over 14 years for 106 couples, and over 21 years for 66 couples. At initial testing, subjects ranged from 22 to 79 years of age. The subjects included in the 21-year analyses (mean age = 42.31 years) were slightly younger than those in the 7-year (mean age = 44.94 years), and 14-year (mean age = 43.18 years) data sets. There were no significant differences in educational, income, and occupational characteristics.

Measures. Variables included in the couples analyses consist of the five PMA subtests (Verbal Meaning, Spatial Orientation, Inductive Reasoning, Number, and Word Fluency), the composite indices of Intellectual Ability and Educational Aptitude, the three factor scores from the TBR (Motor–Cognitive Flexibility, Attitudinal Flexibility, and Psychomotor Speed), and the questionnaire scale of Social Responsibility.

Results of the couples study

The initial correlations among spouses were statistically significant for Verbal Meaning, Inductive Reasoning, and Word Fluency, as well as for the Index of Educational Aptitude and the Social Responsibility scale in all three data sets. The correlations remained significant when controlling for age and educational level of the spouses. Changes (increases) in similarity among couples across time were significant for Verbal Meaning and the Index of Intellectual Ability as well as for the factor scores in Attitudinal Flexibility.

Examination of cross-lag panel correlations suggested that the question of which spouse has more influence on the other may be ability- and time-specific. Husbands' earlier Inductive Reasoning scores positively influenced their wives' Inductive Reasoning scores 7 years later, and wives' Verbal Meaning scores influenced their husbands' Verbal Meaning scores 14 years later.

When couples were divided according to which spouse had the higher initial score, the lower spouses' Attitudinal Flexibility influenced the higher spouses' Motor–Cognitive Flexibility 7 years later. When both age and education were controlled for, the higher functioning spouses' Word Fluency had a positive effect on the lower functioning spouses' Word Fluency and Verbal Meaning scores over both 7 and 14 years.

Couples were also classified on the basis of whether they became more similar or more different or had not significantly changed in magnitude of similarity over a 7-year interval. Couples who became more similar on the ability variables had husbands with higher occupational levels. Couples whose similarity did not change significantly over time had husbands with fewer changes of profession. Couples who became more dissimilar over time had husbands who changed professions more frequently.

Parents and adult offspring

Parent–offspring similarities have traditionally been studied in young adult parents and their children. In this section I describe the first longitudinal data collected on similarity of parents and adult offspring considered specifically as a function of the age of parent–offspring pairs when studied (see Schaie, Plomin, Willis, Gruber-

Baldini, & Dutta, 1992; Schaie, Plomin, Willis, Gruber-Baldini, Dutta, & Bayen, 1993).

Relevance of the SLS to developmental behavior genetics

Developmental behavior genetics has recently begun to focus on change. This is often surprising to those developmentalists who tend to associate the adjectives *genetic* and *stable*. However, longitudinally stable characteristics do not necessarily have a hereditary base, nor are genetically influenced characteristics necessarily stable (Plomin, 1986). The identification of genetic sources of developmental change is important, because change prevails over continuity for most aspects of development. For this reason, a major task for developmental behavior genetics is to explain longitudinal change as well as continuity. It should be emphasized that only longitudinal studies are able to assess genetic change and continuity.

A second issue receiving attention by developmental behavior geneticists is that of nonshared environmental influence. In general, behavior genetic research provides the best available evidence for the importance of environmental influences. This is so because environmental influences have been found to make individuals in the same family as different from one another as are pairs of individuals selected at random from the population. In other words, psychologically relevant environmental influences make individuals in a family different from, not similar to, one another (see Plomin & Daniels, 1987).

The relevance of this issue to our research lies in the usefulness of parent–offspring comparisons for identifying specific sources of nonshared environmental influence by relating experiential differences within pairs to behavioral differences within the pairs. The key question in environmental research is why individuals in the same family are so different from each other. This question can only be addressed by studies that include more than one individual per family (ibid.).

Developmental behavior genetics and adulthood

From a behavior genetic perspective, very little is known about the origins of individual differences in cognitive abilities, personality, and adjustment during the last half of the life span (Plomin & McClearn, 1990). As our analyses have demonstrated, there are vast individual differences in intellectual change across adulthood, ranging from early decrement for some persons to maintenance of function into very advanced age for others; a basic and fundamental research goal must therefore be to account for this individuality in aging. Most behavior genetic research in adulthood involves offspring in their late teens, typically toward the end of high school or at the time of military induction (see Plomin, 1986). In the handful of studies that include older adults, the average age of the sample is typically in the 20s or 30s, and the age range is so great that it is difficult to conduct cross-sectional analyses of family resemblance as a function of age.

The only systematic behavior genetic study in middle and old age is a study organized by Franz Kallman and Gerhard Sander (1948, 1949) in the 1940s. Over 1,000 pairs of twins in New York were studied biennially, with a primary emphasis on physical aspects of aging. Psychological tests were administered to 75 identical and 45 fraternal twin pairs between the ages of 60 and 89 who were selected for cognitive testing on the basis of concordance for relatively good health, lack of institutionalization, and literacy (Kallman, Feingold, & Bondy, 1951). The results were analyzed in terms of intrapair differences rather than correlations: Identical twins show significantly smaller intrapair differences than fraternal twins, with the exception of memory tests involving simple recall of recent material, suggesting the importance of genetic influence on individual differences in cognitive functioning later in life. Small samples of surviving twins were studied again in 1955 (Jarvik, Kallman, Falek, & Kleber, 1957) and 1967 (Jarvik, Blum, & Varma, 1971). In 1967, when the surviving intact pairs were from 77 to 88 years old, 19 pairs – 13 identical and 6 fraternal – were studied again, by means of seven tests of cognitive abilities. This longitudinal sample, however, is so small as to vitiate the comparison of identical and fraternal twin correlations.

One behavior genetic study of older adults has been initiated in Sweden with a sample of twins reared apart and matched twins reared together. In this project, questionnaire data on personality and many other variables were collected for over 300 pairs of twins reared apart and matched pairs of twins reared together, with an age range from 50 to 80 (Pedersen, McClearn, Plomin, Nesselroade, Berg, & DeFore, 1991; Plomin, Pedersen, Nesselroade, & Bergeman, 1988). The second phase of this study involves individual biomedical and behavioral testing of 50 pairs each of identical and fraternal twins reared apart and matched pairs of identical and fraternal twins reared together. A second wave of testing occurred after 3 years, and a third wave, 6 years after initial testing, is in progress. Although the Swedish study will eventually be able to address issues of long-term change, there are currently no longitudinal behavioral genetic studies that extend over extensive portions of the last half of the life span.

By contrast, the research reported here capitalizes on the longitudinal design of the SLS to offer an "instant" longitudinal study of parents and offspring from young adulthood through middle age. Because parents and offspring share family environment as well as heredity, our family design cannot unambiguously disentangle the contributions of heredity and shared environment on familial resemblance. The family design used here, however, has some important advantages over twin and adoption designs. Twins have environmental experiences in common to a much greater extent than do first-degree relatives; furthermore, twin studies estimate higher-order genetic interactions (i.e., epistasis) unique to identical twins. Thus, the results of twin studies may not generalize to the usual case of first-degree relatives either in terms of environmental or genetic factors. Early-adopted individuals are rare, difficult to find later in life, and may differ from nonadopted individuals in terms of the family environments they experience. Also, adoptees are often selectively placed in their adoptive families, which attenuates the separation of genetic and environmental influences when the adoption design is used (Plomin, 1983).

Family studies are valuable because first-degree relatives represent the population to which we wish to generalize the results of behavioral genetic investigations. Furthermore, family studies provide upper-limit estimates of genetic influence – that is, additive genetic influence cannot exceed estimates based on first-degree relatives. Although familial resemblance could reflect family environment as well as shared heredity – which is why estimates of genetic influence are called upper-limit estimates – it appears that shared environmental influences are of negligible importance to personality, psychopathology, and cognitive abilities after adolescence (Plomin, 1987; Plomin & Daniels, 1987). In other words, the important environmental factors in development are no more experienced in common by individuals in the same family than they are by pairs of individuals picked at random from the population. Thus, as a first approximation, it is not unreasonable to assume that familial resemblance later in life is primarily mediated genetically.

Our study is a reasonable first step in understanding the etiology of individual differences in functioning later in life even if a conservative interpretation is taken, in the sense that familial resemblance is not interpreted as exclusively genetic in origin. The family design asks the extent to which individual differences are due to familial factors, whether genetic or environmental, and it provides upperlimit estimates of genetic and shared family environmental influences.

The long-term longitudinal nature of the SLS provides a unique opportunity to study relatives tested at roughly the same age; differences in same-age comparisons of sibling resemblance and parent–offspring resemblance as a function of year of birth yield a novel test of cohort effects. In addition to these same-age comparisons, the SLS data archives make it possible to trace parent–offspring resemblance forward in time by comparing same-age resemblance of parents and offspring to resemblance when the parents are 7, 14, 21, and 28 years older.

Because behavior genetic data during the last half of the life span are virtually nonexistent, it was not possible to propose well-founded hypotheses that could be tested with our data. However, four categories of hypotheses were delineated and addressed in this investigation:

1. *Family similarity in cognitive abilities will be found throughout adulthood, and the relationship will be stronger for verbal ability than for other cognitive abilities.* It is expected that at least modest parent–offspring correlations will be found for all cognitive abilities. However, we also expect that greater similarity will be found for verbal ability. Although evidence is not good that any specific cognitive

ability is more heritable than any other (DeFries, Vandenberg, & McClearn, 1976), there is some evidence that shared family environmental factors are greater for verbal abilities than for other cognitive abilities (Plomin, 1987). This hypothesis seems reasonable when the possibilities for training and modeling are considered – for example, for vocabulary as compared with spatial ability. For this reason, we predict that familial resemblance will be greater for the two verbal tests Verbal Ability and Word Fluency than for other abilities. Further, if this effect is due to shared family environment, we would expect the effect to diminish with age.

2. *Familial resemblance in cognitive abilities is expected to increase from early adulthood to middle adulthood.* It is generally assumed that non-normative experiences increase in importance during development (Baltes, Reese, & Lipsitt, 1980), which would lead to the prediction that familial resemblance for cognitive abilities should decrease during adulthood. However, four recent behavior genetic studies of adoptive siblings all indicate that shared family environmental influences that affect general cognitive ability are of negligible importance after adolescence (Plomin, 1987). This means that the environmental component of familial resemblance does not appear to change during adulthood. In contrast, there is some evidence that genetic influence increases in importance during adulthood (Plomin & Thompson, 1987). If genetic influence increases, we are led to the counterintuitive (from an environmental perspective) hypothesis that familial resemblance in cognitive abilities increases later in life, decades after family members have left their shared family environment. In order to test this hypothesis, familial resemblance will be examined as a function of age.

3. *Familial influences are expected to exert long-term effects on cognitive abilities throughout the adult life course.* If it is assumed that shared environmental influences are relatively unimportant in adulthood (implying that such influences do not contribute to family resemblance), one would not expect to find – strictly from an environmental perspective – familial resemblance with either same-age or cross-age comparisons. However, there is increasing evidence that genetic influence on cognitive abilities shows substantial continuity throughout adulthood (Plomin & Thompson, 1987). For example, model-fitting analyses of adoption data have indicated that genetic

effects in childhood are highly correlated with genetic effects in adulthood for IQ (DeFries, Plomin, & LaBuda, 1987). This leads to the prediction that long-term familial (presumably genetic) effects will produce familial resemblance in cognitive abilities even when one family member is assessed at a very different age from another family member. This hypothesis can be tested by assessing family resemblance cross-sectionally over a wide range of ages, as well as longitudinally within the same data set. The simplest analytic approach to this problem is to test whether familial resemblance differs as a function of the interval at which the family members were assessed (see also Schaie, 1975, for alternative methods of analysis).

4. *Cohort effects will be seen, in that parent–offspring correlations will be greater for earlier cohorts of adult offspring.* The striking finding that shared family environmental influence is negligible for cognitive ability after adolescence has been studied only in recent cohorts. Earlier cohorts will show greater shared family environmental influence if the influence of the family on cognitive scores has declined or if the importance of extrafamilial influences such as television has increased. Older and younger cohorts of parent–offspring relatives yield the same expectation of genetic similarity unless the magnitude of assortative mating has changed (see above, and see Gruber-Baldini, Schaie, & Willis, 1995). As a test of the hypothesis of cohort effects, parent–offspring resemblances were assessed as a function of year of birth.

Method

Subjects. The participants in this study consist of the adult offspring (aged 22 or older in 1990) of members of the SLS panels and their target relatives. Those members who participated in the fifth cycle of the SLS had a total of 3,507 adult children. Of these, 1,416 adult children (M = 701, F = 715) resided in the Seattle metropolitan area.

The adult offspring were recruited in two ways. (1) A letter containing an update report on the SLS was sent to all study participants tested in 1983–84. This letter also announced the

Table 13.1. *Age and sex distribution of parent–offspring study participants*

Age range	Parents (1984)			Offspring (1990)		
	Male	Female	Total	Male	Female	Total
22–28	—	—	—	21	30	51
29–35	—	—	—	52	96	148
36–42	—	11	11	48	82	130
43–49	15	27	42	43	55	98
50–56	34	63	97	25	34	59
57–63	56	59	115	14	17	31
64–70	49	69	118	3	6	9
71–77	35	52	87	2	3	5
79–84	16	28	44	—	—	—
85–91	9	8	17	—	—	—
Total	214	317	531	208	323	531

family resemblance study and requested that panel members provide names and addresses of siblings and offspring. A recruitment letter was then sent to all offspring thus identified. (2) We also searched the participating HMO records to identify offspring and siblings of longitudinal panel members who had dropped out because of death or illness. Offspring of some panel members were also identified because they were included in their parents' service contracts. Surviving spouses were also identified in the same manner and were used as informants to obtain addresses for offspring of deceased panel members. We were able to test 531 adult offspring. Of these study participants, 439 (82.7%) resided in the Seattle metropolitan area; the remaining 92 (17.3%) were scattered through the United States and Canada. The offspring, in 1990, ranged in age from 22 to 74 (mean = 40.43; SD = 10.45). Target parents ranged in age from 39 to 91 at the time they were last tested, in 1984 (mean = 63.66; SD = 10.89). All participants were community-dwelling individuals when tested. This data set includes 99 father–son pairs, 211 mother–daughter pairs, 115 father–daughter pairs, and 106 mother–son pairs. Data on age and gender by subset are provided in Table 13.1.

Measures. The test battery administered to the participants in this study is a subset of measures administered to their parents. It includes the PMA tests of Verbal Meaning, Spatial Orientation, Inductive Reasoning, Number, and Word Fluency. In addition, the ETS Finding A's test was included as a measure of perceptual speed, and the Test of Behavioral Rigidity was used to assess cognitive styles.

Procedure. Potential subjects who agreed to participate were scheduled by telephone for group assessment sessions. Size of the groups ranged from 5 to 20, depending on the age of the subjects. The testing sessions lasted approximately $2\frac{1}{2}$ hours plus a take-home package of questionnaires requiring approximately an additional hour of effort. Each session was conducted by a psychometrist, aided by a proctor whenever more than 5 participants were tested simultaneously. Subjects were paid $25 for their participation.

Analyses. Regression analyses were employed to analyze parent–offspring resemblance and to determine the extent to which familial resemblance differs as a function of other variables, such as age and testing interval, as well as other variables such as gender, time of measurement, and demographic factors (DeFries & Fulker, 1985; Ho, Foch, & Plomin, 1980; Zieleniewski, Fulker, DeFries, & LaBuda, 1987). This least squares model fitting represents a straightforward approach to the analysis of such simple designs as the family design in which we do not attempt to differentiate genetic and environmental components of variance. For example, we may regress out the effects of parent and offspring age to obtain net estimates of the parent–offspring correlations. Alternatively, we may ask the question whether the family similarity differs as a function of offspring age. Using hierarchical multiple regression (Cohen & Cohen, 1975), we regress the parent's score on three predictors: (1) the offspring's score, (2) the offspring's age, and (3) the interaction between offspring age and performance. A significant standard partial regression coefficient for the interaction of offspring score and age indicates that family resemblance differs as a function of offspring age.

Estimation of genetic parameters. In addition to these straightforward analyses of familial resemblance and its interaction with other variables, genetic analyses can be conducted if the assumption is made that shared environment does not contribute to familial resemblance – in other words, if it is assumed that familial resemblance is due solely to hereditary factors. As indicated earlier, this appears to be a reasonable assumption for cognitive abilities in adulthood; however, the novelty of this conclusion and the need for more data to confirm it limit the following genetic analyses to exploratory ventures rather than precise estimates of genetic parameters. If the assumption is made that shared environment does not contribute to familial resemblance in cognitive abilities, doubling parent–offspring correlations provides estimates of heritability: the proportion of phenotypic variance that can be explained by genetic variance (see also Plomin, DeFries & McClearn, 1980). If, for example, a same-age parent–offspring correlation of .30 were obtained for the PMA Spatial Orientation test, it would suggest a heritability of .60 if shared environment does not contribute to the parent–offspring similarity. The rest of the variance is nongenetic; some of the nongenetic variance involves error of measurement, and the remainder is due to nonshared environment. The regression analyses described above provide estimates of heritability across ages, with interactions between familial resemblance and age defining age trends in heritability.

It should again be emphasized that heritability is a descriptive statistic and thus will change as the relative contributions of genetic and environmental influences change in different populations or during development. These statistics imply no more precision than do other descriptive statistics; as for all descriptive statistics, standard errors of estimate need to be consulted to evaluate precision. Most important, heritability does not imply immutability: It simply refers to the proportion of observed interindividual variance in a population that is due to genetic differences among individuals.

Results of the parent–offspring study

Findings on parent–offspring similarity will first be presented in terms of the correlation of parental performance with that of their

Table 13.2. *Correlation of parents and offspring*

Variable	Total ($N = 531$)	Father–son ($N = 99$)	Mother–daughter ($N = 211$)	Father–daughter ($N = 115$)	Mother–son ($N = 106$)
Verbal Meaning	0.14**	0.22*	0.18**	0.00	0.09
Space	0.24***	0.10	0.22**	0.32***	0.27**
Reasoning	0.28***	0.17	0.32***	0.34***	0.40***
Number	0.19***	0.24*	0.19**	0.20*	0.12
Word Fluency	0.27***	0.18	0.33***	0.20*	0.19*
Finding A's	0.10*	−0.09	0.20**	0.12	0.12
Intellectual Ability[a]	0.26***	0.13	0.30***	0.37***	0.20*
Educational Aptitude[b]	0.20***	0.26*	0.23**	0.13	0.16
Motor–Cognitive Flexibility	0.29***	0.07	0.25***	0.43***	0.36***
Attitudinal Flexibility	0.13**	0.08	0.09	0.20	0.21*
Psychomotor Speed	0.21***	0.17	0.23***	0.04	0.36***
Social Responsibility	0.00	−0.07	−0.02	0.09	0.06

[a] Weighted linear combination of first five mental abilities, IA = V + S + 2R + 2N + W (Thurstone & Thurstone, 1949).
[b] Estimate of Educational Aptitude, EA = 2V + R.
*$p < 0.05$; **$p < 0.01$; ***$p < 0.001$.

offspring, as well as of adjusted coefficients when the regression of parental and offspring age on the dependent variables has been removed. We will next consider the stability of parent–offspring correlations across time (and age). The possible effect of shared environment is then reported by considering the correlation of intensity of current contact between parents and offspring. Age/cohort differences in the magnitude of parent–offspring correlation are also examined. Finally, we consider the magnitudes of generational differences in level within families, as well as changes in the magnitude of these differences for successive cohort groupings.

Parent–offspring correlations. As shown in Table 13.2 and Figure 13.1, parent–offspring correlations for the total sample were statistically significant ($p < .05$) for all variables studied except for the trait measure of Social Responsibility. Among the ability measures, correlations were highest for Inductive Reasoning, Word Fluency,

Figure 13.1. Parent–offspring correlations. The value for Social Responsibility is zero. Adapted from Schaie, Plomin, Willis, Gruber-Baldini, & Dutta, 1992.

Table 13.3. *Correlation of parents and offspring, adjusted for age at test*

Variable	Total	Father–Son	Mother–daughter	Father–daughter	Mother–son
Verbal Meaning	0.25***	0.30***	0.30***	0.10	0.21*
Space	0.15**	0.04	0.10	0.27**	0.16*
Reasoning	0.21***	0.19*	0.21**	0.28***	0.31**
Number	0.21***	0.25**	0.22**	0.24*	0.11
Word Fluency	0.27***	0.22*	0.35***	0.21*	0.13
Finding A's	0.07	−0.12	0.15*	0.11	0.08
Intellectual Ability	0.29***	0.21*	0.31***	0.43***	0.17*
Educational Aptitude	0.29***	0.34**	0.32***	0.18*	0.25*
Motor–Cognitive Flexibility	0.21**	0.04	0.16*	0.39***	0.22*
Attitudinal Flexibility	0.15**	0.10	0.10	0.11	0.23*
Psychomotor Speed	0.21***	0.19*	0.25***	0.01	0.26***
Social Responsibility	−0.00	−0.03	−0.04	0.11	0.03

$*p < 0.05$; $**p < 0.01$; $***p < 0.001$.

and the Intellectual Ability composite measure. They were lowest for the measures of Perceptual Speed (the Finding A's test) and Verbal Meaning. Among the cognitive style measures, correlations were highest for Motor–Cognitive Flexibility and lowest for Attitudinal Flexibility.

Because of the wide age range among parents and offspring (and to model the assumption of equal ages), we partialled out the effects of parent and offspring age. The correlations adjusted for age at the most recent test are provided in Table 13.3 and Figure 13.2. Subsequent to the age adjustment, all but the measures of Perceptual Speed and Social Responsibility remain statistically significant ($p < .01$). However, the magnitudes of the correlations change somewhat, with Word Fluency and Verbal Meaning now displaying the highest ability correlations, along with the composite indices of Intellectual Ability and Educational Aptitude. Both Motor–Cognitive Flexibility and Psychomotor Speed continue to show higher family resemblance than does Attitudinal Flexibility.

The correlational findings are not uniform across subsets. When raw parent–offspring correlations are examined (Table 13.2 and

Figure 13.2. Parent–offspring correlations, adjusted for age. The value for Social Responsibility is zero. Adapted from Schaie, Plomin, Willis, Gruber-Baldini, & Dutta, 1992.

Figure 13.1), statistically significant correlations ($p < .05$) between fathers and sons are found only for Verbal Meaning, Number, and Educational Aptitude. For the mother–daughter set, however, statistically significant correlations ($p < .05$) are found for all variables except Attitudinal Flexibility and Social Responsibility. Correlations between fathers and daughters are statistically significant ($p < .05$) for Spatial Orientation, Inductive Reasoning, Number, Word Fluency, the Index of Intellectual Ability, and Motor–Cognitive Flexibility. Finally, for the mother–son set, statistically significant ($p < .05$) correlations are found for Spatial Orientation, Inductive Reasoning, Word Fluency, Intellectual Ability, Motor–Cognitive Flexibility, and Psychomotor Speed.

When age of parent and offspring is controlled for, further differences between subsets are observed (see Table 13.3). Statistically significant correlations ($p < .05$) between fathers and sons are now found for Verbal Meaning, Word Fluency, Inductive Reasoning, Number, Intellectual Ability, Educational Aptitude, and Psychomotor Speed. For the mother–daughter set, however, statistically significant correlations ($p < .05$) continue to be found for all variables except Spatial Orientation, Attitudinal Flexibility, and Social Responsibility. Correlations between fathers and daughters remain statistically significant ($p < .05$) for the same variables as for the raw correlations. For the mother–son set, statistically significant correlations ($p < .05$) are now found for Verbal Meaning, Spatial Orientation, Inductive Reasoning, the composite indices, Motor–Cognitive Flexibility, Attitudinal Flexibility, and Psychomotor Speed.

Stability of parent–offspring correlations over time. One of the critical issues in studying family similarity in adulthood is to determine whether such similarity remains stable or changes as the distance in age at time of assessment between parent and offspring increases. To examine stability of correlations with a sufficiently large sample, we considered for this analysis only those parent–offspring pairs for whom at least four data points (1963, 1970, 1977, and 1984) were available for the parents, yielding a set of 162 participant pairs, who were tested 6, 13, 20, and 27 years apart, respectively. Note that for the first data point (1963), parents are closest to the age at which their offspring were tested in 1990. The top of Table 13.4 and

Table 13.4. *Parent–offspring comparisons across time*

Variable	Parents tested in			
	1963	1970	1977	1984
Correlations as a function of time[a]				
Verbal Meaning	0.24**	0.22**	0.19*	0.20**
Space	0.26**	0.17*	0.30***	0.22**
Reasoning	0.29***	0.34***	0.32***	0.33***
Number	0.13	0.16*	0.14	0.20**
Word Fluency	0.36***	0.22**	0.31***	0.29***
Finding A's	—	—	0.18*	0.21**
Intellectual Ability	0.24**	0.25**	0.23**	0.25**
Educational Aptitude	0.25**	0.27**	0.21**	0.27**
Motor–Cognitive Flexibility	0.14	0.10	0.27**	0.23**
Attitudinal Flexibility	0.16*	0.12	0.13	0.11
Psychomotor Speed	0.40***	0.35***	0.42***	0.40***
Social Responsibility	0.01	0.09	0.12	0.07
Standardized regression coefficients adjusted for parent and offspring age				
Verbal Meaning	0.26**	0.26**	0.23**	0.26**
Space	0.20*	0.10	0.26**	0.13
Reasoning	0.24**	0.30***	0.27**	0.29**
Number	0.15*	0.17*	0.18*	0.24**
Word Fluency	0.36***	0.22**	0.31***	0.29***
Finding A's	—	—	0.15*	0.18*
Intellectual Ability	0.25**	0.26**	0.26**	0.28***
Educational Aptitude	0.18*	0.29**	0.24**	0.31***
Motor–Cognitive Flexibility	0.10	0.05	0.23**	0.20*
Attitudinal Flexibility	0.15*	0.11	0.11	0.12
Psychomotor Speed	0.38***	0.32***	0.42***	0.38***
Social Responsibility	0.00	0.08	0.10	0.06

[a] Offspring ages in 1990 are approximately equal to parental ages in 1963; age differences increase for each successive data point.
*$p < 0.05$; **$p < 0.01$; ***$p < 0.001$.

Figure 13.3 shows the stability results in terms of raw correlations. Note that there is good stability of parent–offspring correlations for all variables. For this data set, however, values for Social Responsibility do not reach statistical significance at any time point, for Attitudinal Flexibility only for the 1963 comparison, and for Number only for 1970 and 1984.

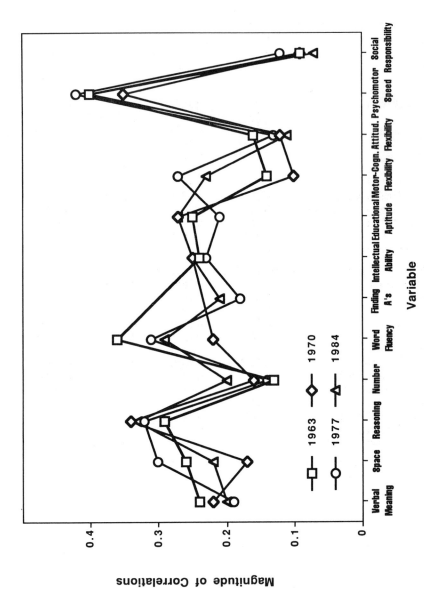

Figure 13.3. Stability of parent–offspring correlations. Adapted from Schaie, Plomin, Willis, Gruber–Baldini, & Dutta,

Table 13.5. *Contact of parents and offspring*

Variable	Total	Father–son	Mother–daughter	Father–daughter	Mother–son
Mean contact	19.01	17.81	19.72	19.17	18.51
SD	3.60	4.09	3.23	3.45	3.64

Note: Contact score is the sum of six Likert scale items; total sum can range from 0 to 41. Actual observed range: 2 to 28.

For comparability with the initial analyses, age was controlled for also in the stability analyses. Relevant data are reported in the lower part of Table 13.4. The observed stability of parent–offspring correlations remains impressive. After age adjustment, values for Social Responsibility continue to fail to reach statistical significance. All values are now significant for Number, but Spatial Orientation is significant only for the 1963 and 1977 comparisons, Motor–Cognitive Flexibility reaches significant levels only in 1977 and 1984, and Attitudinal Flexibility is significant only in the 1963 comparison.

Effects of current family contact. All offspring were asked to indicate the intensity of their current contact with their parents on a multiple Likert scale questionaire. As can be seen from Table 13.5, intensity of contact was slightly greater for daughters than sons; contact was greatest for the mother–daughter and lowest for the father–son sets; the latter two sets differed significantly ($p < .01$). Degree of contact, however, did not significantly correlate with age of parent or offspring.

Magnitudes of parent–offspring resemblance, adjusted for age, were reexamined to consider the effect of contact. This analysis led to slight upward adjustment of some coefficients, but all significant regressions for intensity of contact were negative! That is, parent–offspring resemblance was greater with *less* contact. Significant statistical effects of contact ($p < .05$) were found for the total sample only for Verbal Meaning, Spatial Orientation, Number, and Attitudinal Flexibility.

Table 13.6. *Parent–offspring correlations as a function of cohort*

| Variable | Cohort grouping | | |
	Youngest (1955–68) $N = 199$	Middle-aged (1931–54) $N = 228$	Older (before 1931) $N = 104$
Verbal Meaning	0.21**	0.23**	0.05
Space	0.22**	0.16**	0.11
Reasoning	0.18**	0.29***	0.26***
Number	0.18**	0.25***	0.16
Word Fluency	0.26***	0.29***	0.25**
Finding A's	0.12	0.21**	0.02
Intellectual Ability	0.22**	0.27***	0.26**
Educational Aptitude	0.25**	0.25***	0.11
Motor–Cognitive Flexibility	0.14*	0.06	0.45***
Attitudinal Flexibility	0.13	0.16*	0.07
Psychomotor Speed	0.04	0.36***	0.04
Social Responsibility	0.20**	0.13*	0.07

$*p < 0.05; **p < 0.01; ***p < 0.001.$

Age/cohort differences in parent–offspring correlations. The magnitude of parent–offspring correlations is next considered as a function of age/cohort membership. Because most of our participants (whether parents or adult offspring) were assessed at ages where stability of cognitive performance is the rule rather than the exception (see Schaie, 1983a), it makes sense to organize these data by cohort rather than by age. For this reason we divided the total sample into a youngest cohort (N = 199; birth years 1955 to 1968), a middle-aged cohort (N = 228; birth years 1931 to 1954), and an older cohort (N = 104; birth years before 1931).

As can be seen from Table 13.6 and Figure 13.4, there are substantial differences in pattern and magnitude of correlations. Parent–offspring correlations for the youngest cohort are statistically significant (p < .05) for all variables but Perceptual Speed, Attitudinal Flexibility, and Psychomotor Speed; for the middle-aged cohort, correlations are statistically significant (p < .05) for all variables except for Motor–Cognitive Flexibility. For the oldest cohort, however, correlations are statistically significant (p < .05)

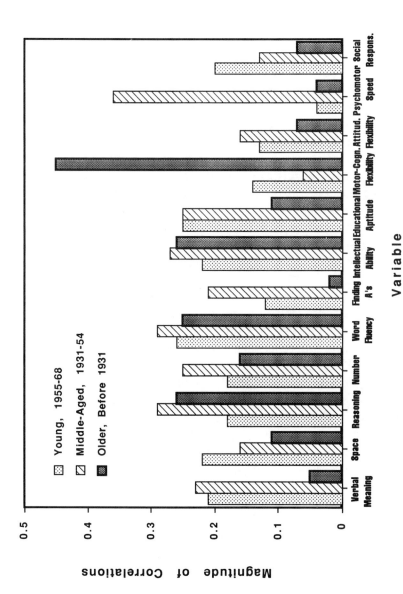

Figure 13.4. Parent–offspring correlations, by cohort. Adapted from Schaie, Plomin, Willis, Gruber-Baldini, & Dutta, 1992.

only for Inductive Reasoning, Word Fluency, Intellectual Ability, and Motor–Cognitive Flexibility. Correlations rise generally from the older to the youngest cohort. However, the correlations drop across cohorts for Inductive Reasoning and Motor–Cognitive Flexibility and show a curvilinear pattern for Psychomotor Speed.

In sum, it does not appear that there are significant differences between the younger and the middle cohort, but there might well be lower relationships for the older cohort, albeit the latter finding might be shaky because of the smaller size of the older group.

The effect of offspring age on family resemblance was tested directly in the total sample by regressing parent performance scores on the interaction of offspring age and offspring performance while controlling for the offspring performance and for the age main effects (hierarchical multiple regression; see Cohen & Cohen, 1975). Only two statistically significant interactions ($p < .05$) were found. They suggest that older offspring showed greater resemblance in Perceptual Speed and Motor–Cognitive Flexibility.

Cohort differences between parents and offspring. To permit comparison with previously determined population values, mean level scores were standardized to T-scores (mean = 50, *SD* = 10). The average parent–offspring differences were then computed in T-score points (see Table 13.7). Note first that there are statistically significant level differences ($p < .001$) for all variables. Raw differences are in favor of the offspring, except differences for Number and Social Responsibility, which favor the parents.

Because of average within-subject age changes, the raw differences must be adjusted before comparison with population cohort differences. This was done by computing the average within-subject age changes found over the range of mean ages for our parents and offspring (using the relevant information provided in Schaie, 1983a). These values are found in the second column of Table 13.7, with adjusted net differences in the third column. After age adjustment, differences are no longer statistically significant for Word Fluency, the Index of Intellectual Ability, and Attitudinal Flexibility. The direction of differences in the remaining variables remains as before the age adjustment.

The fourth column of Table 13.7 provides population cohort

Table 13.7. *Parent–offspring generational differences in performance level*[a]

Variable	Parent–offspring difference	Expected age difference	Net difference	Population difference
Verbal Meaning	2.75***	1.01	1.74**	2.28**
Space	5.06***	1.31*	3.75***	−0.78
Reasoning	6.45***	1.77**	4.68***	2.99***
Number	−1.83***	3.04***	−4.87***	−4.26***
Word Fluency	1.73***	2.46**	−0.73	0.56
Finding A's	2.36***	9.06***	−6.70***	3.55***
Intellectual Ability	2.86***	1.52*	1.34	−0.79
Educational Aptitude	3.73***	1.95**	1.78**	2.67***
Motor–Cognitive Flexibility	6.73***	−0.53	7.26***	5.43***
Attitudinal Flexibility	2.33***	2.03**	0.30	4.42***
Psychomotor Speed	9.19***	3.15***	6.04***	3.22***
Social Responsibility	−3.89***	0.23	−4.12***	−9.43***

[a] Positive values are in favor of the offspring. All values are T-scores, with a population mean of 50 and standard deviation of 10, computed on the basis of 3,442 study participants at first test, except for Finding A's, which is based on 1,628 participants.
$*p < 0.05$; $**p < 0.01$; $***p < 0.001$.

differences over the mean birth years represented by our parents and offspring (also obtained from Schaie, 1983a). Inspection of the third and fourth columns of Table 13.7 (and Figure 13.5) therefore allows us to compare population cohort difference estimates with those found for our "natural" cohort. The cohort difference estimates are quite comparable, except for four noteworthy exceptions: (1) Spatial Orientation provides a significant cohort difference in the present study but not in the population for similar birth years. (2) Perceptual Speed in the natural cohort favors the offspring, but in the population estimate shows an advantage for older cohorts. (3) We find no significant difference in Attitudinal Flexibility in this study, but population values argue for an advantage for younger cohorts. (4) The Social Responsibility difference favoring the older cohort is less than half the value estimated for the population.

We finally address the question whether parent–offspring performance differences might be affected by cohort groupings.

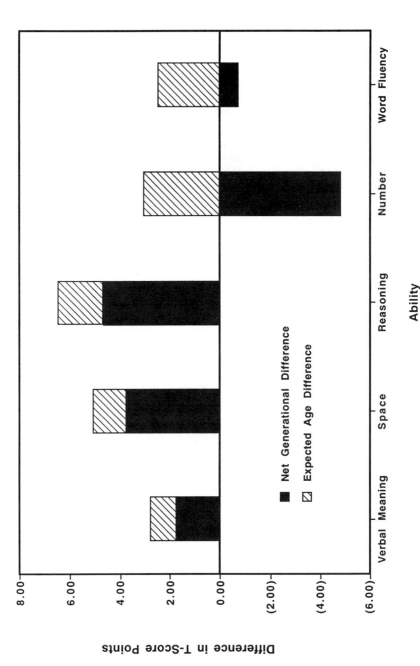

Figure 13.5. Generational differences between parents and offspring, in T-score points. Adapted from Schaie, Plomin, Willis, Gruber-Baldini, & Dutta, 1992.

Table 13.8. *Performance differences between parents and offspring as a function of cohort grouping*

| | Cohort grouping | | |
| | Youngest (1955–69) $N = 199$ | Middle-aged (1931–54) $N = 228$ | Older (before 1931) $N = 104$ |
Variable			
Verbal Meaning	−1.83**	3.83***	9.82***
Space	4.49***	4.57***	7.48***
Reasoning	3.73***	7.56***	9.49***
Number	−5.43***	1.37	2.43**
Word Fluency	−0.74	3.22***	3.89**
Finding A's	2.40*	2.73**	1.40
Intellectual Ability	−0.58	3.85***	7.68***
Educational Aptitude	−0.48	4.98***	10.10***
Motor–Cognitive Flexibility	4.38***	7.06***	10.18***
Attitudinal Flexibility	−0.49	2.70***	7.30***
Psychomotor Speed	6.09***	10.75***	11.99***
Social Responsibility	−6.11***	−3.60***	0.13

Note: Values in T-scores (see Table 13.7).
*$p < 0.05$; **$p < 0.01$; ***$p < 0.001$.

Using the cohort subsets described earlier, we report raw mean differences in Table 13.8 and Figure 13.6. As would be expected because of the increase in age of the parents for the groups, differences here are least for the youngest cohort and greatest for the older. Nevertheless, even in the youngest group, differences in favor of the offspring remain significant for Spatial Orientation, Inductive Reasoning, Perceptual Speed, Motor–Cognitive Flexibility, and Psychomotor Speed; differences in Verbal Meaning, Number, and Social Responsibility favor the parents. For the middle group, all variables favor the offspring, except for Number (nonsignificant difference) and Social Responsibility (which favor the parents). For the older cohort, all differences except Perceptual Speed and Social Responsibility significantly favor the offspring.

Summary and conclusions. Significant family similarities were observed for our total sample for all ability measures except Perceptual Speed

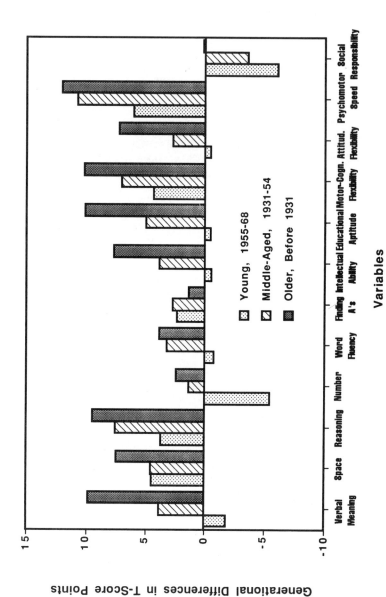

Figure 13.6. Generational differences between parents and offspring, by cohort. Adapted from Schaie, Plomin, Willis, Gruber-Baldini, & Dutta, 1992.

and the cognitive style measures. The magnitude of correlations for the ability measures are comparable to those found between young adults and their children (DeFries, Ashton, et al., 1976). Like the DeFries et al. study, we also found differences in resemblance across subsets. For example, same-gender pairs showed higher correlations on Verbal Meaning, Number, and Word Fluency, but opposite-gender pairs on Spatial Orientation, Inductive Reasoning, and Motor–Cognitive Flexibility. Greater similarity was also found between mother–offspring pairs than between father–offspring pairs on Inductive Reasoning and Psychomotor Speed. Moreover, higher parent–offspring correlations were found for daughters than for sons, suggesting at least the possibility that females may experience greater shared environmental influences than males. Our first hypothesis also argued for the possible effect of early shared environment on offspring performance on Verbal Meaning and Word Fluency. After age adjustment, these were indeed the abilities that showed the greatest parent–offspring similarity.

If shared environmental influences are relatively unimportant in adulthood, then similarity within parent–offspring pairs should remain reasonably constant in adulthood across time and age. Our data strongly support this proposition for all of those variables that displayed significant parent–offspring correlations. Indeed, parent–offspring correlations measured at approximately the same age of parent and offspring and when those ages were 20 years apart had similar magnitudes.

It has been argued that family similarity should decrease with age because of the increasing amount of nonnormative nonshared environment expected as adult life progresses. Counterintuitively, no such decrease in similarity could be observed. Indeed, for two variables there was evidence for increasing similarity as a function of offspring age. This finding makes good sense for our Perceptual Speed variable. Most of our younger offspring typically have not yet experienced age-related decline on this variable, whereas some of their parents have. Both older offspring and parents may have experienced sufficient decline so that once again their observed similarity is increased. The other variable showing an age effect was Motor–Cognitive Flexibility. In this instance, our cross-sectional data may confound substantial cohort effects that could have spuriously inflated the offspring age effect.

Further evidence supporting the absence of shared environmental effects on family similarity were provided by our analyses of the intensity of current parent–offspring contact. All of the few observed significant, but very modest, effects of contact on parent–offspring resemblance in performance (for Verbal Meaning, Spatial Orientation, Number, and Attitudinal Flexibility) were in a negative direction!

We had suspected that cohort effects in parent–offspring correlations would result in higher correlations for earlier cohorts because of a decline in shared environmental influence attributed to an increase in extrafamilial influences in more recent cohorts. This proposition could be supported only for the attitudinal trait of Social Responsibility (systematic cohort differences on this variable have previously been reported; see Schaie & Parham, 1974). For the cognitive abilities, once again counterintuitively, there seems to be stability or even an increase in family similarity for more recent cohorts. And as in the population estimates (Schaie, 1990b) and in other studies (see Sundet, Tambs, Magnus, & Berg, 1988), nonlinear cohort trends were also observed. One plausible explanation for the increase in family similarity in successive cohorts might be the decrease of intrafamilial differences in level of education from our oldest cohort grouping to our youngest.

Finally, we asked whether level differences within families equaled or approximated differences found for similar cohort ranges within a general population sample (see Schaie, 1990b; Willis, 1989a). Comparable differences were found to be the rule, but there were some noteworthy exceptions. Thus the population estimates were found to underestimate the advantage of the offspring cohort for Spatial Orientation and Psychomotor Speed, but to overestimate that advantage for Perceptual Speed. On the attitudinal trait of Social Responsibility, however, the estimated cohort difference in favor of the parent cohort was far greater in the population than that observed in the natural cohort. When broken down by cohort groupings, it became clear that cohort differences became generally smaller for the more recently born parent–offspring pairs, with the exception of increasing differences in favor of the parent generation for Number and Social Responsibility.

Adult siblings

As part of the family study described above, we identified a total of 1,999 siblings, including 779 brothers and 1,020 sisters of our panel members. We were able to assess a total of 304 siblings, resulting in 45 brother–brother pairs, 102 sister–sister pairs, and 157 brother–sister pairs. The newly assessed siblings in 1990 ranged in age from 22 to 89 (mean = 58.26; *SD* = 14.56). Target siblings ranged in age from 24 to 89 when tested in 1984 (mean = 53.26; *SD* = 13.95). All study participants were community-dwelling individuals when tested (see Schaie et al., 1993).

Sibling correlations

In the case of the siblings, the performance of the target sibling is regressed on the index case (the sibling assessed in 1990). The raw correlations are shown in the third column of Table 13.9. Sibling correlations were statistically significant ($p < .01$) for all variables studied except for Perceptual Speed and the trait measure of Social Responsibility. Among the ability measures, correlations were highest for Inductive Reasoning and Verbal Meaning, as well as for the composite measures. They were lowest for the measures of Perceptual Speed (the Finding A's test), Space, and Word Fluency. Among the cognitive style measures, correlations were highest for Motor–Cognitive Flexibility and lowest for Attitudinal Flexibility.

Again, adjustment is needed for the age of siblings to meet assumptions for heritability estimates. The standardized regression coefficients adjusted for the age of both siblings can be found in the last column of Table 13.9. Subsequent to the age adjustment, all but the measures of Perceptual Speed and Social Responsibility remain statistically significant ($p < .05$). However, the magnitudes of the correlations change somewhat, with Verbal Meaning and Number now displaying the highest ability correlations. Correlations for the cognitive style measures are reduced and are now of about equal magnitude.

Table 13.9. *Sibling correlations*

Variable	Raw	Age-adjusted
Verbal Meaning	0.337***	0.256***
Space	0.256***	0.150**
Reasoning	0.470***	0.212***
Number	0.266***	0.262***
Word Fluency	0.270***	0.201***
Finding A's	0.068	0.032
Intellectual Ability[a]	0.351***	0.219***
Educational Aptitude[b]	0.381***	0.239***
Motor–Cognitive Flexibility	0.316***	0.129*
Attitudinal Flexibility	0.163**	0.109*
Psychomotor Speed	0.290***	0.138**
Social Responsibility	−0.044	−0.033

[a] Weighted linear combination of first five mental abilities: IA = V + S + 2R + 2N + W (Thurstone & Thurstone, 1949).
[b] Estimate of Educational Aptitude, EA = 2V + R.
$*p < 0.05; **p < 0.01; ***p < 0.001.$

Stability of sibling correlations over time

Regression coefficients adjusted for age of both siblings were also computed between the index sibling and the performance of the target sibling in 1963, 1970, 1977, and 1984. Because of the relatively small number of pairs for which all four data points were available ($N = 72$), the demonstration of stability is not quite as good as for the parent–offspring pairs. Relevant data are provided in Table 13.10. There is strong evidence for the stability of sibling concordance for Number and Psychomotor Speed. Stable trends seem to prevail as well for Space, Reasoning, and the composite indices.

Summary and conclusions

Just as for parent–offspring pairs, substantial adult family similarity could be documented also for the sibling pairs. The two exceptions to this finding were the attitudinal trait of Social Responsibility and

Table 13.10. *Sibling correlations as a function of time, adjusted for age of both siblings*

Variable	Target siblings tested in			
	1963	1970	1977	1984
Verbal Meaning	0.153	0.114	0.124	0.191*
Space	0.107	0.204*	0.169	0.303**
Reasoning	0.157	0.239*	0.244*	0.043
Number	0.408***	0.276**	0.388***	0.368***
Word Fluency	0.052	0.061	0.155	0.012
Finding A's	—	—	0.107	0.085
Intellectual Ability	0.177	0.176	0.235*	0.164
Educational Aptitude	0.135	0.124	0.116	0.124
Motor–Cognitive Flexibility	−0.018	−0.039	−0.046	−0.075
Attitudinal Flexibility	0.115	0.070	0.211**	0.022
Psychomotor Speed	0.304**	0.259*	0.357***	0.285**
Social Responsibility	0.063	0.178	0.194*	0.149

$*p < 0.05; **p < 0.01; ***p < 0.001.$

the measure of Perceptual Speed; neither seems to display heritable characteristics. In general, parent–offspring and sibling correlations were of similar magnitude. However, after controlling for age, sibling correlations were somewhat lower than those observed for the parent–offspring pairs. Stability data for the siblings could be strongly confirmed only for the variables of Number and Psychomotor Speed. Trends comparable to those observed for the parent–offspring pairs for other variables probably failed to reach significance because of the limited power of the longitudinal sibling sample.

Chapter summary

Married couples were studied for as long as 21 years. They showed significant initial within-couple correlations on Verbal Meaning, Inductive Reasoning, and Word Fluency, on the Index of Educational Aptitude, and on Social Responsibility, even when controlling for age and education. Spousal similarity increased by length of marriage on Verbal Meaning, the Index of Intellectual Ability, and Attitudinal Flexibility. Several reciprocal cross-lag effects were found over time, with husbands influencing wives on Inductive Reasoning, and wives influencing husbands on Verbal Meaning. The higher-functioning spouse was found to influence positively the performance level of the lower-functioning spouse over time on Word Fluency and Motor–Cognitive Flexibility.

Studies of families involved adult parents and their adult offspring as well as adult siblings. Significant correlations (averaging about .30) were found for all mental abilities (except for Perceptual Speed) for parent–offspring pairs, with somewhat lower correlations for the siblings. The within-family correlations are of a magnitude similar to those found in parent–offspring studies at younger ages. Some significant differences were found in the magnitude of correlations between same-sex and opposite-sex parent–offspring pairs, and higher parent–offspring correlations were found for daughters than for sons. The stability of parent–offspring correlations remained high over 7, 14, and 21 years and was not affected by the degree of family contact. Significant within-family cohort ability differences were found in favor of the offspring generation, but generational differences became smaller for more recently born parent–offspring pairs.

14

Subjective perceptions of cognitive change

Research on intellectual aging has typically focused on the objective assessment of study participants' performance. However, more recently interest has developed also in the examination of subjects' subjective appraisal of their cognitive performance. Such subjective assessments are thought to play an important role in the process of intellectual aging. Some studies have linked personal expectations of performance on tests or in real-life situations to actual performance on cognitive tasks (see M. E. Lachman, 1983; Willis & Schaie, 1986a). Several studies examining concurrent relationships between intellectual self-efficacy and ability performance have reported that both young and elderly adults are fairly accurate in estimating their intellectual performance (M. E. Lachman & Jelalian, 1984; J. L. Lachman, Lachman, & Thronesbery, 1979; Perlmutter, 1978). Both age groups, moreover, have been found to make more accurate predictions for tests on which they exhibit higher levels of performance (M. E. Lachman & Jelalian, 1984).

The relationship between perceived and actual performance may also be complicated by age and gender differences. Researchers have differed on the question of whether older adults over- or underestimate their performance on abilities on which they perform poorly. There has been some speculation (e.g., Bandura, 1981, 1982) that the elderly *underestimate* their performance. However, findings from other studies (M. E. Lachman & Jelalian, 1984) indicate that the elderly consistently *overestimate* their performance on measures of fluid abilities. Furthermore, researchers examining concurrent relationships between self-efficacy and ability performance often interpret their findings to suggest that age differences in self-efficacy are ability-specific. Hence, these studies imply that the elderly do *not* subscribe to global negative perceptions of their intellectual competence.

Perception of cognitive change over seven years

Most previous studies have focused on the concurrent relationships between perceived competence and its objective measurement (Cornelius & Caspi, 1986; M. E. Lachman & Jelalian, 1984; M. E. Lachman, Steinberg, & Trotter, 1987). By contrast, in the SLS we asked our study participants to compare their 1984 performance on five mental abilities with their performance 7 years earlier (Schaie, Willis, & O'Hanlon, 1994). In a separate study we also assessed subjects' perception of improvement as a function of cognitive training.

Subjects were asked to rate whether they thought that their current performance was better, the same, or worse; their responses will be referred to as *perceiver* types. Participants were then categorized in a typology based on the congruence between their *perceived* and *actual* performance change over time. Three *congruence* types were identified: realists, optimists, and pessimists.

The questions to be asked were: (1) Are there age and gender differences in perceiver types (better, the same, worse)? (2) Do subjects' current levels of ability performance differ by perceiver type? (3) How accurately can subjects evaluate change in their performance on the five cognitive abilities (congruence between reported perception and actual performance)? (4) Do subjects predict with the same accuracy for all abilities? (5) Are there age and gender differences in congruence types (realists, optimists, pessimists)? (6) Does current level of ability performance differ by congruence type? (7) Does the magnitude of the actual ability change (1977 to 1984) differ by congruence type?

Method

Subjects. The subsample selected for this particular study were those individuals who were tested in 1977 and who returned for the next assessment in 1984. This criterion resulted in a sample of 837 participants (383 men and 454 women) with a mean age in 1984 of 68.36 (SD = 13.34; range: 29 to 95) and a mean educational level of 14.14 years (SD = 3.07). To examine possible age differences among perceiver and congruence types, the sample was divided into three subsets by age in 1984: younger (29 to 49; M = 41.76, SD = 5.20), middle-aged (50 to 70; M = 60.63, SD = 5.73), and older adults (71 to 95; M = 77.24, SD = 5.74).

Procedure. After completing the five PMA tests (V, S, R, N, W), study participants answered the Primary Mental Abilities Retrospective Questionnaire (PMARQ). This questionnaire reminded the participants that they had taken the same five ability tests several years earlier and asked them to reflect on how their performance on the tests just completed (in 1984) compared with their earlier performance (in 1977). Subjects evaluated their relative performance for each of the five abilities using a 5-point scale with the categories (1) much better today, (2) better today, (3) about the same, (4) worse today, (5) much worse today. Because of the small number of persons who chose the extreme categories (1 or 5), these categories were collapsed into a 3-point scale, resulting in three *perceiver types*: better, same, and worse.

Creation of congruence types. Study participants were classified according to how their actual PMA performance had changed between the two test occasions on each of the five abilities. Difference scores between the 1977 and 1984 performance were computed, and subjects were classified into groups showing reliably higher, similar, or lower performance for each ability. The classification criteria for a positive or negative change were that the subject in 1984 performed at least 1 *SEM* below or above his or her 1977 performance (see Dudek, 1979; Schaie, 1989c).

Cross-tabulations between actual performance change and perceived performance change were next examined. Based on the patterns in these tables, the sample was then categorized into three congruence types for each ability: (1) pessimists – individuals who perceived greater negative change, or less improvement in performance relative to their actual change (1977 to 1984); (2) realists – those individuals who accurately predicted change or stability; (3)

Table 14.1. *Schema for classification into congruence types*

Actual change	Reported change		
	Better	Same	Worse
Improved	R	P	P
Same	O	R	P
Declined	O	O	R

R = realist; P = pessimist; O = optimist.

optimists – those who perceived greater positive change or stability than indicated by their actual performance (see Table 14.1).

Results

Age and gender differences in perceiver types. The proportion of subjects who reported that their performance had improved over time ranged from 13.3% for Spatial Orientation to 22.3% for Inductive Reasoning. Those who reported that their performance had remained the same ranged from 47.3% for Spatial Orientation to 71.5% for Verbal Meaning. Those who reported themselves as having performed worse than on the previous test occasion ranged from 8.4% for Verbal Meaning to 39.4% for Spatial Orientation.

For the total sample there was a significant relationship between age and perceiver type for four of the five abilities. On both Verbal Meaning and Inductive Reasoning, more young subjects than old reported that they had become better, whereas more old subjects than young reported having become worse; the middle-aged were in between $(\chi^2(V)[4, N = 818] = 58.35, p < .001; \chi^2(R)[4, N = 818] = 45.18, p < .001)$. On Spatial Orientation, young subjects reported more improvement than did both the old and the middle-aged, and the old reported more decline than did either the young or the middle-aged $(\chi^2[4, N = 818] = 13.61, p < .01)$. However, on Number the age relationship was reversed, with more older individuals reporting that they remained stable or improved and more younger persons reporting that they got worse, with the middle-aged in between ($\chi^2[4, N = 819] = 27.51, p < .001$).

The relationship between age and perceiver type was similar across genders except for a Gender × Perceiver Type interaction for Spatial Orientation ($\chi^2[2, N = 818] = 21.05, p < .001$). On that ability, the proportion of men and women who reported having become better did not differ, but more men than women reported having remained the same, and more men than women reported having gotten worse.

Perceiver type difference in current PMA scores. Differences were examined for participants who had reported that they remained stable, improved, or declined, regardless of the accuracy of their report. A 3 (perceiver type) × 2 (age group) × 2 (gender) ANOVA was run separately for each ability (see Table 14.2 for the associated means). Significant type differences were found for Spatial Orientation ($F[df = 2, 813] = 37.33, p < .001$) and for Word Fluency ($F[df = 2, 811] = 31.49, p < .001$). In both instances, PMA scores were highest for individuals who had reported positive change, in between for those reporting no change, and lowest for those reporting negative change.

Significant Perceiver Type × Age interactions were also found for Spatial Orientation ($F[df = 2, 813] = 3.53, p < .01$) and Number ($F[df = 2, 811] = 2.23, p < .05$). The Type × Age interaction for Spatial Orientation indicated that although there was virtually no performance difference among the three types for the old group, in the young group those who perceived themselves to have improved indeed performed much better than those who perceived themselves to have declined. The Type × Age interaction for Number conversely indicates that whereas there was little difference in performance among the types for either the young or the middle-aged, older adults who perceived themselves to have declined performed at a lower level than did those who perceived themselves to have improved. Significant triple interactions, moreover, were found for Number ($F[df = 4, 811] = 2.75, p < .05$) and Word Fluency ($F[df = 4, 811] = 3.98, p < .01$). The triple interaction on Number reflects the fact that whereas both older adult males and females who perceived themselves to have declined performed at lower

Table 14.2. *Mean T-scores for current performance levels by perceiver type, by ability, age group, and gender*

	Males			Females			Total		
	Better	Same	Worse	Better	Same	Worse	Better	Same	Worse
Verbal Meaning									
Young	57.00	56.53	61.00	56.82	58.40	53.67	56.91	57.47	57.33
Middle	56.09	54.37	52.57	53.24	54.37	51.58	54.67	54.37	52.76
Old	43.86	46.03	39.73	47.25	46.68	42.63	45.55	46.35	41.18
Total	52.31	52.31	51.10	52.44	53.15	49.29	52.38	52.73	50.20
Spatial Orientation									
Young	63.21	58.17	55.58	61.25	57.25	48.32	62.23	57.71	51.95
Middle	54.58	56.87	49.08	54.05	52.82	46.74	54.32	54.85	47.91
Old	43.92	47.92	43.26	45.25	44.67	41.97	44.59	46.29	42.62
Total	53.90	54.32	49.31	53.52	51.58	45.67	53.71	52.95	47.49
Inductive Reasoning									
Young	57.67	57.50	61.62	61.11	58.11	61.14	59.39	57.80	61.38
Middle	53.07	53.52	53.19	52.26	54.45	56.58	52.66	53.99	54.89
Old	45.11	44.90	45.33	47.43	45.29	44.58	46.27	45.10	44.96
Total	51.95	51.97	53.38	53.60	52.62	54.10	52.78	52.30	53.74
Number									
Young	48.80	52.07	58.12	50.22	50.51	46.12	49.51	51.29	52.12
Middle	53.98	52.23	50.64	48.71	49.98	51.00	51.34	51.10	50.82
Old	51.23	48.75	44.32	50.50	47.11	45.31	50.87	47.93	44.82
Total	51.34	51.02	51.02	49.81	49.20	47.48	50.57	50.11	49.25
Word Fluency									
Young	57.00	52.06	50.58	57.90	56.05	52.58	57.45	54.06	51.58
Middle	56.29	50.23	46.98	52.41	53.08	45.49	54.35	51.65	46.23
Old	46.58	46.09	36.92	53.91	47.09	44.43	50.24	46.59	40.68
Total	53.30	49.46	44.83	54.74	52.07	47.50	54.01	50.77	46.16

levels than those who perceived themselves to have improved, young males showed the opposite pattern, in that young males who perceived themselves to have declined actually had higher mean scores than those who perceived themselves to have improved or remained stable. The triple interaction on Word Fluency reflects the finding that men who perceived themselves to have improved or declined showed greater age differences in performance than women; however, the Age × Gender difference in performance was not found for those who perceived themselves as remaining stable.

Correlation between perceived and observed change. Although the correlations between perceived and actual change for the same ability (convergent validity) were statistically significant ($p < .001$) and for the most part were larger than cross-ability correlations (divergent validity), they were quite small (see Table 14.3). Indeed, significantly larger correlations were found among ratings of perceived change across abilities, suggesting that the ratings of perceived change are associated with global perceptions of change in intellectual functioning in addition to the actual observed change on the target ability.

Given the categorical nature of the judgment of perceived change, the correlations do not necessarily give a good picture of the accuracy of the respondents' perceptions. We therefore proceeded next with analyses of the congruence types.

Congruence types in the total sample. Figure 14.1 shows proportions of each congruence type by ability. Assuming that the expected chance probability of being assigned to one of the three response congruence types was .33, chi-square analyses determined that assignment to type differed significantly from chance at or above the 5% level of confidence. Approximately half the participants were *realistic* in their perception of change or stability over the 7-year period. Participants were most accurate (realistic) in estimating stability or change on the Verbal Meaning test. The highest proportion of pessimists (overestimation of decline) occurred for Spatial Orientation (34%), and pessimists were the fewest for Verbal Meaning (10.3%). Approximately 30% of the sample were *optimistic* (underestimation of decline) about their performance change for all abilities except Spatial Orientation.

Table 14.3. *Correlations between perceived and actual change*

	Perceived change				
Actual change	Verbal Meaning	Spatial Orientation	Inductive Reasoning	Number	Word Fluency
Verbal Meaning	0.112***	0.056	0.080*	0.046	0.012
Spatial Orientation	0.068	0.206***	0.055	−0.045	0.037
Inductive Reasoning	0.101**	0.035	0.141***	0.047	−0.030
Number	0.151***	0.076*	0.123***	0.134***	0.064
Word Fluency	0.083*	0.015	0.041	−0.039	0.210***

Note: Convergent validities are underlined.
$*p < 0.05; **p < 0.01; ***p < 0.001.$

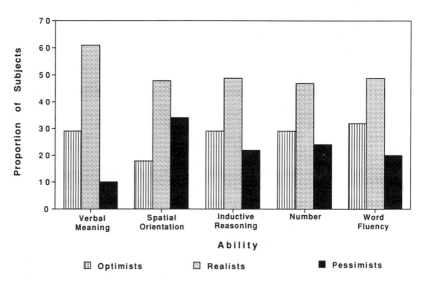

Perceiver Types: 7-Year Change

Figure 14.1. Proportions of congruence types, by ability. Adapted from Schaie, Willis, & O'Hanlon, 1994.

Consistency in congruence types across the five PMA tests was examined, but no consistent pattern was evident. Some study participants who were categorized as pessimistic for one ability were likely to be realistic on another and possibly optimistic on a third. There are 120 possible permutations of congruence types across all five abilities, and virtually all possible permutations were observed. The most frequent permutation ($N = 30$) was the pattern of being realistic across all five abilities.

Age and gender differences in congruence types. Gender differences in the distribution of congruence types were found for only one ability, Spatial Orientation. Here a greater proportion of women were found to be pessimistic about change in their spatial ability than men ($\chi^2[2, N = 818] = 6.4, p < .05$).

As regards age, a greater proportion of the oldest group of subjects were more pessimistic than the young and middle-aged about change in their verbal ability ($\chi^2[2, N = 818] = 19.1, p < .01$) and Inductive Reasoning ability ($\chi^2[2, N = 818] = 13.8, p < .05$). However, a greater proportion of the oldest group were realistic in the assessment of their performance change on the Number test ($\chi^2[2, N = 753] = 26.02, p < .001$).

Congruence type differences in current ability scores. Differences among congruence types in the 1984 PMA scores were also examined by means of 3 (congruence type) × 3 (age group) × 2 (gender) ANOVAs conducted separately for each of the five abilities (see Table 14.4 for associated means). Significant differences by type were found for Verbal Meaning ($F[df = 2, 798] = 11.36, p < .001$) and for Inductive Reasoning ($F[df = 2, 795] = 3.76, p < .02$). Both realists and pessimists had significantly higher 1984 Verbal Meaning scores than optimists. Realists' 1984 Inductive Reasoning scores were significantly higher than those of pessimists.

Significant age main effects occurred for all variables. Gender main effects favored men for Spatial Orientation and Number but favored women for Word Fluency. The only significant Age × Gender interaction occurred for Word Fluency, reflecting greater age differences for women between the younger and middle-aged groups and for men between the middle-aged and old groups.

Table 14.4. *Mean T-scores for current performance levels, by congruence type, age group, and gender*

	Males			Females			Total		
	Pess.	Real.	Optim.	Pess.	Real.	Optim.	Pess.	Real.	Optim.
Verbal Meaning									
Young	60.00	56.66	56.04	57.86	59.51	55.06	58.93	58.08	55.55
Middle	53.14	54.95	54.04	54.52	55.45	50.53	53.83	55.20	52.29
Old	44.46	46.57	41.50	46.72	46.97	43.68	45.49	46.77	42.59
Total	52.53	52.73	50.53	53.03	53.98	49.75	52.78	53.35	50.14
Spatial Orientation									
Young	58.69	57.46	61.40	53.31	54.83	53.96	56.00	56.14	57.66
Middle	54.18	54.67	53.71	48.65	50.60	52.91	51.42	52.63	53.31
Old	45.85	46.82	42.67	43.54	42.94	42.79	44.69	44.88	42.73
Total	52.91	52.98	52.59	48.50	49.46	49.87	50.70	51.22	51.23
Inductive Reasoning									
Young	60.25	59.92	56.73	55.93	60.81	60.29	58.08	60.37	58.51
Middle	52.87	54.13	52.58	56.14	54.74	53.06	54.36	54.44	52.82
Old	42.72	46.33	45.62	43.25	46.38	46.32	42.99	46.36	45.97
Total	51.85	53.46	51.64	51.77	53.98	53.33	51.81	53.72	52.43
Number									
Young	50.62	52.38	52.53	50.26	49.83	49.86	50.44	51.10	51.19
Middle	51.47	51.42	54.15	48.52	51.22	48.49	50.00	51.32	51.32
Old	48.79	48.21	45.62	46.95	46.67	47.33	47.87	47.44	51.19
Total	50.30	50.67	50.77	48.58	49.24	48.56	49.80	50.07	49.60
Word Fluency									
Young	53.59	51.67	55.50	57.05	55.25	56.00	55.31	53.46	55.75
Middle	49.57	51.42	51.72	51.52	52.23	49.79	50.55	51.82	50.76
Old	39.41	44.10	45.53	48.24	47.37	50.04	43.82	45.74	47.79
Total	47.52	49.06	50.92	52.27	51.61	51.94	50.28	50.52	51.07

Congruence type differences in magnitude of ability change. Differences among congruence types in magnitude of ability change (1977 to 1984) were examined via 3 (congruence type) × 3 (age group) × 2 (gender) ANOVAs conducted separately for each ability (see Table 14.5 for the associated mean changes). Significant type differences were found for all abilities: Verbal Meaning ($F[df = 2, 798] = 105.59$, $p < .001$), Spatial Orientation ($F[df = 2, 798] = 53.47$, $p < .001$), Inductive Reasoning ($F[df = 2, 795] = 60.83$, $p < .001$), Number ($F[df = 2, 801] = 53.28$, $p < .001$), and Word Fluency ($F[df = 2, 796] = 47.40$, $p < .001$). For all abilities, each type differed significantly from the others in magnitude of change. As would be expected from the type definitions, the optimists experienced greater average decline (respectively less gain) than either realists or pessimists, and the pessimists experienced objectively the least decline. The difference between pessimists and optimists exceeded 1 *SD* for all abilities and was greatest for Verbal Meaning.

A Congruence Type × Age interaction was found for Verbal Meaning ($F[df = 2, 798] = 3.18$, $p < .001$). The young pessimists gained significantly more over time than did the middle-aged or old pessimists. Likewise, the old optimists declined significantly more than did their young and middle-aged counterparts. Also, the young realists gained significantly more over time than did the middle-aged and old realists. A significant Congruence Type × Gender interaction occurred for Word Fluency ($F[df = 2, 796] = 3.01$, $p < .05$). This interaction reflected significantly greater gain over time for the female than the male pessimists. Finally, a significant triple interaction was obtained for Spatial Orientation ($F[df = 4, 798] = 2.62$, $p < .05$). This interaction reflects significant gain over time for the male pessimists but stability for the female pessimists.

Summary and conclusions

We assume in this study that community-dwelling adults are capable of making appropriate judgments of change in performance on cognitive tests taken 7 years apart. It could be argued that what the subjects actually do is more likely to be a projection of their *feelings* about change in their cognitive competence, with the current test providing no more than a projective stimulus for the expression of

Table 14.5. *Mean T-scores for magnitude of change from 1977 to 1984, by congruence type, ability, age group, and gender*

	Males			Females			Total		
	Pess.	Real.	Optim.	Pess.	Real.	Optim.	Pess.	Real.	Optim.
Verbal Meaning									
Young	-8.83	-0.43	1.35	-7.57	-0.65	2.53	-8.20	-0.54	1.94
Middle	-5.53	0.70	3.55	-3.20	0.53	5.35	-4.27	0.62	4.45
Old	-3.54	1.68	8.63	-0.50	3.13	8.43	-2.02	2.39	8.53
Total	-5.90	0.64	4.51	-3.76	1.01	5.44	-4.83	0.82	4.97
Spatial Orientation									
Young	-1.81	-0.19	3.85	-2.11	1.26	5.25	-1.96	0.53	4.55
Middle	-3.32	2.07	6.00	0.29	2.85	3.87	-1.51	2.46	4.69
Old	0.09	3.02	7.00	0.51	4.51	8.58	0.30	3.77	7.79
Total	-1.68	1.63	5.62	-0.44	2.87	5.74	-1.06	2.25	5.68
Inductive Reasoning									
Young	-3.50	-0.18	2.09	-3.93	0.26	1.66	-3.71	0.04	1.87
Middle	-1.70	0.71	4.58	-2.28	1.12	3.47	-1.99	0.92	4.02
Old	-0.06	1.44	4.38	0.31	2.27	6.35	0.13	1.86	5.37
Total	-1.75	0.66	3.68	-1.97	1.22	3.83	-1.86	0.94	3.76
Number									
Young	-1.42	0.16	1.88	-1.71	1.80	2.48	-1.56	0.98	2.18
Middle	-0.97	1.49	2.74	-1.91	1.04	4.97	-1.44	1.27	3.86
Old	-2.07	1.94	6.44	-1.80	1.81	2.48	-1.94	1.88	5.80
Total	-1.48	1.20	3.69	-1.81	1.55	4.20	-1.65	1.37	3.94
Word Fluency									
Young	-2.41	0.61	1.75	-4.90	0.67	2.78	-3.66	0.64	2.27
Middle	-1.48	0.57	4.41	-3.02	2.03	5.03	-2.25	1.30	4.72
Old	1.56	2.78	5.88	-2.53	1.19	4.89	-0.49	1.98	5.38
Total	-0.78	1.32	4.01	-3.48	1.29	4.23	-2.13	1.31	4.12

Note: Negative values represent mean gain from 1977 to 1984.

such feelings. However, the data suggest that much more systematic judgments are made.

Perceptions of age-related *change* in ability functioning are examined for three age groups (young, middle-aged, and older adults). Furthermore, a typology is proposed for examining the congruence between perceptions of change and actual age-related change in intellectual functioning. The typology categorizes three congruence types: realists, those who correctly estimated change or stability; pessimists, those who thought they had declined more than they actually had; and optimists, those who thought they did better than the objective data reflected. We were able to verify this typology by showing that the three groups differed significantly in absolute magnitude of change in the expected direction on all five abilities; that is, pessimists declined the least or gained, optimists declined the most, and realists were in between.

With respect to subjects' perception of change in ability functioning (regardless of the accuracy of perceptions), we find that a greater proportion of older adults than young or middle-aged adults perceive themselves to have declined on three of the abilities studied (Verbal Meaning, Reasoning, Spatial Orientation). For Number ability, by contrast, a significantly smaller proportion (18%) of older adults perceive themselves to have declined than young adults (38%). No Age × Perceiver Type interaction was found for Word Fluency. There are two possible implications of these findings. Prior research findings (M. E. Lachman & Jelalian, 1984) were supported in that age differences in perceptions turn out to be ability-specific; the old do not hold global perceptions of universal decline across all abilities. Second, the findings suggest a possible cohort effect in ability perceptions. Given our finding on the multidirectionality of cohort differences in Number ability (see chapter 6), it is interesting to note that the older group in the perceptions study represents those cohorts whose Number ability was particularly high compared with more recent cohorts, which may contribute to the age differences in perception of decline on Number ability found in the study.

When perceptions of cognitive change over 7 years are compared with objectively measured change (congruence typology), we find that approximately half our sample could accurately categorize their performance change over time, albeit that the correct attribution in most instances turned out to be their judgment that no change had occurred. Subjects are not only aware of their concurrent levels of performance, but they can make reasonably accurate estimates of change in performance over a 7-year period. However, study participants did not predict change in their performance with equal accuracy across all the abilities measured.

The variables of age and gender were found to moderate accuracy of perceptions of ability change (i.e., congruence typology). Women were found to be more pessimistic than men regarding their decline on Spatial Orientation. In our society, women, particularly older women, frequently report themselves to be less competent at tasks involving Spatial Orientation, such as map reading and giving directions. Our findings suggest that women's overly pessimistic views of decline in Spatial Orientation ability (compared with those of men) may be fostered by negative gender stereotypes, since their individual performance profiles do not warrant such pessimism. Finally, the old (compared with the young) were more pessimistic regarding age-related decline in their verbal and Inductive Reasoning abilities than the performance data would support. Of particular concern is the elderly's pessimism regarding decline in their verbal ability. Since verbal ability remains relatively stable into old age (see chapter 5), it seems reasonable that most older adults should feel fairly confident of their verbal skills.

Perception of short-term cognitive change and of training effects

Perceptions of change in cognitive functioning over a brief period of time were examined for the five basic primary mental abilities as part of the intervention studies described in chapter 7. Here the question of interest was whether subjects can accurately perceive short-term shifts in cognitive performance occurring between repetitions of the same test over a 2- to 4-week period, as well as the question whether subjects who were given cognitive training in a specific ability were more likely to perceive change accurately than those not so trained.

Method

Subjects. Two subsamples selected for this study included those individuals who had taken the PMA battery twice as part of the intervention study. There were 399 individuals (177 men and 222 women), with a mean age in 1984 of 72.55 (*SD* = 6.87; range: 60 to 95), and another 310 individuals (136 men and 174 women), with a mean age in 1991 of 75.2 (*SD* = 6.31; range: 64 to 93).

Procedure. After completing the five PMA tests (V, S, R, N, W) during the posttest, study participants again answered the Primary Mental Abilities Retrospective Questionnaire (PMARQ). Participants were reminded that they had taken the same five ability tests several weeks earlier and were asked to indicate how their performance on the tests just completed (at posttest) compared with their earlier performance (at pretest). Subjects evaluated their relative performance for each of the five abilities using a 5-point scale with the categories (1) much better today, (2) better today, (3) about the same, (4) worse today, (5) much worse today. Again only a few persons chose the extreme categories (1 or 5), and these categories were collapsed into a 3-point scale, resulting in three *perceiver* types: better, same, and worse.

Creation of congruence types. Study participants were classified according to how their actual PMA performance had changed from pretest to posttest on each of the five abilities. Difference scores between the two test occasions were computed, and subjects were classified into groups showing reliably higher, similar, or lower performance for each ability. The classification criteria for a positive or negative change were that the subject at posttest performed at least 1 *SEM* below or above the pretest performance (see Dudek, 1979; Schaie, 1989c). Based on the cross-tabulations between actual performance change and perceived performance change, the samples were again categorized into the three congruence types (pessimists, realists, and optimists) for each ability, as described above (see Table 14.1).

Table 14.6. *Proportion of study participants reporting perceived change in performance from pretest to posttest, by ability and gender*

	1984 study			1991 study		
	Better	Same	Worse	Better	Same	Worse
Verbal Meaning						
Males	20.1	51.7	38.3	30.2	53.7	16.2
Females	17.6	46.6	35.8	27.6	51.2	21.3
Total	18.7	48.9	32.4	28.7	52.3	19.0
Spatial Orientation						
Males	18.8	53.4	27.8	29.4	42.6	27.9
Females	21.7	48.4	16.6	19.0	37.4	43.7
Total	20.4	50.6	29.0	23.6	39.7	36.8
Inductive Reasoning						
Males	22.6	44.1	33.3	24.3	51.5	24.3
Females	16.7	39.2	44.1	32.8	42.5	24.7
Total	19.3	41.4	39.3	29.0	46.4	24.5
Number						
Males	41.2	35.6	23.2	22.6	62.1	15.3
Females	33.3	42.8	23.9	16.7	59.5	23.8
Total	36.8	39.6	23.6	19.2	60.6	20.2
Word Fluency						
Males	30.1	46.6	23.3	54.4	36.8	8.8
Females	23.5	46.2	30.3	37.9	50.0	12.1
Total	26.4	46.4	27.2	45.2	44.2	10.6

Results

Gender and secular differences in perceived change. The proportions of study participants indicating that they had improved, remained stable, or become worse from pre- to posttest are shown in Table 14.6. No significant gender effects were observed in the 1984 study. However, in 1991 there was a significant gender effect for Spatial Orientation ($\chi^2[2, N = 310] = 9.22$, $p < .01$) that reflected more males than females perceiving positive change and more females than males perceiving negative change. Likewise, a significant gender effect for Word Fluency ($\chi^2[2, N = 310] = 8.37$, $p < .01$) indicated that men perceived positive change more frequently than

Table 14.7. *Correlations between perceived and actual change from pretest to posttest*

Actual change	Perceived change				
	Verbal Meaning	Spatial Orientation	Inductive Reasoning	Number	Word Fluency
Verbal Meaning	0.034 −0.023	−0.022 −0.128*	0.000 −0.066	−0.031 −0.028	−0.020 −0.022
Spatial Orientation	−0.007 0.055	0.198*** 0.001	−0.050 0.032	−0.026 0.045	0.004 0.047
Inductive Reasoning	0.012 −0.066	0.107* −0.082	0.199*** 0.242***	0.048 −0.020	0.049 0.015
Number	0.070 0.054	−0.050 −0.033	0.030 0.009	0.015 0.222***	−0.076 −0.025
Word Fluency	0.031 0.018	0.018 −0.050	0.017 0.059	−0.012 0.040	0.323*** 0.234***

Note: First value is for 1984 study; second value, for 1991 study. Convergent validities are underlined.
*$p < 0.05$; **$p < 0.01$; ***$p < 0.001$.

women, whereas women perceived lack of change more frequently than males.

Some interesting secular differences in perceived change were also observed. There was more positive perception of change from pre- to posttest in 1991 than in 1984 for Verbal Meaning, Inductive Reasoning, and Word Fluency but less positive perception in 1991 than in 1984 for Spatial Orientation and Number.

Correlation between perceived and observed change. The correlations between perceived and actual change for the same ability (convergent validity) were statistically significant ($p < .001$) on both occasions only for Inductive Reasoning and Word Fluency. In addition, there was a significant correlation for Spatial Orientation in 1984 and for Number in 1991. These correlations, however, were small, even though, for the most part, they were larger than crossability correlations (divergent validity; see Table 14.7). As for the ratings over the 7-year period, significantly larger correlations were again found among ratings of perceived change across abilities, giving further credence to the conclusion that ratings of perceived change are associated with global perceptions of change in intellectual functioning in addition to the actually observed change on the target ability.

Congruence types. Figure 14.2 shows proportions of each congruence type from pre- to posttest by ability. Again assuming that the expected chance probability of being assigned to one of the three response congruence types was .33, chi-square analyses determined that assignment to type differed significantly from chance at the 1% level of confidence. In 1984, approximately 40% to 50% of the subjects were *realistic* in their perception of change or stability from pre- to posttest. Participants were most accurate (realistic) in estimating stability or change on the Verbal Meaning and Spatial Orientation tests and least realistic on Inductive Reasoning and Number. The highest proportion of *optimists* was found for Number (36.6%) and the lowest for Verbal Meaning (18.7%). A *pessimistic* assessment of performance change was highest for Inductive Reasoning (39.3%) and lowest for Number (23.6%).

Secular shifts were also found in the perceiver types. In 1991, proportions of *realistic* perceivers had increased with a low of 39.7% for Spatial Orientation and a high of 60.6% for Number. The highest proportion of *optimists* now occurred for Word Fluency (45.6%), and the lowest proportion remained for Number (19.2%). Likewise, the highest proportion of *pessimists* now occurred for Spatial Orientation and the lowest for Word Fluency.

Accuracy of perceived change on trained ability. A final question is whether study participants who are trained on a particular ability are likely to perceive greater positive change on that ability than a control group, as well as whether their perception of change (given the fact that they receive feedback during training) is more accurate than that of the controls. Indeed, both in 1984 and 1991 the trained group reports significantly greater positive change than does the control group. The effect is more robust for the Inductive Reasoning training ($\chi^2$1984[2, $N = 228$] $= 15.45$, $p < .001$; $\chi^2$1991[2, $N =$

Perceiver Types: Pre- to Posttest 1984

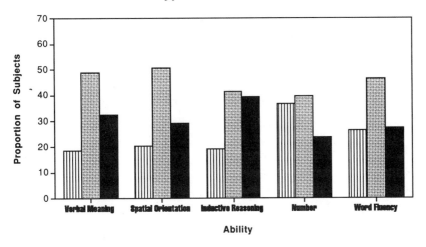

Perceiver Types: Pre- to Posttest 1991

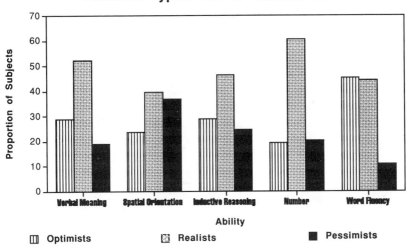

Figure 14.2. Proportions of perceiver types, by ability, in the 1984 and 1991 training studies.

310] $= 34.89$, $p < .001$) than for the Spatial Orientation training ($\chi^2 1984[2, N = 228] = 5.88$, $p < .05$; $\chi^2 1991[2, N = 310] = 5.54$, $p < .06$). However, there were no significant differences between those trained and their controls with respect to perceiver type.

Chapter summary

In this chapter we examine the accuracy of adults' perceptions regarding an issue of increasing concern as we get older – whether or not our intellectual abilities are actually declining. These concerns were investigated by evaluating the accuracy of subjects' assessment of intellectual change over 7 years. The findings suggest that perceptions of ability decline are not limited to old age but that there are also young and middle-aged individuals who perceive that their cognitive abilities have declined. These perceptions vary across abilities, age, and gender. Subjective report of performance change was compared with actual observed change over 7 years. If subjects thought that they had changed less than they actually did, they were designated as *optimists*; if they perceived change status correctly, they were called *realists*; and if they declined less than they reported, they were designated as *pessimists*. Frequency of assignment to these three congruence types varied by age and gender. For some abilities, women tended to be more likely to underestimate their performance, as did the older study participants. However, accuracy of prediction was not strongly related to ability level. Thus it appears that stereotypes of universal intellectual decline with increasing age do not seem to be supported either by adults' perceptions or by the accuracy of their estimates.

We also evaluated judgments of short-term change after repeated testing and training interventions spanning a 4-week period (see chapter 7). Accuracy of prediction was modest, and it varied by ability but was greatest on the ability on which the subjects had actually been trained.

15

Summary and conclusions

The reader has accompanied me through the highlights of the 35-year scientific journey that I undertook together with my colleagues and students to gain a clearer understanding of the progress of adult development in psychometric abilities and related matters. What now remains is for me to attempt a succinct statement of what I think can be concluded from these studies. I begin by reviewing what we have learned in the context of the four questions regarding the life course of intellectual competence raised in the introductory chapter. I then summarize the conclusions reached from our efforts at intervening in the normal course of adult cognitive development, as well as the findings from our efforts to learn more about adult cognition in a developmental behavior genetic and/or family context. Finally, I provide a preview of where my work in the context of the SLS is likely to turn next.

The course of adult intellectual development

Although the development of intellectual competence in childhood and adolescence follows a rather uniform path, with new stages of competence and differentiation of functioning occurring within a relatively narrow band with respect to age, the same cannot be said for the life course of adult intelligence. And of course, in contrast to the major external criterion in early life – the child's ability to master the educational and socialization systems of our public and private schools – adult intellectual competence can be referenced to a multiplicity of outcome variables.

Although I have tried to address many of these issues with the studies described in this volume, I have nevertheless maintained a relatively narrow focus, limited to a number of basic questions that were assessed in considerable depth. Hence, there are many questions we could have asked our study participants had we been satisfied with narrower age ranges and smaller samples but that our strategies involving a large data set placed beyond our reach. Unfortunately, one cannot go backward in a longitudinal study to expand one's inquiry, though one can always add new variables or ask questions in more sophisticated ways as a study progresses. This is what I believe we have done and, building on our rich data set, is what we shall continue to do in order to be able to answer new questions that will arise as time goes on. Here, then, are my conclusions as they seem appropriate at the present stage of our findings.

Does intelligence change uniformly through adulthood, or are there different life course ability patterns?

The answer to this question remains quite unambiguous: Neither at the level of analysis of the tests actually given nor at the level of the inferred latent ability constructs do we find uniform patterns of developmental change across the entire ability spectrum. I continue therefore to warn those who would like to assess change in intellectual competence by means of an omnibus IQ-like measure that such an approach will not be helpful to the basic researcher or to the thoughtful clinician. I have reported some overall indices of intellectual and educational aptitude because they are of some theoretical interest, but I do not think that such global measures have practical utility in monitoring changes (or differences) in intellectual competence for individuals or groups.

At any particular time, a cross-sectional snapshot of age-difference profiles for different abilities will be largely influenced by the interaction of cohort differences and age changes for any given ability. My work in the 1950s began with the observation that there were differences in the age-difference patterns for the five abilities measured in our core battery. However, it is only by observing longitudinal data averaged over several cohorts that definitive conclusions can indeed be reached about whether the nature of these differences is a part of a developmental process of change in adulthood that will be observed whenever the perturbations of time and place are removed. Any single ability measure, moreover, may be unduly influenced by the form and speededness of the particular test. More stable conclusions are therefore likely to be based on ability profiles that compare estimates of the latent ability constructs. The following conclusions are based on the data presented in chapter 5.

From the extensive data on the original core battery, I conclude that Verbal Meaning, Space, and Reasoning attain a peak plateau in midlife from the 40s to the early 60s, whereas Number and Word Fluency peak earlier and show very modest decline beginning in the 50s. In contrast to our earlier conclusions, it now seems that with larger samples the steepness of late-life decline is greatest for Number and least for the measure of Reasoning ability. Verbal Meaning (recognition vocabulary) declines last but also shows steeper decline than the other abilities from the 70s to the 80s. These findings are observed whether we aggregate the large number of observations of individuals followed over 7 years or examine the smaller data sets for those individuals followed over 14, 21, 28, and 35 years.

For the more limited data on the latent construct estimates (obtained only in the fifth and sixth study cycles), it appears that peak ages of performance are still shifting and that we now see these peaks occurring in the 50s for Inductive Reasoning and Spatial Orientation and in the 60s for Verbal Ability and Verbal Memory. By contrast, Perceptual Speed peaks in the 20s and Numeric Ability in the late 30s. Even by the late 80s, declines for Verbal Ability and Inductive Reasoning are modest, but they are severe in very old age for Perceptual Speed and Numeric Ability, with Spatial Orientation and Verbal Memory in between.

Again I must caution that these are average patterns of age-change profiles. Individual profiles depend to a large extent on individual patterns of use and disuse and on the presence or absence of neuropathology. Indeed, virtually every possible permutation of individual profiles has been observed in our study (see Schaie, 1989a, 1989b).

At what age is there a reliably detectable decrement in ability,
and what is its magnitude?

For some ability markers, significant but extremely modest average changes have been observed in the 50s. Nevertheless, I continue to maintain that individual decline prior to age 60 is almost inevitably a symptom or precursor of pathological age changes. On the other hand, it is clear that by the mid-70s significant *average* decrement can be observed for all abilities, and that by the 80s average decrement is severe except for Verbal Ability.

From the largest longitudinal data set, the aggregated changes over 7 years in the core battery, I conclude that statistically significant decrement occurs for Number and Word Fluency by age 60 and for Space and Reasoning by age 67, but for Verbal Meaning only by age 81. For the composite indices, average statistically significant decrement is first observed at age 60 for the Index of Intellectual Ability and at age 67 for the Index of Educational Aptitude.

At the latent construct level, statistically significant decrement is first observed by age 60 for Spatial Ability, Numeric Ability, and Perceptual Speed; by age 67 for Inductive Reasoning; and by age 74 for Verbal Ability and Verbal Memory.

The average magnitude of decrements during the first 7-year period when it becomes significant is quite small, but it becomes increasingly larger as the 80s are reached. The difference in performance for the core battery between age 25 and the age at which the first decrement is observed is less than 0.3 *SD*. However, by age 88 that difference amounts to 0.75 *SD* for Reasoning, approximately 1 *SD* for Verbal Meaning, Space, and Word Fluency, and as much as 1.5 *SD* for Number. For the latent construct measures, initial declines are even smaller (between 0.10 and 0.25 *SD*). The cumulative change from age 25 to age 88 differs widely by ability domain. Because of gains in midlife, it is virtually zero for Verbal Ability, ranges from 0.6 to 0.8 *SD* for Inductive Reasoning, Verbal Memory, and Spatial Orientation, and amounts to approximately 2 *SD* for Numeric Ability and Perceptual Speed.

From these data I conclude that it is during the period of the late 60s and 70s that many people begin to experience noticeable ability declines. Even so, it is not until the 80s are reached that the average older adult will fall below the midddle range of performance for young adults. There are some occupations where speed of performance is important, but since broad individual differences in the speededness of behavior exist, even here there is substantial overlap in the performance of young and old workers until the 80s are reached. This conclusion is reached even independent of the possible compensatory effects of experience in many skilled trades and professions, which may lessen the effect of age declines in the basic cognitive skills. Hence, it turns out that for decisions relating to the retention of individuals in the workforce, chronological age is not a useful criterion for groups, and certainly not for individuals. This conclusion has, of course, been the rationale for abandoning mandatory retirement in the United States.

What are the patterns of generational differences, and what is their magnitude?

Throughout our studies I have been cognizant not only of the fact of individual aging but also of the fact that there have been profound changes in environmental support and societal context that must be part of shaping individual development. I have tried to document the impact of these changes on intellectual development by charting cohort (generational) differences in the intellectual performance measures. These studies have clearly demonstrated that there are substantial generational trends in intellectual performance. As documented in chapter 6, these trends amount to as much as 1.5 *SD* across the 70-year cohort span we investigated.

For the core battery, the form of these generational trends is positive for Verbal Meaning, Space, and Reasoning, but it is concave for Number (with peak performance for the 1924 cohort and decline thereafter) and convex for Word Fluency (with lowest performance for the 1931 cohort and return to the 1889 baseline thereafter). For the latent construct estimates, equally substantial positive cohort gradients were observed for Inductive Reasoning, Spatial Orientation, and Verbal Memory. However, at the factor level the cohort gradient for Verbal Ability takes a concave form, presumably because the added markers are less speeded. Interestingly enough, decline is observed here for the baby-boomer cohorts. Numeric Ability shows a shallow negative cohort trend and Perceptual Speed a shallow concave trend.

An understanding of these cohort differences is important in order to account for the discrepancy between the longitudinal (within-subject) age changes and the cross-sectional (between-group) age differences reported in chapter 4. In general, I conclude that cross-sectional findings will overestimate declines whenever there are positive cohort gradients and will underestimate decline in the presence of negative cohort gradients. Curvilinear cohort gradients will lead to temporary dislocations of age-difference patterns and will over- or underestimate age changes, depending on the direction of differences over a particular time period. Because of these cohort effects, our most recent cross-sectional data suggest much steeper declines on Verbal Meaning, Space, and Reasoning than are found in the longitudinal data while showing far less decline on Number (see Figure 4.4). Similar findings also obtain for the latent construct measures (see Figure 4.7). The slowing of the cohort difference trend suggests that in the next 20 or 30 years concurrently measured age differences will become substantially smaller over that age range where there is little or no within-subject decline. This is fortunate, because there is a need to retain people longer in the labor force because of the demographic reality of the aging of the baby boomers. Stereotypes about age decline will obviously be reinforced less in the absence of the dramatic shifts in ability base levels that were observed for cohorts entering adulthood in the first half of the twentieth century.

What accounts for individual differences in age-related change in adulthood?

Throughout this volume I have stressed the vast individual differences in intellectual change across adulthood. Some individuals, no doubt because of the early onset of neuropathology or particularly unfavorable environments, begin to decline in their 40s, whereas a favored few maintain a full level of functioning into very advanced age.

Not all individuals decline in lockstep. Indeed, although linear or quadratic forms of decline may be detectable for large groups, individual decline appears to occur far more frequently in a stair-step fashion. Individuals will have unfavorable experiences, to which they respond with a modest decline in cognitive functioning, and then tend to stabilize for some time, perhaps repeating this pattern several times prior to their demise. Again the sequence of decline of abilities is not uniform across individuals but may depend on in-dividual circumstances of use and disuse of particular skills. Thus, in actuarial studies of our core battery we have observed that virtually all individuals had significantly declined on one ability by age 60 but that virtually no one had declined on all five abilities even by age 88.

Certainly, genetic endowment will account for a substantial portion of individual differences (see chapter 13 for circumstantial evidence of heritability of adult intelligence). Nevertheless, there are many other important sources of individual differences in intellectual aging that have been implicated in these studies.

To begin with, the onset of intellectual decline seems to be markedly affected by the presence or absence of several chronic diseases. As discussed in chapter 10, cardiovascular disease, diabetes, neoplasms, and arthritis are all involved as risk factors for the occurrence of cognitive decline, as is a low level of overall health. On the other hand, high levels of cognitive functioning seem to be associated with survival after malignancies and late onset of car-diovascular disease and arthritis. Persons functioning at high cognitive levels are also more likely to seek earlier and more com-petent medical intervention in the disabling conditions of late life, and they are more likely to comply more effectively with preventive and ameliorative regimens that tend to stabilize their physiological infrastructure. They are also less likely to engage in high-risk life-styles and to respond more readily to professional advice that maximizes their chances for survival and reduction of morbidity.

My interest next turned to environmental circumstances that might account for individual differences in cognitive aging. Candidates for investigation have been all those aspects of the environment that are likely to enhance intellectual stimulation (see Schaie & Gribbin, 1975; Schaie & O'Hanlon, 1990).

I conclude first of all, from the data presented in chapter 11, that the onset of intellectual decline is postponed for individuals who live in favorable environmental circumstances, as would be the case for those persons characterized by a high socioeconomic status. These circumstances include above-average education, histories of occupational pursuits that involve high complexity and low routine, and the maintenance of intact families. Likewise, risk of cognitive decline is lower for persons with substantial involvement in activities typically available in complex and intellectually stimulating environments. Such activities include extensive reading, travel, attendance at cultural events, pursuit of continuing education activities, and participation in clubs and professional associations.

It does not surprise us that intact families, our most important individual support system, reduce risk of cognitive decline. What was less obvious is the finding that cognitive decline is also less severe for those married to a spouse with high cognitive status. Our studies of cognitive similarity in married couples suggest that the lower-functioning spouse at the beginning of a marriage tends to maintain or increase his or her level vis-à-vis the higher-functioning spouse (see chapter 12).

From the very beginning of our study, we have pursued the question whether the cognitive style of rigidity–flexibility might be associated with differential intellectual aging. I now conclude that an individual's self-report of a flexible personality style at *midlife*, as well as flexible performance on objective measures of motor–cognitive perseveration tasks, does indeed reduce the risk of cognitive decline (see chapter 9). The implication of these findings is that individuals who find themselves having developed rigid response patterns in midlife would be well advised to take advantage of psychological therapeutic interventions that could lead to a more flexible response when it is needed to cope with the vicissitudes of advanced age.

As indicated earlier, aging effects on many cognitive abilities tend to be confounded with the perceptual and response speed required to process the tasks used to measure these abilities. Thus, individuals who remain at high levels of perceptual speed are also at an advantage with respect to the maintenance of such other abilities.

Finally, those individuals who rate themselves as being satisfied with their life's accomplishment in midlife or early old age seem to be at an advantage when assessed at a later age. And those individuals who overestimate the rate of their cognitive decline might well be engaging in self-fulfilling prophecies if they reduce their active participation in life to compensate for perceived but not real cognitive decline (see chapter 14).

I have used event-history methods to develop life tables for the occurrence of decline events on the five single ability markers in the core battery, and I developed a calculus that allows estimation of the most probable age by which an individual can expect to experience decline on each of these abilities (Schaie, 1989a). The most highly weighted variables in this calculus that predict earlier than average decline were found to be a significant decrease in flexibility during the preceding 7-year period, low educational level, male gender, and low satisfaction with success in life.

Intervention in adult intellectual development

Once adult intellectual development has been described and a number of antecedents of individual differences have been identified, it then becomes useful to think about ways in which normal intellectual aging might be slowed or reversed.

In conjunction with Sherry Willis, who analyzed these issues and developed training programs that could be applied to our study samples, we began to initiate a series of cognitive interventions. In contrast to training young children, where it can be assumed that new skills are conveyed, older adults are likely to have access to the skills being trained but through disuse have lost their proficiency. Longitudinal studies are therefore particularly useful in distinguishing individuals who have declined from those who have remained stable. In the former, training should result in remediation of loss; in the latter, we are dealing with the enhancement of previous levels of functioning, perhaps compensating for the cohort-based disadvantage of older persons.

Results from our cognitive interventions allow the conclusion that cognitive decline in old age is, for many older persons, likely to be a function of disuse rather than of the deterioration of the physiological or neural substrates of cognitive behavior. In the initial studies, a brief 5-hour training program succeeded in improving the performance of about two thirds of the participants on the abilities of Spatial Orientation and Inductive Reasoning. The average training gain amounted to roughly 0.5 *SD*. Even more dramatically, of those for whom significant decrement could be documented over a 14-year period, roughly 40% were returned to the level at which they had functioned when first studied. The analyses of structural relationships among the ability measures prior to and after training further allow the conclusion that training does not result in qualitative changes in ability structures and is thus highly specific to the targeted abilities.

The literature is replete with cognitive interventions that show significant pre–post intervention gains but often also report diminution of training effects after brief time intervals. Our follow-up of cognitive training over a 7-year period (including further booster training) has demonstrated that those subjects who showed significant decline at initial training do remain at a substantial advantage over untrained comparison groups. Long-term effects for those who had remained stable at initial training differed by ability. Significant effects were shown to prevail on the intervention for Inductive Reasoning but not on the Spatial Orientation training. Finally, replication of initial training with a new sample confirmed the magnitudes of the training effects obtained in the initial study.

Some might ask how these interventions on laboratory tasks relate to real-life issues. Clearly, the showing of substantial relationships between performance on psychometric ability tests and the measure of practical intelligence or everyday problem solving suggests that these training interventions may be quite useful in a broad sense. The cost of institutionalization for individuals who are only marginally incompetent to live independently because of relatively low levels of intellectual competence is high. Modest educational interventions similar to those described in this volume, on the other hand, are quite inexpensive and deserve to be subjected to large-scale field trials to see whether they can raise competence sufficiently to keep many elders independent for a longer period and so enhance the quality of their lives.

Family similarity in adult intellectual development

Going beyond the study of age in single individuals, we began to be interested in the effects of cognitive aging within families. We began these studies by tracing the impact of shared environment on similarity in intellectual functioning in married couples. Our studies provide some support for the notion of marital assortativity in mate selection by demonstrating substantial within-couple correlations. These relationships persist over time (in our study over as long as 21 years), and indeed in some instances increase in the direction of the spouse who was the higher-functioning at base level.

More recently, influenced by developments in the behavior genetics literature, we began to assess the adult children and siblings of our longitudinal subjects. Significant adult parent–offspring similarities were observed for our total sample for all ability measures (except Perceptual Speed) and for the cognitive style measures. The magnitudes of correlation are comparable to those found between young adults and their children. However, same-gender pairs showed higher correlations on Verbal Meaning, Number, and Word Fluency; opposite-gender pairs on Spatial Orientation, Inductive Reasoning, and Motor–Cognitive Flexibility.

Our data strongly support the hypothesis that if shared environmental influences are relatively unimportant in adulthood, then similarity in parent–offspring pairs should remain reasonably constant in adulthood across time and age.

Given our interest in generational differences in ability, we asked whether level differences within families equaled or approximated differences found for similar cohort ranges in a general population sample. Comparable differences were indeed found to be the rule, but there were some exceptions. The general population estimates underestimated the advantage of the offspring cohort for Spatial Orientation and Psychomotor Speed but overestimated that advantage for Perceptual Speed.

Substantial family similarity was documented also for the adult sibling pairs. In general, parent–offspring and sibling correlations were of similar magnitude. However, after controlling for age, sibling correlations were somewhat lower than those observed for the parent–offspring pairs. Interestingly, stability of sibling correlations across time and age was not as strong as for the parent–offspring data.

What do we still need to learn?

Several additional questions remain that I hope to be able to shed further light on in the context of the next phase of the SLS (which has now been funded through 1998). These questions can be loosely grouped under the topics: differences in rate of aging across generations, cross-cultural generalizability of differential patterns of cognitive aging (see Dutta, Yue, Schaie, Willis, O'Hanlon, & Yu, 1989), effects of retirement on the maintenance of cognitive functioning in old age (see Dutta, Schulenberg, & Lair, 1986), structural invariance of psychometric intelligence, the relation of laboratory measures of intelligence to functioning in the community (as assessed by objective measures of Instrumental Activities of Daily Living [IADL]), the relationship of psychometric abilities to the neuropsychological measures used to detect dementia, the relationship of health behaviors and the maintenance of cognitive functioning, and finally the delineation of the relationship of documented long-term behavior change to neuropathology detected at post mortem.

One of the delights of a broadly conceived longitudinal study is that, far from becoming outdated and obsolete, it often provides the basis for new and exciting questions that could not have been formulated given the state of the art at the study's inception. This exciting voyage of discovery has not only provided me with the basis for an exciting scientific career and an opportunity to train several cohorts of successful students, but also continues to provide encouragement for my trying to shed further light on the dynamics of adult development. I hope the reader will be as eager as I am to see future installments in the account of this odyssey.

References

Adam, J. (1978). Sequential strategies and the separation of age, cohort, and time-of-measurement contribution to developmental data. *Psychological Bulletin, 85,* 1309–1316.

Alwin, D. F. (1988). Structural equation models in research on human development and aging. In K. W. Schaie, R. T. Campbell, W. Meredith, & S. C. Rawlings (Eds.), *Methodological issues in aging research* (pp. 71–170). New York: Springer.

Alwin, D. F., & Jackson, D. J. (1981). Applications of simultaneous factor analysis to issues of factorial invariance. In D. J. Jackson & E. F. Borgatta (Eds.), *Factor analysis and measurement* (pp. 249–278). London: Sage.

American Society of Hospital Pharmacists. (1985). *Drug information 85.* Bethesda, MD: Author.

Anastasi, A. (1976). *Psychological testing* (4th ed.). New York: Macmillan.

Antonovsky, A. (1972). Breakdown: A needed fourth step in the conceptual armamentarium of modern medicine. *Social Science and Medicine, 6,* 537–544.

Baltes, P. B. (1968). Longitudinal and cross-sectional sequences in the study of age and generation effects. *Human Development, 11,* 145–171.

Baltes, P. B. (1987). Theoretical propositions of life-span developmental psychology: On the dynamics between growth and decline. *Developmental Psychology, 23,* 611–626.

Baltes, P. B. (1993). The aging mind: Potential and limits. *Gerontologist, 33,* 580–594.

Baltes, P. B., Dittmann-Kohli, F., & Kliegl, R. (1986). Reserve capacity of the elderly in aging-sensitive tests of fluid intelligence: Replication and extension. *Psychology and Aging, 1,* 172–177.

Baltes, P. B., & Lindenberger, U. (1988). On the range of cognitive plasticity in old age as a function of experience: 15 years of intervention research. *Behavior Therapy*, *19*, 283–300.

Baltes, P. B., & Nesselroade, J. R. (1970). Multivariate longitudinal and cross-sectional sequences for analyzing ontogenetic and generational change: A methodological note. *Developmental Psychology*, *1*, 162–168.

Baltes, P. B., & Nesselroade, J. R. (1973). The developmental analysis of individual differences on multiple measures. In J. R. Nesselroade & H. W. Reese (Eds.), *Life-span developmental psychology: Methodological issues* (pp. 219–251). New York: Academic Press.

Baltes, P. B., & Nesselroade, J. R. (1979). History and rationale of longitudinal research. In J. R. Nesselroade & P. B. Baltes (Eds.), *Longitudinal research in the study of behavior and development* (pp. 1–40). New York: Academic Press.

Baltes, P. B., Nesselroade, J. R., Schaie, K. W., & Labouvie, E. W. (1972). On the dilemma of regression effects in examining ability level-related differentials in ontogenetic patterns of adult intelligence. *Developmental Psychology*, *6*, 78–84.

Baltes, P. B., Reese, H. W., & Lipsitt, L. P. (1980). Life-span developmental psychology. *Annual Review of Psychology*, *31*, 65–100.

Baltes, P. B., Reese, H. W., & Nesselroade, J. R. (1977). *Life-span developmental psychology: Introduction to research methods*. Monterey, CA: Brooks/Cole.

Baltes, P. B., Schaie, K. W., & Nardi, A. H. (1971). Age and experimental mortality in a seven-year longitudinal study of cognitive behavior. *Developmental Psychology*, *5*, 18–26.

Baltes, P. B., & Willis, S. L. (1977). Towards psychological theories of aging and development. In J. E. Birren & K. W. Schaie (Eds.), *Handbook of the psychology of aging* (pp. 128–154). New York: Van Nostrand Reinhold.

Baltes, P. B., & Willis, S. L. (1982). Enhancement (plasticity) of intellectual functioning in old age: Penn State's Adult Development and Enrichment Project (ADEPT). In F. I. M. Craik & S. E. Trehub (Eds.), *Aging and cognitive processes* (pp. 353–389). New York: Plenum.

Bandura, A. (1981). Self-referent thought: A developmental analysis of self-efficacy. In J. H. Flavell & L. Ross (Eds.), *Social cognitive development: Frontiers and possible futures* (pp. 200–239). New York: Cambridge University Press.

Bandura, A. (1982). Self-efficacy mechanism in human agency. *American Psychologist*, *37*, 122–147.

Bayley, N., & Oden, M. H. (1955). The maintenance of intellectual ability in gifted adults. *Journal of Gerontology*, *10* , 91–107.

Bengtson, V. L., Schaie, K. W., & Burton, L. (Eds.). (1995). *Adult intergenerational relations: Effect of societal changes.* New York: Springer.

Bentler, P. M. (1980). Multivariate analysis with latent variables: Causal modeling. *Annual Review of Psychology, 31*, 332–456.

Bernstein, E. (1924). Quickness and intelligence. *British Journal of Psychology, 3*(7).

Binet, A., & Simon, T. (1905). Méthodes nouvelles pour le diagnostic du niveau intellectuel des anormaux. *L'Année Psychologique, 11*, 191.

Birkhill, W. R., & Schaie, K. W. (1975). The effect of differential enforcement of cautiousness in the intellectual performance of the elderly. *Journal of Gerontology, 30*, 578–583.

Blieszner, R., Willis, S. L., & Baltes, P. B. (1981). Training research in aging on the fluid ability of inductive reasoning. *Journal of Applied Developmental Psychology, 2*, 247–265.

Botwinick, J. (1977). Intellectual abilities. In J. E. Birren & K. W. Schaie (Eds.), *Handbook of the psychology of aging* (pp. 580–605). New York: Van Nostrand Reinhold.

Botwinick, J., & Arenberg, D. (1976). Disparate time spans in sequential studies of aging. *Experimental Aging Research, 2*, 55–61.

Brooks, J., & Weintraub, M. (1976). A history of infant intelligence testing. In M. Lewis (Ed.), *Origins of intelligence.* New York: Plenum.

Buss, A. R. (1979–1980). Methodological issues in life-span developmental psychology from a dialectical perspective. *International Journal of Aging and Human Development, 10*, 121–163.

Busse, E. W. (1993). Duke longitudinal studies of aging. *Zeitschrift für Gerontologie, 26*, 123–128.

Campbell, D. T., & Stanley, J. C. (1963). Experimental and quasi-experimental designs for research in teaching. In N. L. Gage (Ed.), *Handbook of research on teaching* (pp. 171–246). Skokie, IL: Rand McNally.

Cattell, R. B. (1957). *Personality and motivation structure and measurement.* New York: World Book.

Cattell, R. B. (1963). Theory of fluid and crystallized intelligence: A critical experiment. *Journal of Educational Psychology, 54*, 1–22.

Cattell, R. B., Eber, H., & Tatsuoka, M. M. (1970). *Handbook for the 16 PF.* Champaign, IL: Institute for Personality and Ability Testing.

Chown, S. M. (1959). Rigidity – A flexible concept. *Psychological Bulletin, 56*, 195–223.

Cohen, J. (1957). The factorial structure of the WAIS between early adulthood and old age. *Journal of Consulting Psychology, 21*, 283–290.

Cohen, J., & Cohen, P. (1975). *Applied multiple regression/correlation analysis for the behavioral sciences*. New York: Academic Press.

Commons, M. L., Sinnott, J. D., Richards, F. A., & Armon, C. (Eds.). (1989). *Beyond formal operations: Vol. 2. Adolescent and adult development models*. New York: Praeger.

Cook, T. C., & Campbell, D. T. (1979). *Quasi-experiments: Design and analysis issues for field settings*. Chicago: Rand McNally.

Cooney, T. M., Schaie, K. W., & Willis, S. L. (1988). The relationship between prior functioning of cognitive and personality dimensions and subject attrition in longitudinal research. *Journal of Gerontology: Psychological Sciences, 43*, P12–P17.

Cooper, L. B. (1975). Mental transformations of random two-dimensional shapes. *Cognitive Psychology, 7*, 20–43.

Cooper, L. B., & Shepard, R. N. (1973). Chronometric studies of rotation of mental images. In W. G. Chase (Ed.), *Visual information processing* (pp. 75–96). New York: Academic Press.

Cornelius, S. W., & Caspi, A. (1986). Self-perceptions of intellectual control and aging. *Educational Gerontology, 12*, 345–357.

Costa, P. T., & McCrae, R. R. (1993). Psychological research in the Baltimore Longitudinal Study of Aging. *Zeitschrift für Gerontologie, 26*, 138–141.

Cronbach, L. J. (1970). *Essentials of psychological testing* (3rd ed.). New York: Harper & Row.

Cumming, E., & Henry, W. (1961). *Growing old: The process of disengagement*. New York: Basic.

Cunningham, W. R. (1978). Principles for identifying structural differences: Some methodological issues related to comparative factor analysis. *Journal of Gerontology, 33*, 82–86.

Cunningham, W. R. (1991). Issues in factorial invariance. In L. M. Collins & J. L. Horn (Eds.), *Best methods for the analysis of change* (pp. 106–113). Washington, DC: American Psychological Association.

DeFries, J. C., Ashton, G. C., Johnson, R. C., Kusi, A. R., McClearn, G. E., Mi, M. P., Rashad, M. N., Vandenberg, S. G., & Wilson, J. R. (1976). Parent–offspring resemblance for specific cognitive abilities in two ethnic groups. *Nature, 261*(5556), 131–133.

DeFries, J. C., & Fulker, D. W. (1985). Multiple regression of twin data. *Behavior Genetics, 15*, 467–473.

DeFries, J. C., Plomin, R., & LaBuda, M. (1987). Genetic stability of cognitive development from childhood to adulthood. *Developmental Psychology, 23*, 4–12.

DeFries, J. C., Vandenberg, S. G., & McClearn, G. E. (1976). The genetics of specific cognitive abilities. *Annual Review of Genetics, 10*, 197–207.

Denney, N. W. (1982). Aging and cognitive changes. In B. B. Wolman (Ed.), *Handbook of developmental psychology* (pp. 807–827). Englewood Cliffs, NJ: Prentice-Hall.

Denney, N. W., & Heidrich, S. M. (1990). Training effects on Raven's Progressive Matrices in young, middle-aged, and elderly adults. *Psychology and Aging, 5*, 144–145.

Donaldson, G. (1981). Letter to the editor. *Journal of Gerontology, 36*, 634–636.

Dudek, F. J. (1979). The continuing misinterpretation of the standard error of measurement. *Psychological Bulletin, 86*, 335–337.

Dutta, R. (1992). *The relationship between flexibility–rigidity and the Primary Mental Abilities*. Unpublished doctoral dissertation, Pennsylvania State University, University Park.

Dutta, R., Schulenberg, J. E., & Lair, T. J. (1986, April). *The effect of job characteristics on cognitive abilities and intellectual flexibility*. Paper presented at the annual meeting of the Eastern Psychological Association, New York.

Dutta, R., Yue, G. A., Schaie, K. W., Willis, S. L., O'Hanlon, A. M., & Yu, L. C. (1989, November). *Age difference patterns in primary mental abilities in China and the U.S.A.* Paper presented at the annual meeting of the Gerontological Society of America, Minneapolis.

Educational Testing Service. (1977). *Basic Skills Assessment Test – Reading.* Princeton, NJ: Author.

Egan, D. E. (1981). An analysis of spatial orientation performance. *Intelligence, 5*, 85–100.

Eichorn, D. H., Clausen, J. A., Haan, N., Honzik, M. P., & Mussen, P. H. (1981). *Present and past in middle life.* New York: Academic Press.

Ekstrom, R. B., French, J. W., Harman, H., & Derman, D. (1976). *Kit of factor-referenced cognitive tests* (rev. ed.). Princeton, NJ: Educational Testing Service.

Elias, M. F., Elias, J. W., & Elias, P. K. (1990). Biological and health influences upon behavior. In J. E. Birren & K. W. Schaie (Eds.), *Handbook of the psychology of aging* (3rd ed., pp. 79–102). New York: Academic Press.

French, J. W., Ekstrom, R. B., & Price, L. A. (1963). *Kit of reference tests for cognitive factors.* Princeton, NJ: Educational Testing Service.

Galton, F. (1869). *Hereditary genius.* London: Macmillan.

Gardner, E. F., & Monge, R. H. (1975). Adult age differences in cognitive abilities and educational background. *Experimental Aging Research, 3,* 337–383.

George, L. K., Siegler, I. C., & Okun, M. A. (1981). Separating age, cohort, and time of measurement: Analysis of variance and multiple regression. *Experimental Aging Research, 7,* 297–314.

Giambra, L. M., & Arenberg, D. (1980). Problem solving, concept learning and aging. In L. W. Poon (Ed.), *Aging in the 1980s* (pp. 253–259). Washington, DC: American Psychological Association.

Glenn, N. D. (1976). Cohort analysts' futile quest: Statistical attempts to separate age, period and cohort effects. *American Sociological Review, 41,* 900–904.

Glenn, N. D. (1981). Age, birth cohort, and drinking: An illustration of the hazards of inferring effects from cohort data. *Journal of Gerontology, 36,* 362–369.

Gonda, J., Quayhagen, M., & Schaie, K. W. (1981). Education, task meaningfulness and cognitive performance in young-old and old-old adults. *Educational Gerontology, 7,* 151–158.

Gough, H. G. (1957). *The California Psychological Inventory.* Palo Alto, CA: Consulting Psychologists Press.

Gough, H. G., McCloskey, H., & Meehl, P. E. (1952). A personality scale for social responsibility. *Journal of Abnormal and Social Psychology, 42,* 73–80.

Gribbin, K., & Schaie, K. W. (1976). Monetary incentive, age, and cognition. *Experimental Aging Research, 2,* 461–468.

Gribbin, K., & Schaie, K. W. (1977, November). *The aging of tests: A methodological problem of longitudinal studies.* Paper presented at the annual meeting of the Gerontological Society, San Francisco.

Gribbin, K., & Schaie, K. W. (1979). Selective attrition in longitudinal studies: A cohort-sequential approach. In H. Orino, K. Shimada, M. Iriki, & D. Maeda (Eds.), *Recent advances in gerontology* (pp. 549–551). Amsterdam: Excerpta Medica.

Gribbin, K., Schaie, K. W., & Parham, I. A. (1980). Complexity of life style and maintenance of intellectual abilities. *Journal of Social Issues, 36,* 47–61.

Gribbin, K., Schaie, K. W., & Stone, V. (1976, August). *Ability differences between established and redefined populations in sequential studies.* Paper presented at the annual meeting of the American Psychological Association, Washington, DC.

Gruber, A. L., & Schaie, K. W. (1986, November). *Longitudinal-sequential studies of marital assortativity*. Paper presented at the annual meeting of the Gerontological Society of America, Chicago.

Gruber-Baldini, A. L. (1991a). *The impact of health and disease on cognitive ability in adulthood and old age in the Seattle Longitudinal Study.* Unpublished doctoral dissertation, Pennsylvania State University, University Park.

Gruber-Baldini, A. L. (1991b, November). *The prevalence of chronic disease from HMO records across age and time.* Paper presented at the annual meeting of the Gerontological Society of America, San Francisco.

Gruber-Baldini, A. L., & Schaie, K. W. (1990, November). *The impact of disease upon cognitive ability functioning in the elderly.* Paper presented at the annual meeting of the Gerontological Society of America, Boston.

Gruber-Baldini, A. L., Schaie, K. W., & Willis, S. L. (1995). Similarity in married couples: A longitudinal study of mental abilities and flexibility–rigidity. *Journal of Personality and Social Psychology: Personality Processes and Individual Differences, 69,* 191–203.

Gruber-Baldini, A. L., Willis, S. L., & Schaie, K. W. (1989, November). *Health and rigidity predictors of cognitive change and training gain.* Paper presented at the annual meeting of the Gerontological Society of America, Minneapolis.

Guilford, J. P. (1967). *The nature of human intelligence.* New York: McGraw-Hill.

Hall, G. S. (1922). *Senescence, the last half of life.* New York: Appleton.

Havighurst, R. J., Neugarten, B. L., & Tobin, S. S. (1968). Disengagement and patterns of aging. In B. L. Neugarten (Ed.), *Middle age and aging* (pp. 161–177). Chicago: University of Chicago Press.

Hertzog, C. (1985). Application of confirmatory factor analysis to the study of intelligence. In D. K. Detterman (Ed.), *Current topics in human intelligence* (pp. 59–97). Norwood, NJ: Ablex.

Hertzog, C. (1989). The influence of cognitive slowing on age differences in intelligence. *Developmental Psychology, 25,* 636–651.

Hertzog, C., & Schaie, K. W. (1986). Stability and change in adult intelligence: 1. Analysis of longitudinal covariance structures. *Psychology and Aging, 1,* 159–171.

Hertzog, C., & Schaie, K. W. (1988). Stability and change in adult intelligence: 2. Simultaneous analysis of longitudinal means and covariance structures. *Psychology and Aging, 3,* 122–130.

Hertzog, C., Schaie, K. W., & Gribbin, K. (1978). Cardiovascular disease and changes in intellectual functioning from middle to old age. *Journal of Gerontology, 33,* 872–883.

Ho, H. Z., Foch, T. T., & Plomin, R. (1980). Developmental stability of the relative influence of genes and environment on specific cognitive abilities in childhood. *Developmental Psychology, 16*, 340–346.

Hollingsworth, H. L. (1927). *Mental growth and decline: A survey of developmental psychology.* New York: Appleton.

Holzman, T. G., Pellegrino, J. W., & Glaser, R. (1982). Cognitive dimensions of numerical rule induction. *Journal of Educational Psychology, 74*, 360–373.

Horn, J. L. (1970). Organization of data on life-span development of human abilities. In L. R. Goulet & P. B. Baltes (Eds.), *Life-span developmental psychology: Research and theory* (pp. 434–466). New York: Academic Press.

Horn, J. L. (1982). The theory of fluid and crystallized intelligence in relation to concepts of cognitive psychology and aging in adulthood. In F. I. M. Craik & S. Trehub (Eds.), *Aging and cognitive processes* (pp. 237–278). New York: Plenum.

Horn, J. L. (1991). Comments on issues in factorial invariance. In L. M. Collins & J. L. Horn (Eds.), *Best methods for the analysis of change* (pp. 114–125). Washington, DC: American Psychological Association.

Horn, J. L., & McArdle, J. J. (1980). Perspectives on mathematical-statistical model building (MASMOB) in research on aging. In L. F. Poon (Ed.), *Aging in the 1980s* (pp. 503–541). Washington, DC: American Psychological Association.

Horn, J. L., & McArdle, J. J. (1992). A practical and theoretical guide to measurement invariance in aging research. *Experimental Aging Research, 18*, 117–144.

Horst, P. (1956a). A simplified method for rotating a centroid factor matrix to a simple structure hypothesis. *Journal of Experimental Education, 24*, 251–258.

Horst, P. (1956b). Simplified computations for the multiple group method of factor analysis. *Educational and Psychological Measurement, 16*, 101–109.

Horst, P., & Schaie, K. W. (1956). The multiple group method of factor analysis and rotation to a simple structure hypothesis. *Journal of Experimental Education, 24*, 231–237.

Hurtado, A. V., & Greenlick, M. R. (1971). Disease classification system for the analysis of medical care utilization. *Health Services Research, 6*, 235–250.

Jarvik, L. F., Blum, J. E., & Varma, A. O. (1971). Genetic components and intellectual functioning during senescence: A 20-year study of aging twins. *Behavior Genetics, 2*, 159–171.

Jarvik, L. F., Kallman, F. J., & Falek, A. (1962). Intellectual changes in aged twins. *Journal of Gerontology, 17,* 289–294.

Jarvik, L. F., Kallman, F. J., Falek, A., & Kleber, M. M. (1957). Changing intellectual functions in senescent twins. *Acta Genetica et Statistica Medica, 7,* 421–430.

Jones, H. E., & Conrad, H. S. (1933). The growth and decline of intelligence: A study of a homogeneous group between the ages of ten and sixty. *Genetic Psychology Monographs, 13,* 223–298.

Jöreskog, K. G. (1971). Simultaneous factor analysis in several populations. *Psychometrika, 36,* 409–426.

Jöreskog, K. G. (1979). Statistical estimation of structural models in longitudinal developmental investigations. In J. R. Nesselroade & P. B. Baltes (Eds.), *Longitudinal research in the study of behavior and development* (pp. 303–351). New York: Academic Press.

Jöreskog, K. G., & Sörbom, D. (1977). Statistical models and methods for analysis of longitudinal data. In D. J. Aigner & A. S. Goldberger (Eds.), *Latent variables in socioeconomic models* (pp. 285–325). Amsterdam: North Holland.

Jöreskog, K. G., & Sörbom, D. (1980). *Simultaneous analysis of longitudinal data from several cohorts* (Research Report No. 80–5). University of Uppsala.

Jöreskog, K. G., & Sörbom, D. (1988). *LISREL VII – Analysis of linear structural equations systems by maximum likelihood methods.* Chicago: International Educational Services.

Kail, R., Pellegrino, J., & Carter, P. (1980). Developmental changes in mental rotation. *Journal of Experimental Child Psychology, 39,* 102–116.

Kallman, F. J., Feingold, L., & Bondy, E. (1951). Comparative adaptational, social, and psychometric data on the life histories of senescent twin pairs. *American Journal of Human Genetics, 3,* 65–73.

Kallman, F. J., & Sander, G. (1948). Twin studies on aging and longevity. *Journal of Heredity, 39,* 349–357.

Kallman, F. J., & Sander, G. (1949). Twin studies on senescence. *American Journal of Psychiatry, 106,* 29–36.

Kamin, L. J. (1974). *The science and politics of IQ.* Hillsdale, NJ: Erlbaum.

Kausler, D. H. (1982). *Experimental psychology and human aging.* New York: Wiley.

Kenny, D. A. (1975). Cross-lagged panel correlation: A test for spuriousness. *Psychological Bulletin, 82,* 887–903.

Kenny, D. A. (1979). *Correlation and causality.* New York: Wiley.

Kertzer, D., & Schaie, K. W. (Eds.). (1989). *Age structuring in comparative perspective.* Hillsdale, NJ: Erlbaum.

Kotovsky, K., & Simon, H. (1973). Empirical tests of a theory of human acquisition of concepts for serial patterns. *Cognitive Psychology*, *4*, 339–424.

Kuhlen, R. G. (1940). Social change: A neglected factor in psychological studies of the life span. *School and Society*, *52*, 14–16.

Kuhlen, R. G. (1963). Age and intelligence: The significance of cultural change in longitudinal vs. cross-sectional findings. *Vita Humana*, *6*, 113–124.

Lachman, J. L., Lachman, R., & Thronesbery, C. (1979). Metamemory through the adult life span. *Developmental Psychology*, *15*, 543–551.

Lachman, M. E. (1983). Perceptions of intellectual aging: Antecedent or consequence of intellectual function? *Developmental Psychology*, *19*, 482–498.

Lachman, M. E., & Jelalian, E. (1984). Self-efficacy and attributions for intellectual performance in young and elderly adults. *Journal of Gerontology*, *39*, 577–582.

Lachman, M. E., Steinberg, E. S., & Trotter, S. W. (1987). Effects of control beliefs and attributions on memory self-assessment and performance. *Psychology and Aging*, *2*, 266–271.

Lankes, W. (1915). Perseveration. *British Journal of Psychology*, *7*, 387–419.

Luchins, A. (1942). Mechanization in problem solving: The effect of Einstellung. *Psychological Monographs*, *54*(6 Whole No. 248).

MacDonald, A. P., Jr. (1972). Characteristics of volunteer subjects under three recruiting methods: Pay, extra credit, and love of science. *Journal of Consulting and Clinical Psychology*, *39*, 220–234.

Maitland, S. B. (1993). *Individual and lifestyle antecedents and concomitants of chronic diseases: Behavioral influences on health.* Unpublished master's thesis, Pennsylvania State University, University Park.

Maitland, S. B., Dutta, R., Schaie, K. W., & Willis, S. L. (1992, November). *Trait invariance and cohort differences of adult personality.* Paper presented at the annual meeting of the Gerontological Society of America, Washington, DC.

Maitland, S. B., O'Hanlon, A. M., & Schaie, K. W. (1990, November). *Activity patterns and dimensions across the life span.* Paper presented at the annual meeting of the Gerontological Society of America, Boston.

Maitland, S. B., & Schaie, K. W. (1991, November). *Individual and lifestyle antecedents of cardiovascular disease.* Paper presented at the annual meeting of the Gerontological Society of America, San Francisco.

Maitland, S. B., Willis, S. L., & Schaie, K. W. (1993, November). *The effect of cardiovascular disease on personality and attitudinal factors.* Paper presented at the annual meeting of the Gerontological Society of America, New Orleans.

Mason, K. G., Mason, W. H., Winsborough, H. H., & Poole, W. K. (1973). Some methodological problems in cohort analyses of archival data. *American Sociological Review, 38*, 242–258.

Matarazzo, J. D. (1972). *Wechsler's measurement and appraisal of adult intelligence.* Baltimore: Williams & Wilkins.

McArdle, J. J., & Anderson, E. (1990). Latent growth models for research on aging. In J. E. Birren & K. W. Schaie (Eds.), *Handbook of the psychology of aging* (3rd ed., pp. 21–44). New York: Academic Press.

McArdle, J. J., & Hamagami, F. (1991). Modeling incomplete longitudinal and cross-sectional data using latent growth structural models. In L. M. Collins & J. L. Horn (Eds.), *Best methods for the analysis of change* (pp. 276–304). Washington, DC: American Psychological Association.

Meredith, W. (1964). Notes on factorial invariance. *Psychometrika, 29*, 177–185.

Meredith, W. (1993). Measurement invariance, factor analysis and factorial invariance. *Psychometrika, 58*, 525–543.

Moos, R. H. (1981). *Work Environment Scale manual.* Palo Alto, CA: Consulting Psychologists Press.

Moos, R. H., & Moos, B. (1986). *Family Environment Scale manual* (2nd ed). Palo Alto, CA: Consulting Psychologists Press.

Mulaik, S. A. (1972). *Foundations of factor analysis.* New York: McGraw-Hill.

Murstein, B. I. (1980). Mate selection in the 1970s. *Journal of Marriage and the Family, 42*, 777–792.

Nesselroade, J. R., Baltes, P. B., & Schaie, K. W. (1972). Ontogenetic and generational components of structural and quantitative change in adult behavior. *Journal of Gerontology, 27*, 222–228.

Nesselroade, J. R., & Labouvie, E. W. (1985). Experimental design in research on aging. In J. E. Birren & K. W. Schaie (Eds.), *Handbook of the psychology of aging* (2nd ed., pp. 35–60). New York: Van Nostrand Reinhold.

Nesselroade, J. R., Stigler, S. M., & Baltes, P. B. (1980). Regression towards the mean and the study of change. *Psychological Bulletin, 88*, 622–637.

Nunnally, J. C. (1982). The study of human change: Measurement, research strategies, and methods of analysis. In B. B. Wolman (Ed.), *Handbook of developmental psychology* (pp. 133–148). Englewood Cliffs, NJ: Prentice-Hall.

O'Hanlon, A. M. (1993). *Inter-individual patterns of intellectual aging: The influence of environmental factors.* Unpublished doctoral dissertation, Pennsylvania State University, University Park.

Owens, W. A., Jr. (1953). Age and mental abilities: A longitudinal study. *Genetic Psychology Monographs, 48,* 3–54.

Owens, W. A., Jr. (1959). Is age kinder to the initially more able? *Journal of Gerontology, 14,* 334–337.

Parham, I. A., Gribbin, K., Hertzog, C., & Schaie, K. W. (1975, July). *Health status change by age and implications for adult cognitive change.* Paper presented at the 10th International Congress of Gerontology, Jerusalem.

Pedersen, N. L., McClearn, G. E., Plomin R., Nesselroade, J. R., Berg, S., & DeFore, U. (1991). The Swedish Adoption/Twin Study of Aging: An update. *Acta Geneticae Medicae et Gemellologiae, 40,* 7–20.

Perlmutter, M. (1978). What is memory aging the aging of? *Developmental Psychology, 14,* 330–345.

Piaget, J. (1972). Intellectual evolution from adolescence to adulthood. *Human Development, 15,* 1–12.

Plomin, R. (1983). Developmental behavior genetics. *Child Development, 54,* 253–259.

Plomin, R. (1986). *Development, genetics, and psychology.* Hillsdale, NJ: Erlbaum.

Plomin, R. (1987). The nature and nurture of cognitive abilities. In R. Sternberg (Ed.), *Advances in the psychology of human intelligence* (Vol. 4, pp. 1–33). Hillsdale, NJ: Erlbaum.

Plomin, R., & Daniels, D. (1987). Why are two children in the same family so different from each other? *Behavioral and Brain Sciences, 10,* 1–16.

Plomin, R., DeFries, J. C., & McClearn, G. E. (1980). *Behavioral genetics.* San Francisco: Freeman.

Plomin, R., & McClearn, G. E. (1990). Human behavioral genetics of aging. In J. E. Birren & K. W. Schaie (Eds.), *Handbook of the psychology of aging* (3rd ed., pp. 67–79). New York: Academic Press.

Plomin, R., Pedersen, N. L., Nesselroade, J. R., & Bergeman, C. S. (1988). Genetic influence on childhood family environment perceived retrospectively from the last half of the life span. *Developmental Psychology, 24,* 738–745.

Plomin, R., & Thompson, L. A. (1987) Life-span developmental behavior genetics. In P. B. Baltes, D. L. Featherman, & R. M. Lerner (Eds.), *Life-span development and behavior* (Vol. 8, pp. 1–31). Hillsdale, NJ: Erlbaum.

Poon, L. W., Walsh-Sweeney, L., & Fozard, J. L. (1980). Memory training for the elderly. In L. W. Poon, J. L. Fozard, L. S. Cermak, D. Arenberg, & L. W. Thompson (Eds.), *New directions in memory and aging* (pp. 481–484). Hillsdale, NJ: Erlbaum.

Pressey, S. L., Janney, J. E., & Kuhlen, R. G. (1939). *Life: A psychological survey.* New York: Hayer.

Price, R. A., & Vandenberg, S. G. (1980). Spouse similarity in American and Swedish couples. *Behavior Genetics, 10,* 59–71.

Quayhagen, M. (1979). *Training spatial rotation in elderly women.* Unpublished doctoral dissertation, University of Southern California, Los Angeles.

Reinert, G. (1970). Comparative factor analytic studies of intelligence through the human life-span. In L. R. Goulet & P. B. Baltes (Eds.), *Life-span developmental psychology: Research and theory* (pp. 468–485). New York: Academic Press.

Riegel, K. F., & Riegel, R. M. (1972). Development, drop, and death. *Developmental Psychology, 6,* 306–319.

Riegel, K. F., Riegel, R. M., & Meyer, G. (1967). A study of the drop-out rates in longitudinal research on aging and the prediction of death. *Journal of Personality and Social Psychology, 4,* 342–348.

Riley, M. W. (1985). Overview and highlights of a sociological perspective. In A. B. Sørenson, F. E. Weinert, & L. R. Sherrod (Eds.), *Human development: Interdisciplinary perspectives* (pp. 153–175). Hillsdale, NJ: Erlbaum.

Riley, M. W., Johnson, M. J., & Foner, A. (1972). *Aging and society: Vol. 3. A sociology of age stratification.* New York: Russell Sage.

Rodin, J., Schooler, C., & Schaie, K. W. (Eds.). (1990). *Self-directedness: Cause and effects throughout the life course.* Hillsdale, NJ: Erlbaum.

Rosenthal, R., & Rosnow, R. L. (1975). *The volunteer subject.* New York: Wiley.

Rott, C. (1990). Intelligenzentwicklung im Alter [Development of intelligence in old age]. *Zeitschrift für Gerontologie, 23,* 252–261.

Salthouse, T. A. (1982). *Adult cognition: An experimental psychology of human aging.* New York: Springer-Verlag.

Schaie, K. W. (1953). *Measuring behavioral rigidity: A factorial investigation of some tests of rigid behavior.* Unpublished master's thesis, University of Washington, Seattle.

Schaie, K. W. (1955). A test of behavioral rigidity. *Journal of Abnormal and Social Psychology, 51,* 604–610.

Schaie, K. W. (1958a). Differences in some personal characteristics of "rigid" and "flexible" individuals. *Journal of Clinical Psychology, 14,* 11–14.

Schaie, K. W. (1958b). Occupational level and the Primary Mental Abilities. *Journal of Educational Psychology, 40,* 299–303.

Schaie, K. W. (1958c). Rigidity–flexibility and intelligence: A cross-sectional study of the adult life-span from 20 to 70. *Psychological Monographs, 72*(9, Whole No. 462).

Schaie, K. W. (1958d). Tests of hypotheses about differences between two intercorrelation matrices. *Journal of Experimental Education, 26,* 242–245.

Schaie, K. W. (1959a). Cross-sectional methods in the study of psychological aspects of aging. *Journal of Gerontology, 14,* 208–215.

Schaie, K. W. (1959b). The effect of age on a scale of social responsibility. *Journal of Social Psychology, 50,* 221–224.

Schaie, K. W. (1960). *Manual for the Test of Behavioral Rigidity.* Palo Alto, CA: Consulting Psychologists Press.

Schaie, K. W. (1963). The Color Pyramid Test: A non-verbal technique for personality assessment. *Psychological Bulletin, 60,* 530–547.

Schaie, K. W. (1965). A general model for the study of developmental problems. *Psychological Bulletin, 64,* 91–107.

Schaie, K. W. (1967). Age changes and age differences. *Gerontologist, 7,* 128–132.

Schaie, K. W. (1970). A reinterpretation of age-related changes in cognitive structure and functioning. In L. R. Goulet & P. B. Baltes (Eds.), *Life-span developmental psychology: Research and theory* (pp. 485–507). New York: Academic Press.

Schaie, K. W. (1972). Can the longitudinal method be applied to psychological studies of human development? In F. Z. Mönks, W. W. Hartup, & J. DeWitt (Eds.), *Determinants of human behavior* (pp. 3–22). New York: Academic Press.

Schaie, K. W. (1973a, August). *Cumulative health trauma and changes in adult cognitive behavior.* Paper presented at the annual meeting of the American Psychological Association, Montreal.

Schaie, K. W. (1973b). Methodological problems in descriptive developmental research on adulthood and aging. In J. R. Nesselroade & H. W. Reese (Eds.), *Life-span developmental psychology: Methodological issues* (pp. 253–280). New York: Academic Press.

Schaie, K. W. (1974). Translations in gerontology – From lab to life: Intellectual functioning. *American Psychologist, 29,* 802–807.

Schaie, K. W. (1975). Research strategy in developmental human behavior genetics. In K. W. Schaie, E. V. Anderson, G. E. McClearn, & J. Money (Eds.), *Developmental human behavior genetics* (pp. 205–220). Lexington, MA: Heath.

Schaie, K. W. (1977). Quasi-experimental designs in the psychology of aging. In J. E. Birren & K. W. Schaie (Eds.), *Handbook of the psychology of aging* (pp. 39–58). New York: Van Nostrand Reinhold.

Schaie, K. W. (1977–1978). Toward a stage theory of adult development. *International Journal of Aging and Human Development, 8,* 129–138.

Schaie, K. W. (1978). External validity in the assessment of intellectual development in adulthood. *Journal of Gerontology, 33,* 695–701.

Schaie, K. W. (1979). The Primary Mental Abilities in adulthood: An exploration in the development of psychometric intelligence. In P. B. Baltes & O. G. Brim, Jr. (Eds.), *Life-span development and behavior* (Vol. 2, pp. 67–115). New York: Academic Press.

Schaie, K. W. (1980a). Age changes in intelligence. In R. D. Sprott (Ed.), *Age, learning ability and intelligence* (pp. 41–77). New York: Van Nostrand Reinhold.

Schaie, K. W. (1980b). Cognitive development in aging. In L. K. Obler & M. Albert (Eds.), *Language and communication in the elderly* (pp. 7–26). Lexington, MA: Heath.

Schaie, K. W. (1980c). Intelligence and problem solving. In J. E. Birren & R. B. Sloane (Eds.), *Handbook of mental health and aging* (pp. 262–280). Englewood Cliffs, NJ: Prentice-Hall.

Schaie, K. W. (1983a). The Seattle Longitudinal Study: A twenty-one-year exploration of psychometric intelligence in adulthood. In K. W. Schaie (Ed.), *Longitudinal studies of adult psychological development* (pp. 64–135). New York: Guilford Press.

Schaie, K. W. (1983b). What can we learn from the longitudinal study of adult psychological development? In K. W. Schaie (Ed.), *Longitudinal studies of adult psychological development* (pp. 1–19). New York: Guilford Press.

Schaie, K. W. (1984a). Historical time and cohort effects. In K. A. McCloskey & H. W. Reese (Eds.), *Life-span developmental psychology: Historical and generational effects* (pp. 1–15). New York: Academic Press.

Schaie, K. W. (1984b). Midlife influences upon intellectual functioning in old age. *International Journal of Behavioral Development, 7,* 463–478.

Schaie, K. W. (1985). *Manual for the Schaie–Thurstone Adult Mental Abilities Test (STAMAT).* Palo Alto, CA: Consulting Psychologists Press.

Schaie, K. W. (1986). Beyond calendar definitions of age, time and cohort: The general developmental model revisited. *Developmental Review, 6,* 252–277.

Schaie, K. W. (1987). Applications of psychometric intelligence to the prediction of everyday competence in the elderly. In C. Schooler & K. W. Schaie (Eds.), *Cognitive functioning and social structure over the life course* (pp. 50–59). Norwood, NJ: Ablex.

Schaie, K. W. (1988a). Ageism in psychological research. *American Psychologist, 43*, 179–183.

Schaie, K. W. (1988b). The delicate balance: Technology, intellectual competence, and normal aging. In G. Lesnoff-Cavaglia (Ed.), *Aging in a technological society* (Vol. 7, pp. 155–166). New York: Human Sciences Press.

Schaie, K. W. (1988c). The impact of research methodology on theory-building in the developmental sciences. In J. E. Birren & V. L. Bengtson (Eds.), *Emergent theories of aging: Psychological and social perspectives on time, self and society* (pp. 41–58). New York: Springer.

Schaie, K. W. (1988d). Internal validity threats in studies of adult cognitive development. In M. L. Howe & C. J. Brainard (Eds.), *Cognitive development in adulthood: Progress in cognitive development research* (pp. 241–272). New York: Springer-Verlag.

Schaie, K. W. (1988e). Variability in cognitive function in the elderly: Implications for social participation. In A. Woodhead, M. Bender, & R. Leonard (Eds.), *Phenotypic variation in populations: Relevance to risk assessment* (pp. 191–212). New York: Plenum.

Schaie, K. W. (1989a). The hazards of cognitive aging. *Gerontologist, 29*, 484–493.

Schaie, K. W. (1989b). Individual differences in rate of cognitive change in adulthood. In V. L. Bengtson & K. W. Schaie (Eds.), *The course of later life: Research and reflections* (pp. 68–83). New York: Springer.

Schaie, K. W. (1989c). Perceptual speed in adulthood: Cross-sectional and longitudinal studies. *Psychology and Aging, 4*, 443–453.

Schaie, K. W. (1990a). Intellectual development in adulthood. In J. E. Birren & K. W. Schaie (Eds.), *Handbook of the psychology of aging* (3rd ed., pp. 291–309). New York: Academic Press.

Schaie, K. W. (1990b). Late life potential and cohort differences in mental abilities. In M. Perlmutter (Ed.), *Late life potential* (pp. 43–62). Washington, DC: Gerontological Society of America.

Schaie, K. W. (1990c). The optimization of cognitive functioning in old age: Predictions based on cohort-sequential and longitudinal data. In P. B. Baltes & M. M. Baltes (Eds.), *Successful aging: Perspectives from the behavioral sciences* (pp. 94–117). Cambridge: Cambridge University Press.

Schaie, K. W. (1992). The impact of methodological changes in gerontology. *International Journal of Aging and Human Development, 35*, 19–29.

Schaie, K. W. (1993). The Seattle Longitudinal Study: A thirty-five-year inquiry of adult intellectual development. *Zeitschrift für Gerontologie, 26*, 129–137.

Schaie, K. W. (1994a). The course of adult intellectual development. *American Psychologist*, *49*, 304–313.

Schaie, K. W. (1994b). Developmental designs revisited. In S. H. Cohen & H. W. Reese (Eds.), *Life-span developmental psychology: Theoretical issues revisited* (pp. 45–64). Hillsdale, NJ: Erlbaum.

Schaie, K. W. (in press). The natural history of a longitudinal study. In M. Merrens & G. Brannigan (Eds.), *The developmental psychologists*. New York: McGraw-Hill.

Schaie, K. W., & Baltes, P. B. (1975). On sequential strategies in developmental research: Description or explanation? *Human Development*, *18*, 384–390.

Schaie, K. W., Baltes, P. B., & Strother, C. R. (1964). A study of auditory sensitivity in advanced age. *Journal of Gerontology*, *19*, 453–457.

Schaie, K. W., Blazer, D., & House, J. (Eds.). (1992). *Aging, health behavior and health outcomes*. Hillsdale, NJ: Erlbaum.

Schaie, K. W., Chatham, L. R., & Weiss, J. M. A. (1961). The multiprofessional intake assessment of older psychiatric patients. *Journal of Psychiatric Research*, *1*, 92–100.

Schaie, K. W., Dutta, R., & Willis, S. L. (1991). The relationship between rigidity–flexibility and cognitive abilities in adulthood. *Psychology and Aging*, *6*, 371–383.

Schaie, K. W., & Goulet, L. R. (1977). Trait theory and verbal learning processes. In R. B. Cattell & R. M. Dreger (Eds.), *Handbook of modern personality theory* (pp. 567–584). New York: Hemisphere/Halsted Press.

Schaie, K. W., & Gribbin, K. (1975). Einflüsse der aktuellen Umwelt auf die Persönlichkeitsentwicklung im Erwachsenenalter [Environmental influences on personality in adulthood]. *Zeitschrift für Entwicklungspsychologie und Pädagogische Psychologie*, *7*, 233–246.

Schaie, K. W., & Heiss, R. (1964). *Color and personality*. Bern: Huber.

Schaie, K. W., & Hertzog, C. (1982). Longitudinal methods. In B. B. Wolman (Ed.), *Handbook of developmental psychology* (pp. 91–115). Englewood Cliffs, NJ: Prentice-Hall.

Schaie, K. W., & Hertzog, C. (1983). Fourteen-year cohort-sequential studies of adult intelligence. *Developmental Psychology*, *19*, 531–543.

Schaie, K. W., & Hertzog, C. (1985). Measurement in the psychology of adulthood and aging. In J. E. Birren & K. W. Schaie (Eds.), *Handbook of the psychology of aging* (2nd ed., pp. 61–92). New York: Van Nostrand Reinhold.

Schaie, K. W., & Hertzog, C. (1986). Toward a comprehensive model of adult intellectual development: Contributions of the Seattle Longitudinal Study. In R. J. Sternberg (Ed.), *Advances in human intelligence* (Vol. 3, pp. 79–118). Hillsdale, NJ: Erlbaum.

Schaie, K. W., Labouvie, G. V., & Barrett, T. J. (1973). Selective attrition effects in a fourteen-year study of adult intelligence. *Journal of Gerontology, 28,* 328–334.

Schaie, K. W., Labouvie, G. V., & Buech, B. U. (1973). Generational and cohort-specific differences in adult cognitive functioning: A fourteen-year study of independent samples. *Developmental Psychology, 9,* 151–156.

Schaie, K. W., & Labouvie-Vief, G. (1974). Generational versus ontogenetic components of change in adult cognitive behavior: A fourteen-year cross-sequential study. *Developmental Psychology, 10,* 305–320.

Schaie, K. W., Maitland, S. B., & Willis, S. L. (1994, October). *Longitudinal and gender invariance of adult psychometric ability factor structures across seven years.* Paper presented at the annual meeting of the Society of Multivariate Experimental Psychology, Princeton, NJ.

Schaie, K. W., & O'Hanlon, A. M. (1990). The influence of social–environmental factors in the maintenance of adult intelligence. In R. Schmitz-Schertzer, A. Kruse, & E. Olbrich (Eds.), *Altern – Ein lebenslanger Prozess der sozialen Interaktion* [Aging – A lifelong process of social interaction] (pp. 55–66). Darmstadt: Steinkopf.

Schaie, K. W., & Parham, I. A. (1974). Social responsibility in adulthood: Ontogenetic and sociocultural change. *Journal of Personality and Social Psychology, 30,* 483–492.

Schaie, K. W., & Parham, I. A. (1975). *Manual for the Test of Behavioral Rigidity.* Palo Alto, CA: Consulting Psychologists Press.

Schaie, K. W., & Parham, I. A. (1976). Stability of adult personality traits: Fact or fable? *Journal of Personality and Social Psychology, 34,* 146–158.

Schaie, K. W., & Parham, I. A. (1977). Cohort-sequential analyses of adult intellectual development. *Developmental Psychology, 12,* 649–653.

Schaie, K. W., Plomin, R., Willis, S. L., Gruber-Baldini, A., & Dutta, R. (1992). Natural cohorts: Family similarity in adult cognition. In T. Sonderegger (Ed.), *Psychology and aging: Nebraska Symposium on Motivation, 1991* (Vol. 38, pp. 205–243). Lincoln: University of Nebraska Press.

Schaie, K. W., Plomin, R., Willis, S. L., Gruber-Baldini, A. L., Dutta, R., & Bayen, U. (1993). Family similarity in adult intellectual development. In J. J. F. Schroots (Ed.), *Aging, health and competence: The next generation of longitudinal research* (pp. 183–198). Amsterdam: Elsevier.

Schaie, K. W., Rommel, L. A., & Weiss, J. M. A. (1959). Judging the relative severity of psychiatric outpatient complaints. *Journal of Clinical Psychology, 15,* 380–388.

Schaie, K. W., Rosenthal, F., & Perlman, R. M. (1953). Differential deterioration of factorially "pure" mental abilities. *Journal of Gerontology*, *8*, 191–196.

Schaie, K. W., & Schooler, C. (Eds.). (1989). *Social structure and aging: Psychological processes*. Hillsdale, NJ: Erlbaum.

Schaie, K. W., & Strother, C. R. (1968a). Cognitive and personality variables in college graduates of advanced age. In G. A. Talland (Ed.), *Human behavior and aging: Recent advances in research and theory* (pp. 281–308). New York: Academic Press.

Schaie, K. W., & Strother, C. R. (1968b). The cross-sequential study of age changes in cognitive behavior. *Psychological Bulletin*, *70*, 671–680.

Schaie, K. W., & Strother, C. R. (1968c). The effects of time and cohort differences on the interpretation of age changes in cognitive behavior. *Multivariate Behavioral Research*, *3*, 259–294.

Schaie, K. W., & Strother, C. R. (1968d). Limits of optimal functioning in superior old adults. In S. M. Chown & K. F. Riegel (Eds.), *Interdisciplinary topics in gerontology* (pp. 132–150). Basel: S. Karger.

Schaie, K. W., & Willis, S. L. (1986a). *Adult development and aging* (2nd ed.). Boston: Little, Brown.

Schaie, K. W., & Willis, S. L. (1986b). Can intellectual decline in the elderly be reversed? *Developmental Psychology*, *22*, 223–232.

Schaie, K. W., & Willis, S. L. (1991a). *Adult development and aging* (3rd ed). New York: HarperCollins.

Schaie, K. W., & Willis, S. L. (1991b). Adult personality and psychomotor performance: Cross-sectional and longitudinal analyses. *Journal of Gerontology: Psychological Sciences*, *46*, P275–P284.

Schaie, K. W., & Willis, S. L. (1993). Age difference patterns of psychometric intelligence in adulthood: Generalizability within and across ability domains. *Psychology and Aging*, *8*, 44–55.

Schaie, K. W., & Willis, S. L. (1994, August). *A life-span approach to adult intellectual development*. Paper presented at the annual meeting of the American Psychological Association, Los Angeles, CA.

Schaie, K. W., & Willis, S. L. (1995). Perceived family environments across generations. In V. L. Bengtson, K. W. Schaie, & L. Burton (Eds.), *Societal impact on aging: Intergenerational perspectives* (pp. 174–209). New York: Springer.

Schaie, K. W., Willis, S. L., Hertzog, C., & Schulenberg, J. E. (1987). Effects of cognitive training upon primary mental ability structure. *Psychology and Aging*, *2*, 233–242.

Schaie, K. W., Willis, S. L., Jay, G., & Chipuer, H. (1989). Structural invariance of cognitive abilities across the adult life span: A cross-sectional study. *Developmental Psychology*, *25*, 652–662.

Schaie, K. W., Willis, S. L., & O'Hanlon, A. M. (1994). Perceived intellectual performance change over seven years. *Journal of Gerontology: Psychological Sciences, 49*, P108–P118.

Scheidt, R. J., & Schaie, K. W. (1978). A situational taxonomy for the elderly: Generating situational criteria. *Journal of Gerontology, 33*, 348–357.

Scheier, I., & Ferguson, G. A. (1952). Further factorial studies of tests of rigidity. *Canadian Journal of Psychology, 6*, 19–30.

Schmitz-Scherzer, R., & Thomae, H. (1983). Constancy and change of behavior in old age: Findings from the Bonn Longitudinal Study of Aging. In K. W. Schaie (Ed.), *Longitudinal studies of adult psychological development* (pp. 191–221). New York: Guilford Press.

Schooler, C. (1972). Social antecedents of adult psychological functioning. *American Review of Sociology, 78*, 299–322.

Schooler, C. (1987). Cognitive effects of complex environments during the life span: A review and theory. In C. Schooler & K. W. Schaie (Eds.), *Cognitive functioning and social structure over the life course.* (pp. 24–49). Norwood, NJ: Ablex.

Schooler, C., & Schaie, K. W. (Eds.). (1987). *Cognitive functioning and social structure over the life course.* Norwood, NJ: Ablex.

Shock, N. W., Greulick, R. C., Andres, R., Arenberg, D., Costa, P. T., Lakatta, E. G., & Tobin, J. D. (1984). *Normal human aging: The Baltimore Longitudinal Study of Aging.* Washington, DC: Government Printing Office.

Siegler, I. E. (1983). Psychological aspects of the Duke longitudinal studies. In K. W. Schaie (Ed.), *Longitudinal studies of adult psychological development* (pp. 136–190). New York: Guilford Press.

Siegler, I. E. (1988, August). *Developmental health psychology.* Master lecture presented as part of a series on "The adult years: Continuity and change" at the annual meeting of the American Psychological Association, Washington, DC.

Simon, H., & Kotovsky, K. (1963). Human acquisition of concepts for sequential patterns. *Psychological Review, 70*, 534–546.

Sinnott, J. D. (1989). *Everyday problem solving: Theory and applications.* New York: Praeger.

Solon, J. A., Feeney, J. J., Jones, S. H., Rigg, R. D., & Sheps, C. G. (1967). Delineating episodes of medical care. *American Journal of Public Health, 57*, 401–408.

Solon, J. A., Rigg, R. D., Jones, S. H., Feeney, J. J., Lingner, J. W., & Sheps, C. G. (1969). Episodes of medical care: Nursing students' use of medical services. *American Journal of Public Health, 59*, 936–946.

Sörbom, D. (1975). Detection of correlated errors in longitudinal data. *British Journal of Mathematical and Statistical Psychology*, *28*, 138–151.

Sternberg, R. J. (1977). *Intelligence, information processing, and analogical reasoning: The componential analysis of human abilities*. Hillsdale, NJ: Erlbaum.

Sterns, H. L., & Sanders, R. E. (1980). Training and education in the elderly. In R. E. Turner & H. W. Reese (Eds.), *Life-span developmental psychology: Intervention* (pp. 307–330). New York: Academic Press.

Stone, V. (1980). *Structural modeling of the relations among environmental variables, health status and intelligence in adulthood*. Unpublished doctoral dissertation, University of Southern California, Los Angeles.

Strother, C. R., Schaie, K. W., & Horst, P. (1957). The relationship between advanced age and mental abilities. *Journal of Abnormal and Social Psychology*, *55*, 166–170.

Sundet, J. M., Tambs, K., Magnus, P., & Berg, K. (1988). On the question of secular trends in the heritability of intelligence test scores: A study of Norwegian twins. *Intelligence*, *12*, 47–59.

Terman, L. M. (1916). *The measurement of intelligence*. Boston: Houghton.

Thorndike, E. L., & Woodworth, R. S. (1901). Influence of improvement in one mental function upon the efficiency of other mental functions. *Psychological Review*, *8*, 247–261, 384–395, 553–564.

Thurstone, L. L. (1938). *The primary mental abilities*. Chicago: University of Chicago Press.

Thurstone, L. L. (1947). *Multiple factor analysis*. Chicago: University of Chicago Press.

Thurstone, L. L., & Thurstone, T. G. (1949). *Examiner manual for the SRA Primary Mental Abilities Test* (Form 10–14). Chicago: Science Research Associates.

Thurstone, T. G. (1958). *Manual for the SRA Primary Mental Abilities 11–17*. Chicago: Science Research Associates.

Thurstone, T. G. (1962). *Primary mental abilities for Grades 9–12*. Chicago: Science Research Associates.

U.S. Public Health Service. (1968). *Eighth revision of the international classification of diseases, adapted for use in the United States* (Public Health Service Publication No. 1693). Washington, DC: Government Printing Office.

Wechsler, D. (1939). *The measurement of adult intelligence*. Baltimore: Williams & Wilkins.

Werner, H. (1948). *Comparative psychology of mental development*. New York: International Universities Press.

Wilkie, F., & Eisdorfer, C. (1973). Systemic disease and behavioral correlates. In L. Jarvik, C. Eisdorfer, & J. E. Blum (Eds.), *Intellectual functioning in adults* (pp. 83–94). New York: Springer.

Willis, S. L. (1985). Towards an educational psychology of the adult learner: Cognitive and intellectual bases. In J. E. Birren & K. W. Schaie (Eds.), *Handbook of the psychology of aging* (2nd ed., pp. 818–847). New York: Van Nostrand Reinhold.

Willis, S. L. (1987). Cognitive training and everyday competence. In K. W. Schaie (Ed.), *Annual review of gerontology and geriatrics* (Vol. 7, pp. 159–188). New York: Springer.

Willis, S. L. (1989a). Cohort differences in cognitive aging: A sample case. In K. W. Schaie & C. Schooler (Eds.), *Social structure and aging: Psychological processes* (pp. 94–112). Hillsdale, NJ: Erlbaum.

Willis, S. L. (1989b). Improvement with cognitive training: Which dogs learn what tricks? In L. W. Poon, D. C. Rubin, & B. A. Wilson (Eds.), *Everyday cognition in adulthood and late life* (pp. 545–569). Cambridge: Cambridge University Press.

Willis, S. L. (1990a). Contributions of cognitive training research to understanding late life potential. In M. Perlmutter (Ed.), *Late life potential* (pp. 25–42). Washington, DC: Gerontological Society of America.

Willis, S. L. (1990b). Current issues in cognitive training research. In E. A. Lovelace (Ed.), *Aging and cognition: Mental processes, self-awareness, and interventions* (pp. 263–280). Amsterdam: Elsevier.

Willis, S. L. (1992). Cognition and everyday competence. In K. W. Schaie (Ed.), *Annual review of gerontology and geriatrics* (Vol. 11, pp. 80–109). New York: Springer.

Willis, S. L. (1995). Competency and everyday problem solving in old age. In M. A. Smyer, M. Capp, & K. W. Schaie (Eds.), *Impact of the law on decision making in the elderly*. New York: Springer.

Willis, S. L., & Baltes, P. B. (1981). Letter to the editor. *Journal of Gerontology, 36,* 636–638.

Willis, S. L., & Schaie, K. W. (1983). *The Alphanumeric Rotation Test.* Unpublished manuscript, Pennsylvania State University, University Park.

Willis, S. L., & Schaie, K. W. (1986a). Practical intelligence in later adulthood. In R. J. Sternberg & R. K. Wagner (Eds.), *Practical intelligence: Origins of competence in the everyday world* (pp. 236–268). New York: Cambridge University Press.

Willis, S. L., & Schaie, K. W. (1986b). Training the elderly on the ability factors of spatial orientation and inductive reasoning. *Psychology and Aging, 1,* 239–247.

Willis, S. L., & Schaie, K. W. (1986c, August). *Training on inductive reasoning with a longitudinal sample.* Paper presented at the annual meeting of the American Psychological Association, Washington, DC.

Willis, S. L., & Schaie, K. W. (1988). Gender differences in spatial ability in old age: Longitudinal and intervention findings. *Sex Roles, 18,* 189–203.

Willis, S. L., & Schaie, K. W. (1992, November). *Maintaining and sustaining cognitive training effects in old age.* Paper presented at the annual meeting of the Gerontological Society of America, Washington, DC.

Willis, S. L., & Schaie, K. W. (1993). Everyday cognition: Taxonomic and methodological considerations. In J. M. Puckett & H. W. Reese (Eds.), *Mechanisms of everyday cognition* (pp. 33–54). Hillsdale, NJ: Erlbaum.

Willis, S. L., & Schaie, K. W. (1994a). Assessing competence in the elderly. In C. E. Fisher & R. M. Lerner (Eds.), *Applied developmental psychology* (pp. 339–372). New York: Macmillan.

Willis, S. L., & Schaie, K. W. (1994b). Cognitive training in the normal elderly. In F. Forette, Y. Christen, & F. Boller (Eds.), *Plasticité cérébrale et stimulation cognitive* [Cerebral plasticity and cognitive stimulation] (pp. 91–113). Paris: Fondation Nationale de Gérontologie.

Willis, S. L., Schaie, K. W., & Maitland, S. B. (1992, August). *Personality factors and cardiovascular disease.* Paper presented at the annual meeting of the American Psychological Association, Washington, DC.

Yerkes, R. M. (1921). Psychological examining in the United States Army. *Memoirs of the National Academy of Sciences, 15,* 1–890.

Zelinski, E. M., Gilewski, M. J., & Schaie, K. W. (1993). Three-year longitudinal memory assessment in older adults: Little change in performance. *Psychology and Aging, 8,* 176–186.

Zieleniewski, A. M., Fulker, D. W., DeFries, J. C., & LaBuda, M. C. (1987). Multiple regression analysis of twin and sibling data. *Personality and Individual Differences, 8,* 787–791.

Zonderman, A. B., Vandenberg, S. G., Spuhler, K. P., & Fain, P. R. (1977). Assortative marriage for cognitive abilities. *Behavior Genetics, 7,* 261–271.

Author index

Subject index